Camden House History of German Literature

Volume 9

German Literature of the Nineteenth Century, 1832–1899

The Camden House History of German Literature

Volume 9

German Literature of the Nineteenth Century, 1832–1899

Edited by
Clayton Koelb and Eric Downing

CAMDEN HOUSE

First published 2005
by Camden House

Camden House is an imprint of Boydell & Brewer Inc.
668 Mt. Hope Avenue, Rochester, NY 14620, USA
www.camden-house.com
and of Boydell & Brewer Limited
PO Box 9, Woodbridge, Suffolk IP12 3DF, UK
www.boydellandbrewer.com

ISBN: 1–57113–250–3

Library of Congress Cataloging-in-Publication Data

German literature of the nineteenth century, 1832–1899 / edited by
    Clayton Koelb and Eric Downing
        p. cm. — (Camden House history of German literature; v. 9)
    Includes bibliographical references and index.
    ISBN 1–57113–250–3 (hardcover: alk. paper)
        1. German literature—19th century—History and criticism.
    I. Koelb, Clayton, 1942– II. Downing, Eric. III. Title. IV. Series.

PT341.G42 2005
830.9′007—dc22

                                                                    2004027939

A catalogue record for this title is available from the British Library.

This publication is printed on acid-free paper.
Printed in the United States of America.

Contents

Part III. Genres

Part IV. Bibliographical Resources

Illustrations

Friedrich Kaiser, Tempo der Gründerzeit, ca. 1875, oil on canvas, depicting building site on the Grenadierstraße (now called Amalienstraße) in Berlin. Courtesy of Stadtmuseum Berlin. Photograph by Christel Lehmann.

Introduction

Clayton Koelb & Eric Downing

THE PERIOD BETWEEN 1832 AND 1900 produced some of the most remarkable writers in the history of European literature, and it includes names that nearly everyone would recognize. There is the poet Heinrich Heine, whose poem about the Lorelei on the Rhine inspired stories and songs known around the world. There is the writer and composer Richard Wagner, whose music dramas are still so popular that eager fans are willing to wait years to get tickets to major performances. There is the philosophical writer Friedrich Nietzsche, whose influence on European thought and culture extends through the twentieth century and now into the twenty-first. But there were also figures not so well known outside Germany whose work deserves wider recognition. This book aims to introduce many of them, and to reintroduce the names already famous throughout the world. It will also introduce the reader to the most important periods, movements, and genres of nineteenth-century German literature.

Periods, movements, and genres: these are the stock-in-trade categories of all literary histories, including this volume of the Camden House History of German Literature. The topic treated by the book as a whole is itself a period, the nineteenth century, though we have defined that period in a way that pays more attention to literary and cultural events than to the pure chronology of the calendar. For us, the signpost that marks the beginning of the century is not the change from 17— to 18— in the first two digits of the date, but instead the end of the "Age of Goethe" with the death of Germany's foremost man of letters in 1832. At the other end, the century ends for us about where the numbers say it should, around the time of the publication of Freud's *Interpretation of Dreams* in 1899 (but dated 1900 by the publisher). Our nineteenth century, then, falls considerably short of a hundred years, encompassing seven decades from the 1830s to the 1890s. It is the literary period that begins with the end of Romanticism and ends with the beginnings of modernism.

Brief Overview of Nineteenth-Century Literary History

Literary historians traditionally divide the nineteenth century into movements roughly as follows:

Junges Deutschland/Vormärz/Biedermeier	1832–1850
Realism/Poetic Realism	1850–1890
Naturalism	1880–1900
Jahrhundertwende	1890–1914

The starting and ending dates of these sub-periods are, of course, not exact: there is considerable overlap, and there is in some cases wide disagreement among scholars about such periodizations. Some, for example, would set the Biedermeier several decades later than Junges Deutschland, and some would start the *Vormärz* — a period of political and cultural unrest — as early as 1815. Also, though it is common practice — followed in this book — to group the three designators Junges Deutschland (Young Germany), Vormärz (Before [the] March [revolution]), and Biedermeier (the untranslatable name of a style) together into a single phenomenon, a few literary historians occasionally insist on separating Biedermeier from the other two. There is also considerable overlap between Poetic Realism and Naturalism, and in this volume the two are treated together. The *Jahrhundertwende* ("Turn of the Century") encompasses the decades immediately before and after 1900 and includes a number of distinct movements, including symbolism, late naturalism and realism, and the beginnings of expressionism and modernism. Because of the limit date of 1900 set for our enterprise, only a portion of the *Jahrhundertwende* is treated in this volume.

It is not always useful, however, to understand the course of nineteenth-century German literature in this traditional way. Instead of regarding the century as chopped up into four or more movements, one can readily see it as divided into no more than two principle periods: the relatively calm, inward-looking mid-century decades between the death of Goethe (1832) and the birth of Thomas Mann (1875); and the intense end-of-century ferment of the 70s, 80s and 90s. Here is a quick sketch of those two sections.

After the death of Goethe the pace of innovative literary production slackened for a time in Germany. The middle years of the nineteenth century — the four decades from roughly 1830 to 1870 — produced a number of significant writers of drama, poetry, and fiction, but the period was by no means so intense as the turn of the century had been. The roster of major figures in these years is not so numerous, and the level of achievement is perhaps not as astonishingly high as it had been during Goethe's lifetime.

A few very talented writers were active in these four decades, however, and one of the most talented among them was the poet Heinrich Heine (1797–1856). His skill was such that some of the poems he composed seemed, from the moment they appeared, to have already existed for centuries. He appealed to a very wide audience, acquiring for his poetry an international following larger than that of any other German poet. Even today, people who know any German poetry at all are likely to know at least one poem by Heine. He expresses himself in terms that are simple, direct, and yet hauntingly allusive: "Du bist wie eine Blume, / So hold und schön und rein; / Ich schau dich an, und Wehmut / Schleicht mir ins Herz hinein." (You are like a flower, so lovely, chaste and pure; I look at you and melancholy creeps into my heart.)

Another, very different, revolutionary talent of the years after Goethe's death, Georg Büchner (1813–37), died too young to have much impact during his lifetime; but his influence on later writers, especially those in the twentieth century, was substantial. Büchner was a playwright who in many ways anticipated the themes and techniques of much later writers. His play about the French revolution, *Dantons Tod* (Danton's Death, 1836), presents a subtle psychological portrait of its central characters and paints a vivid picture of the political and emotional turmoil of the period. Most remarkable among his works is the fragmentary drama *Woyzeck*, first published long after its author's death and little read until the twentieth century. Indeed, with its almost expressionistic technique and its intense interest in the psychopathology of its hero, it seems to belong more to that century than to its own time. That hero is in fact more of an anti-hero, a poor and not particularly bright man who falls apart psychologically and finally commits murder when he finds that his girlfriend is unfaithful to him.

Another major figure of mid nineteenth-century German drama was the Austrian poet and playwright, Franz Grillparzer (1791–1872), whose works for the stage remain among the classics of the German theater. It is worth noting, though, that Grillparzer also wrote an important novella, *Der arme Spielmann* (The Poor Fiddler, 1848), which also has become a classic. While Grillparzer's dramas now seem a bit dated and distant from contemporary literary concerns, his story of the poor fiddler still seems fresh and relevant today. The fiddle player named in the story's title is in fact poor in every sense: not only does he have little money, he has very little musical ability. His playing is so inept that people beg him to stop. But his commitment to art is genuine, and it is informed by a sophisticated concept of the role of the artist and of the place of art in human life. When the fiddler dies after rescuing several of his neighbors during a flood, his fiddle is preserved and revered by those who knew him as the relic of a great man.

The example of Grillparzer's long-term success with his short story is instructive, for this literary form, called the *Novelle* in German, was the most vital genre of the period and perhaps its greatest contribution. Other writers of the time, including those who made their reputations in other areas, produced outstanding and durable examples. The great poet Annette von Droste-Hülshoff (1797–1848), one of the most remarkable women in all German literary history, is a case in point. She wrote many fine poems, but also a single superb *Novelle, Die Judenbuche* (The Jew's Beech, 1842), a disturbing tale of murder and supernatural retribution that was in her lifetime and remains to this day her most widely-read work.

The list of excellent short stories from the mid nineteenth-century is long and impressive, and only a few can be mentioned here. Especially notable are the tales from the collection *Bunte Steine* (Many-colored Stones, 1853) by Grillparzer's fellow Austrian Adalbert Stifter (1805–68); those in the collection *Die Leute von Seldwyla* (The People of Seldwyla, 1856) by the Swiss novelist Gottfried Keller (1819–90); and several of the stories by north German poet Theodor Storm (1817–88) and the prolific prose writer Wilhelm Raabe (1831–1910).

Although not remembered as writer of literary works, one figure from this period became by far the most influential German author of the mid-century. The publication in 1867 of the first volume of *Das Kapital* brought the world's attention to Karl Marx (1818–83), a man of the nineteenth century whose thinking made an incalculable impact, for good or for ill, on the history of the twentieth.

The transition from the quiet mid-century to the intensity of the 1870s, 1880s and 1890s is also marked by a shift in the kinds of cultural activity that dominated the literary scene. Two of the most significant literary figures of the 70s and 80s were not poets, dramatists, or novelists but rather a composer, Richard Wagner (1813–83), and a classical scholar turned philosopher, Friedrich Nietzsche (1844–1900). Though primarily a composer, Wagner had at the heart of his operatic project a very literary ambition: he wanted to reconstruct Greek tragic drama in all its glory as described by Aristotle in his *Poetics*. Wagner's operas were meant to be more than pieces of music performed by singers in costumes; they were fully-formed music dramas in which the music performed a vital *dramatic* function. It is typical of Wagner's goal of writing not only music but also developing wide-ranging if obscure philosophical themes that he wrote all the texts for his operas.

No one understood Wagner's ambition better than the young Nietzsche, whose first important publication, *Die Geburt der Tragödie* (The Birth of Tragedy, 1872), was enormously influenced by the success of Wagnerian opera. The merger of music and dramatic poetry in Wagner's works led the philosopher to the idea that ancient Greek tragedy had been from its inception in ancient Athens an art balanced, through the spirit of music, between form and the formless, between the dark urges of what Nietzsche called the Dionysian (after the Greek god of wine) and the bright clarity of the Apollonian (after the sun god Apollo).

Nietzsche's conception of Greek tragedy — and ultimately all great art — as poised on the edge between the two poles of rational organization (Apollo) and irrational dissolution (Dionysus) influenced nearly every writer who came after, including not least the young Thomas Mann. Mann, too, was intoxicated by Wagner's music and thrilled by the way certain musical figures could transform the emotional impact of a dramatic situation. Both his love of Wagner's music and his admiration for Nietzsche's concept of art would inform his mature writing.

There were, of course, more purely literary developments in the late nineteenth century. In the last decades of the century, a naturalistic strain became dominant in the stories and plays of German writers. The play *Die Weber* (The Weavers, 1892) by Gerhart Hauptmann (1862–1946) offers an apt example. It depicts in heart-breaking detail the uprising of the Silesian weavers in 1844, showing how desperate their economic and social situation was and how hopeless their lives had become. The play has no central character, no hero or heroine: its protagonist is an entire class of people represented by the exploited, alienated weavers. It is a play Karl Marx would have understood and admired.

Social concerns also predominate in the fiction of the period. The novels of Theodor Fontane (1819–98) center around issues of marriage, money, and social standing and often spotlight the problems of the rising middle class in the newly prosperous city of Berlin, Fontane's home. *Frau Jenny Treibel* (1893), for example, explores the conflict between emotions and economics in the marriage plans of a newly rich middle-class Berlin family. The main character, Jenny, professes to have interests in art and in intellectual matters; but when it comes to the marriage of her son, she prefers a daughter-in-law with funds to one with finer feelings. Fontane's characterization of Jenny is one of the most effective social satires in modern German literature, and the next generation of writers, including Mann, learned much from it.

An engagement with social problems also characterizes the work of the dramatist Frank Wedekind (1864–1918). One of the boldest of his plays, *Frühlingserwachen* (Spring's Awakening, 1891), confronts the embarrassing matter of teenage sexuality in an age of repression. Wedekind dares to put on stage scenes involving masturbation, sado-masochistic eroticism, and abortion, shocking his audience into examining a set of problems it would probably have preferred to ignore. Shocking, too, was Wedekind's daring dramatic technique, which begins with realism but drives beyond it by representing the world as an adolescent might see it. A school faculty meeting in *Frühlingserwachen,* for example, depicts the teachers as caricatures straight from a student's fantasy; and the last scene of the play includes among its characters a boy who had died earlier in the action, allowing the dead boy to explain to the audience the circumstances of his death.

The nineteenth century ended with two epoch-making events in German cultural history. The first was the aforementioned publication of Sigmund Freud's *Traumdeutung,* and the second was the appearance of Thomas Mann's novel of family decline, *Buddenbrooks* (1901).

Freud (1856–1939), the founder of psychoanalysis and certainly one of the most influential thinkers of the twentieth century, argued that dreams provided a window on a part of the mind Freud proposed to call the unconscious. This unconscious mind, though almost impossible to detect, was for Freud the origin of much human behavior and the explanation for much mental disease. Freud was convinced that if one could understand what was taking place in the unconscious mind of a patient, it would be possible to effect a cure. Freud's theory had enormous importance for literature, for he believed that literary texts often functioned as a kind of institutionalized dreaming. They could thus, like ordinary dreams, offer a glimpse into the workings of the unconscious.

Mann's novel *Buddenbrooks,* subtitled *Der Verfall einer Familie* (The Decline of a Family), was an equally important event for German letters, but in quite a different way from Freud's theory of dreams. The twenty-five-year-old author achieved the greatest literary sensation in Germany since the publication of Goethe's *Werther* 125 years earlier. The story is set in Mann's own home city of Lübeck in northern Germany and chronicles the events affecting the Buddenbrook family, a fictional family bearing a marked resemblance to the real-life relatives of the author. The lengthy novel has the gripping appeal of a soap opera, as the reader gets to experience in intimate detail the troubled lives of the well-to-do Buddenbrook parents, children, and grandchildren over the period of several decades. Mann showed himself in his mid-twenties already the master of his craft, painting with gentle irony the traits of people he clearly both loved and despised, people clearly deserving of both affection and contempt. The novel was a technical tour-de-force, an artistic breakthrough, and a financial bonanza for both Mann and his publisher. It was both the last great work of the old century and the first great work of the new one.

The Organization and Contents of This Volume

We have chosen to come at our subject from several different angles. Part I provides the necessary contexts — social, cultural, political — without which it would be impossible to understand or assess the literary achievements of the nineteenth century. Part II examines the principle movements, Part III the major genres characteristic of the age. Part IV provides bibliographical tools for further study, including both a bibliographical essay on the secondary literature and a straightforward list, inclusive as practicable, of the primary texts, including information about English translations of these works.

Thus, the primary organization of this book is: Contexts, Movements, Genres, Resources. This seems to us, and we expect to readers as well, a fairly standard approach to the presentation of literary history. And yet, direct and uncontroversial as such categories may appear, they are never neutral. They inevitably bring with them assumptions about the literary material they supposedly only describe. They privilege some authors, works, and features of works as more proper and definitive for the order they represent, and they play down or even neglect others as of lesser representative significance. Hermeneutically aware literary historians must consider the shaping influence of their own methodological categories just as carefully as they consider the literature under interrogation, and all the contributors to this volume prove themselves acutely hermeneutically aware. This fact should help readers to remain alert themselves, to keep in mind the limitations of an enterprise such as this, and to be ready to undertake further reading as inclination and opportunity suggest. That is why this book ends, not with a conclusion that wraps up the history of nineteenth-century German literature in a neat bundle, but with extensive suggestions for additional, more sharply focused study.

The most important function a literary history can serve is to let the reader know what the major texts are, who wrote them, and how and why they reward one's attention. It is this last element that all the contributors to this volume have tried to stress above all others. A bare list can provide the essential information about authors and titles — indeed just such a list, compiled by Thomas Spencer, concludes this book — but the list cannot suggest why these authors and titles are worth the effort of finding and reading them. The essays offered here attempt to do precisely that, and to do it in such a way as to give a sense of how German nineteenth-century literature participates in a larger cultural universe.

That larger cultural and historical context is the special province of the essays in Part I. Because the nineteenth century (as we have defined it) follows directly on the heels of Romanticism, we have opened the volume with Andrew Webber's essay on the afterlife of Romanticism. As Webber's essay reveals, the whole nineteenth century could easily be conceived as the afterlife of the Romantic period, but in a very special sense: the romantic spirit lived on by serving as what he calls the "cultural unconscious" for the age of bourgeois realism. The voices of Romantic writers continued to inhabit nineteenth-century texts in spectral form through a process of "intertextual recall" that preserved the traces of Romanticism in the very act of trying to subvert or overthrow Romantic ideas. For many writers of the nineteenth century, the spectral voices of Romanticism were bad ghosts that could threaten basic nineteenth-century values, including in particular "reality," perhaps the most fundamental of all nineteenth-century values. The "unworldly inwardness" of Romantic thinking posed a constant threat to politically engaged writers like Heine and Büchner because such a perspective runs directly counter to the identification of reality with the world of politics and social history.

The commitment to political and social improvement characteristic of much nineteenth-century writing is also a commitment to the living world of the here and now. Romanticism, on the other hand, was often concerned with the world of the dead and gone, and thus often seemed steeped in melancholy and nostalgia for an irrecoverable past. Although this romantic nostalgia tended to express itself in fantasies of continuity with the past that were inhospitable to bourgeois political engagement, this nostalgia returns again and again in realistic fiction of the nineteenth century. A literature that claims to mirror the world without distortion finds in its mirrors not only the real social and political world it wants to represent but also fantastic "uncanny, secret presences" that seem to sneak in from the romantic past. Even at the very end of the century, at the greatest apparent distance from the Romantic age, we find in a work apparently belonging entirely to the age of bourgeois realism, Thomas Mann's *Buddenbrooks*, what Webber calls "a longing for a lost or inaccessible place" that would seem more at home in Novalis or Eichendorff.

Webber shows that the Romantic impulse not only continues throughout the century but that it develops a new function: it reasserts the claims of subjectivity and the mysterious in life against the false security of nineteenth-century positivism. Romanticism thus becomes the essential "other" of an optimistic and confident sense of what constitutes reality. The most successful and nuanced of nineteenth-century writing thus necessarily incorporates the voice of this spectral other as a necessary, cautionary undercurrent, even in the most concerted attempts to mirror a world of social and political progress.

Indeed, as Lilian Furst indicates, the nineteenth century is "a paradoxical time of contrasts, changes, and reversals that defy reduction to a simple scenario." One of the most striking of nineteenth-century paradoxes actually begins in the eighteenth century, when German Romantic ideas were spreading to the rest of Europe. The figures most Europeans associated with German Romanticism were names like Goethe and Schiller, writers who, because they did not apparently participate in the most radical Romantic experiments in the manner of Friedrich Schlegel or Jean Paul Richter, were not normally classified as Romantic by literary historians. This Romantic iconoclasm was peculiar to Germany, where the aftermath of the French Revolution proved surprisingly hospitable to aesthetic experimentation. Post-revolutionary France found artistic novelty somewhat suspect, but the ruling powers in the German states encouraged radicalism in the arts as a safety valve that could help to prevent radical political ideas from taking root. Ironically, the writers who were thus encouraged, among them Novalis, Wackenroder, and Friedrich Schlegel, believed seriously in the possibility of transforming the political landscape through poetry and hoped to bring about just the sort of political upheaval the tolerant authorities most feared. This Romantic belief in the political effectiveness of literature is one of the most important legacies left to the nineteenth-century realists by Romanticism.

Furst points out that German realism parallels its European counterparts in its opposition to transcendental idealism and its commitment to the here and now. But the "here and now" most prominently displayed in German realist writing tended to be particularized into extreme forms of regionalism. Unlike French realism, which always used standard French as its medium of expression, German realism often chose regional dialects as the most effective way to emphasize the particularity of its subject matter. One result was that French realistic writing was accessible to all Europeans able to read French, whereas much German realistic writing required an intimate knowledge of local variations in spoken German. The extremely sharp focus of German realism during the mid-nineteenth century can also be seen in the rise of peasant literature as an important sub-genre. Although it was immensely popular in its home territory, it did not travel well and had little influence on the rest of Europe. The same could be said of German Poetic Realism, which found complex and often moving ways to depict the human consequences of the small happenings in life. As sophisticated and successful as some of this literature was, it too did not travel well and never became part of the larger European cultural scene.

In the latter part of the nineteenth century, as Furst explains, Germany began to become more prominent in the rest of Europe. Although French was still the most frequently taught second modern language in England, German began to gain ground, especially after the marriage of Victoria to a German prince, Albert, in 1840. At the same time, German scholarship was flourishing and attracting attention all over the world, so that those who desired access to the knowledge available in German scientific literature sought access to the language. Germany was thus becoming increasingly integrated into European culture; German literature of the latter part of the century reflects this. German naturalism was very much in the mainstream of European thought: its guiding spirits (Ibsen, Darwin, Marx, Comte, and Taine) were the same for Germans as for the rest of Europe. Germany at the end of the century is thus very different from the relatively isolated Germany of mid-century; it becomes once again nearly as much a part of the larger European context as it was at the beginning, in the splendid Age of Goethe.

Koch sharpens the geo-political context of Furst's literary parallels and disparities by focusing on the many transformations that mark the political life of the times. Perhaps the most prominent of these was the increasing dominance of large nation-states in central Europe where for centuries relatively small entities had maintained their independence. Of particular concern to Koch is the *Deutsche Bund* (German Confederation), a group of states ranging from the great (Prussia, Austria) to the very small (Liechtenstein), comprising territory roughly coincident with the old Holy Roman Empire. Within the Bund there was a great deal of diversity, politically and ethnically; and outside the confederation there were German-speaking communities, such as Switzerland, that exercised a decisive influence on the members and their relations with each other. Although events in Prussia understandably had powerful repercussions in smaller nations like Switzerland we find a surprisingly strong influence moving in the other direction too, as Swiss democratic institutions and experience with multi-ethnic communities shaped political developments within the Bund.

Expansion of democratic principles was an important element in transforming the German political scene in the nineteenth century, but economic changes were perhaps even more decisive. The Customs Union (*Zollverein*) instituted by Prussia in the 1830s quickly succeeded in establishing Prussian domination in the area covered by this free trade agreement and helped to overcome centuries of insistence on local control. The need to gain access to the rich markets in the states belonging to the Customs Union forced those on the margins to join and thus to bring themselves within the Prussian political sphere. Prussia was thus able to create a kind of economic empire in advance of the political empire that would emerge later in the century. The fact that Austria remained outside the Union had enormous consequences, for it led ultimately to the split between Prussia and Austria that brought with it war in 1866.

In the midst of all this, at the center of the century, came the revolutions of 1848. The forced abdication of Louis Philippe of France in February of 1848 ignited a series of revolutionary uprisings in central Europe with diverse grievances and goals. Although these multiple revolutions failed to bring about any immediate change, they did sow the seeds for a long-term transformation of the political landscape in German-speaking lands. And it sparked a new interest in the problem of German unity, now recognized as an enduring "German question" to be debated for decades to come and made more urgent by the emergence of two competing German powers, Prussia and Austria.

By the end of the century, Prussia and Austria were not just two competing political units; they were two very different cultures. Prussia was dominated by a military aristocracy and developed a politico-social structure equipped to run a large, centralized military-industrial state that could — and, in the Franco-Prussian War, did — dominate its neighbors. Austria, on the other hand, became the multi-national Austro-Hungarian Empire, with a far less centralized system of authority and an ethnically diverse, polyglot population. These differences are reflected in the literary works of the two regions, culminating in a Thomas Mann in the Prussian north and a Franz Kafka in the Austro-Hungarian south.

Part II examines in detail the major literary movements of the years between 1830 and 1900. In his essay on the literary period between 1830 and 1848, Robert C. Holub confronts head on the aesthetic and ideological presuppositions implicit in defining the post-Romantic, pre-realist period by these dates, and in choosing either the rather conservative rubric "Biedermeierzeit," the more leftist-oriented term "Vormärz," or the more apparently neutral "Restaurationszeit" to describe the literature of this one span of literary history. While prudently declining to settle on any one such designation, Holub does note that the difficulties that literary historians face today in defining the period tend to reflect the same struggles that German-language authors themselves faced in defining the role of literature in the early nineteenth century. Holub focuses especially on the competition among authors of this period for profit and control of the literary heritage of Romanticism at a time of rapidly changing political and cultural traditions. In this, he characterizes the period as equally defined by the afterlife of Romanticism, which Andrew Webber discusses in his essay, and by the imperatives of Realism, which Gail Finney makes the subject of hers.

Finney begins her article on German Realism and Naturalism with a thoughtful consideration of the difficulties involved in defining the Poetic Realist movement that dominated German letters during the mid to late nineteenth century. She recalls the two models that have dominated most literary historical analyses: that developed by Erich Auerbach in his widely influential study, *Mimesis* (1946), a model that approaches realism as basically an ahistorical style or orientation that has manifested itself throughout the course of Western literature; and that preferred by Georg Lukács and others that focuses on realism as it manifested itself in the French and English literature of the second half of the nineteenth century, as the serious, verisimilar representation of social, political, and cultural conditions and how they impinge on individual lives. Finney rightly has reservations about both these models: the former tends to overlook the distinctive formal and stylistic features privileged by the German realists, while the latter tends to hold the German tradition to standards by which it can only appear rather second rate, and to ignore the quite different set of interests that shaped the literary endeavors of its most important practitioners. Finney does insist on foregrounding stylistic concerns as central to German realism, and this leads her to an approach that diverges noticeably from that taken in Todd Kontje's *Companion to German Realism* (Camden House, 2002), and to focus on three canonical authors who go largely unmentioned in the Companion volume: Gottfried Keller, Theodor Storm, and Conrad Ferdinand Meyer. While Kontje's volume reflects a view that implicitly applies to its material the more or less extra-literary focus on social, political, and historical conditions that has characterized French and English models of realism, without regard for specifically literary qualities, Finney's article focuses on the innovations in literary technique that peculiarly characterized the work of these German-language authors, innovations that reflected their response to the linguistic skepticism they inherited from the German idealist philosophers, shared with their great contemporary, Friedrich Nietzsche, and shaped into the literary heritage that would become modernism. Like Holub, she sees the idealist inheritance as crucial to the course of German literature in the later nineteenth century, and, like Holub, she sees the seeds for the following dominant literary paradigm already germinating in the present one.

Although Finney's discussion of realism emphasizes the distinctiveness of the German tradition and primarily stresses its literary qualities, her treatment of naturalism focuses instead on its self-conscious ties to the broader European movements of naturalism in literature, Darwinism in science, and socialism and feminism in politics. This does not prevent her from continuing to trace the effects of the realists' linguistic skepticism in the narrative experiments of the German naturalists. It does, however, allow her to discuss alongside the prominent figures of Arno Holz, Johannes Schlaf, and Gerhart Hauptmann the lesser known woman writer, Elsa Bernstein.

Ernst Grabovszki's article suggests much of the continuing force of naturalism in the plurality of literary styles that emerged in its wake at the turn of the century, including the radicalization of its social concerns in the *Arbeiterdichtung* (literature by or about workers) and *Heimatsliteratur* (literature about the homeland of the author) of the period, and of its linguistic skepticism in the work of the impressionists and symbolists. Although Grabovszki delineates some basic differences between the various literary trends of the 1890s, he is careful not to push the distinctions between impressionism, symbolism, aestheticism, or *décadence* too hard, nor to insist on their all-encompassing coverage. Too many of the most interesting authors of this period display influences that could be attributed to a variety of these movements, without being easily situated within any one; and too, many of its most interesting authors, including Karl Kraus and Arthur Schnitzler, do not seem to fall within the literary historian's categories at all. Similarly, while Grabovszki affirms the common perception of the withdrawal of literature from political and social concerns as a hallmark of the several *l'art pour l'art* movements of the *fin de siécle*, he does not push the issue to the point that it blinds us to other matters. Among those other matters are the broadly international orientation of many of these artists, their engagement with the literature of not only France and England but also Russia and Scandinavia, and the self-conscious influence of other cultural spheres on literature at this time, including painting, architecture, science, journalism, philosophy, and medicine. Like both Holub and Finney, Grabovszki manages to display the distortions as well as the clarity that literary history can bring to its literary material.

In Part III, the center of attention shifts from movements to genres. One might expect the points of contention regarding the literary historian's categories to be less prominent in relation to the discussion of the genres of drama, the novel, and lyric, but one would be wrong. Benjamin Bennett's essay on nineteenth-century German drama starts out with the provocative claim that there *is* no drama in this period. His argument is in part that literary historians have tended to approach drama as an exclusively literary phenomenon, and in so doing have fundamentally misrepresented the genre, which is by its nature split between a literary or poetic art and a theatrical, enacted one. Treating drama only as a distinct type of literature has fostered a reading of nineteenth-century drama that privileges some of its most *un*dramatic authors: in particular, Friedrich Hebbel, Franz Grillparzer, and Otto Ludwig. Like Holub, Bennett does suggest that the miscomprehensions that characterize the definitions of literary historians today tend to reflect the confusions of the nineteenth-century authors themselves. Hebbel especially is shown to miss the necessarily double, or split, nature of drama, and to suppress its theatrical identity in order to present it as the literary equivalent of systematic philosophy in its claims to wholeness and unity. To counter the distortions of this "literary" tradition, Bennett offers readings of three authors whose works more honestly confront both the poetic and theatrical dimensions of the dramatic art: Georg Büchner, Johann Nestroy, and Gerhart Hauptmann. Bennett's point is not that these authors thereby achieve a more complete, encompassing, or perfect mode of drama, but that they display the essentially incomplete, disrupted, and defective nature of the genre itself. The admonition against the fantasy of comprehensiveness that Bennett explicitly aims at the dramatist's enterprise he implicitly directs at the literary historian's as well.

In his essay on the novel, Jeffrey Sammons openly laments the distortions and occlusions that literary history has imposed on the rich and varied prose fiction of the German nineteenth century. He identifies two particular tendencies as most responsible for these obfuscations, both of which he associates with a misguided desire to distinguish a peculiarly German literature from that of other contemporary European nations. The first is the enduring critical inclination to view the Bildungsroman as the definitive form of the German novel throughout the nineteenth century, an inclination that has led to a neglect of the broad range of novel types, and especially realist ones, in German that do not differ in any substantial way from those written in French, English, or Russian at this time. The second is the tendency to define a "poetic Realist" tradition in Germany that is fundamentally different from the social realism of other, more worldly and cosmopolitan nations and, as part of that, to emphasize the novella as *the* German prose form in contrast to the novel form that dominated in other literatures. Sammons questions the usefulness of both these claims, arguing for the novelistic quality of many of the best nineteenth-century German novellas, and urging an abandonment of any concept of realism that both isolates and privileges one of its strains over other equally viable ones that existed, and thrived, at the same time. In order to counter the distortions he sees literary history to have inflicted on nineteenth-century German prose fiction, Sammons organizes his own essay in such a way as to discourage notions of either orderly sequence or unified agenda at work in the literature under review. His essay stresses instead the diversity of novel types, and focuses attention on many works that have for the most part been neglected by more canon-oriented contemporary critics. It is, as it were, literary history *contra* literary history.

Thomas Pfau's exposition of the course of lyric poetry over the nineteenth century echoes many of the points made by other contributors regarding other genres or specific periods. Like Bennett's reading of drama, Pfau's reading of lyric proceeds from a counterintuitive starting point — that is, from a sense that lyric poetry was at an end before the period under consideration began. This sense was partly a result of the overwhelming yet no longer useful lyric heritage of the *Goethezeit* that Holub describes. It was also partly a result of the influence of Hegel's aesthetic theory, which seemed to claim that Romantic poetry had been the culmination of a two-thousand year historical process, after which the emotional basis of the lyric was to be superseded by the more abstract form of speculative philosophy — giving rise to a disregard of the material basis in lyric poetry in a manner strictly analogous to the disregard of the theatrical basis in drama described by Bennett. Pfau does not, however, consider that this position only led to an absence of genuine lyric in the changed literary, cultural, and historical landscape of nineteenth-century German-speaking countries. He does note the rash of inferior poetry based on a misguided attempt simply to continue the emotion-based poetry of the Romantic era, as if such poetry had not already ended. He also acknowledges other, equally inferior poetry that tried to enact in lyric poetry itself the Hegelian imperative to overcome emotion with speculative thought (here, too, Friedrich Hebbel serves as whipping boy); and still other all-but-forgotten poetry that abandoned the focus on both emotions and abstract thought and opted for subject matter that was either topically political or historical. But he also calls attention to the truly significant poetry that worked to thematize its own belatedness, its own incongruity in the new, equally incongruent cultural territory. Such poetry also worked to realize lyric emotion as its own, distinct form of self-reflexive cognition, and (of most lasting importance) it strove to overcome the inherited association of lyric poetry and emotional expression in the name of a new, proto-modernist aesthetic of objective constructions, impressionist language, and radically attenuated subject positions. Like Finney, Pfau sees the dominant tendencies of the early twentieth century already far developed in the nineteenth, which is shown to have overcome its own literary history even before it was over.

On the margin of the literary scene — and yet also somehow still at the heart of it — was the music drama of Richard Wagner. As a composer, Wagner has a reputation that seems unassailable as one of the giants of European opera, but as a literary and cultural figure he still stirs controversy. The cult of Wagner seems to go on without any signs of abatement — at the beginning of the twenty-first century there is a seven-year wait for tickets to the Bayreuth festival — in spite of the hostility he engenders among many. His relation to German aesthetics and literature, as Christopher Morris explains, is as complex and troubling as it is vitally important to an understanding of the German nineteenth century.

Although we tend to think of Wagner primarily as a composer, he was also a man of letters. Not only did he write the libretti for his operas, but also wrote numerous prose works setting forth the basis for his great project, the "total work of art" (*Gesamtkunstwerk*). Morris reminds us that Wagner's aim was, in fact, the radical transformation of German culture. The ambition of this project staggers the imagination, for the Wagnerian "total work of art" intended to do nothing less than heal the breach between man and nature by displaying on the stage a "representation of perfect human nature." The music drama, drawing on the primal material of myth, could even transcend history by tapping into a reservoir of mythic truth that was eternally true and eternally fresh. Wagner's operas were thus diametrically opposed to the bourgeois realist novel of the time, with their emphasis on everyday travails and on the details of the quotidian world. Wagner meant to lead his audience back to the roots of Western civilization, to the world of primal myth, a world like the ancient Greece somewhat poetically described by the influential eighteenth-century critic J. J. Winckelmann, as one in which man and nature existed harmoniously.

Also essential to the program was a disturbing political agenda. Wagner's goal of returning to the primal mythic roots of ancient Greece depended on his belief that the Germans were the inheritors of classical civilization and that the German language had a special status as somehow more firmly rooted in authenticity. Wagner's anti-Semitism was part of this same syndrome, in spite of his avowed commitment to what he called the "purely human" elements in German culture. As Wagner made explicitly clear, he considered everything Jewish to be the opposite of what was pure and indeed what was human. "Jewishness" (*Judentum*) needed to be purged from music, if music were to serve appropriately in the great cultural program Wagner had in mind.

Music was essential to this program because of its special status among the arts. Wagner, later in his career, enthusiastically endorsed Schopenhauer's contention that music was closer to the Will, thus to the ground of all being, than any of the other arts. Wagner shared Schopenhauer's belief that music could penetrate through the veil of representations and bring the listener to a state of mind that bypassed normal perception. Music could thus communicate in ways unavailable to the text of the libretto. Even before he read Schopenhauer, Wagner was already composing music that went far beyond the strict demands of the libretto. Morris cautions us to remember, though, that Wagner always ultimately relies on words to ground the meaning of the score. Wagner the musician thus never entirely effaces Wagner the man of letters.

It remains only to say a word about Part IV. The list of Primary Sources, which includes the most important works of the period, together with data on English translations to the extent they exist, is a standard feature in all the *Camden House History of German Literature* volumes. For secondary sources, the reader will benefit, we think, from the expert guidance offered by John Pizer's bibliographical essay. Pizer not only knows his way around the relevant literature, he knows what is likely to be helpful to readers of a work like the *Camden House History of German Literature*. The editors specifically asked him to select only those works which most clearly illuminate the central issues of contemporary scholarship, so there is no comprehensive list on offer. Instead, the reader should learn not only what further reading there is to do, but what the important problems and debates in the field are at the beginning of the twenty-first century.

Philosophy and Other Matters Beyond the Scope of This Volume

Even further removed from the literary center than Wagner's musico-dramatic project was the philosophical writing of the nineteenth century, and here the editors decided to set the boundary of our literary history. It would seem in a sense an easy decision to exclude philosophical writing from a book about literature, since there appears to be as clear a disciplinary boundary between philosophy and literature as there is between, say, physics and literature. But in the case of nineteenth-century Germany the situation is by no means so clear.

The difficulty of separating philosophical discourse from literary or critical discourse had begun in the late eighteenth century, when the two fields were not so distinct. Poets could and did write philosophical essays, and philosophers wrote what would today be called literary criticism. Romantic philosophy and Romantic literature were closely bound together by personal as well as cultural links, since the philosophers and poets were in many cases part of the same social circle. The philosopher Schelling felt not the slightest hesitation in writing about Shakespeare and Dante, and that not in exceptional excursions into literary matters but as a central part of his philosophical discourse. Fichte wrote an important essay "On the Spirit and the Letter in Philosophy" that is just as much a literary as a philosophical text.

The nineteenth century inherited this comfort with an intimate mixing of philosophy and literature. Even philosophers who did not share the literary ambiance of a Schelling expressed important ideas about poetry. Hegel, in his Berlin lectures on aesthetics of the 1820s, proposed a way of understanding drama in terms of conflict that influenced both the theory and practice of stagecraft for more than a century. As Pfau shows in his chapter on lyric poetry, German poets of the decades after 1830 were in many cases responding to Hegelian ideas about emotion. And that most anti-Hegelian of all philosophers, Schopenhauer, not only discussed literature as part of his great work *Die Welt als Wille und Vorstellung* (The World as Will and Idea, 1819) but presented a literary genre, tragedy, as the ultimate expression of the wisdom to be found in his philosophy.

Schopenhauer's work, important as it is for the history of European philosophy, had perhaps its greatest impact in the literary world. We have already discussed the importance of his notions about music to the mature Wagner. Later in the century, with the help of Nietzsche, his influence spread to the young Mann and to others of that generation, such as Hermann Hesse and the somewhat younger Franz Kafka. It is even likely, as Mann himself suggested, that Freud's notion of the unconscious owes something to the Schopenhauerian Will. If Mann's suggestion is correct, then Schopenhauer's influence worked its way through Freud to much of the literature of the twentieth century.

Just how closely philosophy allied itself with literature in the nineteenth century can be seen clearly in no less radical a thinker than Karl Marx, whose work is rarely thought of as particularly literary. Further, it is true that the main line of Marx's thought has little to say about literary matters and that Marx's influence on European letters has been largely mediated through the writings of other theorists who followed him. But it is worth noting that Marx, like other writers of his day, understood poetic texts as having a special claim on truth. When Marx presents his case for the evil effects of money, for example, he marshals as powerful evidence extensive quotations from Shakespeare and Goethe. These citations are not simply rhetorical embellishments intended to spice up an otherwise dry document; they are a vital part of the argument. He understands these poets as colleagues in the enterprise in which he is engaged. Marx would agree with Shelley, a writer whom he greatly admired, that great poets are also great philosophers.

The opposite, we have to acknowledge, has rarely been true. Kant, Hegel, Schopenhauer, even Marx (with some notable exceptions) do not write with anything like poetic flair. One of the few philosophers who might lay claim to a true poetic talent was Nietzsche, one of the most linguistically gifted philosophers since Plato. Some of Nietzsche's writings, such as *Also sprach Zarathustra* (Thus Spake Zarathustra, 1883–85), are so poetic in both form and content that they could just as readily be classified as literature as philosophy.

Unlike Marx, who received formal university training in philosophy, Nietzsche received his doctorate in classical philology. It is not surprising, then, that his first important philosophical work, *Die Geburt der Tragödie aus dem Geiste der Musik* (The Birth of Tragedy from the Spirit of Music, 1872), was intended to inaugurate his career as a professor of Classics at the University of Basel or that the basic thesis of this work is an attempt to answer some fundamental questions about the origin of Greek drama. But from the outset this work shows itself to be as much philosophy as philology, using some of Schopenhauer's ideas about tragedy as a springboard for a reworking of aesthetics into the foundation of a world view. Nietzsche starts by accepting Schopenhauer's fundamentally pessimistic view of human life, claiming that such an existence as ours can only be justified aesthetically. The ultimate human wisdom would be the advice offered by the Greek demi-god Silenus, who proposes that the best possible thing for a human being would be never to be born, the second best thing to die soon. Greek culture, Nietzsche claims, both accepts and inverts this wisdom. It presents in the god Dionysus a force that celebrates the obliteration of individuality in intoxication and ultimately in death; but it also presents in the god Apollo the vision of a life of individual greatness, beauty, and immortality.

The dark, erotic, and deadly world of Dionysus meets the bright, clear world of Apollo on the Athenian tragic stage, where a single Apollonian individual, the actor, confronts a Dionysian mass entity, the chorus. This balanced confrontation is the birth of tragedy. It is the moment in the history of Western culture when two forces, the dark Dionysian wisdom of Silenus and the Apollonian golden dream-world of the immortal Olympian gods, exist together in harmony. In only a single generation, Nietzsche argued, the rise of Socratic philosophy and its reflection in the overwhelmingly Apollonian drama of Euripides would mark the loss of that harmony.

Nietzsche's idea of the two forces, one dark and erotic, the other clear and rational, found its way into the psychology of Sigmund Freud. Although Freud vigorously denied having been influenced by Nietzsche's writings, it seems likely that Mann was right to see in the confrontation between Freud's concept of the Ego and the Id an unmistakable intellectual descendant of the Apollo-Dionysus tension. And both Freud and Nietzsche owe a debt to Schopenhauer's distinction between the world as Will and the world as Representation (*Vorstellung*). Freud's participation in the literary culture of the nineteenth century goes much further, however, as is evident in some of the most famous of his theoretical formulations. Shakespeare and Sophocles are centrally important figures in *The Interpretation of Dreams,* and Freud named perhaps his most daring conjecture about childhood sexuality after Oedipus, a literary character. The core of his notion of the "uncanny" as the return of the repressed is based on a reading of E. T. A. Hoffmann's fantastic tale "Der Sandmann" (The Sandman, 1816). Indeed, one could argue that Freud is perhaps the most literary of all the non-belletristic writers in recent European history.

Thus it would not be difficult to argue that much of the literary and cultural history of the nineteenth century is bound up with the history of its philosophy. One could argue as well that an account of that philosophy properly belongs in a literary history of the period. Granting that, however, it is still necessary for a volume such as this to draw the line somewhere, and we have chosen to put philosophy on the other side of that line. The brief indications in the paragraphs above may perhaps give the reader interested in pursuing matters across the line some notion of where to look.

Part I

Contexts

The Afterlife of Romanticism

Andrew Webber

GERMAN ROMANTICISM is a complex and slippery phenomenon, resisting any straightforward cultural historical periodization or localization. From an early stage in the historiography of the movement, the precocious flourishing of Romantic ideas in the movement's early period (*Frühromantik*) was contrasted with the more mature literary hey-day of high Romanticism (*Hochromantik*) and the often wistfully self-ironic developments of late Romanticism (*Spätromantik*.) In fact, though, the three stages of the life of German Romanticism, broadly spanning the last decade of the eighteenth century and the first three of the nineteenth, are not synchronized in their sequence; the naïve energy of the first often jostles with the more self-conscious, even parodic, disposition of the last, even within individual works. At the same time, a number of groups vied for the proper site of the movement's center, from Jena to Heidelberg, Leipzig, and Berlin; this was a movement that moved, dissolving and reforming in a new location on more than one occasion. Nor does the sequence of phases encompass the full lifespan of the movement: there are distinct trends in eighteenth-century Germany that prefigure Romanticism (both *Empfindsamkeit* and the *Sturm and Drang* can be seen as having proto-Romantic tendencies), and its afterlife, part of which forms the subject of this essay, is extensive and often potent.

The thematic concerns, formal techniques, and political interests of the movement also present a complicated picture. It seems to pursue a quest for metaphysical ends, after the model of the "blaue Blume," the mystical blue flower that is the emblematic object of Romantic yearning in Novalis's frag-mentary novel *Heinrich von Ofterdingen* (1802), but it also invokes the often grossly physical monsters of the Gothic (*Schauerromantik*) tradition. It embraces both a sentimental cult of domesticity, finding special significance in everyday life, and the terrorizing aesthetics of the sublime in the most inaccessible reaches of the experiential world. It celebrates the simplicity of folk culture and yet converts the *Märchen* (fairytale) and the *Volkslied* (folk-song) into their more artful, even esoteric, counterparts — the *Kunstmärchen* (artistic fairytale) and *Kunstvolkslied*. And it makes a cult of medievalism as a fantasy model of primal forms of social relation and aesthetic practice, but comes to complicate that model with the contradictory political and aesthetic demands of contemporary existence. Romanticism is often branded as reactionary, and some of its principal figures were indeed politically conservative, but there were also more liberal, even socialist, tendencies in the movement. If one of the defining aesthetic principles of Romanticism is its attachment to the anti-genre of the fragment, then this signals its resistance to any sustained definition, any grand narrative of its own character and development. It puts emphasis on processes of becoming rather than on established identity. As the principal theorist of early Romanticism, Friedrich Schlegel, has it in the course of his axiomatic definition of the Romantic as "progressive Universalpoesie," the essential nature of Romantic literature is "im Werden," a persistent state of becoming or incompletion.[1]

The process of becoming is not, however, to be mistaken for boundless vitality. While Romanticism pursues a cult of origins, of childhood and the childhood of man, an aspect of it is, more or less from the start, prematurely aged, caught in melancholic or mocking attitudes of looking back at itself. We might consider a description of dreams, taken from *Heinrich von Ofterdingen*, which Freud cites in his *Traumdeutung* (The Interpretation of Dreams, 1899) as an example of the understanding of dreams as refreshing and therapeutic in the manner of a child's game. While Freud sees in this Romantic account of dreaming a position that is appealing in its untroubled, poetic innocence, he fails to note the end of the quotation, which sets the playfulness of dreams against the "Wallfahrt zum Grabe" (pilgrimage to the grave),[2] a journey which is defined from the start by its mortal end. Novalis's text is, in fact, ambiguously cast between recuperation and desolation, the affirmation of creative vitality and a darker view of irredeemable mortality, and the dreams in the text work in both directions. Thus, Heinrich has an anxious dream of his Mathilde being drowned beyond his reach in a whirlpool, awakes into another dream that reunites him with her in death, and then awakes in turn from this, desperately unable to recover the key dream word that she whispered in his ear.[3] Dreams shift dialectically between separation and union in a way that is emblematic for the narrative as a whole, which never reaches the resolution for which it is programmed. Notwithstanding Freud's benign reading of it, Novalis's version of the Romantic view of dreaming might equally well be seen as the more restrained counterpart of the nightmarish account of fantasy that came to inform the Freudian theory of the uncanny in E. T. A. Hoffmann's fantastic novella, *Der Sandmann* (The Sandman, 1817). Novalis's whirlpool has a certain affinity with the circles of fire that are a leitmotif in Hoffmann's text. As we shall see, the afterlife of Romanticism incorporates both the recuperative and the nihilistic versions of the movement's dream-life; the legacies of Novalis and Hoffmann are dialectically intertwined.

Novalis's framing of childlike pleasure through the perspective of death indicates that Romanticism is never fully present or settled in its identity. It seeks to cast itself as a movement of originality, with transcendental reach, but its cult of immediacy is complicated by reliance on forms of mediation, whether in the shape of received cultural models (especially from medieval romance traditions) or of structures of ironic distance. The disposition of Romantic Irony, marking the knowing disjuncture between ideal or fantasy and actual conditions, which becomes such a key element in the writings of late Romantics like Hoffmann, is already anticipated in the earliest stirrings of the movement. While the Idealist philosophy of Fichte could construct the "Ich" as an absolute, sovereign category, its irony a mark of autonomy from the other, subsequent developments in the thinking of Novalis and others drew out the idea of the subject as mobile in its definition, constituted as self-conscious through processes of reflection. The subject, in other words, comes to be the object of its own irony, and this condition, which, on the one hand, promotes the playfulness and creative fantasy of much Romantic writing is also one which is prone to become destructive, following the pathological model of the "chronic dualism" that afflicts so many of Hoffmann's protagonists.[4] Ironic vitality is in contest with ironic morbidity, so that Romanticism was already, while apparently alive, also in its own post-Romantic afterlife. As such, it was peculiarly prepared to live on after its apparent historical demise as a cultural revenant, set to fascinate and to haunt the post-Romantic age proper.

The spirit and rhetoric of Romanticism is a regular, if often marginal, presence in the culture of nineteenth-century Germany when it comes under the sway of Realism, the dominant cultural ideology of the period under review here. The topoi and tropes of Romantic writing, the moonlit magic forest or the architectural ruin, the fantastic transportations and transfigurations, are recurrently in evidence, albeit often ambiguously charged, even disavowed. They are widespread in the popular culture of the period, but they also make themselves felt in some of its most canonical writings, working against their apparent Realist grain. In the current essay, the trajectory of the afterlife of Romanticism will be traced through texts by a number of the most significant writers of nineteenth-century Germany: from Heinrich Heine (1797–1856), through Georg Büchner (1813–37), Annette von Droste-Hülshoff (1797–1848), Theodor Storm (1817–88), Theodor Fontane (1819–98), and Thomas Mann (1875–1955). In each case, the Romantic persists as an intertextual recall: Romantic narratives, poems, and dramas are read by Realist readers, and their haunting effects are felt in the texts that play host to them.

The afterlife began before the movement was properly dead with its unofficial collective obituary, Heinrich Heine's *Die romantische Schule* (1835). This essay is fraught with Heine's own deeply ambivalent attachment to the Romantic. It collects together the principal proponents and exponents of Romantic writing in order at once to create a school after the fact and then to show how inwardly split and moribund that school is. Many of the writers are dead, and Heine supplies their epitaphs in a recurrent rhetorical gesture. And those that are still alive are typically represented as the living dead and furnished with premature epitaphs of their own, so that the spirit of August Wilhelm Schlegel is described as already deceased and his body a spook.[5] While Heine metes out judgments of various kinds, venomous critique, wry mockery, or guarded admiration, the whole is characterized by an overarching version of Romantic irony, a modulation between identification with, and distance from, his object. Heine describes the Romantic school as at base melancholic in attitude, attached to a yearning for what is intrinsically already lost to it. The "blaue Blume" is thus superseded by the passionflower, described as ghostly and melancholic, which elicits the voluptuous cultivation of suffering "in unserer Seele" (in our souls, 126). The first person plural is telling here: Heine shares in the mortified Romantic passion that he exposes. He mocks Friedrich Schlegel for his flight into the "zitternden Ruinen der katholischen Kirche" (trembling ruins of the Catholic Church), but he too in his obsessive necrology seems unable to embrace the suffering of his times as "Schmerzen der Wiedergeburt" (pains of rebirth) rather than as the "Agonie des Sterbens" (agony of dying) (166). He recognizes the vampiric character of the cult of medievalism, but again has to include himself in the circle of victims of the undead ghost that "saugt uns das rothe Leben aus der Brust" (sucks the red life out of our breast, 241). The post-Romantic Heine cannot help but be a parasite upon the parasitic affliction of the Romantics, compulsively re-enacting the return of the vampire in his own works much as he revives the ghosts and golems of the Romantic school in his essay.

Heine's morbid preoccupation with Romanticism incorporates both the ghost and the golem, the supernatural or transcendental aspects of the movement and its more earth-bound fantasies. The dichotomy is nicely in evidence in the encounter that he organizes between Novalis and Hoffmann. Behind the ethereal disposition of the former and the dogged attachment to materialism of the latter, even in his most esoteric fantasies, Heine diagnoses a shared condition of pathology: Novalis the consumptive meets Hoffmann the febrile fantasist. But the diagnostic role of the doctor-critic irks with Heine, who is bound to see in his "patients" indications of a disease that is endemic in the age and not least in the symptomatic shape of his own poetic writings. Instead, Heine reads *Heinrich von Ofterdingen* through a strategy of identification or, in psychoanalytic terms, transference, inhabiting through projection the text under scrutiny. Novalis's tubercular muse takes on the form of the girl, called Sophia (after Novalis's beloved Sophie), who introduces Heine to the text, and is found living with her sister, a very physical postmistress whose passion is reading Hoffmann. When Heine revisits this house inhabited by the two forms of

Romantic reading, he finds both touched by death. The vitality of the postmistress has been lost, her powerful breasts now in Romantic ruins, and she has ceased to read Hoffmann. The very touch of the physical object of a Hoffmann text is like death for the ethereal Sophia, but she also contracts her eventual death from the Novalis book, reading her consumption out of the consumptive text: "sie hatte sich die Schwindsucht herausgelesen" (196). Heine meanwhile transcribes the poetry in the style of Novalis that this Romantic reader speaks. He becomes a medium for a revived but death-marked embodiment of the muse of Novalis, thus spreading the consumptive contagion into newborn texts. Sophia's spirit passes into death, but she passes on her copy of *Heinrich von Ofterdingen* to the necrologist of the Romantic movement, who has this physical embodiment of the transcendental death-cult on his desk as he writes over her dead body.[6] The spirit of Novalis is thus introduced intertextually into the writing practices of his necrologist as ghostwriter. Heine, the would-be post-Romantic, remains intimately involved in the reading and writing network of Romantic fantasy.

For Heine, Romanticism, implicitly including his own Romanticism, remains politically suspect, regressive in its tendencies. He sees the Romantic School as following the reverse tide of restoration politics in the Germany of that time, the "Strom, der nach seiner Quelle zurückströmte" (river that flowed back to its source, 141). This is also how the rhetoric of Romanticism appears in the works of the later Heine's chief political mentor, Karl Marx. In the *Eighteenth Brumaire* (1852), written in response to the dictatorship of Louis Bonaparte, Marx famously arrogates the supernatural language of the "rotes Gespenst," the red ghost that Communism represents for the *ancien régime,* as his leitmotif to describe the failure of the 1848 revolution, which he sees as reviving not the spirit of the French Revolution but its phantom.[7] He invokes figures from the Romantic repertory to describe the revolutionary struggles of 1848–1851 as a mock-Gothic theatre: its protagonists are inverted Schlemihls,[8] shadows that have lost their bodies (136), or the victims of the bourgeois order as a vampire which sucks the blood from their hearts and the marrow from their brains in order to cast it into the alchemical cauldron of capital (201). The ghost of empty, theatrical repetition that Marx sees as the great counter-revolutionary danger at work in history is figured as a return of the repressive potential of Romanticism, its otherworldly fantasies and demons. Not for nothing does he represent the art historian and poet Gottfried Kinkel (1815–82), the first of his targets for opprobrium amongst the émigré figures of 1848, in *Die großen Männer des Exils* (The Great Men of Exile, written 1852, first published 1930), as playing the role of a latter-day Heinrich von Ofterdingen in a pseudo-Romantic amateur theatre.[9] Marx's mobilization of Romantic tropes to figure the repetitive character of history also implies that the Romantic itself may have a constitutional tendency toward repetition.

The ghost as revenant is a repetitive figure par excellence. Whether it is in the character of the historical repetition of Romanticism to be in the mode of farce, as Marx argues of the repetition of revolution, is another question. A more ambiguous mixture of earnest and irony, such as that exhibited by Marx's text in its invocation of Gothic figures, is the abiding characteristic of the ghostly afterlife of Romanticism.

In the work of Georg Büchner, too, the radical agenda for social change has a tendency to be converted into a theatrical rehearsal of the Romantic fantasy world. While Büchner sets out an anti-idealist agenda for a theatre devoted to "Menschen von Fleisch und Blut" (people of flesh and blood) and driven by their material concerns,[10] the program for an early form of politically engaged Realism is recurrently seen to play host to forms of self-serving theatricality. The ghost of the revolution Marx seeks to exorcise is already abroad in the stage-managed version of the French Revolution that Büchner represents in *Dantons Tod* (Danton's Death, 1835), where the revolutionaries are haunted by Gothic specters of the Terror and entertain elaborate Romanticist fantasies of transcendental lyricism.[11] The scenes where these fantasies are contrived introduce into the materialist drama of the revolution a form of Romantic theatre that will then take over the stage in Büchner's satirical fantasy drama *Leonce und Lena* (1838).

As Heine with his death-kissed Sophia, and Marx in his satirical biography of Kinkel enact the afterlife of the biographical novel *Heinrich von Ofterdingen*, in *Leonce und Lena* Büchner stages a pastiched revival of Romantic drama. While the drama is confected out of an extensive inter-textual network, Brentano's comedy, *Ponce de Leon* (1801), is its prime source. Büchner's title in itself, eliding Ponce and Leon into the figure of Leonce, indicates that the play will be an echoing fabrication after Brentano's model, an exercise in the playful performance of citation. Büchner develops a fantasia on the principal themes of Brentano's drama, with Leonce following the eponymous Ponce in cultivating aristocratic melancholy born of existential *far niente*, and a plot that leads through playful, masquerading diversions toward a resolution of the intrigue. While Brentano borrows the clothes for his drama from the *commedia dell'arte*, Büchner's text is a borrowing at second hand, one that takes the figures of ambiguous or artificial identity in *Ponce de Leon* and subjects them to hyperbolic reworking. In particular, the mask and the automaton, which Brentano employs as theatrical devices in order first to complicate, and then to resolve riddles of identity and relationship in his drama, are redeployed by Büchner to leave the distinction between artifice and authenticity profoundly unclear to the end. While the couples at the end of *Ponce de Leon* are revealed and made ready for true wedding in the conventional romance style, the marriage of Leonce and Lena is conducted under false pretences, a performance by automata that is set to be replayed at will. And the figure of the masked performing automaton also stands for a fabricated, repetitive performance of human discourse. Büchner adopts the wordplay of Brentano's characters, their playful linguistic masquerading, and produces out of it an intense self-reflexiveness, in the style of an elaborate *mise-en-abyme*. The broken mirrors, which are one of the figures that Büchner cites from *Ponce de Leon,* serve as an emblem of the fragmentary reflection of his source text and its Romantic conventions that Büchner undertakes.

This reiterative Romantic theatricality has a profoundly ambivalent character. As Heine's invocation of his Sophia develops an afterlife of its own, exceeding the purposes of the satirical intention, so *Leonce und Lena* too is in excess of its ideological critique. While the engineering of comedy under the sign of romance is certainly mocked here, and this used as a vehicle for the satirical exposure of feudal structures, the comic drama seems ready to take on a less instrumental life of its own. Romantic fantasy is certainly parodied in the play, but it also exerts a seductiveness that threatens to become autonomous, freeing itself from the playwright's declared political agenda. The rhetorical postures of the Romantic prince and princess or the exuberant playfulness of Valerio's punning create an aesthetic surplus that seems to be produced for its own sake, perhaps not without a degree of nostalgic indulgence in the creative license and political irresponsibility which the Romantic model allows.[12]

At the same time the figure of the masked automaton embodies a darker side to the appropriation of the Romantic model. While in *Ponce de Leon* the automaton is unmasked at the end as a figure in the role of *deus ex machina,* resolving the play of false identities and introducing order into the play's relationships, *Leonce und Lena* effects a different sort of resolution *ex machina,* transforming its protagonists into repeating machines. Büchner appears to expose here the sort of cultural apparatus of fantasy that sustains prevailing systems of oppression (not for nothing does Leonce propose to build a theatre and fashion his puppet subjects after his own fantasies), but he also perhaps recognizes, in a more uncanny sense, the limitations of his own attempts at theatrical intervention in the course of history. The marriage of the automata Leonce and Lena incorporates into the mock-Romantic drama the writer's real sense of Romantic hauntedness, the idea that he is surrounded by human automata and might himself be nothing more than an undead character in a *Fantasiestück* by Hoffmann.[13] In other words, Büchner's text seems to be inwardly transformed by its Romantic intertext, unable to keep it at an ironic distance. In the terms of the somewhat bowdlerized version of the verse from "Die Blinde" (The Blind Woman) by the Romantic poet Chamisso that stands as a motto to the second act, a dark voice resonates within and consumes all memory (174). "Erinnern" (remembering) is reduced to "Innern" (inside) in Chamisso's rhyme-scheme; and, by analogy, the demands of the outside world, not least that of political-historical memory, are under threat of being turned to oblivion by a compulsive, blind identification with the unworldly inwardness of the voice of Romanticism.

While Romantic fantasies work against the grain of the writing of politically engaged writers like Heine and Büchner, they have another kind of function within the more conservative Poetic Realist tradition of mid to late nineteenth-century Germany. In the works of Annette von Droste-Hülshoff, for instance, Romantic fantasies represent a strand of continuity with the past in the face of the ascendancy of the bourgeoisie and the cultural ideology of Realism. Droste's early work, such as the novel fragment *Ledwina* (written in 1824) is produced when Romanticism is still at its peak and is substantially under its influence. The eponymous protagonist of the text is a hybrid spirit-woman to rival the iconic Romantic figure Undine (from Fouqué's 1811 tale of that name). Indeed, she is explicitly cast as a latter-day Undine figure after her graveyard dream, a Romantic tour de force that appears to prefigure, and so in some sense bring about, the drowning outside her window as well as foreshadowing her own demise. Ledwina embodies both the magnetic allure of Romantic fantasy and its deathly threat. After the model of Novalis's muse Sophie, she is barely embodied, a *femme fragile* drawn to life beyond the grave. While the novel remains unfinished, its specter revisits much of Droste's later work in an age when the more restrained aesthetics of Biedermeier have superseded the dream-life of Romanticism. Her poetry recurrently invokes Romantic scenarios, attached especially to the primal territory of the moors and to the ruins of aristocratic dwellings. In the landscape, the sounds and appearances of nature are invested with supernatural spirits, as in the famous "Am Moor" (On the Moor), and the ruins become sites of living death, inhabited by somnambulistic survivors of the old order. The spirit of Romanticism gives pursuit in nature and sleepwalks uncannily through Gothic architecture. While a poem like "Das alte Schloß" (The Old Castle) apparently ironizes the Romantic topos, inherited from Hoffmann and others, of the "öde Haus" (abandoned house) as a site of haunted inhabitation, the rhyming of "Romantik" with a "Genick" (neck) which might be broken, seems to exercise a double irony. It at once acts bathetically on the idea of Romantic fantasy and reinvests it with a real danger to the life and limb of the subject who has conjured it up in ironic fashion.

Two of the ballads that Droste submitted for Freiligrath and Schücking's *Das malerische und romantische Westfalen* (Picturesque and Romantic Westphalia, 1842) illustrate that her investment in Romantic visions is not reducible to the picturesque or mere ethnographic interest in the popular beliefs of her native Westphalia. "Vorgeschichte (Second Sight)" and "Das Fräulein von Rodenschild" both indulge in the fantasy scenario of the obsolescent aristocratic castle, its last inhabitants cast between life and death. They were among the poems that were based on ghost stories which Droste would recount to circles of relatives and friends, derived at once from her own experiences, dreams, and fantasies and from the local oral tradition. The protagonists of both poems are tormented by visionary powers, the first a baron who is fed upon by a vampiric moon and foresees the death of his son and thus of his family line, and the second a young woman who touches death in the form of her spectral reflection in the mirror which leaves her with the hand of a corpse. The temporal logic of these poems is nicely indicative of the hold that Romanticism retained over the post-Romantic writer. While "Vorgeschichte" translates here as premonition, it also carries its primary meaning of pre-history: the Romantic fantasy belongs to the prehistory of the mid nineteenth-century writer and her culture but it also previews what is to come, exercising a determining effect on history in the making. The Romantic cult of death is above all attached to the idea of death both as prefigured in life and as sustaining an afterlife in the figure of the restless revenant.

Droste's best-known work, the novella *Die Judenbuche* (The Jew's Beech, 1842), is also host to revenant figures. Its late eighteenth-century setting gives her the license to incorporate into her anthropological portrait of the moral life of a Westphalian community the sort of gruesome figures that still exercise fascination in her own post-Romantic time. The mirror motif, which runs through her works, is in part a device for reflecting that fascination. The version of the Romantic *Doppelgänger* that Droste revives here is emblematic of a questioning of the basis of identity at every level.[14] If the body of the double found hanging in the tree at the end of the novella is identified on the basis of a scar for which no history is provided, then this is indicative of the narrative's attachment to trauma, to forms of violence which determine identity but which are not properly knowable. The death by hanging is apparently effected by a sort of spell that realizes the curse cut into the tree, but it also revisits on the body a mysterious violence which the scar indicates has happened before and was predestined to happen again. By virtue of the omission of its provenance, the scar becomes a final mark less of secure identity than of the text's traumatic attachment to the darker mysteries of the Romantic imagination.[15]

This act of ending in mystery is characteristic of Droste's writerly imagination and of its revival of the Romantic. It is telling that her contemporary Adele Schopenhauer was troubled by the fact that the protagonist in "Das Fräulein von Rodenschild" lives on at the end of the ballad, but with an icy hand as the mark of the touch of death.[16] That the Fräulein should neither die nor be released by a reasoned resolution into proper life offends this reader's enlightened instincts. Instead, what she calls the "Aufklärung," or elucidation, of the "Rückspiegelung" (the reflecting back of the deathly mirror image onto its alter ego) is left wanting at the end. The mystery of Romantic compulsion is reflected back into the real and its uncanny symptom remains. What Adele Schopenhauer calls the end losing itself in indeterminacy is exactly the sort of afterlife effect that Droste appears to wish to achieve. The poem thus also effects another kind of "Rückspiegelung," taking on the reflection of the magic mirror of Romanticism which lies behind it, and projects this into the future by leaving the ending open.

If for Droste-Hülshoff, the aristocratic survivor in the age of bourgeois realism, Romanticism is attached at once to a primal experience of nature and to the legacy of the feudal order, the same is true for one of the model bourgeois writers of the second half of the nineteenth century, Theodor Storm. Droste's supernaturalized moor has an equivalent in Storm's native heath, intensively invested as it is with superstitious beliefs, even as it is reclaimed for material human use. And the Ledwina figure is brought back to ambiguous life in a series of elusive or mortified female protagonists, not least in the person of Anna Lene, the last survivor of a local family of minor aristocrats in Storm's novella *Auf dem Staatshof* (On the Staatshof Estate, 1858), who in life is already a ghost of herself. The young bourgeois protagonist and narrator, ironically bearing the name Marx, is in thrall to this otherworldly figure, but his grasp of her in living experience and of her story through the mediation of failing memory is decidedly uncertain. Only when he dances with her does she seem to become physical, the spirit brought to life, but this could be seen to revive the lifeless automaton in Hoffmann's *Sandmann* or the demonic Wilis conjured up in Heine's *Florentinische Nächte* (Florentine Nights, 1836), suggesting an uncanny fate for the dancers. Even as she falls to her death by drowning, Anna Lene eludes Marx's grasp, as he remains caught on the threshold, a recurrent feature of the narrative of their virtual relationship. In a way that is paradigmatic for Storm, the bourgeois narrator remains fascinated by the world of the Romantic in a sort of melancholic death-cult.

In the writings of both Droste and Storm, the ubiquitous mirror provides reflections of another world both in nature and in human habitation. Thus, Ledwina is introduced in disembodied form by her reflection in the mirror of the stream, which exerts a deathly pull upon her, and Fräulein von Rodenschild is touched by her dead mirror image. If the mirror is espoused as the emblematic device of authentic reflection in the mimetic order of Realism, it is also recurrently appropriated by powers that are more unreal. The mirror becomes a key instrument for the projection of the effects of the uncanny, which, as Freud argues in his essay on *Das Unheimliche* (The Uncanny, 1919), finds its archetypal residence in the family home. Freud shows how the "unheimlich" and the "heimlich" (the homely or secret) converge at their roots, and this convergence can be seen in the liability of the domestic mirrors of post-Romantic literature to reflect uncanny, secret presences.

In Storm's writing, too, mirrors are susceptible to uncanny effects, to forms of the sort of mirroring-back of the other onto the subject at which

Adele Schopenhauer balked. When Anna Lene dances, her little feet are described as gliding across the floor as if over the surface of a mirror. Upon the death of her grandmother, the mirror is marked as a device of death, following the custom of covering mirrors after a death in the house to ensure that the spirit rests. In a form of narrative "mirroring-back" Anna Lene's dance is thus retrospectively invested with uncanny reflections. A similar structure prevails in *Der Schimmelreiter.* The same mirror in the old Deichgraf's house that is covered up after his death is that in which Elke Haien makes her husband see himself as the new Deichgraf. The mirror is at once an item of Realist décor, carefully placed between the windows in both scenes in the interests of mimetic continuity and reflecting the rites of the local community, and yet also, by dint of the realistically described superstition, converted into a version of the magic mirrors of Romanticism. What the mirror projects, therefore, is the image of the Deichgraf who will become a restless ghost with an apparently unbounded afterlife. It seems that, after the death of Romanticism, the mirrors in the house of bourgeois realism have to be covered up if its ghosts are not to come back to haunt the new order.

Like Droste, Storm was an avid collector and accomplished oral narrator of ghost stories. He had a project to publish these in the form of a *Neues Gespensterbuch* (New Ghost Book),[17] and he incorporated several of them in his fictions. If Büchner feared that he was becoming a figure out of the pages of E. T. A. Hoffmann, Storm actively seeks to cultivate a revival of the Hoffmannesque and not least of the scenario of the Romantic symposium, the gathering of narrators and listeners around a hearth in order to exchange stories of the strange and the paranormal. Romantic fantasy becomes an object of melancholic attachment for the post-Romantic Storm. He rues his inability to project fantasy in the same colors as Hoffmann and his magic lantern; in his own writing it appears in more oblique forms and muted tones. Just as Droste caused perplexity by not furnishing a decisive end to her ghost ballad, Storm likewise provokes his readers and listeners, both real and fictional, by keeping his stories open-ended. One of those who experienced Storm as a charismatic, if idiosyncratic, teller of ghost stories, and was also one of his most enthusiastic readers, was Theodor Fontane. Fontane relates the ambivalent reactions of the circle of listeners to Storm's narration, at once fascinated and left unsatisfied at the end. His example is a story about ghostly dancing in an abandoned house, where the neighbors see only a delicate pair of feet with laced boots when they look through the keyhole, and where the narrator also refuses to let his listeners see any more than this.[18] This example suggests that the technique can be called fetishistic, focusing on a partial object rather than the whole story that the reader/listener craves and which must be denied them. The little feet correspond to those that enthrall the young Marx as he watches Anna Lene's mirror-dance. In

Fontane's account, this is Storm's strategy for the telling of ghost stories in a post-Romantic age. Storm insists that the "unfinished" character of the stories is of their essence and that their achievement of aesthetic satisfaction is contingent on the dissatisfaction they produce at the level of the listener's desire to know in full what has happened. Indeed, this model extends to Storm's narrative technique as a whole, where oblique indications or symptomatic gestures recurrently substitute for the full story. Thus, the specular dancing feet in *Auf dem Staatshof* represent the way in which that narrative relies on the highly charged part, unable as it is to recuperate the whole.

This model of teasing, partial information is particularly characteristic of the function of tales of the supernatural in Storm's fictional work. In *Am Kamin* (At the Hearth, 1857) a sequence of ghost stories is told, three of them derived from the *Neues Gespensterbuch* collection. While their incorporation into the fictional text is managed by a framework narrative, this is kept strangely open; the characters in the frame narrative are never properly introduced, and its recording entirely as conversation rather than third-person account gives a troubling sense of partial representation which imitates the stories told. There is something ghostly about the gathering as well as the stories. The narratives adopted from the *Gespensterbuch* are all elaborated somewhat in their new context, but they also retain a sense of elusiveness and interruption. The model deployed by the narrator is one of reflection or shadow play: dream-life is seen as a form of second sight, foreshadowing uncanny events in real life or playing host to the dead. The most acute effect of the uncanny arises when these two functions collapse, and with them distinctions between past and future, where what is foreseen is what will have happened when the dreamer awakes. Characters in the stories thus adopt the uncanny, glassy gaze of the necromantic ghost-horse of popular mythology, which is described in the frame narrative as looking in through the window of a house where death is imminent.[19]

The first of the stories from the *Gespensterbuch* describes a young man who is suddenly struck rigid and glassy-eyed as his party pass a certain spot out on the heath. This turns out to be the place where he will die from a stroke while out riding. He becomes, in other words, an uncanny horseman in the style of Hauke Haien in Storm's late masterpiece *Der Schimmelreiter* (The White Horse Rider, 1888). If one of his fellow travelers describes the coach as traveling past the "schlimme Stelle" (bad spot) as smoothly as if over floorboards (55), then this reflects the uncanny scene back into the home that will be devastated by the death. The second story also inverts the model of the uncanny gaze into the house, as a young journeyman is finally driven from his apparently haunted adopted home when he sees a ghostly figure looking down at him out of the window. In the third, the narrator gives an example of the vision as reflection or shadow and the real event coinciding: a young man has been tending his mother at her death-bed; when he finally goes to bed himself he suddenly awakes and has a vision of a hand with a handkerchief emerging from his bedroom door. He finds his mother dead in her bed, a handkerchief clutched in her hand. As with the added reference to the floorboards in the first story, Storm modifies his source here to bring the uncanny effect home: as the young man bends down to kiss his dead mother's hand, so he finds himself holding the handkerchief as well as the hand. Like Droste's Fräulein von Rodenschild, the visionary is touched by the death he has foreseen.

On the model of these and the other stories of *Am Kamin*, Storm sets up his post-Romantic magic lantern and achieves uncanny effects of his own by training it back on the viewer, suggesting that the late nineteenth-century homes which play host to narrative reenactments of the Romantic uncanny are prone to harbor shades of it themselves. The narrator's principal interlocutor in *Am Kamin* is the suitably named Clärchen, like the Klara of Hoffmann's *Der Sandmann,* representing a down-to-earth, domestic version of Enlightenment clear-sightedness in the face of the fantastic. As the story closes, however, she is pictured checking under her bed and cupboards in case of ghosts in the home of bourgeois realism.

Fontane's account of Storm's ghost story-telling highlights a key aspect of this Romantic genre. Designed for narration in the round, it is also set to be transmitted from one narrative community to the next. Fontane describes Storm's oral narration as a form of writing on the imaginations of his listeners, as the narrator seeks to "read" his effects in their faces. The intertextual echoes of Romantic fantasy in post-Romantic writing are indicative of this sort of transmission. The ghost that haunts the marital home of the Innstettens in *Effi Briest* (1895) shows that some version of the effects that Storm wishes to read in the face of Fontane are in turn sought by him in the responses of his readers. This anachronistic spook has a profoundly ambiguous function in the world of the novel. On the one hand, it works on the model of what one of the figures in *Am Kamin* calls the "Rüstzeug der Reaktion" (armory of reaction, 52). That is, Innstetten, the Prussian official with a secret life as narrator of ghost stories, is taken to use it as an instrument of control over his wife, an "Angstapparat" (apparatus of fear) with which to maintain the status quo of patriarchal power relations.[20] But it also becomes a focus for Effi's seduction, an embodiment of the lure of fantasy in a world that is dominated by the demands of social order. Not for nothing does Fontane deem the ghost to be pivotal for the whole narrative.[21] Its power derives, much as with the model provided by Storm, from its incompleteness, its reduction to a fetishistic structure: an image on the back of a chair, a gravestone, and a story which is never fully told.

No less than Storm, Fontane is conscious of the spell of the Romantic in all its forms, even as he feels an inevitable distance from it. His early novel *Irrungen, Wirrungen* (translated as *Delusions, Confusions,* 1888) is characteristic of the dialectical character of that relationship. The protagonist Lene is at once a real bourgeois girl and constructed as a Romantic fantasy figure, comparable to Storm's Anna Lene, but at a further remove from the origins of Romanticism. The opening page of the work indicates this tension, establishing the narrative in a scene that is, in every sense, transitional. The scene, liminally set between culture and nature, is marked as already of the past in the present of the narrative, described as still in place in the middle of the 1870s and so implicitly now gone.[22] What the narrative sees from the point of view of a passer-by, a little house standing in front of a bigger building visible only through its tower, is a Romantic composite construction. The small house is described according to Romantic convention, using the language of withdrawal from the world and miniature dimensions (through the proliferating suffix "-chen") which characterize the *Märchen* genre. The tower, which gives Frau Nimptsch the license to call the larger building a castle, is marked by a broken clock-face, suggesting that the scene is lifted out of time, a fairy-tale gesture that is, however, ironically twisted by the historical transience factored into the opening sentence. By introducing the scene through the language of theater scenery (the twice-mentioned "Kulisse"), the narrator seems to suggest that this alluring, semi-hidden site is as likely to be a place of staged illusion as one of real Romantic attractions. A form of dramatic, or theatrical irony is cast over the story from its start.

Fontane thus employs Romantic effects in order to draw his reader into the narrative, but always through ironic mediation. The peace of the front garden is tellingly described as "halb-märchenhaft" (320), and this halfway division between fairy-tale fantasy and sober reality is maintained throughout. Lene, the adopted "princess" with her painfully keen sense of reality, is drawn into a masquerade form of Romantic love affair, complete with references to Cinderella and Sleeping Beauty (336), which she pursues but also sees through. In fact, as with the ghost story derived from an illicit romance, which is at once the focus of *Effi Briest* and, like the adulterous affair, left strategically under-narrated, so the Romantic scenario of *Irrungen, Wirrungen* cannot be allowed to develop into the sustained material of the narrative. While this novel has no ghosts returning from beyond the grave, it repeatedly accompanies the stations of the love affair with the language of mortality and the ritual objects of death, wreathes and graveyard statuary. The love story that is its putative focus is finished long before the end, leaving the novel to mark time in a melancholic afterlife.

Thomas Mann was an enthusiastic reader of both Storm and Fontane, admiring in each their distinctive forms of allegiance to the Romantic. In Storm he recognized the North-German cultural tradition of mists and mysticism but also an attachment to the idea of "Heimat" or homeland that he says a philistine might judge to be hysterical because residing in lack, in a yearning "Heim*weh*" (home*sickness* [Mann's emphasis]).[23] Fontane, on the other hand, is seen not as a Romantic in the German sense (musical, metaphysical, and melancholic), but, as he suggests himself, in the Romance tradition of fantasy, based in reason (488). Mann conjures up the scene of Fontane leaving a production of Wagner's *Parsifal* at Bayreuth because he feels sick during the overture (487). Wagner represents for Mann the heir to the mystical hallucinations and synesthesia of the *Hoch-* and *Spätromantik,* reviving the dreams of Hoffmann's musical maestro Kreisler (405). Mann's own attachment to Romanticism is an ambivalent mixture of these different modes, by turns enthusiastic and critical, and its effects can be traced in his first major novel, written between 1897 and 1900, *Buddenbrooks* (1901).

Buddenbrooks charts the period under review in the present volume and reflects nicely the lack of synchrony in the cultural historical developments of the nineteenth century. While it measures itself against key historical moments, the dynastic history of the Buddenbrook family is as much a story of recurrence and reversion as of progressive development. This is most palpably marked in the return of the family members to the sea, which they encounter described in the same language as had been used for their predecessors. By the time that Hanno returns to the sea near the end of the novel, the family's attachment to it has been transmuted into a sort of sickness on the model of Romantic "Heimweh."[24] Although the family relies on a combination of tradition and change (as ritually recorded in their chronicle), their narrative all too often casts their experience as fundamentally regressive. A key aspect of this attachment to the past is the cultivation of Romanticism in its various forms, marked by its distinctive lexicon which resonates through the text in the language of yearning ("Sehnsucht") and Gothic horror ("Grausen," "schauerlich," etc.). *Buddenbrooks* incorporates an intertextual network of Romantic literature through the reading habits of its characters as well as figuring the eventual demise of the family through a hyper-Romantic, Wagnerian understanding of what, since Hegel, has been considered the most Romantic of art forms, music. While much of the novel sustains the method of Realism, at its end it is increasingly overtaken by the neo-Romantic cultural fashion of decadence.

The Buddenbrook family crest, featuring what is described as a melancholic moorland scene, provides an emblematic representation of a Romantic yearning that haunts many of the family members to different degrees. When Tony is made to mishear the name Morten, confusing it with "Moor" and "Mord," she also indicates the sort of mortal darkness that can attach to the emblematic moor. This confused, romantically charged figure will be the object of her version of melancholic "Sehnsucht" (217), the longing for a lost or inaccessible place or experience that is the keynote of Romantic writing, through the remainder of the novel. Tony is represented as a derivative character, reproducing the speech and ideas of others, and her personal catastrophe appears ironically to repeat her Romantic reading habits. Morten calls her a "Romantikerin" who has read too much E. T. A. Hoffmann (131), and when her future first husband appears, she is reading Hoffmann's *Serapionsbrüder* (The Serapion Brothers, 1819), a work that relates a sequence of strange and disastrous tales in the mode of *Schauerromantik*. When Grünlich enters to interrupt her reading and the family circle, he does so after the style of many an uncanny intruder in Hoffmann's writing, not least the eponymous visitor of the story "Der unheimliche Gast" (The Uncanny Guest) in the book that Tony is reading. Grünlich, a professed admirer of Hoffmann, seems to be anything but uncanny, but the calamitous effect that he will have on Tony and her home-life echoes its Romantic equivalent. When he returns to propose to her, she is once more reading. The novel is unidentified, but it seems to be a trivial, Romantic text where young women are overwhelmed by passionate men in frock coats, so that Grünlich appears to her as a character from a novel who has entered her life.

This pattern of other texts entering into the lives of the characters recurs in Mann's novel. Mann follows Fontane in *Effi Briest* in establishing Heine as an ambiguous textual model for his characters to follow. Fontane's Crampas uses Heine's poetry of passion and death as an instrument in his seduction of Effi; for Thomas Buddenbrook, the introduction of Heine quotations into business dealings also indicates the susceptibility he will have to a wife who is compared, among other mythical figures, to the archetypal Romantic combination of *femme fatale* and *femme fragile*, the otherworldly Melusine (295), related both to Undine and to the sprites and sirens of Heine's poetry. If Heine appears to provide an ironically distanced access to the Romantic domain, the child who comes of Thomas's union with his Melusine, Hanno, communicates more immediately with its passions and phantasms. When Hanno is racked by the phantom visions of his *pavor nocturnus,* the uncanny guest who visits his bedside is the "bucklicht Männlein," the little hunchback who has stepped out of the archetypal Romantic poetry anthology, *Des Knaben Wunderhorn* (463).[25] If his elders find themselves unwittingly repeating the scenarios of Romantic texts, Hanno is gripped by a more virulent compulsion to repeat, reciting the lines in his sleep, and seeing the figures they invoke. Afflicted by Romantic ghosts, he is unable to recite the more innocent "Schäfers Sonntagslied" (Shepherd's Sunday Song) when called upon to do so for social purposes. Hanno is sick with Romanticism. While his death from typhus is recorded as an exercise in Naturalistic description, the psychosomatic excesses of Wagnerian fantasy suggest an alternative diagnosis. When Hanno contracts his Romantic pathology, he embodies the effects of a contagion that is already present in his uncle and father, the odor of death which he is able to intuit in the manner of one with second sight. While Christian becomes, from an early age, hystericized, increasingly subject to psychosomatic disorders and hallucinatory visions, Thomas develops a form of the Romantic disease of melancholia, which eventually overwhelms his ironic control. When he reads Schopenhauer's *Welt als Wille und Vorstellung* (The World as Will and Idea, first edition 1819), therefore, it is as a reader programmed by Romanticism, so that the epiphany he experiences is expressed in the intoxicated language of "Sehnsucht" (655).

Thomas, in other words, reads Schopenhauer in the same ecstatic Wagnerian style as his son plays the piano. The second chapter of the eleventh section of the novel represents the apotheosis of this Romanticization of the world of bourgeois Realism. Cast as a satire on the educational system of late nineteenth-century Germany, modulating between tragedy and farce, it is rife with the ghosts of Romanticism. The chapter begins with a visit to see Wagner's *Lohengrin,* which duly leaves Hanno with a fever in his bed. When he has to return to the world of bourgeois order, it is invested for him with a hysterical sense of anxiety. The school, which represents the epitome of that order, is run by a grotesque troupe of teachers, with names redolent of the *Schauerromantik* tradition (Todtenhaupt [Deathshead] and Modersohn [Rottingson]). The shadowy figure of the custodian is ironically named Schlemiel (after Chamisso's Romantic protagonist who was a favorite of Mann's own school-days) and the geography teacher, Herr Mühsam, models himself after the sick but witty Heine. Against the framework of this nightmarish burlesque, the latter-day Romanticism of Hanno and his friend Kai is presented in a more serious tone. Kai's writing is thus in the mode of Edgar Allan Poe's *Fall of the House of Usher* (1839), a Gothic counterpart to the fall of the house of Buddenbrook, or it describes the quest for esoteric underground secrets (721), after the model, perhaps, of the mines in *Heinrich von Ofterdingen* or the darker one of Hoffmann's "Bergwerke zu Falun" (translated as *The Mines at Falun,* 1819).[26] And Hanno plays his final fantasia on a fragmentary musical idea in the mode of the Romantic sublime, figuring heroic adventure, phantasmatic terror, irresistible yearning, and mortifying pain. The purple pages that describe the development of that improvised fantasia after Wagner also represent Mann's own susceptibility to the Romantic style, just as the sober etiology of typhus that follows seems to be as much a stylistic corrective for his text as the comeuppance for his young protagonist having followed the demonic tune of exalted Romanticism.

Mann's performance of Hanno's performance represents the return of Romanticism as decadence at the end of the nineteenth century and a tension between social order and the lure of inner disorder that characterizes that period divided between Naturalist and Symbolist tendencies. It marks a form of continuity between the Age of Romanticism at the start of the century, which was also so often diagnosed as a pathological phenomenon, most famously by Goethe,[27] and a culture on the brink of twentieth-century industrial and technological modernity that finds Romantic ghosts in its machinery and is perversely drawn to diseases and disorders it cannot heal. The painful disjuncture between the textbook description of typhus and the aesthetic rendering of Hanno's inner condition indicates how inimical and yet interdependent the voices of rationalist modernity and of Romantic fantasy are. Mann's position can be compared to that of two of the thinkers who were most influential for him. Like Nietzsche, who first champions Wagner's mythopoeic vision then becomes an avowed critic of neo-Romantic decadence in the Wagnerian style, or Freud, the psychopathologist of everyday life who persistently exposes the dark underworld of the mind but in the interests of a more enlightened understanding, Mann moves between the positions of critical rationality and the lure of those ideas which are subsumable as Romantic. He exposes neo-Romantic tendencies to critique but also cultivates them in an ironic resistance to that critique.

The various forms of the afterlife of Romanticism that have been reviewed here all indicate that its function is a complicated and dialectical one. It certainly embodies, in part, a reactionary fixation on old social and aesthetic orders, so that Nietzsche can accuse it of attempting a cultural "Rückbildung": a regressive formation with a contradictory temporal structure, at once ahead of its time, prematurely symptomatic of the cult of decadence developing later in the nineteenth century, and yet profoundly belated in its yearning for lost times.[28] But Romanticism can also be said to serve to unsettle new orders that are in danger of becoming fixed in damaging ways, making claims for subjectivity and mystery against the false security of a culture under the hegemony of positivism. It can perhaps best be described as a sort of cultural unconscious for the Age of Bourgeois Realism, representing what is repressed by that order of things and is, according to psychoanalytic logic, bound to be returned upon it. If Freud finds a major source for his understanding of the unconscious in a classic text of German Romanticism, *Der Sandmann*, then the post-Romantic texts which have been discussed here all provide evidence of the uncanny endurance of that unconscious and its mysterious disorders against the grain of the empiricist culture of the mid to late nineteenth century. The protagonists of Storm's *Am Kamin* could certainly feature as easily in the Freudian casebook as in the book of ghosts. Thus, there is a boy with a wolf-dream that resembles the psychic world of Freud's Wolf Man; and the dream of the dying mother merges the world of dream and waking life in a way that is strikingly reminiscent of the traumatic dream of the burning son recounted in *Die Traumdeutung*, which one recent critic has seen as key evidence for reading Freud's dream-book as a Gothic novel.[29] At the same time, the compulsively disordered behavior of Droste's Ledwina or her Fräulein von Rodenschild with the hystericized hand and of the final generations of the Buddenbrooks, is uncannily close to the forms of psycho-social disorder which Freud was beginning to record in his case histories at the end of the nineteenth century.[30] Freud and Breuer famously described hysterics as suffering from reminiscences,[31] and the recurrence of the disorders of Romanticism in the period from the middle of the nineteenth century to the fin-de-siècle can perhaps be viewed as symptomatic of a type of hysterical culture, one suffering from the compulsive reminiscence of the traumatic fantasies of a foregone generation.

The afterlife of Romanticism in the nineteenth century is, then, a contradictory phenomenon. It incorporates by turns a secondary form of nostalgia, a longing for a mode of longing which is past; the knowing and satirical debunking of dreams and visions no longer tenable in the modern age; and the haunting and often profoundly painful revisiting of nineteenth-century culture by obsessive desires and mysteries from its prehistory. If Friedrich Schlegel claimed that Romanticism was always in a state of becoming, he failed to note that part of what it is becoming is regressive, an often morbid repetition of the past. At the end of the nineteenth century, long after its supposed cultural historical demise, Romanticism still inheres in cultural developments, ambivalently cast between progression and regression, life and death.

Notes

[1] *Kritische Friedrich-Schegel Ausgabe,* vol 2. ed. Ernst Behler (Munich: Ferdinand Schöningh, 1967), 183.

[2] Sigmund Freud, *Die Traumdeutung, Gesammelte Werke,* vol 2/3, ed. Anna Freud et al. (Frankfurt a. M.: Fischer, 1999), 86.

[3] *Werke, Tagebücher und Briefe Friedrich von Hardenbergs,* vol. 1, ed. Richard Samuel (Munich: Carl Hanser, 1978), 326.

[4] See the chapter on Hoffmann in my *The Doppelgänger: Double Visions in German Literature* (Oxford: Clarendon, 1996), 113–94.

[5] Heinrich Heine, *Historisch-kritische Gesamtausgabe der Werke,* vol. 8/1, ed. Manfred Windfuhr (Hamburg: Hoffmann und Campe, 1979), 176.

[6] Sophia lies in her grave as her book lies metonymically for her on the desk. She conforms to the model of the dead muse discussed by Elisabeth Bronfen in *Over Her Dead Body: Death, Femininity and the Aesthetic* (Manchester: Manchester UP, 1992), 360–83.

[7] Karl Marx, *Der achtzehnte Brumaire des Louis Bonaparte,* in Karl Marx and Friedrich Engels, *Werke,* vol. 8 (Berlin: Dietz, 1960), 116–17.

[8] As derived from Adelbert von Chamisso's famous Romantic tale, *Peter Schlemihls wundersame Geschichte* (The Strange Story of Peter Schlemihl, 1814).

[9] Karl Marx, *Die großen Männer des Exils,* in Karl Marx and Friedrich Engels, *Werke,* vol. 8 (Berlin: Dietz, 1960), 243 & 250.

[10] In a letter of July 1835 to his family, in: Georg Büchner, *Werke und Briefe,* ed. Karl Pörnbacher et al. (Munich: dtv, 1988), 306.

[11] The ghosts that haunt Robespierre in I.vi. return to visit Danton in a similar scene and with similar language in II.v. Lucile's song of Death at the end of the drama, "Es ist ein Schnitter" (There is a Reaper), is derived from the key Romantic sourcebook, *Des Knaben Wunderhorn* (The Boy's Magic Horn, 1805–8).

[12] Thus Büchner writes of the poems in the Romantic style by Stöber that he sends to Gutzkow that they may have recourse to the Middle Ages because they can find no proper place in the modern world, but that they nonetheless remain dear to him (*Werke und Briefe,* 311).

[13] In a letter of March 1834 to his fiancée, he describes a feeling of living death and a morbid fear of himself such that he could pose for "Herrn Callot-Hoffmann" (*Werke und Briefe,* 287). The elision of Hoffmann with the artist Jacques Callot, whose etchings inspired his *Prinzessin Brambilla* (Princess Brambilla, 1820), indicate the sort of chain of identification which Büchner's own citational practices establish, not least in relation to Romantic sources.

[14] See my argument in *The Doppelgänger,* 243–57.

[15] For a development of this argument, see my essay "Traumatic Identities: Race and Gender in Annette von Droste-Hülshoff's *Die Judenbuche* and Freud's *Der Mann Moses,*" in *Harmony in Discord: German Women Writers in the Eighteenth and Nineteenth Centuries,* ed. Laura Martin (Berne: Lang, 2001), 185–205.

[16] In a letter to Droste of 27 June 1841. Annette von Droste-Hülshoff, *Historisch-kritische Ausgabe,* vol. 12, ed. Winfried Woesler (Tübingen: Niemeyer, 1995), 42.

[17] While Storm calls his book of ghost stories new, its sources are often old; many are drawn from a classic text of Romantic counter-science, Stilling's *Theorie der Geister-Kunde* (1808). See, Theodor Storm, *Neues Gespensterbuch,* ed. Karl Ernst Laage (Frankfurt a. M.: Insel, 1991).

[18] Theodor Fontane, *Sämtliche Werke: Aufsätze, Kritiken, Erinnerungen,* vol. 4, ed. Walter Keitel (Munich: Carl Hanser, 1973), 369.

[19] Theodor Storm, *Sämtliche Werke,* vol. 4, ed. Karl Ernst Laage and Dietrich Lohmeier (Frankfurt a. M.: Deutscher Klassiker Verlag, 1988), 54.

[20] Theodor Fontane, *Effi Briest,* in *Sämtliche Werke: Romane, Erzählungen, Gedichte,* vol. 4, ed. Walter Keitel (Munich: Carl Hanser, 1963), 134.

[21] Theodor Fontane, *Werke, Schriften und Briefe: Briefe,* vol. 4, ed. Otto Drude and Helmuth Nürnberger (Munich: Carl Hanser, 1982), 506.

[22] Theodor Fontane, *Irrungen, Wirrungen,* in *Sämtliche Werke: Romane, Erzählungen, Gedichte,* vol. 2, ed. Walter Keitel (Munich: Carl Hanser, 1962), 319.

[23] Thomas Mann, *Adel des Geistes: Sechzehn Versuche zum Problem der Humanität,* in *Stockholmer Gesamtausgabe* (Stockholm: Fischer, 1967), 455.

[24] Thomas Mann, *Buddenbrooks: Verfall einer Familie* (Frankfurt a. M.: Fischer, 1974), 638.

[25] This is the same figure that comes from underground to haunt the fin-de-siècle childhood of Walter Benjamin, as recorded in his *Berliner Kindheit um*

Neunzehnhundert in *Gesammelte Schriften,* vol. 4/1, ed. Rolf Tiedemann and Hermann Schweppenhäuser (Frankfurt a. M.: Fischer, 1972), 302–4.

[26] Hoffmann's scenario of the embalmed and disinterred corpse of a Romantic fantasist who went mining for the inner secrets of the world provides a nice model for the afterlife of Romanticism, exhumed as it was in various later treatments of the Falun theme.

[27] *Goethes Gespräche mit Eckermann* (Leipzig: Insel-Verlag, 1920), 460.

[28] Friedrich Nietzsche, *Kritische Studienausgabe,* vol. 13, ed. Giorgio Colli and Mazzino Montinari (Munich: dtv, 1988), 463.

[29] Robert J. C. Young, 'Freud's Secret: *The Interpretation of Dreams* was a Gothic Novel', in *Sigmund Freud's The Interpretation of Dreams: New Interdisciplinary Essays,* ed. Laura Marcus (Manchester/New York: Manchester UP, 1999), 206–31, 223.

[30] Hanno's *pavor nocturnus* and Christian's physical tics directly recall the symptoms recorded by Freud in his early work on hysteria and anxiety neuroses.

[31] Sigmund Freud, *Gesammelte Werke,* vol. 1, ed. Anna Freud et al. (Frankfurt a. M.: Fischer, 1999), 86.

Parallels and Disparities: German Literature in the Context of European Culture

Lilian Furst

To PLACE GERMAN LITERATURE in the context of European culture is a tall order. What René Wellek called "the 'foreign trade' of literatures"[1] has been examined with extraordinary thoroughness in regard to nineteenth-century German literature and its European connections because they are so numerous, so dense, and so influential. The impact particularly of Goethe and the Romantics has been the subject of countless studies.[2] The processes of transmission are supported by other types of documentation: for instance, the reports of such travelers as Henry Crabb Robinson,[3] Charles de Villiers,[4] and Mme. De Staël,[5] and the mapping of the demography of translations.[6] To these analyses of specific aspects must be added more wide-ranging surveys like Rosemary Ashton's *The German Idea* (1980) on Coleridge, Carlyle, G. H. Lewes, George Eliot, and German thought, her subsequent book, *Little Germany: Exile and Asylum in Victorian England* (1986), and my own *Romanticism in Perspective* (1969) and *Counterparts* (1977). There is, therefore, ample scholarly evidence of the wealth of contacts between German and European writers in the nineteenth century.

Nevertheless, Wellek's objection to an exclusive concentration on "the 'foreign trade' of literatures" remains a valid warning. The mere fact of an established contact says nothing about its meaning; the sheer quantity of contacts between German and European writers must always be tempered by consideration of their quality. For example, when Wordsworth and Coleridge visited Klopstock, they were able to converse only in schoolboy Latin, a fact that must arouse misgivings about the productivity of this meeting. Graver still are the implications of Mme. de Staël's skewed image of German literature that spread throughout Europe with the popularity of *De L'Allemagne* (1802) in which she presented Goethe and Schiller as the German Romantics. The persistence of this misconception contributed significantly to the long neglect of Early Romanticism. Likewise, translations may not provide the receiver with a genuine sense of the power of the original. Both Coleridge and Benjamin Constant translated Schiller's *Wallenstein,* but Coleridge's version was hampered by his poor German[7] as well as by the onset of revulsion against German melodrama as represented, for example, by the plays of Kotzebue in England, while Constant domesticated Schiller's mighty trilogy to conform to French expectations by reducing it to a play in five acts and in regular hexameters.[8] Most hazardous of all is the vague concept of influence which proves open to alternative interpretations. Thus, Coleridge's enthusiasm for Schiller's *Die Räuber* (1781, The Robbers) is more a rediscovery of the native Shakespearean tradition than a grasping at a foreign model.

Knowledge of "the 'foreign trade' of literatures" is at best a tentative starting-point for an assessment of cross-cultural interactions. Detailed information is unquestionably useful, even when it perpetuates a distortion, as Mme. De Staël did, for the nature of the distortion itself uncovers national prejudices. But studies of discrete contacts are too limited and fragmented by virtue of their very specialization to give a coherent, overall picture of the larger contours of the comparative position of German literature in the context of European culture. I therefore propose to approach this vast topic through an appraisal of the parallels and disparities in the three major literary movements of the nineteenth century, Romanticism, realism, and naturalism. The patterns of similarity and difference facilitate a broader understanding of the place of German literature in the European setting.

The politico-social situation in Germany was a fundamental determinant of its literary life, and perhaps never more so than in the nineteenth century. Indeed, to speak of "Germany" is erroneous for it was not a unified country until 1871. Up to then it consisted of thirty-nine states, each with its own ruler, despotic or enlightened at will, and its own legal and educational structures. Sagarra summarizes the political system as being "antiquated and complex."[9] Even after the advent in 1835 of railroads which expanded to a network of fifteen thousand miles within ten years, the improvement of roads, and the increasing use of rivers and canals for transportation, travel from one jurisdiction to another was difficult because of the necessity for police permits. Before Grillparzer could go to Italy in 1819, he had to obtain the emperor's personal permission. Stringent censorship was enforced, particularly of any opinions suspected of being subversive of the ruling regime. Publication abroad was also forbidden without censorial clearance. The only possible subterfuge was to write fictitious memoirs purporting to comment on abuses witnessed abroad. The 1789 revolution in France and its successors in 1830 and 1848 throughout Europe heightened suspicion of foreigners and journalists, especially in the 1830s and 1840s. The thwarting of both mobility and free speech resulted in stasis and the isolation of self-enclosure. Germany, Sagarra points out, "was not well-known to outsiders in 1830, nor even to the Germans themselves."[10] Organization was in small units, almost entirely on the land; in the first third of the century only thirty-four towns had a population over twenty thousand, with Berlin and Vienna as yet not above a quarter of a million. The inhabitants' horizons were normally bounded by the Residenz (court), their interests and attention confined to local affairs. This compartmentalization had a major consequence for cultural life in the lack of a capital, a magnetic focus for intellectual and artistic exchange comparable to Paris or London.

In the absence of a capital, writers and thinkers clustered in a series of provincial towns. During the first third of the century, in Goethe's lifetime, Weimar was the focal point. German and foreign travelers alike flocked to the tiny principality in what amounted to pilgrimages to see the star of German as well as of European culture.[11] Besides Weimar, Jena, the home of the early Romantics, and Heidelberg, that of the High Romantics, were also active artistic hubs, although in contrast to Weimar they were hardly sought out by curious visitors from abroad. The incidence of European interest in German writers was extremely uneven; Goethe's contemporaries certainly suffered from his overshadowing fame. Only in the final third of the century, after unification, did Germany have a national capital. In the later 1880s and early 1890s Berlin became the primary center of naturalism with the establishment of the *Freie Bühne* (Free Stage) in 1891. From September 1892 to May 1893 Strindberg lived in Berlin, frequenting the group that congregated at the bar, "Der schwarze Ferkel" (The Black Sow). Ibsen, too, spent considerable time in Germany, including visits to Berlin to attend performances of his plays. But his favorite German residence was Munich, which in the late nineteenth and into the twentieth century was a major center of artistic life, offering a more congenial, easygoing milieu for Bohemianism than the austere atmosphere of Prussian Berlin.

Prussia became the dominant force as Germany was transformed in the course of the nineteenth century from a motley collection of states that favored sleepiness as a bastion against revolution into a dynamic, militant (and militaristic) nation under Bismarck's leadership. In Sagarra's words, "from being a nation long regarded as philosophic, a-political and unpractical, she [Germany] became highly organised and excessively self-conscious."[12] Beginning with the Customs Union of 1834 that facilitated the movement of goods, national consciousness grew at an incremental pace. The institution of the classical Humboldtian Gymnasium had a potent standardizing effect, although its emphasis on Latin and Greek acted as a disincentive to the acquisition of modern foreign languages, as did the schooling offered by the religious orders. Still, French continued to be the lingua franca of polite society throughout Europe and beyond, and Germans turned to France for models in fashion, which were always copied with a time-lag. On the other hand, North Germany, particularly the so-called Wasserkante (Edge of the Sea), traditionally more cosmopolitan because of its trading connections, tended to be oriented toward England. Hamburg businessmen sent their sons to England to gain experience there.[13] Long after unification Germany continued to remain essentially heterogeneous. Nationhood by no means put an end to diversity, so that the picture of Germany in the nineteenth century is not only shifting but also often contradictory. Any generalization must be qualified in light of time and location.

This inherent complexity immediately becomes apparent in German Romanticism, which was far more multifaceted than its European counterparts. On the one hand, German Romanticism runs parallel to the Romantic movements in other countries in its basic affirmation of individualism, the centrality of the imagination, and the spontaneous expression of personal feeling.[14] On the other hand, it differs from its equivalents in several respects: in its temporal expanse, its innate intricacy, and its tendency to extremism. The argument can be put forward that the primacy of individualism throughout Romanticism was bound to lead to multiformity. Wordsworth's tone is distinctive from Coleridge's, even in their cooperative work, the *Lyrical Ballads* (1798), while Blake and Byron, though both classed as Romantics, are utterly dissimilar. In German Romanticism, however, the discrepancies run deeper; the ideals dominant in successive phases are quite divergent, and the artistic output of a range beyond that in other countries.

Temporally, German Romanticism extends from the later 1790s to the early 1830s in two separate waves, early Romanticism from around the turn of the century and the high Romanticism from 1805 onward. A case can be made for an even greater expansiveness if Goethe and Schiller are subsumed into Romanticism on the grounds that they certainly subscribed to what was to crystallize as the Romantics' creed of individualism, imagination, and feeling. But they also upheld classical forms, and except for a phase in their youth did not partake of Romantic iconoclasm. Indeed, Goethe became ever more conservative, partly in response to the destructiveness of the French revolution. While Goethe and Schiller are regarded in Germany as the representatives of the classical period in its literature, throughout the rest of Europe they were read as the foremost German Romantics. No doubt this (partial) misreading can be ascribed to Mme. De Staël's interpretation, which was highly influential. Banned from France by Napoleon, she traveled widely on the Continent and to England, where *De l'Allemagne,* published there in 1813, sold out its entire fifteen hundred copies (a sizable number at that time) in under a year. The acceptance of Goethe and Schiller as the major German Romantics produces a fundamental disparity between native and foreign perceptions of German literature.

The disparity is evident too in the far shorter time span of both English and French Romanticism. Wordsworth's and Coleridge's *Lyrical Ballads* (1798) is generally taken to mark the breakthrough of Romanticism in English literature; it comes to an abrupt end with the deaths of Keats, Shelley, and Byron in the early 1820s. The tempestuous Romantic outburst in France was more short-lived still, spanning from 1820 to the early 1830s. Its lateness, compared to Germany and England, is largely due to the intervention of the 1789 revolution, which diverted innovative thinking into the politico-social arena. To risk one's head — literally — for the sake of an unpatriotic literary opinion was simply not worth it. Romanticism was decried as a foreign invasion, a threat to the native neoclassical tradition. Spain and Italy, in the wake of France, were also late in the timing of their Romantic movements.

The very tenuousness of the anterior tradition in Germany fostered the bold adventurousness of its Romantics. Devastated economically by the Seven Years' War (1756–63) when marauding bands laid waste to the land, Germany was in the mid to later eighteenth century the poor relation in Europe culturally too, with no great writer of international stature such as England had in Shakespeare and Milton, France in Racine and Molière, Italy in Dante, and Spain in Cervantes. Goethe, born in 1749, was to redress the balance, but around the turn of the century German writers had less to lose and more to gain by experimentation than their European peers who venerated the glories of their respective national heritages. In contrast to France, where artistic novelty was suspect, after the French Revolution the rulers of the German states encouraged the exploration of aesthetic notions as posing no danger to the political status quo that they sought to preserve. Thus, paradoxically, the same forces that retarded Romanticism in France were conducive to its flowering in Germany. Its artistic backwardness in the late eighteenth century made Germany so open to, indeed avid for, new ideas and styles of writing as to catapult it into the avant-garde.

This thrust to innovation was most prominent among the early Romantics, partly no doubt because they were so overshadowed from the international perspective by the towering figure of Goethe. Important though they subsequently became, in their lifetime they were a marginalized sideshow on the German literary scene, which was dominated by Goethe and Schiller. While Goethe and Schiller were, like the Romantics, disillusioned with the present, they turned their gaze to classical models and themes as a refuge in their joint *Xenien* (1796), Goethe's *Römische Elegien* (1796) and his *Iphigenie auf Tauris* (1787). The Romantics, in averting their eyes from a dismal present, invested their hopes either in the restoration of a golden age, posited in the past, or, above all, in the coming of utopia through the reign of poetry in the future. Thus, their idealism took extreme forms. In Novalis's (1772–1801) novel fragment *Heinrich von Ofterdingen* (1802), the titular figure, a youthful poet, makes a journey to Augsburg that is simultaneously a symbolic journey into the future realm of poetry. Heinrich embodies Novalis's aphorism in his collection *Blütenstaub* (Pollen Dust, 1798), "Nach Innen geht der geheimnisvolle Weg" (The secret path leads inward), a pronounced affirmation of the inwardness characteristic of the early Romantics. This inwardness expresses in part the urge to flee present reality but even more the belief in the creative writer's capacity to transfigure the world.

The possibility of transfiguring the world through poetry is the major theme of early Romanticism in contrast to other European Romantic movements where it hardly appears at all. Besides *Heinrich von Ofterdingen* it figures in Novalis's *Hymnen an die Nacht* (Hymns to the Night, 1800) and in Wackenroder's (1773–98) and Tieck's (1773–1853) *Herzensergiessungen eines kunstliebenden Klosterbruders* (Outpourings of an Art-loving Friar, 1797). Insofar as this ideal is codified, it comes not in the systematic form of treatises such as were produced in England by Wordsworth and Shelley, and in France by Hugo and Sainte-Beuve, but in provocative fragments, notably those of Friedrich Schlegel (1772–1829), who stands at the intellectual core of early Romanticism. His *Athenäum* (1798) fragments center on the conceptualization of Romantic poetry as "eine progressive Universalpoesie" (116th fragment, a progressive universal poetry) open to an infinite ascendance toward the ideal by means of Romantic irony whose function was to deconstruct and reconstruct the work in an upward spiral.

In light of Schlegel's frequent invocation of supranational models it is perplexing to find the German Romantics denied receptivity to foreign cultures.[15] Admittedly, the German Romantics were opposed to the rigid generic distinctions of French neoclassicism. However, in articulating his program Friedrich Schlegel freely invokes Dante, Cervantes, and Shakespeare, and among the moderns Sterne and Diderot. His brother, August Wilhelm Schlegel (1767–1845), in his *Vorlesungen über dramatische Kunst und Literatur* (Lectures on Dramatic Art and Literature, 1809) cast his net even wider, covering in his survey of the development of drama Aeschylus, Sophocles, Euripides, Aristophanes, Plautus, Terence, Ariosto, Goldoni, Corneille, Racine, Molière, Voltaire, Shakespeare, Marlowe, Ben Jonson, Beaumont and Fletcher, Dryden, Otway, Cervantes, Lope de Vega, and Calderón, to name only the major figures. This impressive list, together with Friedrich Schlegel's laudatory references to European writers, invalidates the accusation that the German Romantics ignored foreign literature. On the contrary, in this respect they were more sinned against than sinning. For long they were not heeded in other countries where Goethe monopolized attention. Carlyle's *Sartor Resartus* (1833) is a witty but deflating attack on the mystical German philosopher, Diogenes Teufelsdrökh. In France early Romanticism did not become known until the Symbolist movement of the late nineteenth century when the Romantics' belief in transcendentalism and their technique of synesthesia were widely adopted. The mediating force in France was primarily musical, via the operas of Wagner which are in their concept of the *Gesamtkunstwerk* (totalizing work of art) a summation of the early

Romantic creed. Wagner enjoyed immense popularity in France from 1861 onward.[16]

The early Romantics' radicalism undoubtedly contributed to their long neglect. Their works are not easily accessible because they were so committed to experimentation. Friedrich Schlegel himself, only half jokingly, deemed his *Athenäum* an "Ideenigel" (a hedgehog of ideas), and in an early instance of promotional advertising, suggested that a slice of gingerbread be given to every buyer! His novel *Lucinde* (1799) suffers from shadowy characters and a confusing plot. The *Herzensergiessungen,* too, is as eccentric as its title suggests. The principle animating these bizarre works is the advocacy of the *Mischgedicht,* the mingling of the genres and styles in opposition to the neoclassical doctrine of their strict separation. In fact, Friedrich Schlegel went so far as to affirm the grotesque, even the monstrous in pursuit of the ideal of an all-encompassing *Poesie.* When Victor Hugo (1802–85) attempted to practice the grotesque in France in his play *Hernani* (1830), the stage was pelted with eggs. The authority of decorum in literature was an obstacle to the reception of early Romanticism's experimentation.

High Romanticism to some extent continued this vein of unconventional writing, notably in the narratives of E. T. A. Hoffmann (1776–1822) although to an attenuated, more acceptable degree. Hoffmann's satirical momentum stands recognizably in the lineage of eighteenth-century social criticism of the stolid bourgeois. Also, his stories, despite their fundamental seriousness, are imbued with a humorous playfulness that made them more attractive than the earnest solemnity of early Romanticism. Hoffmann was the first of the German Romantics to be well received abroad. In France he enjoyed almost immediate and enormous success from his introduction in the early 1820s; following the translation of his complete works, his fame probably equaled Goethe's.[17] Through Jacques Offenbach's opera *Les Contes d'Hoffmann* (1881) he gained a popularity that lasts to this day. Appropriately, since he was himself a musician and composer, his work was broadly disseminated through the medium of music. His stories inspired Delibes's ballet *Coppélia* (1870) and Tchaikovsky's *Nutcracker* (1892). In Russia Hoffmann was all the rage from the 1820s to about 1850. By the second half of the 1820s every writer was acquainted with him, and many of his themes and motifs were being reiterated in Russian writings. In the 1830s and 1840s, when the press abounded in references to him, it was considered good taste to have read him. By 1840 sixty-two of his stories had appeared in translation as well as fourteen articles about him. Indeed, the claim was made that Hoffmann did not die but moved to Russia![18]

The only other German Romantic poet to achieve such international fame in his lifetime was Heinrich Heine (1797–1856). From 1830 until his death Heine lived in Paris as a high profile exile; he moved in literary circles and was an astute reporter on French political and cultural life. In

Ideen: Das Buch Le Grand (Ideas: The Book of Le Grand, 1827) he celebrated Napoleon as the representative of revolutionary politics. In 1833 he
published *Französiche Maler* (French Painters) and *Französiche Zustände*
(French Conditions) which mediated between German thought and
French social action. His critical stance toward Germany, exemplified in
Deutschland: Ein Wintermärchen (Germany: A Winter's Tale, 1844) was
intensified by the failure of the 1848 revolution. Banned in Prussia in
1835, the work attacked both the aristocracy and clericalism on personal
and idealistic grounds. As a Jew, albeit converted to Lutheranism in 1825,
he was unable to find employment in public administration or the universities in Germany. Ultimately Heine's reputation rests on his bittersweet
lyrics, superficially simple, yet often full of irony, His work was crucial in
initiating the growing interest in the German Lied in France in the middle
of the century. Gérard de Nerval's translations, *Poésies allemandes* attracted
little attention on its appearance in 1830; then, however, between 1848
and 1868 came a whole spate of anthologies and studies of the German
lyric.[19]

High Romanticism differed fundamentally from early Romanticism in
regard to the important role played by political factors. Decidedly conservative in outlook, yet alienated from the post-Napoleonic reactionary age,
High Romanticism sought traditional values in this destabilized period. In
practical terms this meant a return to the past not as a golden age but as
the repository of a Germanic culture that had been overlaid and forgotten.
In place of the utopianism and millenarianism of the earlier generation, the
second generation of Romantics took refuge in historical continuity,
nationhood, and Catholicism. In their patriotic fervor they paved the way
for the *Jungdeutschland* (Young Germany) movement and for the formation of national consciousness. This emphasis on continuity contrasts with
the situation of French Romanticism which denoted a break away from the
native tradition. In England, too, Romanticism meant innovation
although not necessarily at the expense of continuity for as in Germany,
neoclassicism had never been firmly entrenched since Shakespeare had
initiated freedoms not tolerated in France.

The High Romantics concentrated on the retrieval of the national
heritage by collecting (and in many instances elaborating on) folk-songs
and -tales. In this they had a precedent in Great Britain where Bishop
Percy had published *Reliques* (1765) and Macpherson had had great
success with the partly spurious *Poems of Ossian* (1762). Clemens Brentano
(1778–1842) and Achim von Arnim (1781–1857) culled the two volumes
of *Des Knaben Wunderhorn* (The Youth's Wondrous Horn, 1805–1807),
an anthology of German folk poetry largely from oral sources. Similarly,
Joseph Görres (1776–1846) compiled German legends in *Die teutschen
Volksbücher* (Germanic Chapbooks, 1807), deliberately using the archaic
form *teutsch* in its title to project authenticity. The Grimm brothers'

Kinder- und Hausmärchen (Children's and Folk Tales, 1812–15) form part of the same endeavor. The Grimms' tales were slow to catch on, seeming to be addressed to a scholarly audience because of the appended notes. The fact that many of the primary informants were of French Huguenot background placed the *Tales* in a more cosmopolitan European context as a manifestation of an increasing interest in folklore not merely as a fascination with the Germanic past. The Grimms' *Tales* attained popularity in England from the first translation in 1823 onward with illustrations by George Cruikshank. Thus, they inaugurated the vogue in England for German children's books that reached its peak between 1840 and 1860.[20] With these works of the brothers Grimm, Hoffmann, and Heine aspects of German culture spread into the European domain not because of parallels between the various national movements but precisely because of the distinctiveness of Romanticism in Germany.

This distinctiveness continues in realism; however, in this instance, the differences between the German and European versions were an obstacle to diffusion so that the greatest disparity between German and European literature occurred round the middle of the century. Nonetheless, some fundamental parallels do exist that warrant the use of the same name. The term realism, derived from *res*, the Latin for thing, denotes a concentration on the commonplace lives, circumstances, and surroundings of ordinary people generally of the middle classes socially. The primary thrust of realism is in sharp contradistinction to the idealistic transcendentalism of Early Romanticism or the predilection of the High Romantics for the historical; instead, the setting is in the present or the recent past. In this respect German realism parallels its European counterparts.

But Germany in mid-century differed radically from England and France where realism flourished. Both countries were undergoing rapid industrialization and were also in a phase of expansionist imperialism. Germany, too, witnessed the beginnings of industrial capitalism in the 1840s but its response to the emergence of capitalist means of production was affected by the unsuccessful 1848 revolution and the subsequent sense of disillusionment. That disillusionment led to a strengthening of the distrust of the great world already evident after the failure of the Wars of Liberation (1813–15). The movement known as Biedermeier (1820–50) which, significantly, has no direct equivalent in other literatures, evokes above all the narrow environment of that period. That narrowness was reinforced by the continuing absence of a national capital and the concomitant cultivation of regionalism.

It is regionalism that most deeply distinguishes German from European realism. Many writers withdrew into their home area, producing vivid descriptions of local life. Gottfried Keller's (1819–98) cycle of tales *Die Leute von Seldwyla* (The People of Seldwyla, 1856–74) is framed by its setting in the little Swiss town of Seldwyla, whose quirky inhabitants misbehave in a seriocomic manner. Conrad Ferdinand Meyer (1825–88) was also Swiss, while Adalbert Stifter (1805–68) wrote lyrically about his native Austria. A whole cluster of significant writers was centered in North Germany: Theodor Storm (1817–88), Fritz Reuter (1810–64), Klaus Groth (1819–99), and Willibald Alexis (1798–1871). All these wrote, as it were, from within and about the rural societies in which they were embedded. Symptomatic of their immersion in their environment is their predilection for local dialect as their means of expression. On the one hand recourse to dialect heightens the impression of realism, but on the other it limits the audience to those familiar with it.

Another variant on regionalism was peasant literature, which became a serious literary genre and an important strand of German realism. It found its model in the stories published in the early years of the century by Peter Hebbel (1760–1826) who wrote about simple country folk in both dialect and standard German. His foremost successors were the Swiss Jeremias Gotthelf (1797–1854) whose best known work is *Die schwarze Spinne* (The Black Spider, 1845) and Fritz Reuter, who came from Mecklenburg and won the admiration of all who could read the dialect of that area. Peasant literature in standard German commanded a wider readership, some of it enjoying immense popularity such as the *Schwarzwälder Dorfgeschichten* (Black Forest Village Tales, 1843–54) by Berthold Auerbach (1812–82), the stories of the Austrian Peter Rosegger (1843–1918), and the dramas of peasant life by his countryman Ludwig Anzengruber (1839–89). But peasant literature, especially that in dialect, was seldom translated and did not reach far beyond local boundaries.

This regional limitation was not the only factor that hampered the diffusion of German realism — often termed "poetic realism" because it focuses in a gentle manner on the small happenings, tragedies, and heroisms of humble life rather than on the impact of public social and political issues addressed by the mid-nineteenth-century French and English novelists. The preferred form of the German poetic realists was the novella. Though often complex in form and artistically sophisticated, it does not have the broad sociological horizon of the European novel of the time. Its ideological thrust is away "from direct interaction or engagement with the reader."[21] In other words, it looks inward onto itself in antithesis to the novels of, say, Balzac or Dickens that open up a vista from the particular to the universal. The retreat from the reader in the novella is reiterated in the relatively few novels of German realism such as Stifter's *Witiko* (1865–67), Wilhelm Raabe's (1831–1910) *Stopfkuchen* (1891), Friedrich Spielhagen's (1829–1911) *Problematische Naturen* (Problematic Characters, 1861), and Gustav Freytag's (1816–95) *Soll und Haben* (Debit and Credit, 1855). Their tendency to a mannered style and archaic expressions removes them from the spoken language or the press. The historicizing idiom, like dialect, seems an attempt to hold back the age or at least to attain distance from it.

In this retreat, too, German realism differs from its European counterparts. "For the German realist writers," Sagarra comments, "the 'modern world' signified potential chaos rather than opportunity, and his first task was to discover coherence in what he saw around him."[22] This imperative clearly underlies the attraction to regionalism. Perhaps it also inspires the often noted greater preoccupation with ethical foundations than with social issues. Dogged by an elegiac sense of loss, German writers emphasized the aesthetic and ethical over the social implications of the changes in the world they did not feel capable of reforming. They did not have the self-confidence about the artist's role in a capitalist society characteristic of Balzac, Zola, Dickens, or George Eliot. German realism has nothing to correspond to Balzac's *Human Comedy* (1842–48) of striving ambition for wealth and success, nor the thoughtful confrontation of the problems of the day in George Eliot's oeuvre. Only toward the very end of the century did Germany produce a writer whose novels are of a stature to take their place in the context of European literature. It is surely no coincidence that Theodor Fontane (1819–98) spent the middle thirty years of his life in England as a reporter. The substantial novels of his last years address the ethical problems of his time such as class distinctions and codes of behavior from a social angle. Although set in North Germany, they transcend regionalism in their subtle analysis of universal issues.

Yet even while German realism had little resonance abroad, other facets of German culture at the time were an important presence, especially in England. The marriage of Queen Victoria to Prince Albert of Saxe-Coburg in 1840 marks the start of the positive reception of things German in England. The importation of the Christmas tree is an emblem of the openness to Germany in spheres not necessarily literary. The middle years of the century until Albert's untimely death in 1861 correspond to the high point of the German presence in England. This is the period of the popularity of German children's books; apart from the *Tales* of the brothers Grimm, Heinrich Hoffmann's *Struwwelpeter* appeared in an English translation in 1845, and in 1847 E. T. A. Hoffmann's *History of a Nutcracker,* adapted from a French version by Alexandre Dumas the Elder. But the stories, often by unnamed translators, were domesticated to British perceptions of Germany so that they did not acquaint readers with what Germany was actually like.[23]

The influx of German refugees after the failure of the 1848 revolution gave further impetus to the awareness of German ideas in England.[24] Since the refugees were primarily intellectuals and political activists, they drew attention to German thought and scholarship. George Eliot had translated David Friedrich Strauss's important *Das Leben Jesu* (1835–36, *The Life of Jesus*) in 1846, and it was followed in 1854 by her translation of

Ludwig Feuerbach's *Das Wesen des Christentums* (1841, *The Nature of Christianity*). Eliot maintained a profound and protracted fascination with Goethe, traveling to Germany in 1854 with George Henry Lewes to engage in research for Lewes's *Life and Works of Goethe* (1854–55). Goethe remained an icon among the small but intellectually high-powered group of leading British thinkers. German scholarship, especially the Higher Biblical criticism, was scrutinized and discussed notwithstanding the fact that the study of German was "still mainly an occupation for cultured individuals and the intellectual circles surrounding them."[25] The school curriculum retained a bias toward the classics, and among modern languages German was outdone by the continuing predominance of French. However, chairs of German were established at University College and King's College, London in 1828 and 1831 respectively, and the Northern provincial universities also offered instruction in the German language.

The motivation to learn German in the mid to later nineteenth century stemmed less from interest in its literature than in its scholarship. The reform of German education in the earlier half of the century paved the way for the efflorescence of science in its second half. In the new Realgymnasium priority was given to the sciences in order to prepare men for industrialization and research. The German medical schools with their emphasis on chemistry, physics, botany, and zoology, and the addition of histology and embryology in the 1850s and 1860s became models for the medical curriculum in London (and in the United States). Signal advances were made in bacteriology, microscopal anatomy, neuropsychiatry, and instrumentation that brought Germany into the forefront of medical progress. The work of Robert Koch (1843–1910) in infectious diseases is preeminent. Although Sagarra asserts that "the view has been widely held that the nineteenth century was a period of decline, even decadence in the history of German literature,"[26] in other spheres of endeavor that were to assume increasing importance into the twentieth century Germany was undoubtedly in the forefront.

With the advent of naturalism the picture changes once more, this time to a preponderance of parallels over disparities as German literature moved into the European mainstream. The unification of Germany and the consequent establishment of a capital in Berlin had a decisive effect on both ideological and practical levels. Ideologically, in the wake of the military victories in the Franco-Prussian War (1870–71) and the proclamation of William I, King of Prussia as German Emperor (at Versailles!), the Germans acquired, together with statehood, a new pride and self-confidence as a European power. Prussian military rule set the tone for the emerging nation as a hard-headed confrontation of reality ousted a quiescence and placidity now regarded as antiquated. The guiding spirits of naturalism were outspokenly anti-metaphysical: Darwin, Marx, Engels, Feuerbach, and two French thinkers, the philosopher Auguste Comte, who championed the mathematical method, and the critic Hippolyte Taine, who believed in the formative impact of heredity, environment, and the pressure of immediate circumstances on the individual's behavior.

In practical terms, Berlin provided a focal point for naturalism in contrast to the dispersal of realism into the regions. It was one of the cities that grew most rapidly in the transition from agrarian to factory production. As in London and Paris, poorly paid, disenfranchised workers huddled in the slums that arose around the mechanized factories. With the widening of the gap between the exploited proletariat and the complacent bourgeoisie that was being enriched by industrialization, the optimism characteristic of the Gründerzeit (foundation years) was dampened in certain quarters by concern for the wretched misery of large segments of the population. German naturalism therefore runs parallel to its European equivalents in its strong social consciousness and its zeal for reform.

The combative momentum of the German naturalists is similar to but even more pronounced than that of their precursors in France and Scandinavia. Emile Zola's (1840–1902) cycle of novels about various members of a sprawling family with a legitimate and an illegitimate branch, *Les Rougon-Macquart* (1871–93) was extolled as the implementation of the scientific principles governing human behavior. Although Zola at first met with hostility on account of his alleged immorality, he was greeted with increasing enthusiasm from 1880 on, and translations of his works proliferated.[27] Wilhelm Bölsche's *Die naturwissenschaftlichen Grundlagen der Poesie* (The Scientific Bases of Poetry, 1893) is an attempt to systematize the analogy between science and literature along the same lines as Zola had done in *Le Roman expérimental* (The Experimental Novel, 1880). Arno Holz's treatise, *Die Kunst: Ihr Wesen und ihre Gesetze* (Art: Its Essence and its Laws, 1891) goes further still in seeking to spell out the fundamental laws of art which he posited as nature minus x, x representing the shortfall in the artist's capacity to copy nature perfectly. Thus, in his slice of life sketch *Papa Hamlet* (1891) he uses hyperrealistic devices including the phonetic notation of personal idiosyncrasies in speech and the mimetic recording of sounds such as the drip from a leaking roof to achieve the closest approximation to reality. In theories and experiments such as these, German naturalism parallels but also exceeds its European counterparts.

It is in the theater that German naturalism comes closest to its sister movements in other European countries, partly because they all imported the same models from Scandinavia. Ibsen's *Ghosts* (1881) was the play chosen to inaugurate successively the *Théâtre libre* in Paris in 1887, the *Freie Bühne* (Free Stage) in Berlin and the *Independent Theatre* in London both in 1891. There can be no better demonstration of the unanimity in European naturalism than this agreement on the foundation of the new drama. The social problems and dirty secrets of the middle as well as of the lower classes were exposed by Gerhart Hauptmann (1862–1946) in an impressive series of plays: *Vor Sonnenaufgang* (Before Dawn, 1889), *Das Friedensfest* (The Festival of Peace, 1890), *Einsame Menschen* (Lonely People, 1891), and *Die Weber* (The Weavers, 1892), originally in Silesian dialect and subsequently in standard German. "Seen in retrospect and from an international perspective, the movement [naturalism] produced only one author of lasting significance," Maurer asserts of Hauptmann.[28] Certainly in prose Germany was no match for the wealth of works, many of them distinguished, in France. The novels of Michael Georg Conrad (1846–1927), editor of the journal *Die Gesellschaft* (Society) in Munich, the secondary locus of German naturalism, are pretty well forgotten nowadays. Nevertheless, "naturalism is usually regarded as the beginning of the phase of modern German literature"[29] as Maurer points out. It marks the point where German literature, with Hauptmann, Fontane, and just a little later Thomas Mann, attained full parity in Europe.

Das schwierige neunzehnte Jahrhundert (The Difficult Nineteenth Century) is the title of a recent international interdisciplinary conference whose proceedings were published in 2000. *Schwierig* is an evocative word, less weighty than the outright *schwer* (hard), yet implying a peculiar awkwardness and intricacy. Was the nineteenth century really particularly *schwierig* in Germany? The political situation with its struggles between pressures to conservatism or progressiveness as the country moved toward unification is definitely a complicating factor in its literary and cultural history. The nineteenth century in Germany is above all a paradoxical time of contrasts, changes, and reversals that defy reduction to a simple scenario. The position of German literature in the context of European culture offers a cogent example of paradoxicality. For instance, Goethe was for most of the century perceived as the only German poet of international stature, while the Romantics, engaged in experimentation vital to modernism and postmodernism, were with few exceptions, neglected. As were the realists, though for opposite reasons. If the Romantics ventured too far beyond then accepted literary and aesthetic norms, the realists retreated too far into their niches in localized precincts remote from the world at large. As a result, German literature was largely undervalued in the context of European culture in the nineteenth and even into the twentieth century. Some of its most original writers, such as Novalis and Friedrich Schlegel did not reach an audience commensurate with their importance.

Notes

[1] René Wellek, "The Crisis of Comparative Literature," *Concepts of Criticism*, ed. Stephen J. Nichols, Jr. (New Haven: Yale UP, 1963): 283.

[2] See, for example, Catherine W. Proescholt-Obermann, *Goethe and his British Critics: The Reception of Goethe's Works in British Periodicals 1795–1855* (Frankfurt,

Bern & New York: Peter Lang, 1992; J. Simpson, *Matthew Arnold and Goethe* (London: Modern Humanities Research Association, 1979); Walter H. Bruford, "Goethe and some Victorian Humanists," *Publications of the English Goethe Society* 18 (1949): 34–67; Albert Fuchs, *Goethe et l'esprit français* (Paris: Les Belles Lettres, 1958); E. M. Vida, *Romantic Affinities* (Toronto, Buffalo, and London: U of Toronto P, 1993); Oliver Boek, *Heine Nachwirkungen* (Göppingen: Kümmerle, 1972); Elizabeth Teichmann, *La Fortune de Hoffmann en France* (Geneva: Droz, 1961).

[3] Edith J. Morley, *Crabb Robinson in Germany 1800–1805* (London: Oxford UP, 1935).

[4] Ruth Anne Crowley, *Charles de Villiers: Mediator and Comparatist* (Frankfurt: Peter Lang, 1978).

[5]. Lilian R. Furst, "Mme. de Staël's *De L'Allemagne:* A Misleading Intermediary," *Orbis Litterarum* 31 (1976): 41–58.

[6] Bayard Q. Morgan, *A Critical Bibliography of German Literature in British Translation 1481–1927, with a supplement for 1928–35* (Stanford: Stanford UP, 1938); Susanne Stark, *"Behind Inverted Commas": Translations and Anglo-German Relations in the Nineteenth Century* (Clevedon, UK: Multilingual Matters, 1999).

[7] His inability to grasp the difference between *heiraten* and *sich verheiraten* led him to marry off the wrong pair of characters.

[8] Lilian R. Furst, "Two Versions of Schiller's *Wallenstein,*" in *Modern Miscellany: Festschrift for Eugène Vinaver,* ed. T. E. Lawrenson, F. E. Sutcliffe, and Gilbert Gadoffre (New York: Barnes & Noble, 1969): 65–78.

[9] Eda Sagarra, *Tradition and Revolution: German Literature and Society 1830–90* (New York: Basic Books, 1971), 3.

[10] Sagarra, *Tradition and Revolution,* 3.

[11] Karl S. Guthke, *Goethes Weimar und "Die grosse Öffnung' in die Welt* (Wiesbaden: Harrassowitz Verlag, 2001), 147–54 on British travelers.

[12] Sagarra, *Tradition and Revolution,* 65.

[13] Cf. Christian in Thomas Mann's *Buddenbrooks.*

[14] See Furst, *Romanticism in Perspective* (London: Macmillan, 1969; New York: Humanities Press, 1970).

[15] Roger Paulin, "'In so vielseitiger Wechselwirkung': Some Problems in Nineteenth-Century Anglo-German Literary Relations," *Das schwierige neunzehnte Jahrhundert,* ed. Jürgen Barkhoff, Gilbert Carr, and Roger Paulin (Tübingen: Niemeyer, 2000): 571.

[16] Cf. Furst, *Counterparts* (London: Methuen, 1977; Detroit: Wayne State UP, 1977), 99–173, especially 120–32 on Wagner.

[17] Cf. Teichmann, *La Fortune de E. T. A. Hoffmann en France.*

[18] A. B. Botnikova, *E. T. A. Hoffmann and Russian Literature* (Voronezh: Voronezh UP, 1977). I am most grateful to my research assistant Marina Alexandrova for reading this book for me in Russian and providing the information as well as many other biographical and bibliographic facts.

[19] Cf. Furst, *Counterparts*, 114.

[20] Cf. David Blamires, "German Children's Books in England 1840–1860," in *Das schwierige neunzehnte Jahrhundert*, 559–65.

[21] Duncan Smith, "Realism," *Encyclopedia of German Literature*, ed, Matthias Konzett (Chicago: Fitzroy Dearborn, 2000) II, 806. I am indebted to Clayton Koelb for lending me his copy as well as for stimulating conversations and useful suggestions for this piece.

[22] Sagarra, *Tradition and Revolution*, 222.

[23] Cf. Blamires, "German Children's Books in England 1840–1860" in *Das schwierige neunzehnte Jahrhundert*.

[24] Cf. Ashton, *Little Germany*, 93–108.

[25] Cf. Stark, *"Behind Inverted Commas,"* 31.

[26] Sagarra, *Tradition and Revolution*, 69.

[27] Winthrop H. Root, *German Criticism of Zola 1875–93* (New York: Columbia UP, 1929).

[28] Warren R. Maurer, "Naturalism," *Encyclopedia of German Literature*, II: 750.

[29] Ibid.

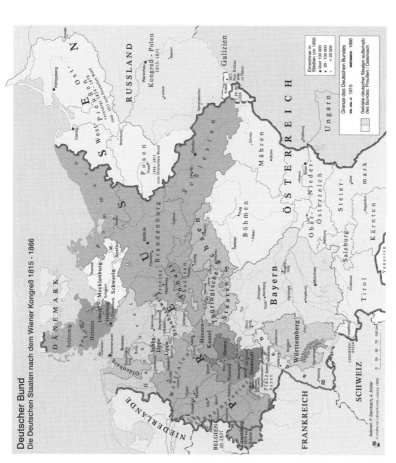

The German Federation: The German states after the Congress of Vienna, 1815–1866. Courtesy of Institut für Länderkunde, Leipzig.

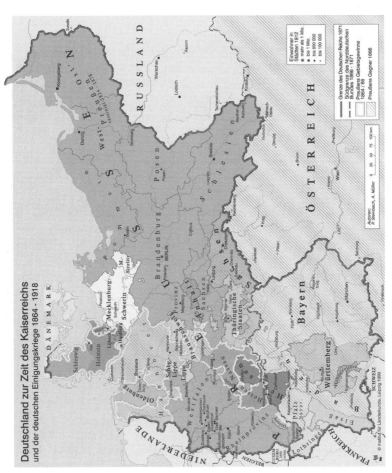

Germany during the Wilhelmine Empire and the German Wars of
Unification 1864–1918. Courtesy of Institut für Länderkunde, Leipzig.

Revolution and Reaction: The Political Context of Central European Literature

Arne Koch

THE NINETEENTH CENTURY was an age marked by countless transformations. By the end of the 1800s, the patchwork of German-speaking kingdoms, principalities, and dominions had been drastically altered. Geographically, the unifying façade of the nation-state replaced the previously fragmented map of Central Europe. Economically, industrial advances succeeded the seeming backwardness of traditional agriculture. Politically, multi-party parliamentary systems took the place of individual absolute rulers. And socially, innovations in transportation, city planning, social welfare and other areas radically modernized German-speaking Europe. The population's reaction to these changing political and social conditions were manifold and often dependent on individuals' religious beliefs, social standing, regional loyalties, gender and age. Inevitably, artists supported, critiqued, escaped, and contemplated many of the transformations during "The Long Nineteenth Century"[1] through literature, paintings, and musical compositions. This survey traces many of the political and social factors writers encountered during this period; to do so, it focuses on major historical moments between 1830 and 1899. Possible causes and relationships of political and social developments during this time-span are brought to light: the geopolitical position of the German-speaking states will resurface repeatedly as we look at links between seemingly distinct historical episodes — from the status quo in the year 1830 to the watershed 1848 revolutions, from the origins of diplomatic differences between Prussia and Austria to the series of wars between 1864 and 1870, and from the creation of the German Empire in 1871 to the coexistence of two German-speaking empires at the end of the century.

The German States in 1830

The territorial contours of Central Europe help account for many of the differences, tensions and desires that this essay accentuates for political, social and cultural spheres alike. In 1830, none of the German-speaking countries with which we are familiar today existed, let alone one unified Germany in the fashion of the Western European nation-states England and France. Instead, maps comprised countless sovereign entities. Following the end of the Napoleonic era and the treaty of the Congress of Vienna, which had produced a peaceful balance among the European powers in 1815, the uncompromising leadership of Austria's foreign minister and later chancellor, Clemens von Metternich (1773–1859), had created the *Deutsche Bund* (German Confederation) with thirty-nine member states ranging in size from the Kingdom of Prussia down to the duchy of Liechtenstein with only 5000 inhabitants. As a loosely-joined federation of states and cities (*Staatenbund*), however, not a federal state (*Bundesstaat*), the *Bund* preserved the boundaries of its precursor, the Holy Roman Empire of the German Nation, which had come to an end in 1806. A lack of central administrative and executive bodies disappointed premature hopes for the creation of a unified national structure. The Confederation's permanent ambassadorial congress, the *Bundesversammlung* (Federal Diet) in Frankfurt, had little more than nominal representative functions, which consequently aided the Austrian Empire (created in 1804), whose Emperor presided over the *Bund,* and Prussia in maintaining and expanding their positions as the two dominant states. With the creation of the *Bund,* several smaller political units had been absorbed by others. For example, the acquisition of the Rhineland and Westphalia in the west had given Prussia previously absent economic powers. Some of the *Mittelstaaten* (middle states) also had recorded territorial gains. Among these states, Bavaria, Baden, and Württemberg had introduced written constitutions as part of the sovereignty granted by the *Bund*. Unlike the enduring absolutist monarchies in Prussia, Austria and middle states such as Hanover and the Mecklenburgs, these southern and southwestern states now granted more participatory rights to individuals.

That the *Bund*'s exterior borders did not correspond to the makeup of its nationality groups proved to be significant later in the century. The *Bund* did not follow a sense of national belonging as an organizing principle. Some non-German minorities were included, for instance Czech nationals as part of Austria, while Prussia's easternmost province of East Prussia with its large German population and substantial parts of the multinational Austrian Empire including Hungary were left out. Switzerland also remained outside the *Bund*. It had not been a part of the Holy Roman Empire and continued to maintain a neutral stance between France, Italy and the *Bund* throughout the 1800s. As the writings of the Swiss novelist Gottfried Keller (1819–1890) nonetheless revealed, developments in Prussia, Austria and elsewhere impacted the Swiss imagination, and as the later dissemination of Swiss democratic ideals in Europe reveal, the flow of ideas clearly moved in the opposite direction as well. Other territories, however, were much less resolute about ties to the *Bund*. On occasion there existed deep divisions over national affiliations exemplified by the duchies of Schleswig and Holstein. Holstein with its predominantly German-speaking population was part of the *Bund,* while Schleswig and its Danish residents remained excluded. This discord was a recurring theme for Theodor Storm (1817–1888) and other writers from Schleswig-Holstein. Politically, the division resurfaced again and again in crucial points of dispute, which the following discussion of the 1848 Revolution and the Wars of Unification between 1864 and 1870 will underscore. Significant connections between the order within the *Bund* and the rest of Europe were further shaped by the kings of England, the Netherlands, and Denmark and their rule over the states of Hanover, Luxembourg, and Schleswig-Holstein respectively. Located in the center of Europe, the German Confederation was thus not a unified power, but a product of a European balancing act.

This territorial composition polarized the power brokers Austria and Prussia throughout the nineteenth century. Thus, Austro-Prussian relations largely shaped the history of Central Europe until the 1870s. We will see how the conservative reactions in these two states to revolutionary events in the 1830s and in 1848, their division over economic cooperation, the culmination of their competition in the war of 1866, all amplified this crucial struggle. Yet, as differences crystallized, it became apparent how nonetheless the Confederation articulated great consensus on interior politics. Following the lead of Prussia and Austria, the *Bund* agreed on controlling demands for political and social change as potential threats to their rule. Under Metternich's conservative influence, the *Bund* had passed the *Karlsbader Beschlüsse* (Carlsbad Decrees, 1819) in response to the murder of the playwright August von Kotzebue (1761–1819) who had mocked the ideals of nationalist yearning. Consequently, persistent threats of censorship, bans on political associations, limitations on freedom of speech, and secret trials were among the restrictive measures that affected the intellectual climate and everyday life. As the seven-year incarceration in 1833 of the Mecklenburg dialect-writer Fritz Reuter (1810–1874) for his youthful political associations illustrated, an individual's protection from the long arm of the state was at risk throughout the century. Often callous responses to attempted change and public criticism underscored the influence of a reactionary alliance confirmed at the beginning of the *Restaurationszeit* (Restoration Era) in 1815 between monarchy, Church, and nobility.[2] It was an alliance that endured for a long time. Yet commencing with the year 1830, the restrictive measures of the Restoration were challenged as never before.[3]

The 1830s and '40s: Revolutionary Decades

Scholars use the designations *Restaurationszeit* and *Vormärz* (Pre-March) at times interchangeably for the period between 1815 and 1848.[4] The latter describes, however, more accurately the second half — the years between 1830 and 1848. As an allusion to the period leading up to the 1848 Revolution that broke out all over Central Europe in March of that year, the term *Vormärz* also incorporates the constant scrutiny of any opposition to the structures and regulations of the *Bund*. Precisely this suppression stimulated further political curiosity and antagonism, making the pre-March period a time in which society became increasingly politicized and polarized. As social disparities grew between classes, causing such phenomena as pauperism (impoverishment of the lower social strata) and stimulating radical and socialist thinkers, this period was marked by revolutionary activities, demands for social and political reforms, civil unrest and, in due course, conservative reactions to uphold the existing order.

The events of the July Revolution of 1830 in France unleashed the potential for change in many European states. Bourgeois unrest had culminated in the establishment of a constitutional monarchy in place of the Restoration regime of Charles X (1757–1836), King of France. Although news from Paris together with meager harvests and ensuing high food prices fueled growing discontent within the *Bund*, the few rebellious eruptions in places like Saxony, Hesse-Darmstadt and Brunswick did not represent the most noteworthy impacts of the July Revolution on the German lands. Unquestionably, revolts in these states resulted in the implementation of written constitutions, but more important was how the revolution affected the political consciousness of individuals and the increasing growth of *Vereine* (clubs and organizations). Ostensibly related yet conflicting ideological orientations began to find broader support. Liberalism (economic and individual emancipation from feudal structures, although often within monarchical configurations), nationalism (transformation from *Kulturnation* to nation-state as the possibility to transcend limitations of state particularism), and democracy (belief in sovereignty of the people as a ruling body) were organizing principles for like-minded groups.[5]

In spite of this politicizing atmosphere, as the case of Hanover illustrated, the *Vormärz* offered only limited political freedom and change did not come with a guarantee of permanence. After Hanover's transition to a constitutional state in 1833, King Ernst August (1771–1851) single-handedly eliminated rights granted by his predecessor, which drew forceful criticism from the *Göttinger Sieben* (Göttingen Seven), a group of university professors, including the fairy-tale collectors and Germanists Jacob (1785–1863) and Wilhelm Grimm (1786–1859) and the historian Friedrich Dahlmann (1785–1860), who had once sworn to defend the old charter but now publicly objected to the king's directives. Their reactions ultimately resulted in their dismissal and subsequent exile in 1837. This famous case drew so much attention throughout the *Bund* that it illustrated the mounting challenges for governments to contain unwanted dissension.

It revealed, in addition, how events previously relevant to individual territories began to translate into issues of broader and potentially national relevance. The growth of the *Bildungsbürgertum* (educated middle class) and the increase in literacy rates made possible the dissemination of various reformist pleas and publications.[6]

Disturbances: Social and National Questions

Substantial population increases, a rise in poverty — approximately 60% of the Prussian population lived below the poverty line in the 1830s and early 1840s — and the burgeoning proto-industrialization of textile homemakers in regions such as Bohemia, Silesia, and southwest Switzerland all posed latent threats of instability to the existing order.[7] The social question and the emerging proletariat only became increasingly significant by the mid 1840s.[8] For now, governments were more concerned with a noticeable increase in the public's concern with issues of governance. Organizations such as the southwest *Vaterlandsverein zur Unterstützung der freien Presse* (Fatherland Association for the Support of the Free Press) endorsed calls for greater freedom, which was celebrated at the *Hambacher Fest*. With the support of several *Burschenschaften* (student societies or fraternities) more than 20,000 people attended this symbolic gathering in Hambach in 1832. Certainly while this event generated an often emphasized pro-democratic atmosphere, it was in fact staged by small groups with often-conflicting views.[9]

Sentiments regarding political reform were expressed quite differently by members of the bourgeoisie. While many contemplated possibilities for change within the privacy of their homes, in small circles and often with an unstated belief in the basic integrity of the system,[10] more outspoken groups exposed political views in form of poetry, plays and journalistic pieces such as the feuilleton. This thematization of social and political turmoil demanded explicit criticism. While this overview does not provide analyses of the various tendentious characteristics of the *Junges Deutschland* (Young Germany), it is nevertheless important to underscore how this literary orientation at times directly impacted the social-historical reality. The playwright Georg Büchner (1813–1837) caused uproar with his pamphlet *Der Hessische Landbote* (The Hessian Messenger, 1834) in which he encouraged outright revolts among the oppressed peasant population in Hesse-Darmstadt. The daring motto of his tract, *Friede den Hütten, Krieg den Palästen* (Peace to the huts, war to the palaces!), blatantly conveyed the imagery of what many feared, revolution. Other writers, including Georg Herwegh (1817–1875) and Ferdinand Freiligrath (1810–1876), disseminated leaflets in numerous cities and used the operative possibilities of their poetry with uncompromising candor.[11]

Alongside these revolutionary manifestations during the *Vormärz* coexisted another reaction, declared by some historians as even more characteristic for its time. The terms *Bürgertum* (bourgeoisie), extensively discussed for its divisions into *Bildungs-* and *Wirtschaftsbürgertum* (educated and commercial bourgeoisie) as well as *Beamten-* and *Kleinbürgertum* (civil servant and petty burgher), imply a resigned quiescence to the philistine world instead of a social challenge to it. This *Biedermeier Verbürgerlicherung* (the process of becoming bourgeois)[12] is important for an understanding of how many citizens responded to an increasingly complex reality.[13] Contemporary thinkers lamented this process, such as the writer and ethnographer Wilhelm Heinrich Riehl (1823–1897) in his study *Die bürgerliche Gesellschaft* (1851). The stereotypical figure of the *deutsche Michel* (poor Mick), a popularized self-image of the German, conveyed the characteristic ineffectiveness of society and drew attention to the pessimistic and unpolitical *Biedermeier* world of the bourgeoisie.[14] The Bavarian painter Carl Spitzweg (1808–1885) made this withdrawal into the private domain famous with his portrait of a penniless poet who seeks shelter from raindrops dripping into his loft while writing on his bed. Spitzweg's *Der arme Dichter* (The Poor Poet, 1839) also found its equivalent in the world of letters. The notorious silence and tranquility of a writer such as the Austrian Franz Grillparzer (1791–1872) in due course became a target for historians.[15] Yet, this outward appearance of *Biedermeier* prevented a full recognition of veiled elements of a political discourse.[16]

A key historical episode illustrated the state of the political consciousness among many citizens. During the *Frankfurter Wachesturm* (the raid of the police station in Frankfurt am Main, April 3, 1833) a small group of former students and political activists did not gain the support expected and faced instead an uninterested public. In the end, this dilettantish effort to generate widespread revolution triggered an unexpected reaction. The *Bund* exploited the events to justify the elimination of various forms of political assembly and extended censorship to previously exempt monographs exceeding 320 pages. Between 1832 and 1842, the *Bund* conducted over 2000 investigations of political activities. In Prussia alone, thirty-nine people were sentenced to death for subversive activities and around 170 were incarcerated.[17] Most death sentences were later reduced to life and eventually to amnesty in 1840. Nonetheless, the *Wiener Ministerialkonferenzen* (Vienna Ministry Conferences) in July 1834 still further intensified the persecution of writers and intellectuals categorized as demagogues. In 1835, the *Bundestag* (Federal Diet) banned *Junges Deutschland* outright for blasphemous and immoral writings. This ban affected writers as different as Georg Büchner, Georg Herwegh, Heinrich Heine (1797–1856), and the Viennese comedic playwright

Johann Nepomuk Nestroy (1801–1862), and forced many writers to emigrate. Ironically, the formation of exile groups in Paris, London, and Switzerland later on generated an influx of radical ideas during the 1848 Revolution.

In part due to this influx of political refugees from Italy, France, and the *Bund*, Switzerland experienced noteworthy changes during the *Vormärz*. The *Regeneration*, a *nom de plume* for the democratic movement, successfully deposed the aristocratic leadership in several cantons by means of petitions and public assemblies in 1830. That same year, ten cantons established indirect, democratic voting alongside the guarantee of civic rights. Similar demands in Basel however led to civil war between city and rural areas and ultimately a creation of two *Halbkantone* (half cantons) in 1833. Despite Switzerland's democratic reorganization, Basel's partition and ensuing conservative attempts to restore aristocratic governments in Zurich and Lucerne highlighted continued political uncertainties.

The Customs Union

Democratic impulses from Switzerland were certainly important during the 1830s and 1840s, but more significant was an economic expansion that took place January 1, 1834. This extension greatly impacted both the structure and politics of the *Bund* for decades to come. As this discussion of the revolutionary events in 1848 and consequent Prussian-Austrian relations will later illuminate, the creation of the *Zollverein* (Customs Union) far exceeded Prussia's initial expectation of a simple free trade area to bridge its geographically removed territories Westphalia to Silesia and East Prussia. As early as 1842, Prussian control in the *Zollverein* meant its virtual economic domination of the *Bund* and an increasing political influence. Critics disagree about the actual influence of this economic phase on Germany's eventual unification and industrialization. It is accurate to say, however, that the *Zollverein* was a step in advancing broader, unifying notions against protective attitudes of state particularism.[18] After all, the desire of manufacturers in the *Mittelstaaten* to gain access to Prussian markets compelled many states to join the Union. But as much as economic and infrastructure expansion contributed to drawing multiple states together — railway construction stood out as one of the objects promoted by the Prussian economist Friedrich List (1789–1846) — some states remained on the outside. Austria's decision not to join the Union and instead to concentrate exclusively on the protection of its empire proved to be of great consequence. In effect, the open discord over the *Zollverein* set in motion the competition of Habsburg Austria and Hohenzollern Prussia for leadership within the *Bund*. The following discussion of the 1848 Revolution will further reveal the significance of the

Zollverein and its economic and diplomatic division for the political tone up until the 1866 war between the two states.

Despite the tension, common patriotic enthusiasm throughout the *Bund* reached a high point in 1840. Widespread protest against France's demands for a reestablishment of the Rhine as its eastern border stimulated calls for German unity and even preemptive military engagement. A profusion of political and nationalist poems, for example the *Rheinlieder* (Rhine Songs), written by Robert Prutz (1816–1872) and many by lesser-known poets circulated widely and suggested a growing collective consciousness.[19] That same year, the ascent of Friedrich Wilhelm IV (1795–1861) to the Prussian throne further encouraged supporters of liberal ideals and national unity. Initial changes included amnesty for prisoners, reduction of political investigations, and appointments of moderate ministers. Friedrich Wilhelm's yearning for popularity even led him to participate in the *Kölner Dombaufest* (consecration of the Cologne Cathedral) in September 1842. For many, this public festivity celebrating the cathedral as a national symbol anticipated an overcoming of the divisions between popular and patriotic groups, Catholic, liberal, and nationalist organizations alike. However, Friedrich Wilhelm disappointed most people. His firm belief in society's God-given order and in the king's primacy deviated from his initial populist stance. Consequently, he opposed actual change when he denied a written Prussian constitution pledged by his predecessor in 1815. Friedrich Wilhelm's rationalization of his objections appears today as rather facetious, yet aptly exposes his traditional, reactionary course: a written constitution simply obstructed the bond between God, king and people.[20]

As public opinion swayed between enthusiasm and frustration, social inequality had become a vital force by the mid to late-1840s. High food prices and poor harvests in 1846–47 once again led to disquiet throughout the *Bund*. With over 70 percent of the population still working in rural areas in Prussia in the 1840s, peasants emphatically demanded the elimination of aristocracy's remaining feudal privileges.[21] In the months of April and May 1847, uneven demographic growth contributed to revolts and to 158 food riots in Prussia. The most notorious disturbance, the so-called *Weberaufstand* (Weaver Revolt), took place in Upper Silesia in 1844 and has been depicted since in the critical poems of Heinrich Heine and the Saxon writer Louise Otto (1819–1895) and, most famously, in 1892 by the playwright Gerhart Hauptmann (1862–1946). The revolt was not provoked directly by the deaths of over 50,000 people who had succumbed to malnutrition related illnesses over the years. Instead, the abusive working conditions and frequent cases of child labor triggered the uprising and the demolition of small textile mills and of factory owners' properties. Comparable uprisings in the textile industry had occurred a decade earlier in Great Britain (Birmingham and Newport in 1838) and also in

Switzerland. Although small insurgencies in places such as Uster in 1832 did little to prevent Switzerland's position as the most industrialized country on the continent by 1850. The transition of the country's economy from the traditionally agriculture to an industrial one greatly affected Swiss political debates and became a thematic undercurrent in several works by the novelist Gottfried Keller and the short-story author Jeremias Gotthelf (1779–1854), whose tale *Käthi die Großmutter* (Käthi the Grandmother, 1847) described poverty-stricken regions in Switzerland.

Swiss Civil War

Since 1838, the Swiss democratic movement had tried to force additional amendments to the *Kantonsverfassungen* (constitutions of the cantons). These efforts did not significantly impact economic progress, but tensions between liberal-Protestant and conservative-Catholic districts did lead to tumultuous years. Following the 1844 attack of centralist volunteer corps on the Catholic stronghold Lucerne, several cantons, mostly Catholic, created the *Sonderbund* (Separate League, 1845) as a defense pact to prevent further centralization. Historical overviews sometimes neglect to stress the importance for Central Europe, primarily for the southwest German states, of these early revolutionary events in Switzerland.[22] It is important, therefore, to note that the ensuing *Sonderbundskrieg* (War of the Confederation of Seven Catholic Cantons) of 1847 captured the imagination of many parts of the *Bund* well before the Italian civil unrest and the French Revolution in 1848. Possible explanations for an omission of Switzerland as an inspiring model for unrest in the German states may be attributed simply to the swift resolution following the Swiss disputes. In the war's aftermath, the *Neue Bundesverfassung* (New Federal Constitution) was introduced by early 1848. Patterned after the United States constitution, Switzerland established a balance between central interests of the Federation and distinct privileges of the cantons.[23]

The 1848 Revolution and Its Aftermath

1848 became the year of the revolution throughout most of Europe. News of the February Revolution in France and of the abdication of the bourgeois King Louis Philippe (1773–1850) soon awakened the continent. The causes for rebellion, however, differed considerably: uprisings in France mostly targeted the one-sided interests of the upper classes; Eastern European regions were incensed by the consequences of foreign rule, while events in Italy and the *Bund* focused on remaining feudal, absolutist structures as well as the lack of national cohesion. Differences abounded, yet the revolution became a pan-European experience that proved pivotal. One significant feature of the 1848 Revolution involved the widespread articulation of competing ideals, which ranged from liberal economic and political demands to nationalist yearning. Even as this plurality of ideologies created disarray and weakened efforts to unite against established authorities, the taste for political activity it bestowed on the public generated significant long term consequences. Within the *Bund,* the events of 1848 contributed to the political emancipation of society in a number of ways. The creation of a democratic parliament in Frankfurt, in the *Frankfurter Paulskirche,* albeit short-lived, was a key impulse for the future initiation of political parties and societies. Resolute political and social demands during these revolutionary moments brought about major triumphs, such as the eventual abolition of feudal dues. This latter advance may have been motivated by the authorities' desire to slow the dispersion of revolutionary ideals by satisfying the masses, yet it was an accomplishment to be ascribed to the episodes in 1848.

In spite of and perhaps because of such positive accomplishments, the revolution as a whole failed to change instantly the political culture and structure of the *Bund.* Divisions among revolutionaries and the silence of a broad majority aided the pre-revolutionary powers' dominance. Yet as a result of the events in 1848, the cooperation between various German states changed dramatically. Parliamentary discussions concentrated on boosting the rights of every citizen and addressed social concerns. The Frankfurt Parliament is notable for the degree to which it evolved into more than just the body and the symbol of the 1848 Revolution. As competition between Austria and Prussia intensified politically and economically (over the *Zollverein*), the Frankfurt Parliament became the first site for and perhaps also the first casualty of a dualism that determined Central Europe's course for decades to come.

The Frankfurt Parliament: Between German Question and Zollverein

A chain reaction quickly swept through the *Bund* after the revolution unfolded in Paris.[24] Five hundred representatives from all over Germany were summoned to form the *Frankfurter Vorparlament* (Pre-Parliament) after southern assemblies petitioned the convening of a German assembly. Differences between radicals and moderates immediately created a rift that soon led to a declaration of a republic by a small group of parliamentarians. Federal troops swiftly defeated this mini-revolution and related uprisings in the southwest. Despite such military success, between March 31 and April 3 the *Bund* voted to hold elections for a national assembly, which convened later in the Frankfurter Paulskirche on May 18. In the absence of political parties, many notables among the 585 deputies dictated the debate, including the brothers Grimm and the poets Ludwig Uhland (1787–1862) and Ernst Moritz Arndt (1769–1860). The presence of legal scholars and academics in the Paulskirche illustrated the influence of the educated bourgeoisie, now confronted with the task of crafting its own modus operandi. This *Parlament der Professoren* elected an imperial administrator to appoint a provisional central government. Through October 1848, this parliament continued intensive debates on the basic rights of the people, but an increasing division into political factions foretold the impending dissolution of the assembly.

Negative sentiments among monarchists toward the assembly deepened with internal turmoil in Prussia and Austria. As early as March 13, 1848, uprisings had forced Metternich's emigration to London. News of Metternich's departure intensified unrest throughout the multinational empire. Until the end of 1849, violent conflicts in Hungary, Bohemia, the Piedmont (northern Italy) and other regions dominated Austrian politics and military. It prefigured, as we will discuss shortly, some of the domestic tribulations within the Austrian-Hungarian multi-cultural empire and would be exposed implicitly and explicitly by Austrian writers as diverse as Adalbert Stifter (1805–1868), Marie von Ebner-Eschenbach (1830–1916), Ferdinand von Saar (1833–1906), and Franz Kafka (1883–1924). For now, the abolition of statutory labor through a newly established Austrian assembly simply appeased large parts of the rural population. The combination of liberal demands, ethnic fighting and peasants' aspirations confirmed how the German constituent in Austria was far more concerned with their own territory than with events in Frankfurt. In the meantime, in Prussia, Friedrich Wilhelm was taken aback by public protests that reached Berlin in early March. During the king's celebrated announcement of the repeal of censorship regulations on March 18, inadvertent gunshots ignited a confrontation between military and civilians. The street battle, in which some writers including Louise Aston (1814–1871) participated, left 230 dead. The following day, Friedrich Wilhelm moved his troops out of Berlin. As part of a tribute to the victims, he assured the creation of a Prussian National Assembly to deliberate a new constitution and define Prussia's role within Germany.

Historians repeatedly invoke the dual objectives of the Paulskirche, the focus on the creation of a constitution and on Germany's becoming a nation-state as necessary for understanding fully in what ways Prussia and Austria contributed to the collapse of the parliament. In March 1848, tensions with Denmark over its occupation of Schleswig had triggered a Prussian military campaign. The Schleswig-Holstein Question was now synonymous with the German Question as immense enthusiasm spread throughout the German states and among writers such as Theodor Storm and Klaus Groth (1819–1899). The declared effort was to remove Danish influence from Schleswig and to secure the duchy's association with the *Bund*. But when France, England and Russia forced an armistice in Malmø, Sweden, Prussia's decision to cease the battle against the wishes of the Paulskirche created great disillusionment. The subsequent acceptance of the armistice by the assembly provoked unexpected attacks against this institution. In the end, only Prussian and Austrian troops could subdue the rioters. Before this revolt, the parliament had projected a sense of calm and authority with its protracted but steady course of action. Now it was clear that a lack of real power and presence of divergent political decisions in Berlin and Vienna could mean the end of the revolutionaries' efforts.

Counter-Revolutions

This collapse of common goals occurred when Austria and Prussia forcefully orchestrated their respective counter-revolutionary campaigns. Imperial and Croatian troops surrounded Vienna and the 100,000 revolutionary troops inside, before reoccupying the city by mid-November 1848. Immediately, the re-established authorities executed many revolutionaries, including some Frankfurt delegates. By the end of the year, Prince Felix von Schwarzenberg (1800–1852), Chancellor of Austria, had empowered Franz Joseph I (1830–1916) as Emperor. Less violent but equally effective was the Prussian response. It commenced with Friedrich Wilhelm's disbanding of the Prussian National Assembly and the re-entry of his troops into Berlin in December 1848. A substitution of the restrictive three-class indirect franchise for the recently introduced manhood suffrage immediately fortified the dominance of rank and wealth. This arrangement endured until the end of the First World War. In the meantime, Schwarzenberg further polarized the Paulskirche. He rejected closer cooperation with parliament and instead demanded the inclusion of the entire Habsburg Empire into the *Bund*, including its eastern and Slavic regions. At stake was therefore the question, which of the two powers would take the leadership role within the *Bund* and by extension in the pursuit for German unity. Prussian-Austrian competition over the *Deutsche Frage* now significantly influenced the politics of the Frankfurt Parliament. What had been previously regularly debated in parliament — namely two opposing approaches to German unity: *großdeutsch* (a large Germany including Austria and all its dominions) versus *kleindeutsch* (a small Germany without Austria under Prussian leadership) — now had become a key issue for the Paulskirche and for Austrian-Prussian relations. In the end, a *kleindeutsch* majority in parliament defeated proponents for a *Großdeutschland*. An immediate vote offered the King of Prussia, Friedrich Wilhelm the title of German *Kaiser*, which he subsequently rejected. Describing it as a "Hundehalsband, mit dem man mich an die Revolution von 1848 ketten will,"[25] the king's refusal accelerated the end of the parliament. Before long, Austria and Prussia recalled its delegates. Despite the resulting dispersal of the Paulskirche in March 1849, a rump parliament remained intact between May and June, when in a final symbolic act of force Prussian troops broke up the remaining delegates.

The Quest for Germany: 1850–1871

Austro-Prussian division over German unity was evident since the Frankfurt Parliament and the continued economic exclusion of Austria from the *Zollverein* revealed Prussia's increased dominance. The period leading up to German unity in 1871 hinged at first however on the cooperation between the two states during renewed international disputes over Schleswig-Holstein in the early 1860s. As will be seen, the initial acceptance of a dynastic dualism between Prussia and Austria cemented by their joint effort in the war against Denmark in 1864 evolved into open competition for hegemony and the Austro-Prussian war in 1866. Theodor Fontane's (1819–1898) *Kriegschroniken,* the novelist's accounts of the three wars, illuminates many details of these developments. His reports also disclose how the resulting defeat and exclusion of Austria from the *Bund* in 1866 was instrumental in solidifying Prussian control of the German states under the auspices of Otto von Bismarck. It opened the door for Prussia in 1870 with the war against France to appeal to the remaining *Mittelstaaten,* mostly in the south, as the only leader in the *Bund.* This third military campaign in less than a decade became the final stage in uniting the German states, with the exception of Austria, to create one German nation-state in 1871.

Following the failed revolution, transformations went beyond political concerns at first. Between 1816 and 1850, the population had increased from about thirty-three million to forty-nine million, which was now about evenly divided between Prussia, the German parts of Austria, and the *Mittelstaaten.*[26] This growth contributed to a period of sustained industrial advances until the early seventies.[27] News of available labor reached poor rural populations and urban artisans; many relocated to industrial areas in the northwest, around Berlin and in Saxony. Despite this surge that also brought agricultural advances and production increases, large sections of the population, especially in the southwest and in Mecklenburg, were unable to maintain their small homesteads. Mounting feelings of rootlessness and uncertain communal structures among the itinerant population now advanced often conflicting ideologies that promised a needed sense of meaning. The first workers' parties formed in the 1860s. The visions of Friedrich Engels (1820–1895) and Karl Marx (1818–1883) and the publication of the *Manifest der Kommunistischen Partei* (1848) impacted the

Bund far beyond merely offering workers a surrogate religion. Whereas socialist movements aimed at the growing working class's yearning for solidarity, desires for economic and political self-determination led others to regard a unified nation as the necessary solution. Nonetheless, heightened by poor harvests between 1852 and 1855, a sizeable number, around 1.2 million, left between 1850 and 1859 — mostly for the United States — second only to the 1880s when about 1.3 million left for the New World. Fritz Reuter's *Kein Hüsung* (No Home, 1858) was one of several literary works depicting this emigration as the only solution to social disparities. Yet, the emigration of 80,000 from the revolutionary center of Baden suggest causes beyond social inequities prompting the decision to leave. The uprisings in the late 1840s had drawn many who were now affected by the ensuing persecutions. This reduction of the revolutionary movement further shifted the concerns of large parts of the population away from democratic reforms to predominantly economic affairs and the emotional topic of German unity.

Constitutional Crises

The seeming Prussian-Austrian political agreement on the future of the *Bund* was misleading. In 1850, the *Bund* had been formally restored under permanent Austrian chairmanship, yet the *Zollverein* emerged as Prussia's key to expanding its influence. In addition to the economic setback of a continued exclusion from the Customs Union, Austria faced many challenges. Persistent opposition by liberal factions and nationalist groups compelled Austria to create a neo-absolutist government under the auspices of the democrat-turned-monarchist Minister Alexander Bach (1813–1893), who helped propagate a centralized bureaucracy until the late 1850s. The diplomatic decision to demonstrate neutrality during the Crimean War (Russia versus the alliance of Turkey, Britain and France, 1853–1856) propelled Austria's growing isolation within Europe. Although Prussia too remained neutral, it faced fewer geopolitical losses. Not only did Austria slight its former ally (Russia had helped suppress rebellions in the eastern Habsburg territories in 1849), but its neutrality also enabled France to forge a secret pact with the Piedmont in 1858.

In Prussia, the 1850s came to a close with a number of highly symbolic events. The recurring image of the French as archenemy revived during the *Rheinkrise* and again in 1848–49, resurfaced during the many festivities for Schiller's centennial birthday in 1859. The commemoration represented a highpoint for the national movement throughout the *Bund,* despite open divisions between *kleindeutsch* and *großdeutsch* supporters. With the appointment of Wilhelm I as regent in 1858, parliamentarians initially tied their beliefs in national unity to the prospect of reforms following the selection of liberal cabinet members. This early bond between the Prussian *Landtag* (Lower House) and Wilhelm quickly soured over budgetary differences and the role of the military. The military reforms proposed by Albert von Roon (1803–1879), Prussian Minister of War, served only to incense the parliament. While delegates conceded a necessary expansion of the military due to Prussia's massive population increase, they objected to the planned military service extension. The *Landtag* also opposed the abolition of the *Landwehr* (civilian militia), which had held a mythical status ever since its successes against Napoleon during the Wars of Liberation from 1813 to 1815. In the year of his succession to the throne following his brother's death (1861), Wilhelm therefore dissolved the opposing Lower House. The king's effort the following year to increase the influence of *Junker* (large landowners), employers and pastors, resulted instead in the almost complete exclusion of conservative representatives from the newly elected chamber.

This escalation, known as the *Verfassungskonflikt* (Constitutional Conflict), reached its decisive pinnacle in 1862 with the government's resignation and the king's threat of abdication. Aside from issues of constitutionality, the conflict represented a struggle between bourgeois interests in free industrial and agrarian ventures vis-à-vis concerns shared by the traditional elites of nobility, army and landowners.[28] Fontane's celebrated novels accurately captured the prevalence of this latter coalition, which fortified its political dominance with Bismarck's appointment as minister president in September 1862.[29] Following appointments as Prussian ambassador to the Federal Diet, to Russia and to France, Bismarck, who had taken a reactionary stance in 1848, was regarded as a stern defender of royal privileges. Without the parliament's permission, Bismarck proceeded to collect the resources needed for expanding the military through customs revenue and taxes. His decision to govern without a budget represented a triumph of the monarchical authority and continued to be feasible partly because Bismarck pursued economic policies that matched the interests of many parliamentarians and large parts of the bourgeoisie.

Competing for Hegemony: German Dualism and the Wars of Unification

During Bismarck's ascent, a national movement emerged alongside the growing desire for economic liberalization. The *Deutsche Nationalverein* (National Association) openly promoted Prussian leadership. Given the internal strife of such associations and their limited number of members, their impact on plans for unity should not be overrated. National sentiments were nonetheless widespread, as pro-national events in the late fifties and the popular reception of Italy's unification in 1861 suggest. In this context, Bismarck's promotion of *Blut und Eisen* (blood and iron) — in a speech on the possibility of redrawing Prussia's frontiers delivered to the *Landtag* in October 1862 — could have appeared as a firm resolution to achieve unity. Only later was it evident that Bismarck's primary aim was to expand Prussia's hegemony; the interests of a national movement were only secondary. The Wars of Unification between 1864 and 1871 eventually revealed the conflicting interests of Prussia and the rest of the *Bund*.

Prompted by disagreement about a line of succession to the throne, the death of the King of Denmark in 1863 reignited tensions that dated back to the 1848 campaign. Danish nationalists in Schleswig claimed the duchy for their monarchy, while German nationalists in Holstein insisted on the indivisibility of the duchies and their association with the *Bund*. After Prussian and Austrian troops invaded Schleswig in the wake of Denmark's incorporation of the duchy and the *Bund*'s resolution to send in troops to Holstein, war broke out in January 1864. Before long, Denmark ceded Schleswig to Vienna and Berlin in the Treaty of Vienna. Together with the *Bund*'s acceptance to leave Prussian and Austrian forces in charge of the two duchies, this concession disappointed many German nationalists and also writers such as Storm, whose oeuvre is alive with subtle criticism of how the Schleswig-Holstein question was handled. Nevertheless, war and diplomacy made possible the Austrian and Prussian occupations of Holstein and Schleswig respectively. For now, the rivalry for leadership in the *Bund* had been settled more or less affably. However, the renewal of the *Zollverein* in January 1866, with even lower tariffs, affirmed Austria's exclusion from full participation in the Confederation. At that point, a Prussian proposal for democratic reforms in the *Bund* further provoked Austria. Its decision to refer the future of Schleswig and Holstein to the *Bund* was interpreted by Bismarck as a breach of their treaty and a cause for invading Holstein in June 1866. Bismarck's concurrent expansion of diplomatic contacts in Europe led to the Austro-Prussian War.[30] The Battle of Königgrätz in Bohemia sealed Austria's defeat. The subsequent Treaty of Prague in October 1866 highlighted Austria's recognition of its formal exclusion from the *Bund*. Annexations of Schleswig and Holstein, of the Austrian ally Hanover, Hesse-Kassel, Nassau, and the city of Frankfurt now also territorially strengthened Prussia's supremacy among the German states.

Prussia's leadership still was not yet secured within political parameters of the *Bund*. In fact, the *Bundestag* had supported an Austrian motion in June 1866, calling for Prussia's withdrawal from Holstein. Only Prussia's successful push for the dissolution of the *Bund* and the creation of a new confederation, the *Norddeutsche Bund* in late 1866 and early 1867, cemented Prussian power. Comprised of all German states north of the

River Main, this confederation was effectively under Prussian control and the leadership of its king. Prussia did not attempt overtly to integrate the southern states, in part because of the independent position of the governments in Bavaria and Württemberg, which had fought alongside Austria in 1866 and in part due to their predominantly Roman Catholic populations. Instead, Bismarck tied the remaining *Mittelstaaten* to Prussia economically through a customs agreement in July. Bismarck's course of action and his resolution of the Verfassungskonflikt though tenuous and dubious was ultimately successful as the passing of the Indemnity Bill attests. It was a success that further secured the subsequent dominance of a military culture in Prussian society, which writers including Theodor Fontane and later Heinrich Mann (1871–1950) critically depicted for the next five decades.

The Formation of the Second German Reich

Despite reservations in southern German states, Bismarck recognized and utilized growing national sentiments — once more against France. Another dispute concerning succession to a European throne eventually resulted in the creation of a German empire.[31] After Queen Isabella's II (1830–1904) resignation in 1868, Spain offered the throne to a relative of Prussia's Hohenzollern family. On the acceptance of the candidature in 1870, France pressured Spain to withdraw the offer since it feared a Hohenzollern presence east and south of its borders. The French ambassador failed to have Wilhelm guarantee that the Hohenzollern family would never again seek the Spanish throne. In July, Wilhelm informed his chancellor of his meeting through the famed *Emser Depesche* (Ems telegram). Bismarck edited Wilhelm's simple account of the refusal into a more inciting newspaper publication. The published telegram reached the French public and was received — as intended — as an insulting rebuttal. The response was swift for already on July 19 France declared war. Yet the Prussian army had the support of the *Norddeutsche Bund* along with the southern states who had signed a secret military defense pact two years earlier. The Franco-Prussian war evolved into a Franco-German war and became the critical link for Bismarck to convince the entire *Bund* of Prussia's leadership. The strengthening of Prussian hegemony was Bismarck's goal and was crowned with Germany's unification. The Prussian-led German army defeated Napoleon III (1808–1873) in the Battle of Sedan, which was celebrated as a national holiday until 1918.[32] As the war continued, primarily in dispute over Alsace-Lorraine, enthusiasm in southern Germany for national unity generated the necessary political agreement for a creation of the *Deutsches Reich* (German Empire). With a ceremonial announcement in the Hall of Mirrors at the Palace of Versailles on January 18, 1871, King Wilhelm I was proclaimed German Kaiser. Ten days later, French and Prussian commands signed an armistice, and in March the first *Reichstag* (Imperial Diet) convened in Berlin.

The Imperial Age: 1871–1899

In 1870, Germany had still been a patchwork of states in the heart of Europe consisting of the *Norddeutsche Bund* and the southern *Mittelstaaten* from the Palatine to Bavaria. One year later the map had changed drastically. Now there was one German Empire whose fortune rose and fell with its most dominant state, Prussia. This new Central European map was completed by a new Austria as well. Since 1867, Austria had been the *königlich-kaiserliche Donaumonarchie* (royal-imperial Danube Monarchy) following the reorganization of the so-called *Ausgleich* (compromise). The compromise had been a constitutional mediation between Hungary's ambitions for independence and Vienna's desire for a strong, centralized empire to reassure its power after the defeat in 1866. Hungary gained control of internal affairs in exchange for acceptance of a centralized foreign policy and a continued union of the Austrian and Hungarian thrones under Habsburg leadership. This arrangement exemplified Austria's now overt eastward concentration to secure its power. With this geopolitical change, two major political units now dominated Central Europe — the German Empire and the Austro-Hungarian Empire. The remaining decades of the nineteenth century illustrate to what degree the internal concerns of these two empires and their international cooperation would shape Europe's future.

The Founders' Years: Kulturkampf
and Economic Downturn

There were now only twenty-five states within the German Empire. Despite public support and popular confirmation of unity, the creation of the empire had in fact been achieved from above by the old monarchical order and by the force of arms, not by democratic and political consensus. Some states retained autonomous privileges, such as postal services, but were in reality subordinated to an imperial structure that expanded Prussia's authority. The new imperial constitution assured the title of *Kaiser* to the Prussian king, who in turn appointed the *Reichskanzler* (imperial chancellor). Real political power remained with the authority of the monarch, who firmly controlled the military and supported the interests of noble and wealthy elites. Despite the concentration of rule in Prussia and its increasing influence on all levels of German society, one cannot initially speak of a centralization that undermined the existing particularities of the states. Still, the Prussian government was determined to maintain control of numerous social, economic and political changes associated with population increases in the empire from 41 million to 56.3 million between 1871 and 1900.

Bismarck's plan to exploit the increasingly polarized landscape of political parties and to utilize the previously successful strategy of uniting against enemies of Germany, set in motion the famous *Kulturkampf* (cultural struggle). Bismarck effectively deployed the papal declarations of 1864 and 1870, which proclaimed papal infallibility and greater authority over Catholics of every nation, to target Catholicism as an enemy within the empire. He thus tapped into the liberal parties' disdain for the Church. Yet, many measures designed to restrict the Catholic Church also affected Protestants. The ban on the Jesuit Order, the end of church jurisdiction over schools (1872), the imposed minimum education requirement for clergy and the power of the state to appoint clergy (1873–74) were all results of the *Kulturkampf*. Required state registrations of births, marriages and deaths highlighted the bureaucratic face of this struggle (1874–75).[33] These actions also prompted federal censorship laws in 1874, which transferred questions of freedom of expression and the press to the jurisdiction of the courts. The *Kulturkampf* indirectly affected many. The sentencing of the playwright Frank Wedekind (1864–1918), for example, for his satirical verses written about the *Kaiser* in 1899, was a notable result of the new censorship laws. While Switzerland, Austria and other European countries witnessed similar tensions between state and church, the vilification of Catholics in the German Empire later expanded to include different sets of enemies of the empire including socialist groups.[34]

Bismarck soon turned his attention away from liberal parties toward conservative ones for political gain and after initiating a reduction of anti-Catholic legislation the *Kulturkampf* came to an end in 1879. This reorientation was also motivated by the abrupt halt of the economic boom of the *Gründerzeit* (founders' years). Depression set in and cheap imports worsened economic conditions after the markets crashed in 1873. Prompt payment of war indemnities after 1871 and the economic burden of the iron and steel production in Alsace-Lorraine ceded by France had contributed to this economic crisis. Concurrently, a great number of *Aktiengesellschaften* (public companies) had been established from 1871 to 1873. This craving for financial success, which the novelist Wilhelm Raabe (1831–1910) so compellingly depicted in his story *Pfisters Mühle* (Pfister's Mill, 1884), along with a diminished awareness for increasing social

inequities, urban overpopulation, and the onset of environmental pollu-
tion, all characterized the *Gründerzeit*. Industrialists and landowners
meanwhile continued to demand import tariffs on competing foreign
grains and manufactured goods; conservative parties openly represented
these special interests. A launch of general protective tariffs and indirect
taxes therefore effectively isolated the liberal parties in parliament (1879),
producing a conservative alliance between industry and landowners that
lasted into the early 1900s.

Similar economic holdups in the early 1870s had stimulated demands
in Switzerland for a more unified national market. The formation of many
agricultural cooperatives was one result. This crisis also contributed to the
creation of a new *Bundesverfassung* (1874), which accentuated federal
social welfare components. The eventual population decline in the agriculture sector from 36% in 1888 to only 25% by the early 1900s reflected
Switzerland's fast development into a democratic nation increasingly
dependent on its burgeoning banking system and industries.[35] As
Switzerland settled in for a period of relative economic and political tranquility and Austria-Hungary continued to be preoccupied by internal
nationality disputes in its broad multi-cultural empire, Germany witnessed
a conservative reorientation called *die große Wende* (the big transformation) or the Second Founding (1878–79).[36] Historians may disagree about
the impact of a single person on this political evolution, yet the chancellor's manipulation of policy shifts reaffirmed the impact of Bismarckian
Realpolitik, a notion in which the end often appeared to justify the
means.[37]

Socialist Legislation and
Diplomacy Games

Having achieved German unity, Prussian dominance and a conservative cultural reorientation, Bismarck's politics now focused on socialist parties and
associations and deployed the old strategies of isolating internal enemies.
August Bebel (1840–1913) and Wilhelm Liebknecht (1826–1900) had
created the SDAP (Social Democratic Workers Party) as early as 1869. The
later established SAP (Socialist Workers Party in Gotha, 1875; precursor of
present-day SPD) had proven itself a small but growing parliamentary party.
For Bismarck, social democratic parties and organizations posed threats to
the existing monarchical order, but the parliament resisted his request to
outlaw the SAP. In the end, Bismarck succeeded in moving forward with
the *Sozialistengesetz* (antisocialist law) after two assassination attempts on
Wilhelm by alleged socialists (1878). The laws were renewed at intervals
until 1890 and banned venues for socialist activity including meetings,

organizations, newspapers and periodicals. Yet just as the *Kulturkampf* had failed to eliminate the designated enemy, the antisocialist law generated the opposite of the intended goal. Since the law did not directly affect socialist political parties, consistent membership gains throughout the 1880s enabled the parties to transform German socialism into a parliament-oriented force. Growing disparities between rich and poor — a literary topic depicted by established writers such as Fontane as well as more strident Naturalists such as Gerhart Hauptmann and Hermann Sudermann (1857–1928) — along with the political hope of culling favor with the industrial and rural working classes and abating their socialist fervor, were factors that, in combination, motivated Bismarck's introduction of progressive social security measures in the eighties. In the 1880s, health insurance (1883), accident insurance (1884), and old age and invalidity insurance (1889) were introduced to alleviate social welfare, creating legislation that far surpassed in its generosity other European states. In fact, Austria upheld many extreme conservative policies, including the *Ausnahmegesetze* (emergency laws, 1884) that precluded the founding of the SPÖ (Austrian Social Democratic Party) until 1889. The effective autocratic pact between Kaiser Franz Joseph and the bureaucratic state apparatus noticeably contributed to this prolonged obstruction.

Shifting majorities and the formation of extra-parliamentary interest groups forced Bismarck to make concessions in domestic and international policies throughout the 1880s. The creation of the *Kolonialverein* (Colonial League, 1882) and the *Gesellschaft für deutsche Kolonisation* (Society for German Colonization, 1884) helped fuel a period of active colonial policies. Colonialization and the desire for a "place in the sun" had already inspired a tradition of "colonial fantasies" in German culture long before the 1880s.[38] But the last decades of the century exposed an almost ever-present thematization and discussion of this political and cultural phenomenon in practically every societal domain. Moreover, it was implicitly and explicitly depicted in popular journals such as *Die Gartenlaube* (The Arbor) and by distinct writers such as Theodor Storm, Wilhelm Raabe, and Felix Dahn (1834–1912). Yet politics within the *Reich* were intricately tied to politics within the colonies. Bismarck's colonial decisions, for instance extending protection for German traders in Africa, functioned in essence to secure support from conservative parliamentarians in domestic issues. Such balancing acts also laid the foundations for foreign policies within Europe. Bismarck constantly renegotiated existing alliances. This intricate system highlighted the complexities behind Bismarck's concern for preventing anti-German alliances. By the 1890s however, this diplomatic chess game left very little room for error.[39]

Even though elections in February 1887 had established Bismarck's most substantial majority with the so-called *cartel* coalition between conservatives and National Liberals, elections just three years later undermined the cartel dominance. Following the deaths of Wilhelm I and of his son Friedrich III (1831–1888) in March and June 1888, the accession of Wilhelm II (1859–1941) to the throne that year effectively ended the twenty-eight-year-period of Bismarckian domination. Wilhelm's insistence on the non-renewal of the antisocialist law following the election (February 1890) marked the first sign of Bismarck's diminished authority. In contrast to his grandfather, Wilhelm II did not accept his exclusion from government decisions — domestic or international. As a result, Bismarck offered his resignation to the emperor in March 1890 who consequently appointed General Leo Graf von Caprivi (1831–1899) as Chancellor.

The End of an Age: The Wilhelmine Era and the Austrian *Vielvölkerstaat*

Wilhelminian Germany, a term commonly referring to the reign of Wilhelm II, experienced enormous growths in agricultural and industrial productions until 1912 alongside an increasing economic diversification. Migration from rural communities contributed to even more rapidly growing urban populations.[40] Germany became a progressively more heterogeneous society. Berlin grew swiftly with ornate and ostentatious buildings next to *Mietskasernen* (rental barracks) and housing projects sponsored by corporations such as Siemens. Despite visible signs of growing disparities, a sense of commonality and even political loyalty has been repeatedly observed for the German society prior to 1914.[41] This intriguing discrepancy between recognizing an unbalanced reality and accepting the status quo could explain why some of the more critical voices in the arts never attained the same popular status as contemporary escapist writers. The majority simply preferred the docile and nostalgic depictions of *Heimatliteratur* (a type of provincial literature emphasizing the qualities of a given geographic region) by writers such as the Austrian Peter Rosegger (1843–1918) and Clara Viebig (1860–1952) instead of the explicit depiction of urban milieus by the Naturalists Gerhart Hauptmann and Arno Holz (1863–1929).[42] Notwithstanding these reading habits, social tension — punctuated by the rise of the social democrats — unstable parliamentary politics, and the emperor's primary concern with foreign relations, all characterized the Wilhelmine Era. Political and economic interest groups continued to influence most policies and the decision making of the four men who followed Bismarck as chancellors between 1890 and 1914.

Until his retirement in 1900, Chlodwig von Hohenlohe-Schillingfürst (1819–1901), chancellor since 1894, represented the agreements reached by the emperor and the elites of military, landowners and industry. A conservative reconstruction of government took place in 1897 with key appointments of new cabinet posts, including the Secretary of the Navy. Different groups including the *Alldeutscher Verein* (Pan-German League, 1893) and the *Flottenverein* (Navy League, 1898) rallied against perceived threats in this period. Unionization and working class interests were among the declared enemies. The phrase *Sammlungspolitik* (policy of concentration), coined by Prussia's Finance Minister Johannes von Miquel (1828–1901), described the banding together of interests against branded *Reichsfeinde*. Consensus was also attained for a more aggressive foreign policy, further fueling Wilhelm's imperialist desires. Not only did the growing economy view the development of foreign markets as a possible solution, but industrialists also saw an expansion of the military, primarily the naval fleet (1898), as an opportunity for economic gain. Germany's almost exclusive concentration on colonial interests at that point coincided with a seeming disregard for political developments within Europe. Germany was now diplomatically isolated.

Austria-Hungary was Germany's only ally. However, it continued to face domestic volatilities as a result of its multi-ethnic makeup. Austria-Hungary remained the most extensive *Vielvölkerstaat* (multinational state) in Europe up until the First World War. Of its four principal ethnic groups (Germans, Hungarians, Slavs, and Italians), however, only the first two received full partnership. Since the establishment of the Dual Monarchy in 1867, the sheer topographical vastness between Switzerland and the eastern Carpathian Mountains and the great ethnic diversity of that vast area had been both the strength and the weakness of the empire. Many facets of this multicultural undertaking in Central Europe inspired artists from the mid-1800s well into the twentieth century. Although literary illustrations by writers as Adalbert Stifter, Marie von Ebner-Eschenbach, Franz Kafka, Joseph Roth, and Robert Musil (1880–1942) disagree in terms of how they analyze and express their Austrianness and the turmoil within their empire, it is through their different perspectives that one can shed light on the diverse realities of Austria-Hungary. The ongoing national aspirations of different nationalities in the empire determined political reality for Emperor Franz Joseph as much as the competition with Russia for hegemony over the Balkans did. The return of the Viennese authorities to autocratic rule at the end of the 1890s generated no solution for the ongoing demands for independence by minorities or for the underlying disputes over territorial rights and autonomy, and eventually helped spark the First World War.

Whereas both empires entered the twentieth-century as modernized industrial nations with all the positives and negatives thereof — Germany perhaps more strikingly so than Austria — their political arrangements revealed dated structures. The influence of ruling small elites (military, landowners, and industry) exposed how the actual social makeup with its growing working and lower middle classes and its multi-ethnicity was not properly represented. As the developments since 1830 demonstrated, many social and political changes had nonetheless dramatically altered the face of Central Europe. Numerous political modifications had taken place since the beginning of the century when Europe was first shaped by individuals like Napoleon and Metternich and later by the overbearing figure of Bismarck. Bismarck's social legislation and his changing stance on German unity underline why change was not necessarily the result of personal convictions. As Nipperdey fittingly observed, the Iron Chancellor had been an opportunist who transformed nationalism from an ideology of opposition into an ideology of integration (I, 802). Similar opportunistic decisions over the next decades would continue to reveal the dangerous distance of the ruling members from the reality of society as an unsolved problem at the beginning of the twentieth century.

Notes

[1] For a discussion of this widely used descriptive term see David Blackbourn, *The Long Nineteenth Century: A History of Germany, 1780–1918* (New York & Oxford: Oxford UP, 1998). Very useful historical and literary studies of the period between the French Revolution and the beginning of the First World War also include: *Nineteenth-Century Germany: Politics, Culture and Society 1780–1918*, edited by John Breuilly (London: Arnold, 2001); Alan Sked, *The Decline and Fall of the Habsburg Empire, 1815–1918* (London: Longman, 1989); Georg Kreis, *Der Weg zur Gegenwart: Die Schweiz im 19. Jahrhundert* (Basel and Boston: Birkhäuser, 1986); Eda Sagarra, *Germany in the Nineteenth Century: History and Literature* (Frankfurt: Peter Lang, 2001); *Zur Sozialgeschichte der deutschen Literatur von der Aufklärung bis zur Jahrhundertwende: Einzelstudien*, edited by Günter Häntzschel et al. (Tübingen: Niemeyer, 1985). Other important studies that cover select periods of nineteenth-century political and social history include: Barbara Jelavich, *Modern Austria: Empire and Republic 1815–1986* (Cambridge: Cambridge UP, 1987); James Sheehan, *German History 1770–1866* (Oxford: Clarendon P, 1989); Gordon A. Craig, *Germany 1866–1945* (Oxford: Oxford UP, 1981). In German: Thomas Nipperdey, *Deutsche Geschichte*, 3 vols. (Munich: C. H. Beck, 1983–93); Hans-Ulrich Wehler, *Deutsche Gesellschaftsgeschichte*, 3 vols. (Munich: C. H. Beck, 1987–95).

[2] The Swiss political philosopher and publicist Carl Ludwig von Haller (1768–1854) first introduced this term in his six-volume *Restauration der Staats-Wissenschaft* (Winterthur: Steiner, 1816–1834).

[3] A characterization of the time from 1830 to 1848 as "Repressionspolitik" instead of Restoration can be found in Peter Stein, "Sozialgeschichtliche Signatur 1815–1848" in *Zwischen Restauration und Revolution 1815–1848*, edited by Gert Sautermeister and Ulrich Schmid (Munich: Hanser, 1998) 16–37 (30).

[4] Discussions on accurately designating this period, both with regard to historical and literary analyses, can be found in Sagarra, 21, Blackbourn, 91, and Christopher Clark, "Germany 1815–1848: Restoration or pre-March?" in Breuilly, 40–65.

[5] For more detailed explanations of concurrent political principles, see Stein, 29–35.

[6] The complexities of the reading culture along with the variations of literacy rates are discussed by Ulrich Schmid, "Buchmarkt und Literaturvermittlung" in Sautermeister, 60–93.

[7] The most detailed discussions of demographic changes during the 1800s can be found in Wehler, *Gesellschaftsgeschichte* and Nipperdey. More concise overviews can be found in Sagarra 43–69 and 247–272.

[8] Sagarra, 32.

[9] A detailed overview of the events surrounding the *Hambacher Fest* can be found in Nipperdey I, 366–77.

[10] See Clark, 51–52.

[11] See the excellent discussion by Peter Stein, "Operative Literatur," in Sautermeister, 485–504.

[12] A comparative analysis of the concept *Bürgertum* can be found in *Bürgertum im 19. Jahrhundert. Deutschland im europäischen Vergleich,* edited by Jürgen Kocka, 3 vols. (Munich: dtv, 1988).

[13] Nipperdey I, 533.

[14] The reinvention of *der deutsche Michel* as a successful and brawny character by the early twentieth century is discussed in Sagarra, 273.

[15] See Golo Mann, *Deutsche Geschichte des 19. und 20. Jahrhunderts* (Frankfurt a.M.: Fischer, 1958), 158.

[16] Gordon A. Craig's aptly titled collection of essays points to this hidden principle in *The Politics of the Unpolitical: German Writers and the Problem of Power, 1770–1871* (Oxford, New York: Oxford UP, 1995). See also Karin Friedrich, "Cultural and Intellectual Trends" in Breuilly, 96–116.

[17] Nipperdey I, 373.

[18] Sagarra, 37.

[19] An excellent discussion of the *Rheinlieder* can be found in Lorie A. Vanchena, "The Rhine Crisis of 1840: *Rheinlieder,* German Nationalism, and the Masses" in *Searching for Common Ground: Diskurse zur deutschen Identität 1750–1871,* edited by Nicholas Vazsonyi (Cologne, Weimar, Vienna: Böhlau, 2000), 239–251.

[20] Nipperdey I, 398.

[21] The following statistics are discussed in detail in Clark, 56–60.

[22] Two studies that stress the key role of Switzerland are Blackbourn, 140–41 and Wolfram Siemann, "The Revolutions of 1848–1849 and the Persistence of the Old Regime in Germany (1848–1850)" in Breuilly, 117–37.

[23] See Dieter Fahrni, *Schweizer Geschichte: Ein historischer Abriß von den Anfängen bis zur Gegenwart* (Zurich: Pro Helvetia, 1996), 70–71.

[24] An excellent historical discussion of the events in 1848–49 can be found in Nipperdey I, 594–673. The following overview draws on his chapters.

[25] Friedrich Wilhelm compared the parliament's offering of the crown to "a dog-collar with which one intends to chain me to the Revolution of 1848." Original quoted in Nipperdey I, 660.

[26] Breuilly, 140.

[27] Historical analyses of Germany's delayed industrialization sometimes distinguish between the years 1850 to 1873 as *Hochkonjunktur* (economic boom) and the second phase between 1873 and 1895 as *Hochindustrialisierung* (high industrialization). See Hans-Ulrich Wehler, *Das Deutsche Kaiserreich 1871–1918* (Göttingen: Vandenhoeck & Ruprecht, 1977) 41–2.

[28] Sagarra, 120.

[29] An expansive account of Bismarck's impact on Prussian and German politics and culture is the study by Otto Pflanze, *Bismarck and the Development of Modern Germany*, 3 vols (Princeton: Princeton UP, 1990).

[30] A detailed overview and analysis of the diplomatic and military schemes leading to the Austro-Prussian war can be found in Nipperdey I, 768–803.

[31] Cf. Nipperdey III, 55–84.

[32] For a discussion of Sedan Day as part of the German national imagination, see Alon Confino, *The Nation as Local Metaphor: Württemberg, Imperial Germany, and National Memory, 1871–1918* (Chapel Hill: The U of North Carolina P, 1997).

[33] Cf. Nipperdey III, 364–381.

[34] Nipperdey II, 380.

[35] Fahrni, *Schweizer Geschichte*, 87.

[36] A concise overview of the conservative changes is provided by K. D. Barkin, "1878–1879: The Second Founding of the Reich, a Perspective," *German Studies Review* 10 (1987): 219–35.

[37] For further discussion of the concept of *Realpolitik*, see Peter Stemmler, "'Realismus' im politischen Diskurs nach 1848. Zur politischen Semantik des nachrevolutionären Liberalismus," in *Bürgerlicher Realismus und Gründerzeit 1848–1890*, edited by Edward McInnes and Gerhard Plumpe (Munich and Vienna: Hanser, 1996), 84–107 (85–95).

[38] An already classic investigation of colonialism's impact on the artistic (and collective) colonial imagination is that of Susanne Zantop, *Colonial Fantasies: Conquest, Family, and Nation in Precolonial Germany, 1770–1870* (Durham: Duke UP, 1997).

[39] A very brief overview shows the chess-game-like back-and-forth of Bismarck's shifting alliances: With the conclusion of the 1872 *Dreikaiserabkommen* (Three Emperors Alliance) between Germany, Austria and Prussia, a *Zweibund* (Dual Alliance, 1879) was formed between Prussia and Austria and later expanded by Italy with the *Dreibund-Vertrag* (Triple Alliance Treaty, 1882). In 1881 and again in 1884, the old *Dreikaiserabkommen* was renewed for three years each time. The prevention of attacks from two fronts motivated Bismarck to seek alliances with Russia and Austria. However, as the Austro-Russian conflict of interest for the Balkan region intensified, Bismarck secured Russia as an ally with the signing of the

Reinsurance Treaty in 1887 to preclude a possible Franco-Russian pact. A detailed discussion of Germany's foreign policy, including Bismarck's exploitation of colonial issues, can be found in Nipperdey III, 426–470.

[40] For brief overview of the changing social dynamics until 1914, see Volker Berghahn, "Demographic Growth, Industrialization and Social Change," in Breuilly, 185–198.

[41] Nipperdey II, 425.

[42] See Horst Thomé, "Modernität und Bewußtseinswandel in der Zeit des Naturalismus und des Fin de siècle" in *Naturalismus, Fin de siècle, Expressionismus: 1890–1918*, edited by York-Gothart Mix (Munich and Vienna: Hanser, 2000), 15–27.

Part II

Movements

Literary Controversy: Naming and Framing the Post-Romantic, Pre-Realist Period

Robert C. Holub

H OW DO WE DEFINE the periods of German literature? In traditional literary histories the labels assigned to periods by former generations of German scholars include an odd assortment of features. The sixteenth and seventeenth centuries, for example, which are usually taught under the tripartite designation Renaissance-Reformation-Baroque, mix movements that were originally associated with architecture and art history (Renaissance and Baroque) outside German borders with a religious movement identified primarily with a native revolt against the Roman-Catholic church. Although each of these terms may describe some characteristics of the literary production of the early modern era, none relates specifically to literature; they are drawn from a more general view of ideological currents and applied then to specific works of poetry, prose, or drama. Similarly the Enlightenment as a period in German letters occurring primarily in the eighteenth century describes a larger intellectual tendency, one that was extremely broad and not shared in all of its particulars by the writers whose works are subsumed under that rubric. With the "Storm and Stress" (*Sturm und Drang*) we encounter for the first time in the post-medieval era a label that was developed for, as well as from, the literary sphere. As a period, however, the Storm and Stress encompasses only a small clique of writers publishing during the seventh and eighth decades of the eighteenth century and describes a mood of rebellion connected with a younger generation; authors whose works are not included in this period designation are either missing from literary history or shoe-horned into another period that overlaps with the Storm and Stress. Classicism is even more restrictive, referring in essence to the writings of Goethe and Schiller in a particular phase of their careers, and occasionally to a few ancillary figures. In this instance two domineering figures, who evidenced interest in classical antiquity, are justification for an entire period designation. Romanticism involves a greater range of writers and includes a European dimension not always present in earlier periods, and the name itself relates more specifically to works of the imagination, primarily literary works, and by extension, other products of human creativity. What we can conclude from this brief survey of period designations over three centuries is that the mixture of labels from the fifteenth to the early nineteenth century is anything but uniform: periods are drawn from the pictorial arts in other countries, from religious protests, from generational rebellions, from the inclinations of a restricted group of writers, and from general ideological considerations. The common thread for all of these periods is that literary historians were convinced that they could locate in a particular term a dominant tendency, which then justifies the somewhat artificial designation of a period. Authors who do not partake of this tendency are cast aside or, in unusual cases, integrated uncomfortably into a historical category that has become the structure through which we understand the course of literary achievement.

Although literary historians have generally agreed about the periodization and rubrics from around 1500 through the early nineteenth century, there has been no such concord about the period immediately following Romanticism and preceding realism. Indeed, there is no epoch in German literary history that has been subject to as much dispute. Even the years in question are far from certain. While various scholars would extend Romanticism into the second, third, or even fourth decade of the century, and others would locate realist tendencies well before its midway point, the only thing on which previous critics have generally agreed is that there was something different, something worthy of a separate label that occurred after the demise of Romanticism and before the advent of realism. At issue here are not simply the duration and boundaries of the period, but, more important, the nature of its literary production. Commentators who have found the writings of Heine and Büchner the most significant accomplishments in the post-Romantic era propose a different label and canon from those who believe that Droste-Hülshoff, Mörike, and Grillparzer were the trend-setting writers of their times. Those who view literary works in an historical context may argue that historical markers are most valid and may assert that the spirit that animates literary production should be identified with the historical movement or ideological currents of the times. On the other hand, those who focus on more formal features of literary texts may contend that the unity of the period lies in a style or a mode of representation. In all, one can find more than a dozen designations for the post-Romantic, pre-realist period in German literature, and although the matter has received extensive attention, no single designation has emerged as the most favored in literary historiography to date.

In the postwar era three viewpoints have dominated the discussion, each of which is based on a slightly different understanding of literary history, its goals, and its relationship to its putative object of study. Emerging in the early twentieth century as a major candidate to describe post-Romantic literature is the rubric "Biedermeier." Originally a term from the area of fashion, design, and painting, Biedermeier vied for canonical status after 1945 with the publication of Friedrich Sengle's monumental *Biedermeierzeit,* which appeared in three volumes from 1971 to 1980. Sengle is conscious of the controversy surrounding his attempt to unify a period that has formerly been considered fragmented, contending at the very outset that his study is the first to consider the period from 1815–1848 as an independent, separate entity. His selection of the boundary dates for the period indicate a heavy reliance on historical events as markers — the defeat of Napoleon and the Congress of Vienna at one end, and the Revolution of 1848 at the other — and he even calls the period in his opening remarks the age of "Metternich's restoration."[1] Sengle emphasizes that he intends his study and the title that adorns it to be inclusive, encompassing conservative, liberal, and radical authors of the three decades he has delineated. However, he has difficulties explaining why his putative inclusiveness led him to choose the controversial and traditionally conservative term *Biedermeier* as the unifying label. His explanation for his alternative demonstrates clearly the discomfort he feels, especially in the stormy atmosphere of the student movement when his initial volume appeared: the reader is asked to distinguish *Beidermeierzeit* from *Biedermeier;* the latter refers to a tendency identified with particular authors in the period; the former designation is meant to be a purely descriptive designation for a larger unity. "Biedermeierzeit ist nichts weiter als ein Sammelbegriff, dessen Inhalt erst geklärt werden muß"[2] (The Age of Biedermeier is nothing more than a composite notion whose content must then be clarified). Sengle continues apologetically to claim that the title is a matter of relative indifference; it is, after all, only a name. He recalls that he had formerly opted for the term *Restaurationszeit,*[3] which he now rejects because a restoration is a general historical notion that does not specify the early nineteenth century. Nonetheless, the unity he detects appears to be related to historical circumstances rather than style; his justification for the choice of "Biedermeier," however, rests on the perception that the conservative writers of the period were more significant than their liberal or radical counterparts.

The radically inclined student movement viewed Sengle's book as a provocation, and it was answered most incisively by a small volume devoted solely to a discussion of the "problem" of the period from 1815–1848. Peter Stein's *Epochenproblem Vormärz* (1974) boldly proclaims in its title the challenge to an allegedly conservative literary historiography. Stein points out first that *Vormärz* is a term used shortly after the revolution in the context of both historical and literary works; around 1900 it was employed by liberal scholars to designate the literary period of the Metternich restoration. *Biedermeier* and *Vormärz* thus represent competing conceptions in the earlier twentieth century, and

Stein reintroduces that competition in the 1970s. Supported above all by literary scholarship in the German Democratic Republic and by Marxist scholarship in the West, Stein posits *Vormärz* as the appropriate period designation for a materialist conception of literature. It performs the double function of criticizing bourgeois methods in literary studies and embedding literature appropriately in its time: "Mit der Wahl des Begriffs 'Vormärz' als Epochenbezeichnung ist nicht nur die Kritik am Prinzip der bürgerlichen literaturhistorischen, sprich: literaturimmanenten Periodisierung verbunden, sondern wird zugleich zum Ausdruck gebracht, daß die Geschichte der Literatur im Kontext der gesamtgesellschaftlichen Geschichte zu sehen ist"[4] (The selection of the concept "Vormärz" as designation for the epoch not only critiques the principle of bourgeois, literary-historical periodization, which is literature-immanent, but also emphasizes that the history of literature must be seen in the context of a larger social history). Particularly important for Stein is the economic history of the nineteenth century: the *Vormärz* distinguishes itself as a phase of bourgeois emancipation from feudalism during which one observes a pronounced contradiction between the delayed bourgeois revolution and the growth in industrialization. Like Sengle, Stein views the period as a unity; indeed, he rejects attempts to divide the years 1815–1848 into segments that delineate a dominant tendency. He criticizes Sengle's unifying principles, however, for being historically pessimistic. Reliance on the waning of Christianity and the resulting "Weltschmerz," which, Sengle avers, capture the essential mood of the period, only betrays his bourgeois prejudices. Proceeding from a worldview inspired by faith in the march toward an inevitable triumph of socialism, Stein posits a period dominated by writers who contributed to a revolutionary spirit. Thus, although Sengle believes that conservative authors produced more seminal writing and were dominant in this period, Stein opts for a canon that emphasizes the creative activities of the leftist and liberal camp, understood by him as the forerunners of the ultimate victors in world-historical struggle.

Although there is little room for a middle ground between Sengle and Stein, there are other alternatives, and the postwar scholar who has contributed most to elucidating the issues surrounding post-Romantic periodization is Jost Hermand. A student of Sengle who has great sympathy for Stein's general outlook, Hermand proposes the more neutral term *Restaurationszeit* (restoration period) for the years 1815 to 1848. For Hermand, Metternich's restoration was decisive for both conservatives and liberals alike: "Kraß gesagt, läßt sich weder Stifter noch Heine ohne Metternich begreifen"[5] (Crassly stated, neither Stifter nor Heine can be understood without Metternich). Agreeing with Sengle that realism is an appropriate label for literary endeavor only after the 1848 revolution, Hermand contends that the chief characteristic of the previous period is the vacillation between pro-Biedermeier and anti-Biedermeier forces. For this reason he disagrees with Stein's argument that the entire period should be accorded the progressive name "Vormärz," since Hermand would reserve this term for the decade of the 1840s. Indeed, although Hermand advocates the more general term *Restaurationsperiode,* he subdivides the period into smaller segments that capture the ideological fluctuations with greater precision. The initial four years, which close with the issuance of the Karlsbader decrees, are characterized by the spirit of disappointed nationalists following the Napoleonic Wars and the Congress of Vienna. The span from 1819 until 1830 is marked by the most severe repressions of liberal sentiments and qualifies as the decade most accurately described by the word "Biedermeier." After the Young German outburst following the July Revolution in 1830, the prohibition of this group after five years marks a return to the quiescence of the 1820s, although one detects a more restive disposition in intellectual life and a greater tension with authorities. Only the fifth segment of the "restoration period" merits the name "Vormärz," since Hermand argues that the rise of the Hegelian left, the ascent to the throne of Friedrich Wilhelm IV, and the shift to more operative genres separate these years from the preceding decades. In general, Hermand argues against the continuity that Stein seeks to establish on the level of historical and economic development. Few nationalists were active in the liberal Young German revolt of the 1830s, and by and large the Young Germans in turn did not join forces with the radical writers of the 1840s. Thus the period designation "Restaurationsepoche" suggests only a vague unity for post-Romantic literature in Germany, whose essence is its alternation between conformity and opposition, resignation and rebellion, in the intellectual and literary world.

Postwar disputes over the apposite designation for the post-Romantic, pre-realist literary period provide us with some insight into the nature of that epoch. There exists in the critical literature a sharp divergence of opinion about the essence of creative endeavor after the Congress of Vienna, and scholars have sought to defend their views, sometimes with sharp polemics, against countervailing sentiments. Often the differences involve political and ideological issues, and the intensity of disagreement correlates directly with the commitment to a given Weltanschauung. This sense of struggle over naming and definition recapitulates precisely the conflicts in which authors of the early nineteenth century were engaged. Post-Romantic writers, whether conservative, liberal, or radical, were acutely aware of the contested nature of the literary public sphere. Whether we select 1815 as a starting point, when early Romanticism had all but vanished as a force, or 1820, when the nationalist "Romantics" of the war of liberation were effectively silenced, or 1830, when revolutionary uprisings across Europe and the deaths of notable figures such as Goethe (1832) and

Hegel (1831) brought to consciousness the end of a era, authors began to vie for control over a heritage created by an older generation and responsive to a quite different set of social, political, and cultural imperatives. The result is a literature that appears disparate because new literary norms — as well as the social and political norms — have not yet been established, and various parties assert, sometimes implicitly, but on occasion programmatically, an agenda considered most appropriate for the age. No doubt the economic transformations that Stein prominently cites and the demise of formerly hallowed ideals, thematized in Sengle's work, contributed to the intensity of the struggles. The magnitude of the controversies is indicated by their duration: it took over three decades before relative calm was restored on the literary battlefield. After the defeat of the revolution in 1848 and the elimination of social unrest for many years one encounters a cessation of conflict with the advent of "poetic" or "bourgeois" realism. Literature had divested itself of its idealist trappings and entered the modern age.

During the post-Romantic epoch contention can be seen in many areas of literary activity, but a pronounced struggle in the realm of literary language can be noted. During the eighteenth and early nineteenth century, writers had developed a vocabulary and style that distinguished their creative endeavors from the conventions of their predecessors. The new, more dynamic language of love and nature, codified in central poetic images and phrases, appeared in now recognizable patterns and variations; a level of literary decorum commensurate with the norms of the era accompanied works by authors of various persuasions. This heritage became a focal point for subsequent writers, whose energies were perforce occupied with the appropriate manner to act as heirs to this tradition. Perhaps the most important writer in the post-Romantic tradition — if he was a post-Romantic at all — was Heinrich Heine, whose attitude toward the hallowed traditions of past generations was irreverent and ironic. His most celebrated volume of poetry, the *Buch der Lieder* (1827), makes ample use of the poetic lexicon of the Romantics, and in a certain sense the poems in this collection can be understood as a compilation of the emotions experienced by the young intellectuals of the 1820s. But this work is also a mosaic of motifs, symbols, and figures that have become slightly outdated and consequently do not precisely fit the sentiments of those born at the turn of the century and thereafter. The consciousness of this linguistic belatedness is manifested in Heine's poetry in his celebrated irony, which is perhaps his outstanding stylistic feature. The irony in Heine's literary language is manifested in the distance between the figures formerly employed to conjure an impression of authenticity and the recognition that they no longer ring true, that they are, after all, merely figures. Yet there is no other language in which to express feelings. The authenticity that remains a part of Heine's work is thus a function of the undecidability in his ironic stance. At certain moments, Heine opines at the close of the *Harzreise* (The Harz Journey, 1824), "I no longer know where irony leaves off and heaven begins."[6] And it is this uncertainty inscribed in the poet's language that allows Heine's writings to comprehend at once a nostalgia for the past, an affirmation for the present, and a utopian image of the future to come.

Heine's exemplary manipulation of literary language is perhaps most readily observed in the third poem of the collection "Die Heimkehr" (The Homecoming).

> Mein Herz, mein Herz ist traurig,
> Doch lustig leuchtet der Mai;
> Ich stehe, gelehnt an der Linde,
> Hoch auf der alten Bastei.
>
> Da drunten fließt der blaue
> Stadtgraben in stiller Ruh';
> Ein Knabe fährt im Kahne,
> Und angelt und pfeift dazu.
>
> Jenseits erheben sich freundlich,
> In winziger, bunter Gestalt,
> Lusthäuser, und Gärten, und Menschen,
> Und Ochsen, und Wiesen, und Wald.
>
> Die Mägde bleichen Wäsche
> Und springen im Gras' herum;
> Das Mühlrad stäubt Diamanten,
> Ich höre sein fernes Gesumm'.
>
> Am alten grauen Thurme
> Ein Schilderhäuschen steht;
> Ein rothgeröckter Bursche
> Dort auf und nieder geht.
>
> Er spielt mit seiner Flinte,
> Die funkelt im Sonnenroth,
> Er präsentirt und schultert —
> Ich wollt', er schösse mich todt.[7]
>
> [My heart, my heart is saddened,
> But May glows joyously,
> I lean at the high old bastion
> Against a linden tree.
>
> Below me the blue waters
> Flow gently in the moat.
> A boy is fishing and whistling,
> Leisurely rowing his boat.

And colorful in the distance,
Friendly and small, one sees
Cottages, gardens, and people,
And oxen, and meadows, and trees.

In the grass some maids bleach laundry
Joyful and frolicsome.
The mill wheel sprays clear diamonds,
I hear its distant hum.

There's a sentry box by the tower
That's gray and of old renown;
A lad with a scarlet tunic
Is pacing up and down.

He's playing with his rifle,
It shines in the sun so red,
He shoulders and presents it —
I wish he would shoot me dead.]

The first lines of this poem recall all the Mays from poetry of the past two generations, among them, of course, Goethe's "Mailied" (May Song), where the blossoming of nature coincides with the burgeoning of love. Heine, by contrast, immediately contradicts this correspondence between the inner and the outer world; the "Doch" of the second line, which comes much too early in the poem to signal such an abrupt change, removes us, however, from the poetic persona's troubles and feelings, which are described only with the clichéd notion of a sad heart, and thrusts us into the external scenery. The remaining lines of the stanza merely describe the poet's position with regard to his surroundings: he is a detached observer, "high" above the objects and people he surveys, leaning in a disengaged fashion on a linden tree. Around him we encounter not only May as the glorious time of natural renewal, but also the accouterments of an idyllic country landscape and population. At least we are initially led to believe that the poem is going to present a simple contrast between a sad poet and his beautiful environs. The portrayal of the young boatman in the second stanza appears innocent enough, but the polysyndeton of the third stanza, with its syntactic equation of human beings and the beast of the fields signals that the idyll is one in which habit and mindless activity predominate. This impression is confirmed by the fourth stanza, when we find the maidens hopping around performing their daily chores, and in the fifth, where we not only encounter the mechanical conduct of the soldier, but also are reminded of the oppressive force that underlies the apparent peaceful order of the German villages during the restoration. Heine's dramatic ending, in which the potential violence threatens to be realized, undermines the imagery that precedes it: even the heartbroken poet, a hackneyed image drawn from the canon, must be reinterpreted in light of the turnaround. The shift announced by "Doch" at the outset is mild compared to the reversal after the final dash; the language that the poet has borrowed to create his idyll is now exposed as part of the same mindless activity whose image it conjures. The critique of the apparent calm in the German landscape is simultaneously a critique of the language that reinforces this calm.

Alternatives in the struggle for an appropriate literary language are encountered in a variety of conservative writers who endeavor to continue the traditions of their predecessors, in so doing reinforcing the lexicon of nature and love, and sometimes expanding its purview. Heine's efforts to estrange the figurative language of the *Goethezeit* are countered by poets contesting his ambivalence or outright hostility to idealization on the linguistic, as well as the social and political level. At approximately the same time that Heine's lyrics in *Heimkehr* announced an ironic departure from tradition while still using its vocabulary, we can read a quite different response to spring and nature in a poem by Joseph Freiherr von Eichendorff:

> Wem Gott will rechte Gunst erweisen,
> Den schickt er in die weite Welt,
> Dem will er seine Wunder weisen
> In Berg und Wald und Strom und Feld.
>
> Die Trägen, die zu Hause liegen,
> Erquicket nicht das Morgenrot,
> Sie wissen nur vom Kinderwiegen,
> Von Sorgen, Last und Not um Brot.
>
> Die Bächlein von den Bergen springen,
> Die Lerchen schwirren hoch vor Lust,
> Was sollt' ich nicht mit ihnen singen,
> Aus voller Kehl' und frischer Brust?
>
> Den liben Gott laß ich nur walten;
> Der Bächlein Lerchen, Wald und Feld
> Und Erd' und Himmel will erhalten,
> Hat auch mein' Sach' auf's Best' bestellt![8]
>
> [The man who in God's favor stands,
> Has His command to wander free
> And seek the wonders of His hands,
> Revealed in wood and flower and tree.
>
> The listless man who sleeping lies
> Knows not the joy of morning's red;

> He only knows of children's cries,
> Of burdens, cares and daily bread.
>
> The streamlets from the mountains flow,
> The larks above make cheerful song;
> And in my joy of heart below
> I fain would join their happy throng.
>
> My guide in life is God alone,
> Who stream and lark and sea and land
> And earth and Heaven alike doth own:
> My life and fate lie in His hand.]

We recognize this poem from the first chapter of the novella *Aus dem Leben eines Taugenichts* (Memoirs of a Good-for-Nothing, 1826), where the eponymous hero has just been admonished by his father that he should seek his fortunes in the wide world. The beginning of wandering and adventure is here coterminous with the start of a new life cycle for the natural world. There is no discrepancy between nature, which is presented in the stereotypical images of Romanticism, and the feelings of the ne'er-do-well, whose life and ambition appear similarly cheery. The polysyndeton of the first stanza, in contrast to Heine's ironic use of the figure, contains no hint of discord or mockery, no inappropriate equation, but is instead a simple enumeration of elements in the external world suitably highlighted in a conjunctive string; the same figure in the final stanza allows for a recapitulation of natural bounty, while extolling its creator. Indeed, the harmony and tranquility of the poem are obtained through the intervention of the godhead, who guarantees a favorable outcome for those he chooses, as well as a beneficent natural world in which the chosen can wander and prosper. With such a guarantee of success why shouldn't the ne'er-do-well mimic his surroundings and chirp like a lark? The absent irony in the poem is located in the tension between narrative and lyrical insert: the lazy ones, admonished in the second stanza and found to be underprivileged when compared with the more ambitious wanderers, are obviously more like our hero, whose verses provide a rationale for his departure and signal a faulty self-assessment. But the poem itself, which appeared without the narrative context as early as 1823, can be considered Eichendorff's salvo in the implicit dispute around control of the inherited literary language in German-speaking countries during the restoration. He champions a continuity with past traditions, even if poetry must now be situated in a world of fairy tales and fantastic coincidence.

Other wanderers appropriate the lexicon of past generations in a slightly different fashion. While Heine's irony cleaves image and reality, and Eichendorff welds them together again in a utopian space blessed by the deity, a poet like Eduard Mörike, some twenty years later, could employ a literary language designed to affirm precisely what Heine disdains and Eichendorff escapes: the idyll of the German countryside. Theodor W. Adorno, commenting on the poem "Auf einer Wanderung" (On a Hike) notes that it does not partake in the kitsch and sentimentality of a typical Biedermeier portrayal, that it retains a dignity and high style that separates it from the clichéd works of the time:[9]

In ein freundliches Städtchen tret ich ein,
In den Straßen liegt roter Abendschein.
Aus einem offnen Fenster eben,
Über den reichsten Blumenflor
Hinweg, hört man Goldglockentöne schweben,
Und *eine* Stimme scheint ein Nachtgallenchor,
Daß die Blüten beben,
Daß die Lüfte leben,
Daß in höherem Rot die Rosen leuchten vor.

Lang hielt ich staunend, lustbeklommen.
Wie ich hinaus vors Tor gekommen,
Ich weiß es wahrlich selber nicht.
Ach hier, wie liegt die Welt so licht!
Der Himmel wogt in purpurnem Gewühle,
Rückwärts die Stadt in goldnem Rauch;
Wie rauscht der Erlenbach, wie rauscht im Grund die Mühle!
Ich bin wie trunken, irrgeführt —
O Muse, du hast mein Herz berührt
Mit einem Liebeshauch![10]

[I enter a friendly little town,
On the streets lies the red evening light,
From an open window,
Across the richest profusion of flowers
One hears golden bell-tones hover,
And *one* voice seems to be a choir of nightingales,
So that the blossoms quaver,
So that the breezes are lively,
So that the roses glow forth in a higher red.

I stood a long while marveling, oppressed with pleasure.
How I got out beyond the city gate,
I really do not know myself,
Oh, how bright the world is here!
The sky surges in purple turbulence,
At my back the town in a golden haze;
How the alder stream murmurs, how the mill roars below!

> I am as if drunken, led astray —
> Oh muse, you have touched my heart,
> › With a breath of love!]

Adorno focuses his attention initially on the combination of the high style with its hint of classical forms and dignity (in the apostrophe to the muse in the final lines and the free rhythms reminiscent of an ode), and the language and images of the poet's surroundings: his claim is that the poem successfully accomplishes what Goethe's *Hermann und Dorothea* (1797) ultimately fails to do.[11] But in our present context, the struggle over the literary vocabulary in post-Romantic times, we cannot help but notice the contrast with Heine's outlook on language and irony. While Heine employed the images of the peaceful idyll in order to expose their vacuousness and oppression, Mörike, despite the quality of his language and his consciousness of avoiding the "kleinbürgerliche Dumpfe" (petty-bourgeois dullness)[12] of the *Biedermeier*, nonetheless disregards any discord, stressing instead the harmony and natural wonder of village existence. In contrast to Heine, whose estrangement from the scenes he describes is evident even from the body position assumed by his poetic persona, Mörike and his poetic persona feel at home in the constructed small-town idyll, where we encounter no inhabitants, but only the clues of their existence: voice, mill. It is odd that Adorno lauds Mörike's successful integration of language and sentiment in an artificial, utopian, and affirmative construct, while he deprecates Heine's ironic reception of the tradition with its consciousness of the very tensions Adorno himself recognizes are the essence of the times. More insightful are Adorno's further remarks on the historical embeddedness of Mörike's verse. Entangled in the paradox of lyrical poetry in the advancing times of industrialization, Mörike, like his contemporaries, must negotiate between the poetic language of the heritage and the reality it is used to describe, avoiding the triviality of Biedermeier and the false pathos of a superannuated rhetoric. In this context we can situate not only Mörike, but also Heine and Eichendorff, who are similarly confronted with the paradoxical demands of modernity. Their poems, understood here as combative alternatives to deal with their historical predicament, vie with each on the level of literary language, asserting the superiority of their respective solutions to a perhaps insoluble dilemma.

We notice a second area of contention in character portrayal. Classicism and Romanticism displayed a tendency toward idealization of types. The protagonists in Schiller's plays in particular are often the personification of one or another ideal; they are less the reproduction of historical persons than the mouthpieces of a particular view. Goethe's characters may appear more realistic, especially in his early years, but the idealization during his classicist period, most noticeable in *Iphigenie*

(1787), is evident. Romantic figures, often bordering on the fantastic, are similarly removed from mundane reality. The further we move into the nineteenth century, however, the more writers appear to depart from obvious idealization, or else to account for idealization in a different fashion. This trend is shared by writers of radically divergent political persuasion. Heine, once again, offers one alternative in that he frequently retains Romantic or classical types only to expose them to his satirical wit. In *Ideen: Das Buch Le Grand* (Ideas: The Book of Le Grand, 1826), for example, Heine runs through a series of characters found in Romantic literature, including his first-person persona, who begins as a love-sick poet and playwright, transforms himself into a medieval knight only to wind up as the Count of the Ganges. In chapter 5 of this work he leads us through a mock Romantic landscape, introducing us to the beautiful Gertrud, the beautiful Katharine, the beautiful Hedwig, the beautiful Johanna, and "tiny, dead Veronica."[13] Heine's method of subverting the character types found in his predecessor's writings, however, is only one way in which writers diverged from tradition. If we examine an author with more conservative proclivities, for example, Annette von Droste-Hülshoff, we encounter a similar distancing from the stock figures of the *Goethezeit*. In *Die Judenbuche* (The Jew's Beech Tree, 1842), which recounts the life of Friedrich Mergel and includes unflattering portrayals of poverty among the lower classes, bands of thieves, and the Jewish community in the eighteenth-century, Droste avoids the ideal and airy qualities found in past portrayals, developing instead a series of depictions that provide a more realistic view of village life. In part the change here is one of class: the idealized middle and upper classes had occupied the attention of serious literature in previous generations, while Droste's novella selects a different social stratum for its focus.

Certainly the most radical departure from idealized treatment of characters can be seen in the writings of Georg Büchner, who combines Droste's inclusion of the lower classes with Heine's distancing reflection on tradition. Büchner's protagonists range from the debauched revolutionary Danton, who is pathologically unable to defend himself against the ascetic fanatic Robespierre; to the schizophrenic playwright J. M. R. Lenz, whose journey to the philanthropist Johann Friedrich Oberlin cannot prevent the further deterioration of his already precarious hold on reality; to the common soldier Franz Woyzeck, who is bullied by his sergeant, exploited by a pretentious doctor, and cuckolded by his girlfriend Marie. In each case Büchner appears to be flaunting a stereotypical hero from the classicist or Romantic tradition. Danton is neither valorous nor particularly admirable; while his companions plead with him to fight for his and their survival, he appears bored with existence, preferring to associate with prostitutes rather than dedicating himself to a defense of revolutionary ideals. Lenz is an obvious contrast to the exalted artist hero frequently found in the works of previous generations: he has lost his former creativity and artistic drive; indeed, he is barely able to survive in a world that escapes his comprehension. And Woyzeck, although he has no direct counterpart among protagonists of earlier times since he stands at the lowest rung of the social order, is, perhaps for this very reason, the paradigmatic anti-hero. Exhibiting neither bravery nor intelligence, he is the prototypical victim whose life is wholly determined by the forces around him: nature, which controls his drives and desires, and the institutions of the early nineteenth century, which manipulate his behavior in the most unsavory fashion. His complete lack of freedom, his inability to exercise an autonomous will, makes him the very antithesis of the literary figures who had preceded him in the *Goethezeit*. But perhaps the anti-idealization in Büchner is nowhere more evident than in his female figures, from the prostitutes in *Dantons Tod* (Danton's Death, 1835) to the odd assortment of women in the vicinity of Waldbach, or Marie, Woyzeck's unfaithful and headstrong companion. Indeed, Marie provides a stark contrast with almost every female character in the plays of German classicism. Conscious of her own sexual needs, she is more the brazen seductress of the drum major than his innocent victim. What Büchner provides for his reader, therefore, is an assortment of figures constructed in opposition to the literary standards of his predecessors. In the struggle for appropriate literary representation he implicitly demands that the idealistic characters populating literary works be replaced with figures exhibiting mental instability, hopeless penury, unbridled carnality, and utterly non-heroic behavior.

The conservative alternative to these departures from the idealized figures of the *Goethezeit* could sometimes entail a simple attempt to recapture the features of a timeless classicism, as in the plays of Franz Grillparzer, or a continuation of Romanticism on a more mundane level, as in the novellas of Ludwig Tieck. But these continuities with the past, although they reveal the reluctance with which authors relinquished traditional modes of representation and the values inherent in them, are not as interesting as the more innovative, albeit still conservative, strategies of Adalbert Stifter (1805–68). He, too, adhered to a conventional view of character portrayal, but he did not always simply revert to superannuated practices. Rather, Stifter, by stylistic and other means, sought to outdo the heritage he obviously revered. A good illustration of Stifter's artistry with regard to characterization occurs in the novella *Brigitta* (1844). In this work the eponymous heroine departs from the stereotypical women of classicism and Romanticism in three important respects: she is physically unattractive; she is alone and independent; and, when we meet her, she is already middle-aged. Her counterpart, Stephan Murai, known also as "the major," is a man who could have qualified as a ideal protagonist in an earlier era, since we are informed that he was handsome, honorable, and courageous in his youth; but the reader knows him for the most part as an aging, settled owner of an estate in the region of the Hungarian steppes. Both Brigitta and Stephan are thus past the prime age for the ideal of a Romantic pair, and Brigitta's external appearance would seem to disqualify the two from any mutual attraction. Indeed, Stifter stacks his tale against the conventions of an earlier era precisely to propagate all the more emphatically an ideal notion of love. The attraction between Brigitta and Stephan raises the stakes of prior idealized portrayal since it removes the bond between man and woman from its customary association with physical qualities. What characterizes their relationship, and what the narrator does not explicitly state, but everywhere suggests, is that it is emotional involvement without passion, love without sexual desire. The ideal of the beautiful soul in Goethe's writings and of ideal love from the Romantic tradition is here retained, but raised to a new level of idealization. Stifter's counter-thrust to the realist trend in writers such as Droste and Büchner is a criticism of the *Goethezeit* as too materialist, too carnal, as not ideal enough.

Finally, we might consider how struggles in the literary sphere of the post-Romantic era focused on the appropriate place for literature and culture in general. Creative works of art were accorded an elevated status by writers of the *Goethezeit* and viewed by most theorists and aestheticians as the epitome of human accomplishment. Typical in this reverential attitude toward literature and art was Friedrich Schiller, whose theoretical writings extol "aesthetic education" as a panacea for the ills of his contemporary times. Drawing on his understanding of Kantian philosophy, Schiller sketches a role for beauty that mediates between the realm of the senses and the sensual and the realm of material necessity: "Durch die Schönheit wird der sinnliche Mensch zur Form und zum Denken geleitet; durch die Schönheit wird der geistige Mensch zur Materie zurückgeführt und der Sinnenwelt wiedergegeben"[14] ("Through Beauty the sensuous man is led to form and to thought; through Beauty the spiritual man is brought back to matter and restored to the world of sense"). The ultimate goal for humankind is freedom, which includes for Schiller political liberty as well as abstract philosophical freedom, but this goal can be achieved only via the beautiful appearance associated with the aesthetic sphere. Genuine works of art therefore solve not only the philosophical conundrum contained in Kant's first two critiques and in the assumed dual nature of the human being, but also contemporary issues surrounding the French Revolution and its violent manifestations. The "total revolution"[15] posited by Schiller in his closing remarks to *Über die ästhetische Erziehung* (On the Aesthetic Education, 1795) is a process initiated and fostered by art and beauty. Schiller's close associate during his Weimar period, Goethe, may not have subscribed to all the philosophical underpinnings in Schiller's discussion of aesthetic education, but he certainly agreed with their general tendency. And the early Romantics, although they understood themselves in part as opposed to the classicist movement in German letters, concurred that literary endeavor was an ultimate value for humankind. Friedrich Schlegel's notion of "universal poetry" captures well the ambitions for Romantic authors, who should seek not only to combine features from various genres, but also to comprehend diverse aspects of life. In this ideal role assigned to the highest type of literary work, life itself becomes poetic, encompassing everything from the most complex systematic thoughts to the sighs and kisses contained in a children's ditty.[16] Schlegel and the Romantics, like their predecessors in German classicism, thus assign a supreme value to literature and the arts and bequeath this heritage to the generations born around 1800.

Writers of the post-Romantic era had difficulty maintaining this lofty view of literature. Particularly among the liberal and radical writers we find an outright rejection of the tenets of their predecessors. In this regard the views of the Young Germans are revealing. Typically the members of this group recognized that the aesthetic principles of the older generation were simply no longer appropriate for the changed conditions of the Restoration. Goethe and his works, for example, were respected by some, disdained by others, or treated with ambivalence; but the consensus view was that his writings were simply untimely. A figure in Theodor Mundt's novel *Moderne Lebenswirren* (Modern Life of Turmoil, 1834) captures this sentiment well: "Vergebens lese ich in jetziger Stimmung meinen alten geliebten Goethe, um mich durch ihn wieder in die gute goldene altväter- liche Ruhe eines literarischen Deutschlands hineinzuwiegen und einzul- ullen"[17] (In vain I read in my present mood dear old Goethe, to try to rock and lull me once more into that good old golden, grandfatherly quiescence of a literary Germany). The aesthetic values of the older generation were no longer timely because the Young Germans believed they were living in an age of transition. Karl Gutzkow, one of the prominent members of the group, stresses in this regard the liberation from the past and the aspira- tions for the future: "Wir emanzipieren uns von der Sitte und Tradition und schaffen uns neu aus unserm Herzen heraus. Wir haben keine Schule und kein Vorbild; aber wir wissen, daß das, was wir ausathmen, Poesie ist. Hier noch Zerrissenheit, dort schon keimende Objektivität"[18] (We are emancipating ourselves from customs and traditions and creating ourselves anew out of our hearts. We have no school and no models; but we know that what we are breathing is poetry. While there is still internal conflict, we already sense budding objectivity). Heinrich Laube calls his times "eine Durchgangsepoche"[19] (an epoch of transit); Theodor Mundt labels it an "Übergangs-Epoche" (a transitional epoch) or "Uebergangsperiode"[20] (transitional period); Heine refers to "die Endschaft der goetheschen Kunstperiode"[21] (the end of the Goethean art period). And the theorist Ludolf Wienbarg in his *Aesthetische Feldzüge* (Aesthetic Campaigns, 1834), which he dedicated to "Young Germany," expatiates on the transitory nature of his times as follows:

> Das ist der Fluch der Zeit, der auf einer Übergangsepoche wie der unsrigen ruht, das ist der Schmerz, der die edelsten Geister durchdringt, der in so vielen Stunden die Hoffnung übertäubt und die Unruhe, die Zerrissenheit, den Zweifel erzeugt, Plagegeister der Menschheit, wenn sie nächtlich mit neuen Geburten schwanger geht.[22]

> [That is the curse of the times that is based on a transitional epoch such as ours; that is the anguish that penetrates the most noble spirits, that in so many hours deadens hope and produces restlessness, internal conflict, and doubt: tormentors of humanity, when it walks around at night pregnant with new births.]

To be timely in this transition phase the authors of Young Germany embraced "Zerrissenheit" (internal conflict), rather than pretending that there existed a false harmony and that literature's function was to ennoble through aesthetic education. The result was works that often consist of fragments and confusion, such as Heine's *Reisebilder* (Travel Pictures, 1825–30), Gutzkow's *Briefe eines Narren an eine Närrin* (Letters from One Fool to Another, 1832), Gustav Kühne's *Quarantine im Irrenhaus* (Quarantine in the Mad House, 1835), Mundt's *Moderne Lebenswirren,* or Laube's *Reisenovellen* (Travel Novellas, 1834–37) and *Die Poeten* (The Poets, 1835). This literature implicitly critiques the idealistic aesthetics of the *Goethezeit*, positing instead a fiction grounded in the discord and turmoil they believed characterized their era.

The radical writers of the 1840s took this rejection of past practice one step further. Poets in the decade immediately preceding the 1848 revolution obviously no longer conceived of their poems as an appeal to some timeless realm of beauty and grandeur. Instead, the preferred genre for verse was the "Zeitgedicht" (poem of the time; political poem), which often amounted to simply agitational poetry. Georg Herwegh, one of the leading writers of oppositional verse, summarizes at the beginning of the 1840s the attitude that soon gained widespread acceptance. Speaking of the change in literary sensitivities as coterminous with the opposition to Goethe, he explains his own views on the venerated writers in a manner reminiscent of Young Germany:

> "Ich liebe Göthe, ich weiß, daß er der größte Künstler ist, den Deutschland geboren; ich weiß, daß seine Gedanken das lautere Gold des Herzens und der Vernunft — ich finde die Grundsätze fluchwürdig, aus denen ihn z. B. Menzel angefochten; aber Göthe war kalt, indifferent, er sympathisirte nur mit der Ewigkeit, nicht auch mit der Zeit, die ein integrirender Theil von jener ist."[23]

> [I love Goethe; I know that he is the greatest artist that Germany has produced; I know that his thoughts are the pure gold of the heart and

reason — I find the principles despicable that, for example, Menzel used against him. But Goethe was cold, indifferent; he had sympathy only with eternity, not with the times that are an integral part of everyone.]

It was in the same spirit that Herwegh countered Ferdinand Freiligrath, who had written in a poem "Aus Spanien" in 1841: "Der Dichter steht auf einer höhern Warte, / Als auf den Zinnen der Partei"[24] (The poet stands on a higher vantage point / Than on the battlement of the party). Herwegh's response in the polemical lyric rejoinder "Die Partei"[25] defends partisanship as a necessary element of creative endeavor. Freiligrath eventually agreed and signaled his conversion in the collection *Ein Glaubensbekenntnis* (A Confession of Faith) in 1844. From Herwegh's *Gedichte eines Lebendigen* (Poems of Living Soul, 1841), Franz Dingelstedt's *Lieder eines kosmopolitischen Nachtwächters* (Poems of a Cosmopolitan Night Watchman, 1842) and Hoffmann von Fallersleben's *Unpolitische Lieder* (Unpolitical Songs, 1841), which included the famous and — in the twentieth century — misused "Deutschlandlied," to Max Schenkenberger's notorious "Wacht am Rhein" (The Watch on the Rhine, 1840) or Niklas Becker's "Der deutsche Rhein" (1841), poets sought to inspire, provoke, or inform their readers about contemporary events and issues. Writers repudiated the purely aesthetic attitudes of former times, insisting that the value of literature was not its timeless beauty, but its partisanship for a specific cause. Heine, who transformed his poetics several times during his career, captures this sentiment well in the opening verses of his mock epic, *Deutschland: Ein Wintermärchen* (Germany. A Winter's Tale, 1844):

> Ein neues Lied, ein besseres Lied,
> O Freunde, will ich Euch dichten!
> Wir wollen hier auf Erden schon
> Das Himmelreich errichten.[26]
>
> [A new song, and a better song,
> O friends, I'll sing for you.
> Here on earth we mean to make
> Our paradise come true.]

Gone are the thoughts of a poetry that appeals to eternity and eternal truths; the poets of the 1840s are pragmatically interested only in the here and now. The sacred poetic values of the *Goethezeit* are replaced with an insistence on relevance, reality, and revolution.

Other post-Romantic authors of less radical persuasion often appear to have ignored the altered historical situation and sought to preserve the lofty role of the writer as an aesthetic educator. Certainly Freiligrath's remark prior to his conversion is evidence for the persistence of such an attitude, and one could point as well to the dramas of Franz Grillparzer, which were modeled on his classicist predecessors, or the lyrics of August Graf von Platen-Hallermünde, whose Orientalized verse continues a trend popularized from a previous generation. The general sentiment among most writers, however, was that even these efforts to forge a continuity with the past were themselves exhausted. Paradigmatic for the mood of a generation that felt itself to be in the shadow of more illustrious precursors is Karl Immermann's novel *Die Epigonen* (1836), whose original title of *Die Zeitgenossen* (The Contemporaries) gives some indication of the feeling that writers during the restoration could at best aspire to be imitators of past achievements. Indeed, *Die Epigonen* is significant in that it performs its title. A clear reworking of Goethe's *Wilhelm Meister* (1795–96), the novel deviates from its model only by introducing more forcefully certain features that could not have been foreseen in the late eighteenth century, such as the rise of industrial production on German soil. In this sense, as Immermann himself recognized, this work is, like its more radical counterparts, the product of an age of transition, where former values no longer hold sway, but new ones have not yet been realized. Perhaps the most poignant reflection on the changed role of literature and art came from Grillparzer in his late novella, *Der arme Spielmann* (The Poor Fiddler, 1847), which appeared at the very close of the period we have been examining and in some sense summarizes the conflicted nature of more conservative writers. The main figure, the inept violinist Jakob, strives for ideality in his musical compositions, while simultaneously trying to earn his living by playing popular songs for the masses. But in the reality of post-Romantic Vienna he is able to satisfy neither his yearnings for artistic perfection nor the desire for quotidian commendation. Like the liberals of Young Germany and the radicals of the *Vormärz*, Grillparzer thus recognizes that literary endeavor has undergone a radical transformation. Originally following the aesthetic principles of an earlier age, he finally concedes with the melancholy message in this novella that literature must accommodate itself in new ways to the contentious, transitional times.

The writers of the period from 1815 to 1848 evidence a divergence of opinion about central issues relating to literature. The defining characteristic for the period is precisely their difference of opinion on, and their struggles over, such central matters as poetic language and its employment, characterization and idealization, and the role of literature in a changing social environment. It is perhaps discomforting for literary history that we are compelled to identify the unity of a period in its disunity, and surely the lack of a dominant coterie of authors, compositional principle, or ideological direction contributes to the conflictive situation mentioned at the outset, according to which any name for the post-Romantic period is viewed as necessarily partisan or false from an equally legitimate, but differing perspective. If we were pressed to select a single designation for the post-Romantic, pre-realist period, we would have to reject *Biedermeier* as well as *Vormärz* as too misleading, since each suggests a clear predominance of a certain type of literature — and perhaps implicitly a set of aesthetic and political views — that falsifies the discord that lies at the heart of these decades. The "Restoration epoch" has the advantage of remaining neutral with regard to the disputed issue of ideological direction and artistic preferences; its great disadvantage, besides the fact that historically there have been several restorations and it is therefore ambiguous, is that it captures little of the dynamics of the times. Certainly authors wrote in the context of social and political parameters set by Metternich's restoration, and they responded to the exigencies of their times. But this tells us about as much as saying that Günter Grass wrote in postwar Germany, or Gotthold Ephraim Lessing composed his works in the eighteenth century. Preferable because they suggest the tension of the era are the various suggestions that indicate the transitional nature of the period, for example, Walter Höllerer's monograph *Zwischen Klassik und Moderne* (Between Classicism and Modernism, 1958), whose subtitle, *Lachen und Weinen in der Dichtung einer Übergangszeit*[27] (Laughing and Weeping in the Literature of a Transitional Period), indicates something of the variety of literary endeavor as well as the feeling of instability expressed by many authors sensitive to the transition from times of firm literary values to an unknown future. But Höllerer's book title produces no period designation: the age of transition or the age of conflicting aesthetic values are too long-winded and ultimately as vague in historical reference as the Restoration epoch. Perhaps the only real lesson that can be gleaned from our dissatisfaction with the various alternatives is that some periods, particularly those in which no school or person or ideology predominates, are impossible to describe in a word or short rubric. Ultimately our continued fascination with the literary sphere in the years 1815–1848 is linked not to a period designation, but to our appreciation of struggles whose final consequence was the relinquishing of traditional literary values and the introduction of the precarious aesthetic standards of industrialized modernity.

Notes

[1] Friedrich Sengle, *Biedermeierzeit: Deutsche Literatur im Spannungsfeld zwischen Restauration und Revolution 1815–1848* (Stuttgart: Metzler, 1971), 1: VII.

[2] Sengle, *Biedermeierzeit*, 1: X.

[3] In Friedrich Sengle, "Voraussetzungen und Erscheinungsformen der deutschen Restaurationsliteratur," *Deutsche Vierteljahrsschrift* 30 (1956): 268–94.

[4] Peter Stein, *Epochenproblem "Vormärz" (1815–1848)* (Stuttgart: Metzler, 1974), 28.

[5] Jost Hermand, "Allgemeine Epochenprobleme," *Zur Literatur der Restaurationsepoche 1815–1848,* ed. Jost Hermand and Manfred Windfuhr (Stuttgart: Metlzer, 1970), 16.

[6] Heinrich Heine, *Sämtliche Werke,* ed. Manfred Windfuhr, vol. 6, ed. Jost Hermand (Hamburg: Hoffmann und Campe, 1973), 138.

[7] Heine, *Sämtliche Werke,* vol. 1.1, ed. Pierre Grappin (Hamburg: Hoffmann und Campe, 1975), 209–11. Trans. Max Knight, cited from *Heinrich Heine: Poetry and Prose,* ed. Jost Hermand and Robert C. Holub (New York: Continuum, 1982), 11.

[8] Joseph von Eichendorff, *Sämtliche Werke,* Historisch-Kritische Ausgabe, ed. Wilhelm Kosch et al., vol. 5.1, Erzählungen, ed. Karl Konrad Polheim (Tübingen: Niemeyer, 1998), 86. Cited from "Memoirs of a Good-for-Nothing," trans. Ronald Taylor, *German Romantic Stories,* ed. Frank G. Ryder (New York: Continuum, 1988), 190.

[9] Theodor W. Adorno, *Gesammelte Schriften,* vol. 11, *Noten zur Literatur* (Frankfurt: Suhrkamp, 1997), 60–64. (From the essay "Rede über Lyrik und Gesellschaft)

[10] Eduard Mörike, *Sämtliche Werke,* ed. Herbert G. Göpfert (Munich: Hanser, 1981), 1: 102. Cited from Theodor W. Adorno, *Notes to Literature,* vol. 1, ed. Rolf Tiedemann, trans. Shierry Weber Nicholsen (New York: Columbia UP, 1991), 47–48.

[11] Adorno, "Rede über Lyrik und Gesellschaft," 62.

[12] Adorno, "Rede über Lyrik und Gesellschaft," 61.

[13] Heine, vol. 6, 179–181.

[14] Friedrich Schiller, *Werke,* National Ausgabe, ed. Benno von Wiese, vol. 20, Philosophische Schriften, Erster Theil (Weimar: Hermann Böhlaus Nachfolger, 1962), 365. Translation cited from Friedrich Schiller, *On the Aesthetic Education of Man,* trans. Reginald Snell (New Haven: Yale UP, 1954), 87.

[15] Schiller, 405.

[16] Friedrich Schlegel, *Kritische Friedrich-Schlegel-Ausgabe,* ed. Ernst Behler, vol. 2, *Charakteristiken und Kritiken I (1796–1801),* ed. Hans Eichner (Munich: Schöningh, 1967), 182.

[17] Theodor Mundt, *Moderne Lebenswirren* (Frankfurt: Athenäum, 1973; orig. 1834), 12.

[18] Karl Gutzkow, "Wolfgang Menzel und der deutsche Tierspartei," *Phönix: Frühlingszeitung für Deutschland,* Nr. 102, Literatur-Blatt Nr. 17, 30 April 1835, in Athenäum Reprints Series, *Die Zeitschriften des Jungen Deutschland,* ed. Alfred Estermann (Frankfurt: Athenäum, 1971), 1: 408.

[19] Heinrich Laube, *Kritiken von Heinrich Laube,* selected and edited by S. D. Stirk, Sprache und Kultur der germanischen und romanischen Völker, D. Texte, vol. 1 (Breslau: Verlag Priebatsch's Buchhandlung, 1934), 74–75.

[20] Theodor Mundt, "Die Dichtung der Übergangs-Epoche," *Charaktere und Situationen: Novellen, Skizzen, Wanderungen auf Reisen und durch die neueste Literatur* (Wismar and Leipzig: H. Schmidt und v. Cossel's Rathsbuchhandlung,

1837), 1: 313–28; and Theodor Mundt, *Madonna: Unterhaltung mit einer Heiligen* (Frankfurt: Athenäum, 1973; orig. 1835), 410.

[21] Heine, vol. 8.1, ed. Manfred Windfuhr (1979), 125.

[22] Ludolf Wienbarg, *Aethetische Feldzüge* (Hamburg: 1834; rpt. Berlin and Weimar: Aufbau, 1964), 75–76.

[23] Georg Herwegh, "Die Literatur im Jahre 1840," *Über Literatur und Gesellschaft (1837–1841)*, ed. Agnes Ziegengeist (Berlin: Akademie Verlag, 1971), 117.

[24] Ferdinand Freiligrath, *Sämtliche Werke,* ed. Ludwig Schröder (Leipzig: Max Hesse, 1906), 5: 15.

[25] Georg Herwegh, *Gedichte eines Lebendigen* (Stuttgart: G. J. Göschen'sche Verlagshandlung, 1877), 201–3.

[26] Heine, vol. 4, ed. Winfried Woesler (1985), 92. Cited from *Heinrich Heine: Poetry and Prose,* trans Aaron Kramer, p. 232.

[27] (Stuttgart: Klett).

The agony in Silesia. Hunger and despair. The official remedy.
Courtesy of Bildarchiv Preußischer Kulturbesitz, Berlin.

Poetic Realism, Naturalism, and the Rise of the Novella

Gail Finney

Introduction

AS A STYLISTIC MODE, realism has long been with us. For Aristotle, whose *Poetics* (fourth century B.C.) remained the bible of dramatic theory in the West for more than 2000 years, the arts, including literature, are based on imitation, or mimesis. This definition yields the criterion of verisimilitude, or trueness to life, which is equivalent to realism in its most general sense: the truer a work of art is to nature — the more faithful the artistic imitation — the more realistic the work is. This criterion can be applied to texts of any period and genre, although it is of course far from absolute or objective, since verisimilitude can lie in the eye of the beholder.

Realism as a diachronically universal stylistic mode reaches a synchronic high point in the nineteenth century, when it acquires the status of a historical period or movement. At this time its definitions become numerous and complex. In this chapter they will be seen to crystallize around three principal dichotomies:

1) Realism as a nineteenth-century movement vs. realism as a timeless stylistic mode; I will designate these as "Realism" and "realism," respectively.

2) Realism in non-German-speaking countries, above all, France, England, and Russia (referred to in this chapter as "European Realism") vs. Realism in Germany, Switzerland, and Austria, often known as Poetic Realism.

3) Realism vs. naturalism.

Two of the first critics to confront these dichotomies systematically are Erich Auerbach and Georg Lukács. Although first published in 1946, Auerbach's *Mimesis: The Representation of Reality in Western Literature* remains a point of departure for any discussion of realism. Auerbach undertakes a series of close textual analyses of carefully selected passages from works ranging from Homer's *Odyssey* to Marcel Proust's *Du côté de chez Swann* (1913) and Virginia Woolf's *To The Lighthouse* (1927). He uses these analyses to illustrate his definition of realism as a mixed style — mixed in social content as well as in linguistic form, and above all a mixture of the everyday with the sublime. For Auerbach, realism is a style in which readers always know where they are, where the characters have come from and where they are; descriptive details clearly establish setting and time, and all these elements are placed within a clearly ordered framework. Realism breaks down, in Auerbach's view, with Woolf and her contemporaries, with the introduction of multiple perspectives and random, banal detail which seems to be present for its own sake rather than as part of a coherent synthesis of character and environment.

Auerbach is obviously writing about realism as a stylistic mode. As he shows, realism came into full flower in the nineteenth century, when it was historicized: Realism designates the interweaving of a literary character's personal development with the social, political, and economic conditions of his or her time. This is precisely the definition of Realism celebrated by the Marxist critic Lukács. For Auerbach and Lukács, the Realists par excellence are the nineteenth-century French writers Balzac and Stendhal; Lukács would also include Tolstoy. Where does this leave the Germans, the focus of our interest in this chapter? I have touched on Auerbach and Lukács because the views put forth in Auerbach's chapter in *Mimesis* entitled "Miller the Musician" and in Lukács's ˙writings, notably *Deutsche Realisten des 19. Jahrhunderts* (Nineteenth-Century German Realist Writers, 1951), set the tone for the subsequent critical view of German Realism as anachronistic, narrowly provincial, and inward in its orientation.

In brief, the two critics argue that, because there existed no unified nation or society in Germany until the establishment of Bismarck's Second Reich in 1871, there was no common basis for the kind of socially-oriented literature that epitomizes Realism. Furthermore, the belated founding of the German nation led to a prolongation of feudalism and the delayed arrival or consolidation of modern capitalism, whose ramifications lie at the heart of so many Realist novels. Finally, the shadow of Weimar classicism still hung over nineteenth-century German writers, so that timeless, universal values took precedence over the depiction of contemporary social conditions. In the view of Auerbach and Lukács, the result of these circumstances was that nineteenth-century writers wrote from within the context of their own province or state and had an inward orientation that was at odds with the sociocritical thrust of European Realism.

Although these features are conventionally associated with "Poetic Realism," the term as originally coined by the German writer Otto Ludwig (1813–65) had little to do with them. Rather, in his critical writings Ludwig imagines "poetic" or "artful" realism to be a middle realm between the subjectivity of the writer's mind and the objectivity of things in and of themselves, between the unified worldview associated with (Schillerian) idealism and the multiplicity characteristic of naturalism, by which he means the political literature of the 1830s and 1840s.[1]

It is therefore telling that the first major critic to challenge the status of Poetic Realism as the disadvantaged little sister of European Realism illustrates his argument in part with Ludwig's novella *Zwischen Himmel und Erde* (Between Heaven and Earth, 1856). Richard Brinkmann's pioneering *Wirklichkeit und Illusion* (Reality and Illusion, 1957) argues that it is misleading to base a definition of Realism on the portrayal of external reality, since nineteenth-century literature increasingly reflects the awareness that reality is little more than our perceptions of it, which are necessarily subjective. For Brinkmann, Realism consists of the progressive subjectivization of the external world. He demonstrates this thesis through close analyses of narrative technique — point of view, narrative distance, tone, and voice — in selected prose texts.

Shifting the object of critical attention from content to form in this way can alter the judgments, current since Auerbach and Lukács, that subordinate Poetic Realism to European Realism. During the past dozen or so years several prominent scholars, notably Robert Holub, Martin Swales, and Eric Downing, have returned to an emphasis on formal aspects in studying nineteenth-century German fiction, and the results have been surprising and refreshing: these critics illuminate a self-consciousness and narrative reflectiveness in nineteenth-century prose texts that show them to be not backward but in many ways forward-looking.[2] As will be seen, the combination of provincialism, inwardness, and sentimentality, on the one hand, and formal innovation on the other, produces a unique body of fiction. When all is said and done, it perhaps makes more sense to characterize German Poetic Realism as neither inferior nor superior to European Realism, but as simply distinctive.

Poetic Realism

Although the term "Poetic Realism" has been disparaged and even rejected on occasion, its two poles in fact form a spectrum across which German prose from the second half of the nineteenth century can usefully be discussed, reflecting a tendency to idealize, sentimentalize, provincialize, or look back to earlier periods and models at one extreme, and an interest in contemporary socioeconomic conditions, growing industrialism and urbanization, scientific developments of the day, and politics at the other. This essay focuses on three authors whose work spans both poles, who are both lyric poets and writers of Realist fiction, Gottfried Keller (1819–90), Theodor Storm (1817–88) and Conrad Ferdinand Meyer (1825–98).

The Swiss poet and fiction writer Keller is perhaps best known for his Bildungsroman *Der grüne Heinrich* (Green Henry, first version 1854–55, second version 1879–80), the greatest novel of Poetic Realism. As a

Bildungsroman, or novel of education or development, *Der grüne Heinrich* charts the growth of the protagonist Heinrich from childhood to adulthood. The "greenness" announced in the title refers not only to the fact that Heinrich is decidedly naïve, innocent, and idealistic and that he wears green clothing, but also to the hopefulness with which he is repeatedly associated, traditionally symbolized by the color green. This hue is appropriate as well to the markedly regional backdrop of *Der grüne Heinrich*. Set largely in the author's own country, it is enlivened with portrayals of the Swiss landscape. Keller's fondness for his homeland as a setting for his work endures throughout his life, still prominent for instance in his late cycle of novellas, *Züricher Novellen* (1876–77), based on stations in the history of Zürich from the Middle Ages to the nineteenth century.

The German Bildungsroman is perhaps better translated as the novel of self-cultivation, since it is typically influenced by the great Goethean model, *Wilhelm Meisters Lehrjahre* (Wilhelm Meisters Apprenticeship, 1795–96). Accordingly, the central tension of *Der grüne Heinrich* is that characterizing Poetic Realism in general: the conflict between idealism and realism. In contrast to Eugène de Rastignac of Balzac's novel *Père Goriot* (1835) or Pip in Dickens's *Great Expectations* (1860–61), who take on the social world in Paris and London, respectively, as a kind of opponent, Keller's Heinrich is content to participate in local theatrics and to spend forty days at home reading the collected works of Goethe. Distinguished already as a child by his vivid imagination, which prefers his subjective conceptions of things to their actuality, Heinrich decides to become a landscape painter. In this regard, too, realism is an ideal not attained by Heinrich, first because his subjective fantasy prevents him from capturing the objective reality of the natural world, and then because he eventually abandons a traditional mimetic aesthetic and creates non-representational canvases that foreshadow abstract art.

The tension in Heinrich between idealism and realism is reflected as well in his romantic life. He resists his strong physical attraction to the older, earthy and sensual Judith because of his platonic interest in the pure, delicate Anna. But Keller explodes this conventional dichotomy, so common in works by male writers, between the (usually dark-haired) desirable yet dangerous woman and the (usually fair-haired) innocent, more conventional female figure through his creation of Dortchen Schönfund, whom Heinrich meets after Anna dies and after his break with Judith. Dortchen, whose personality embraces spiritual, sensual, and even intellectual elements, introduces Heinrich to the works of the atheistic philosopher Ludwig Feuerbach (1804–72), in so doing attempting to bring the dreamy young artist down to earth. Because Heinrich fails to propose to her, however, this relationship too comes to naught. His life takes a pragmatic turn when he becomes employed in the civil service and reunites with Judith, but not in a romantic sense.

Heinrich's unfulfilling amorous experience constitutes only one of the novel's parallels to the life of its author, who had a number of unhappy love affairs but never married. Other autobiographical echoes are Heinrich's sojourn in Munich and the financial hardship he endures there in attempting to become a painter, his aforementioned reading of Feuerbach, and his close but vexed relationship with his mother.

Keller's encounter with the work (and the person) of Feuerbach while a student in Heidelberg in the late 1840s represents one of the most decisive experiences that he chose to weave into his autobiographical Bildungsroman. Feuerbach's attempts to direct attention away from a disembodied divinity and toward concrete social problems resonated with Keller, whose orientation became increasingly secular and liberal. This perspective was fueled by his enthusiasm for the Revolution of 1848, an unsuccessful effort to found a unified, democratic Germany. Keller's emphasis on the earthly realm finds one of its pithiest and most memorable formulations in his poem "Abendlied" (Evening Song, 1879), which ends with the lines, "Trinkt, o Augen, was die Wimper hält, / Von dem goldnen Überfluß der Welt!" (Drink, oh eyes, as much as your lashes can hold of the world's golden abundance!).

An extensive manifestation of Keller's worldly, realist side is the two-volume collection of novellas entitled *Die Leute von Seldwyla* (The People of Seldwyla, 1856, 1873–74). In his talent for rendering the details of food, clothing, setting, and, especially, objects — a talent everywhere in evidence in these novellas — Keller is comparable to the European Realists; when one considers the etymological origin of the word "realism" — from the Latin *res,* for "thing" — he is a consummate realist. Monetary factors play a key role in these tales. Moreover, as is perhaps appropriate for a citizen of the nation that gave birth to Jean Jacques Rousseau and Johann Heinrich Pestalozzi, Keller endows each tale with a folksy didacticism, a down-to earth moral that further enhances the realistic quality of the collections. The characters — for example, Pankraz, a boy given to sulking, or the son of the disciplined, sensible Frau Regel — typically learn a lesson, and one has the sense that the reader is supposed to learn it as well. The (often satiric) humor infusing these novellas, a trait that distinguishes Keller from the other writers discussed in this chapter, is counterbalanced in most of the tales by a decidedly dark note, as when, for example, attention is drawn to Pankraz's isolation or when the titular "three righteous combmakers" meet a harsh end, one through suicide, one through dissolution, and one through domination by his wife.

As the latter title suggests, some of the novellas in these collections contain fairy-tale motifs, one of the poeticizing features that set *Die Leute von Seldwyla* apart from European Realist fiction. The most fully developed example is the novella *Spiegel, das Kätzchen,* expressly subtitled *Ein Märchen* (Mirror, the Cat: A Fairy Tale, 1856), which has a cat as its protagonist and includes other talking animals, a witch, and a sorcerer. In a similarly fantastic and idealizing vein, "Seldwyla" does not designate an actual place but stems from the Middle High German word *saelde,* meaning "blissful" or "sunny."

One of the richest illustrations of the dichotomy between poetic and realistic tendencies characteristic of *Die Leute von Seldwyla* is the well-known novella *Romeo und Julia auf dem Dorfe* (A Village Romeo and Juliet, 1856). The idyllic, provincial setting previewed in the title belies both the universality of the theme of star-crossed lovers and the materialistic nature of the force that comes between them, greed, in this case the quarrel between their fathers over a piece of land between their fields. This dichotomy is epitomized in the inn, the *Paradiesgärtlein* ("Paradise Garden"), to which the lovers, Sali and Vrenchen, flee in a desperate attempt to be together despite their fathers' feud. Contrary to its idyllic name, the inn is revealed to be a haven for bohemians, unwed lovers, and the poor and homeless, in other words, for those rejected by respectable society. Unwilling to join this class of people and yet prevented by filial loyalty from legitimizing their union, Sali and Vrenchen drown themselves. Here as elsewhere in his oeuvre, Keller shows his awareness of dark sides of human existence that no amount of poeticization or sentimentality can mask. In contrast to the quaint archaism associated by many critics with Poetic Realism, these works by Keller anticipate the existential despair of much twentieth-century literature.

The tales in Keller's *Die Leute von Seldwyla* represent some of the most memorable examples of the dominant genre of Poetic Realism, the novella. As a systematic genre the novella was born in Italy, in Giovanni Boccaccio's cycle of one hundred short narratives known as the *Decameron* (1349–51); in the frame narrative a group of Florentines who have fled the city because of the plague entertain themselves by telling stories. Two key features of these stories remain attached to the form even through the nineteenth century: the dichotomy between novelty and credibility, reflected in the Italian word *novella* ("news"), and the embedding of the narrative within a frame, ostensibly in order to heighten the impression of objectivity. As we will see, however, the level of complexity to which the Poetic Realists develop the frame technique can produce very different results.

The Boccaccian dichotomy between the striking and the believable is fundamental to one of the most famous pronouncements about the novella, Goethe's definition of the form in a 1827 conversation with his secretary Johann Eckermann (1792–1854). In that conversation he described the novella as "ein sich ereignete, unerhörte Begebenheit," an unheard-of event. Throughout the nineteenth century German writers sought to identify the defining features of the genre. Ludwig Tieck (1773–1853) emphasized the importance of the *Wendepunkt* (turning point); Paul Heyse (1830–1914) focused on an object or thing, which he called the "falcon" after a tale in the *Decameron,* that is central to the narrative and distinguishes it from others; Friedrich Theodor Vischer (1807–87) drew attention to the pithy quality of the novella; and in an unpublished preface of 1881 Theodor Storm called the novella the "sister of the drama" because of its conciseness and seriousness.

In Storm one sees another author who, like Keller, excels both as a lyric poet and as a writer of Realist fiction and who therefore also merits the label "Poetic Realist." As with Keller, much of Storm's poetry and prose work are colored by the atmosphere of his regional homeland, in this case his small hometown of Husum in Schleswig, a northern province that belonged to Denmark until 1864. His poetry, among the finest written in German, can be divided into thematic categories: patriotic poetry supporting the German cause in opposition to Denmark, and poems on love, death, nature, and transience. His nature poems, often evoking the North Sea landscape around Husum, are especially atmospheric. Notable examples are "Die Stadt" (The City, 1851) and "Meeresstrand" (The Seashore, 1854), both of which represent a marked departure from the nature poetry celebrating forest landscapes that had been so popular in the German tradition.

The lyrical talent so evident in Storm's poetry leaves its mark on his early novellas as well. One of the most popular of these, *Immensee* (1850), actually interweaves poetry into the narrative, which tells the story of Reinhard, an aspiring poet who loses his beloved, Elisabeth, to another, more affluent man because of pressure from the girl's mother. This dynamic exemplifies one of the dominant themes of German literature from Goethe onward, the conflict between the artist figure and the bourgeois. *Immensee*'s lyricism is further heightened by its nature imagery, such as the linnet that Reinhard gives to Elisabeth, the titular lake, and the water lilies on its surface, all of which are endowed with symbolic significance.

The frame structure of *Immensee,* in which the love story from Reinhard's youth is narrated as a flashback triggered by a picture of Elisabeth he encounters as an elderly man, recurs often in Storm's oeuvre. He steadily increases the narrative complexity of the frame technique, above all in his historical or chronicle novellas, as two examples will demonstrate. Most strikingly, in both *Aquis submersus* (Submerged Beneath the Waters, 1876) and *Der Schimmelreiter* (The Rider on the White Horse, 1888) the frame structure ostensibly intended to add an element of objectivity to the inner story in fact colors the narrative with the subjective viewpoint of the narrator. It is because of this paradox and the epistemological uncertainty it creates that many of the novellas of Storm and Meyer anticipate modernist fiction and remain so fascinating today.

As in *Immensee,* the "narrative trigger" in *Aquis submersus* is a picture, in this case a seventeenth-century painting of a man holding a dead boy, which the primary narrator encounters in a house in his hometown.

He had seen a portrait of the same child a few years before in a church, alongside that of a priest, and had been intrigued by the letters C.P.A.S. at the bottom of the child's portrait. Asking about the painting in the house, he is given a seventeenth-century manuscript written by the painter, Johannes. This secondary narrative comprises the greater part of the novella and tells the story of a love doomed, as in *Immensee*, by class and economic differences. We learn that the artist Johannes's love for Katharina, the daughter of his aristocratic patron, was thwarted by her family, but that the two managed to spend one night together before being separated. This union produces a son, who drowns five years later during a chance reunion between Johannes and Katharina. Katharina's husband, the priest in the church portrait, forces Johannes to paint the dead boy's picture as a warning. The primary narrator's curiosity is satisfied at last as he deciphers the abbreviation: "Culpa Patris Aquis Submersus" (Submerged beneath the Waters through the Guilt of the Father).

Despite its resemblance to a painted Russian doll that contains numerous smaller dolls, each embedded inside the other, *Aquis submersus* is not a mannered construction, and does not make use of complex narrative technique for its own sake. In addition to its many evocations of transience — not only of human life but even of the artistic creations that human beings produce — this novella succeeds through the distance created by its multiple frames in rendering guilt impenetrable and thus in questioning the ability of human beings, joined by their fallibility, to judge each other.

Der Schimmelreiter raises the narrative distancing structure of *Aquis submersus* by one power. The most deeply embedded narrative is the story about the title character and protagonist, the dike master Hauke Haien, told by a village schoolmaster in North Frisia (Storm's home territory) in the 1820s, retold by a traveler in a magazine article in the 1830s, and in turn recalled some fifty years later by the primary narrator. Although the multiple frame technique is typically characterized as intensely objective, it should be kept in mind that both the retellings and the recollection of the inner narrative necessarily involve a degree of reinterpretation and that the schoolmaster's narrative is itself highly subjective. Hence, the picture that ultimately emerges of Hauke Haien, while not colored by his own subjectivity, is marked by inevitable limitations in the perceptions and memories of those who attempt to tell his story, with the result that that picture is called into question. This attention to the subjectivity of perception and to the resulting difficulty of knowing other human beings represents a marked contrast to the pose of omniscience so common in the European Realist novel and looks ahead to the epistemological uncertainty characteristic of modernist fiction.

Considering the effects of the multiply embedded narrative technique on the reader's image of Hauke Haien sheds some light on apparent ambiguities and contradictions in the text. The title itself is ambiguous, referring both to the Hauke Haien of the past, internal tale and to his ghost, reputed to ride in the present along the dikes on his white horse. Similarly, dikes were Hauke Haien's major preoccupation beginning in childhood and are his driving force as an adult, but they ultimately lead to his demise, when the town dike bursts during a tidal wave because he did not have it repaired properly. Furthermore, although as a brilliant innovator in dike construction he is associated by many critics with the heroic, enterprising ideal of the *Gründerzeit* (early part of Bismarck's reign, 1871–73), in his isolation from family and community he is more reminiscent of a Romantic hero. No doubt in part because of mysteries like these, *Der Schimmelreiter* is usually regarded as Storm's masterpiece and is one of the best-known of all German novellas.

Conrad Ferdinand Meyer is the most significant lyric poet among the Poetic Realists. Although Swiss like Keller, Meyer brings to his work a cosmopolitanism that sets it apart from that of the other Poetic Realists. His travels to France, Italy, Germany, and other parts of Switzerland than his native Zurich leave their mark on his poetry and fiction. He has a distinctly more aesthetic inclination than Keller and Storm, and many of his poems treat works of art. Rejecting the Romantic tendency to project human feelings onto inanimate objects, in his so-called *Dinggedichte* ("thing-poems") Meyer develops an aesthetic of objectivity and impersonality in which he strives to convey objects in and of themselves, or from the inside out, free from all marks of human subjectivity. The central objects are often indicated in the poems' titles, "Der römische Brunnen" (The Roman Fountain, 1860–82) and "Zwei Segel" (Two Sails, 1870–82) being two of the best-known examples. His poems were of crucial importance for Rainer Maria Rilke's (1875–1926) further refinement of the *Dinggedicht*.

Meyer's cosmopolitanism also colors his eleven novellas, set in France, Italy, England, Sweden, and Switzerland. Reflecting the author's extensive knowledge of European history, they take place in periods ranging from the eighth through the seventeenth century. Most feature actual historical personages, such as Ulrich von Hutten, the French kings Charles IX and Louis XIV, the Borgia family, Dante, King Gustavus Adolphus of Sweden, Saint Thomas à Becket, and the English King Henry II. While the historical character of Meyer's novellas would seem to contrast sharply with the attention to contemporary social condictions typical of the novel of European Realism, Meyer often employs historical settings as a mask through which to criticize institutions of his day indirectly, notably the Church.

The attention to the subjective and restricted nature of human perceptions that we discern in Storm's later work occupies a central place in Meyer's oeuvre. These concerns are especially visible in two of his most powerful novellas, *Der Heilige* (The Saint, 1879–80) and *Die Hochzeit des*

Mönchs (The Wedding of the Monk, 1883–84). As in Storm's late novellas, in these two works Meyer employs a frame structure that distances the authorial voice from the object of the narrative by means of a secondary narrator, thereby heightening the ambiguity of the inner tale.

The frame narrator of *Der Heilige* is a servant of King Henry II, Hans the bowman, who tells his tale some twenty years after the murder of Thomas à Becket in Canterbury Cathedral by Henry's knights in 1170. This fact of the murder is known, but Meyer's novella shows that what is not known — because Hans could not know it — is the precise nature of the relationship between the king and his chancellor Becket. To further complicate this relationship, Meyer adds a fictitious figure, Becket's beautiful and adored daughter Grace, whom Henry seduces. When political differences between Becket and Henry later arise after Becket has become the archbishop of Canterbury, Hans's narrative leaves the reader uncertain about the extent to which Becket's actions are motivated by a desire for revenge. Rage, guilt, fear, revenge, loyalty — all these feelings contribute to the actions of Becket and Henry, but as *Der Heilige* shows, there are limits to our ability to describe human emotions because of our restricted ability to perceive and understand them. Hans says this, in effect: "Es kommt . . . beim Urteilen wie beim Schießen lediglich auf den Standpunkt an" (In making judgments, as in shooting a bow, everything depends on your point of view).[3]

Die Hochzeit des Mönchs features the master storyteller Dante himself, who entertains the court of his patron Can Grande in Verona with a sensational tale: a monk breaks his vows by marrying for family reasons, then rejects his new wife for a woman to whom he has long been attracted, bringing on both their murders. But in telling the story Dante makes no judgments, claiming that it is impossible to read the minds of others. The tale's presumed objectivity and truthfulness is further undermined by the fact that Dante names its characters after his listeners and that the latter frequently interrupt Dante's narrative and question his facts. In this novella, the omniscient stance of the European Realist novel is stood on its head.

The extent to which language, communication, and epistemological certainty are thrown into question in the work of Storm and Meyer places them in a longstanding and important line of thinking that can be characterized as linguistic skepticism. Given that the use of language is one of the main properties that distinguishes us from animals and makes us human, it can be said that there exist in literature and philosophy two major attitudes toward language, and that these can be seen to form two traditions: linguistic faith, which celebrates language as a vehicle of communication, and linguistic skepticism, which laments that language is inadequate to express our thoughts and feelings and can even interfere with communication. Linguistic skepticism often goes hand in hand with epistemological resignation, or an awareness of the limitations of human perception and knowledge.

Prominent in German literature and philosophy from the eighteenth century on, epistemological resignation and linguistic skepticism find expression for example in Immanuel Kant's *Kritik der reinen Vernunft* (Critique of Pure Judgment, 1781), the work of idealist philosophers Johann Gottlieb Fichte (1762–1814) and Friedrich Wilhelm Schelling (1775–1854), Heinrich von Kleist's fragmentary essay "Über die allmähliche Verfertigung der Gedanken beim Reden" (On the Gradual Production of Thoughts While Speaking, 1805; pub. 1878), Friedrich Nietzsche's essay "Über Wahrheit und Lüge im außermoralischen Sinn" (On Truth and Lying in an Extra-Moral Sense, 1873), the writings of the philosopher Wilhelm Dilthey (1833–1911) on what we today call "body language," Sigmund Freud's *Zur Psychopathologie des Alltagslebens* (The Psychopathology of Everyday Life, 1901), and the Austrian writer Hugo von Hofmannsthal's "Ein Brief" (A Letter, 1902). At the turn of the century, epistemological resignation is often manifested as perspectivism, or the belief that perception — necessarily subjective and limited — is reality. As we will see, this way of thinking colors much of naturalist literature.

Naturalism

German naturalism is a much more self-conscious and international literary movement — indeed, much more of a movement — than is Poetic Realism, whose exponents did not come together to theorize. The origins of German naturalism lie in the literary journals and critical manifestoes published in Berlin in the late 1870s and early 1880s by the brothers Heinrich and Julius Hart (1855–1906, 1859–1930). Rejecting the bourgeois thesis plays popular in the 1870s, they advocate greater attention to contemporary life and the treatment of working-class figures, two elements that were to become paramount in naturalist literature. The Munich critic Michael Georg Conrad (1846–1927), who in 1885 founded the first major naturalist periodical, *Die Gesellschaft* (Society), championed the French novelist Émile Zola, who became a prominent influence on German naturalism. Zola's influence was dominant during the 1880s, when naturalism in Germany was represented largely by prose works, whereas the Norwegian dramatist Henrik Ibsen (1828–1906) was the decisive model during the 1890s, when the drama was the prevailing genre of German naturalism. Partly under the influence of Zola, who embraces the entire range of humanity in his twenty-volume *roman fleuve Les Rougon-Macquart* (1871–93), German naturalists came to include in their purview subjects previously considered too negative and base for literary treatment — disease, poverty, squalor, alcoholism, and a spectrum of other physical and mental pathologies.

Like other intellectuals of their time, German naturalist writers were fascinated by revolutionary developments in nineteenth-century science. The evolving doctrine of scientific determinism, or the belief that the human being is a product of heredity and environment, found an increasing number of adherents, among them — to varying degrees — Zola, Ibsen, and the German naturalists. As a result, their work is often set within a family, as the natural, living laboratory within which the influence of heredity and environment on its members can be charted.

A further historical development that left its mark on naturalist literature was the women's movement. Having received its original impetus in 1848 at the first Women's Rights Convention in Seneca Falls, New York, the drive for equal rights, above all the fight for women's right to vote, had spread by 1900 to countries around the globe. Women writers made memorable contributions to naturalism.

The remainder of this chapter will examine works by Arno Holz and Johannes Schlaf, Gerhart Hauptmann, and Elsa Bernstein (pseud. Ernst Rosmer), texts that exemplify features characteristic of much naturalist literature: emphasis on contemporary subjects, inclusion of working-class characters, attention to physical and mental pathology, exploration of the influence of heredity and environment in determining characters' actions, and interest in the psychology and situation of women in society.

The novella *Papa Hamlet* (1889) was a collaboration by Arno Holz (1863–1929), one of the principal theorists of naturalism, and Johannes Schlaf (1862–1941). In keeping with the vogue for Scandinavian literature, largely inspired by Ibsen, they published the novella as the work of a fictitious Norwegian author named Bjarne P. Holmsen. The title is an ironic reference to the novella's central figure, a Norwegian actor called Niels Thienwiebel, who previously played the role of Hamlet but is now unemployed and living in poverty with his wife Amalie and baby Fortinbras. The repeated references to Amalie as the "reizende Ophelia" (charming Ophelia), like the many quotations from Shakespeare's *Hamlet* that are either spoken or thought by Thienwiebel, underline by contrast the impotence and victimization of these decidedly unheroic characters.

Papa Hamlet abounds in details of squalor and misery. Amalie is ailing and dirty; the family is starving, freezing, and on the verge of eviction for non-payment of rent; and Thienwiebel drinks, mistreats his wife, and abuses the baby, finally strangling him because of his continuous crying. At the novella's end Thienwiebel is found frozen to death, a liquor bottle clutched in his hand.

Such a synopsis tells a banal naturalist tale and does not do justice to the formal innovations of *Papa Hamlet*. The authors sought to achieve the greatest possible objectivity by reducing to a minimum the role of the subjective narrator. The bulk of the work consists of the characters' dialogue and thoughts, so that the text approaches the unmediated portrayal of drama. This quality is part of Holz's so-called "konsequenter Naturalismus" (consistent naturalism), an aesthetic doctrine based on his understanding of art as highly imitative of nature; in his schematic formula, "Kunst = Natur – x" (Art = Nature – x), meaning that the less visible the artistic media employed in a work are, the more naturalistic the work.[4] In *Papa Hamlet*, this elliptical conception of literary representation leads to fragmentation. In contrast to the Poetic Realist novella, often cohering around a central symbol and carefully structured around a turning point, *Papa Hamlet* consists of a series of novella-like sketches.

This fragmentary quality also characterizes the text's dialogue and method of description, both of which exhibit a stylistic technique called *Sekundenstil*, or the attempt to render the details of events or speech in a second-by-second fashion.[5] In describing this style Holz uses the example of leaf falling from a tree. Whereas older means of description simply observe that a leaf falls, or turns over while falling, his new microscopic style dissects the leaf's subtle movements and shadings; documents the way the sunlight colors now this side, now that; takes note of the leaf's changing position. Similarly, *Papa Hamlet* attends to the tiniest details of its squalid setting — an overturned cup; a sock in the middle of a table containing dirty dishes; the soft sputtering of the lamp, from whose wick a spark leaps off and floats black in the thick yellow oil.

This attention to minute detail is one of the features of naturalism that renders it tantamount to hyperrealism. The last example cited above reflects the way in which the photographic hyperrealism of Holz and Schlaf moves into what might be called their phonographic hyperrealism — their attempt to convey minuscule particles of sound and speech in written language, more than thirty years before James Joyce was to bring this technique to a global audience in *Ulysses* (1922). The dripping of melting snow in the roof gutter is represented as "Tipp Tipp Tipp," Amalie's fondling of the baby as "Kuß! Kuß, Kuß, Kuß, Kuß!!" (Kiss! Kiss, kiss, kiss, kiss!!), the baby's gurgling as "Grrr . . . grrr . . . äh!," all without mediation by a narrator.[6] Exclamations, expressions of disgust and rage, pauses within characters' sentences and even within their words — all these nuances are conveyed through the creative orthography and punctuation of Holz and Schlaf.[7] The fragmentary, grunting language and ineffectual thoughts and gestures of the characters in *Papa Hamlet* reflect their passivity, perhaps most obvious in the infirm, weary Amalie, who scarcely moves.

Despite its desire for the utmost objectivity, achieved through minimal artistic mediation, through its narrator *Papa Hamlet* furthers the process of subjectivization already evident in much of the prose of Poetic Realism. Rather than assuming an objective stance, the narrator of *Papa Hamlet* constantly makes judgments about the characters, usually of a sardonically negative nature. Often the narrator's opinions are similar to Thienwiebel's, and indeed it is at times impossible to determine whether the perspective is that of an "omniscient" third-person narrator or that of Thienwiebel's narrated monologue (*erlebte Rede*). It does not really matter which is the case, since the — rather paradoxical — point is that a highly naturalistic narrative turns out to be highly subjective, or vice versa. Harking back to the argument of Richard Brinkmann, this insight about the conjunction of naturalism and subjectivity in fact looks ahead to the central role of perspectivism in modernism.

If one wanted to sum up briefly (and alliteratively) some of the dominant figures treated by Naturalism, one could talk of the "three Ws": wastrels, workers, and (new) women. Because the drama is the predominant genre of naturalism during the final decade of the nineteenth century, I will examine one major play dealing with each of these types or figures. The shocked reactions of many readers to *Papa Hamlet*, while retrospectively justifying Holz and Schlaf's use of a pseudonym, pale in comparison to the furor evoked by the drama which Gerhart Hauptmann (1862–1946) dedicated to *Papa Hamlet*'s supposed author, *Vor Sonnenaufgang* (Before Sunrise, 1889). The five-act drama was not only Hauptmann's first play but the first German naturalist play to be staged. It was performed by the *Freie Bühne* (Free Stage), a society established in Berlin in 1889 on the model of André Antoine's *Théâtre Libre* in Paris, founded two years earlier. These two societies, and later the Independent Theatre in London (est. 1891), can be thought of as midwives to naturalist drama. As private societies operating on the basis of subscription, they were not subject to official censorship and could thus stage plays that had been or were likely to be banned by public theaters. Yet even at the *Freie Bühne*, the premiere of *Vor Sonnenaufgang* was controversial, nearly causing a riot.[8]

A look at the play's plot explains why. Maintaining the scientific model and metaphor so prominent in naturalism, the laboratory within which Hauptmann is working here is his native Silesia, and the experiment is the transition from agriculture to mining, which causes some of the local farmers to become wealthy overnight from the sale of rights to the rich coal deposits discovered beneath their land. Hauptmann demonstrates the effects of these developments by dramatizing the decline of one nouveau riche family, the Krauses, formerly farmers. This attention to decline, degeneration, and decadence as microcosmically portrayed in one family links Hauptmann to Holz and Schlaf as well as to other realist and naturalist writers. One of the most fully developed examples is Thomas Mann's novel *Buddenbrooks: Verfall einer Familie* (Buddenbrooks: Decline of a Family, 1901).

The Krause household is a veritable hothouse of degeneration. In keeping with the deterministic belief at the time that alcoholism is unavoidably hereditary, Krause's staggering alcoholism has been passed down to his daughter Martha and even to her first child, who dies because of it at age three. Krause's brutish, ill-bred wife takes comfort in the arms of her loutish nephew Kahl, an affair of which the entire family is aware. Most disturbing is the fact that Krause sexually pursues his daughter Helene. Educated at a Pietist boarding school, she has escaped the effects of this pathological environment and can therefore be seen — sustaining the metaphor of a scientific experiment — as the control. Yet she functions in the play as the quintessential victim. Her mother has forced her into an engagement with Kahl, and she is the sexual prey not only of her father but of Martha's imperious and corrupt husband Hoffmann.

The only breath of hope for Helene is offered by Loth, an old friend of Hoffmann's who visits him to study the plight of the region's coal miners. In Loth the viewer recognizes the Ibsenesque figure of the character whose arrival from the outside sets in motion the action of the drama, most often turning upside down the world he initially encounters. He is "der Retter aus der Ferne," the rescuer from a distance, the only figure who can possibly bring about change in a determined, naturalistic world. Revealed to be an idealistic and abstemious socialist concerned with global suffering and, locally, with the exploitation of the working class, Loth is nevertheless receptive to Helene's needs. The love that swiftly develops between the two is cut short by the revelations of Schimmelpfennig, the doctor who arrives to deliver Martha's baby and enlightens Loth about the kind of family he is about to join. Schimmelpfennig thus shows himself to be a cousin of the numerous medical doctors who serve as a philosophizing voice of reason in plays by Ibsen and Anton Chekhov (1860–1904). Since physical and mental health in a mate is of paramount importance to Loth, he abruptly leaves Helene, apparently forgetting despite his socialism that charity begins at home. Schimmelpfennig's dire existential diagnosis — "die Menschheit liegt in der Agonie"[9] (humankind lies in its death throes) — is dramatically borne out at the play's conclusion, when Martha's baby is born dead and Helene Krause, now with no way out of her trapped circumstances, ends her life with a hunting knife, her drunken father's lascivious rantings forming a grotesque offstage counterpoint to her despair.

Its melodramatic elements notwithstanding, stylistically *Vor Sonnenaufgang* is in most respects a classically naturalistic drama. It strives for the utmost linguistic verisimilitude. The Silesian-tinged speech of the servants, workers, and *nouveau riche* farmers imbues the play with much local color; the speech impediment of Frau Krause's companion Frau Spiller is also conveyed orthographically; and the effects of passion on Loth and Helene are reflected in their halting, fragmented dialogue. Most graphically — and most shockingly for the time — the extremely detailed stage directions indicate that the audience should hear the cries of Martha as she gives birth, prompting one outraged spectator to hurl a pair of forceps onto the stage during the play's turbulent premiere.

Although *Vor Sonnenaufgang* bears the subtitle *Soziales Drama*, its criticism of industrial capitalism as illustrated in the exploitation of the miners remains on the margins of the play. In Hauptmann's *Die Weber* (The Weavers, 1892) the workers' cause moves into the foreground. Subtitled *Schauspiel aus den vierziger Jahren* (A Play of the Eighteen-Forties), the five-act drama is based on a revolt by textile workers that actually occurred in 1844 in several towns at the base of the mountains called the Eulengebirge, in a part of lower Silesia that today belongs to Poland. Not surprisingly in light of its incendiary subject matter, this play too was first staged by the *Freie Bühne*.

The weavers' rebellion of 1844, which unleashed a heated reaction among the public after the Prussian military shot down many of the workers, inspired numerous literary treatments at the time, the most famous being Heinrich Heine's poem "Die schlesischen Weber" (The Silesian Weavers, 1844). Typical of the *Vormärz*, or pre-revolutionary, period, this poem's political direction is reflected in the fact that it was first translated into English by Friedrich Engels. Hauptmann had a personal relationship to the subject matter: his dedication of the play to his father states that his father's stories of *his* father's memories as a weaver who experienced the revolt were the germ of the drama. Hauptmann fleshed out his father's stories with documentary evidence, traveling to the site of the rebellion to talk to elderly weavers, acquaint himself with weaving terminology, and gather eyewitness evidence in the manner of Zola. In further naturalistic fashion he wrote the first version of the play in Silesian dialect, entitled *De Waber*. Since this thick dialect is virtually incomprehensible to anyone not from the working class in Silesia, Hauptmann rewrote the play as the version now usually performed, which is in High German with marked dialect traces.

The driving force of *Die Weber* is the capitalist system and the friction inherent in it between labor and management. The situation of the former is depicted as lamentable: the weavers are overworked and either egregiously underpaid or unemployed. Several factors contribute to their collective plight, including the hiring of additional workers and the mechanization of their craft through power looms, thus reducing the need for their labor, and the arbitrary lowering of their wages. Hauptmann portrays the unhealthy and starving condition of the weavers in naturalistic detail; they are described as ashen-faced, hollow-chested, coughing frequently, and so hungry that they are reduced to eating dog meat.

Management — the agent of the weavers' exploitation — is embodied in the cotton manufacturer Dreissiger. A self-pitying man who complains that the manufacturers are blamed for all the ills of the workers, he in turn attempts to shift responsibility to his manager Pfeiffer, who is portrayed in an equally negative light. Pfeiffer, himself formerly a weaver, treats the workers imperiously, yet is unmasked as a coward in the face of their rebellion. Their attack on Dreissiger's residence, during which they drive out his family and wreak havoc on the house, is strikingly reminiscent of the scene in Zola's novel *Germinal* (1885), in which rebelling miners surround the home of the mine's manager. Especially noteworthy is the attention in both works, as a raging mob of workers looms, to the marital unhappiness of the respective industrialists. In both cases the reasons for juxtaposing the private unhappiness of the wealthy with the mass misery of the poor are not simple and provide food for thought, demonstrating the extent to which both Zola and Hauptmann are not only naturalist but also humanist writers. But the end is the same for the weavers and the miners, since in each case the military are called up to put down the workers' rebellion.

The existentialist element introduced in the scene of the weavers' attack on Dreissiger's house recurs even more forcefully at the end of the play. The elderly weaver Hilse, a fervently patriotic, dutiful, religious man who vehemently opposes the rebellion and prefers thinking about the afterlife, is fatally shot by a soldier while sitting at his loom. Much has been written about the possible meaning of this conclusion to Hauptmann's drama. Whether one sees it in religious terms, regarding Hilse as a martyr, or as utterly cynical and nihilistic, what is certain is the modern character of this ending, pointing forward in its ambiguity and apparent randomness to much twentieth-century literature.

Die Weber is a landmark drama in many respects. Although earlier German plays had treated proletarian characters — Georg Büchner's *Woyzeck* (written 1836–37) is a memorable example — in *Die Weber* the workers are featured, playing key roles in every act. Moreover, no single one of them can be regarded as the protagonist of the play; instead, the mass functions as the hero. *Die Weber* is the first mass drama in German literature to be performed. Another striking element of *Die Weber* is its use of music. The so-called "Dreissiger's Song," a passionate evocation of the weavers' cruel treatment by their overseers, recurs in leitmotific fashion, sung by the weavers to create solidarity. This integration of songs into politically serious subject matter anticipates the distancing techniques of the dramatist Bertolt Brecht (1898–1956), who was in many ways a follower of Hauptmann. In contrast to the Marxist inspiration of much of Brecht's oeuvre, however, Hauptmann insisted that *Die Weber,* while socially motivated, was not socialistic. The play was nevertheless banned because of its relevance to Hauptmann's own era, which had witnessed proletarian uprisings against Bismarck's antisocialist laws not long before the premiere of *Die Weber.*

Although *Die Weber* offers an especially powerful portrayal of the proletariat, it is not Hauptmann's only work to treat this class. Others include the novella *Bahnwärter Thiel* (1888) and the plays *Der Biberpelz* (1893), *Fuhrmann Henschel* (1898), *Hanneles Himmelfahrt* (1893), and

Rose Bernd (1903). His depictions of the working class remain some of the most memorable in the German tradition.

Turn-of-the-century feminism, defined as the drive for equal rights between the sexes and often referred to as the "old" or "first" feminist movement, comprises an important piece of the backdrop to naturalist literature. In its early stages in the eighteenth and early nineteenth century, feminism centered on economic issues, working for example to secure means for unmarried women to earn their livelihood. Later, reflecting the influence of the middle class and of Protestant thinking, the women's movement became more concerned with moral considerations. Suffrage, which lay at the heart of the first feminist movement, was seen as both an end and a means to these considerations, since it was not only morally right that women should have the vote; the vote would help women achieve other morally just ends through legislation.

The German feminist movement was the largest and best-organized in the world after the corresponding movements in the United States and Britain.[10] In *Vor Sonnenaufgang* Hauptmann makes fun of women's emancipation, Loth pays lip service to it, and Schimmelpfennig supports it. But a more profound treatment of naturalism and feminism, specifically of the New (liberated) Woman, is found in three plays that can be seen to form a triad about triads: Ibsen's *Rosmersholm* (1886), Hauptmann's *Einsame Menschen* (Lonely Lives, 1891), and *Wir drei* (The Three of Us, 1891) by Elsa Bernstein, pseud. Ernst Rosmer. The three plays, each built around a love triangle, form a kind of chain of determinism, but in these naturalist works characters are shown to be driven primarily by emotional rather than by bodily needs.

Ibsen's atmospheric play *Rosmersholm* features the memorable Rebecca West (whose name the actual twentieth-century feminist journalist Cicily Andrews took as her pseudonym), a free spirit and New Woman living with John Rosmer as his mistress. It is gradually revealed that Rebecca committed psychic murder, as Strindberg later termed it in an article on the play, on Rosmer's melancholy, neurasthenic wife Beata, that is, Rebecca's power of suggestion induced Beata to take her own life. But at the end of the play Rebecca and Rosmer, unable to escape Beata's ghost and their guilt, drown themselves together.

In Hauptmann's *Einsame Menschen,* visibly influenced by *Rosmersholm,* the psychic vulnerability of Ibsen's Beata is split, so to speak, between the unstable, hypochondriacal scholar Johannes Vockerat and his timid, self-effacing wife Käthe. The visit of the student Anna Mahr, who embodies a hybrid of the emancipated woman and the femme fatale, brings the dissatisfaction simmering in the Vockerat household to a boil: captivated by Anna, Johannes comes to realize the painful magnitude of his loneliness with Käthe, who is not his intellectual equal. After Anna leaves, he commits suicide, bearing out Käthe's earlier fatalistic pronouncement, itself a virtual watchword of naturalist doctrine: "Aber man kann eben nicht gegen seine Natur: das ist das Unglück!" (But people can't act against their nature — what a misfortune that is!)[11]

Although not included in the canon of German dramatic writers in recent decades, Elsa Bernstein (1866–1949) was one of the most successful women dramatists of the *fin de siècle*. She wrote some fifteen plays, most of them in everyday, naturalistic language. Bernstein is often regarded as an epigone of Hauptmann, but the close timing between the appearance of *Einsame Menschen* and the beginning of her work on *Wir drei,* along with her pseudonym, Ernst Rosmer, point toward *Rosmersholm* as the more important influence here. Yet *Wir drei* offers a quasi-feminist variation on the third of the "three Ws" of naturalist drama, the depiction of women, and concomitantly on the doomed love triangles of Ibsen and Hauptmann. Like several of Bernstein's other plays, it dramatizes the clearly autobiographical conflict between marriage and career, reflecting an increase in the number of working women figures in drama between 1870 and 1900.[12] This tension is centered in the character Sascha, an independent, passionate, sometimes shocking writer, who is friends with the couple Agnes, a conventionally passive, self-sacrificing wife, and Richard, a self-involved, rather insensitive writer with whom Sascha becomes involved.

But *Wir drei* offers some surprising twists on the plots of *Rosmersholm* and *Einsame Menschen*. After Richard and Agnes separate because of his affair, Sascha returns to care for Agnes, who it turns out was pregnant at the time of the separation. Moreover, Agnes and Richard's marriage is restored, leaving the intelligent, creative woman alone with her writing, denied the satisfaction of combining a career with personal happiness. Thus, although the wife/mother figure is neither sacrificed, as in Ibsen's play, nor bereft of her husband, as in Hauptmann's play, we encounter here one of the dominant topoi of German literature by men: the theme of renunciation. This instance is not atypical of the fact that, as women move into positions comparable to those occupied by male writers, their stance remains largely transitional. Not until the twentieth century would German women writers break away fully from male models and travel their own literary paths.

Notes

[1] Otto Ludwig, "Shakespeare und Schiller," in *Otto Ludwigs Werke in sechs Bänden,* ed. Adolf Bartels, vol. 6 (Leipzig: Hesse, 1906), 156–59.

[2] Robert Holub, *Reflections of Realism: Paradox, Norm, and Ideology in Nineteenth-Century German Prose* (Detroit: Wayne State UP, 1991); Martin Swales, *Epochenbuch Realismus: Romane und Erzählungen* (Berlin: Erich Schmidt,

1997); and Downing, *Double Exposures: Repetition and Realism in Nineteenth-Century German Fiction* (Stanford: Stanford UP, 2000).

[3] C. F. Meyer, *Der Heilige*, in *Sämtliche Werke in zwei Bänden*, vol. 1 (Munich: Winkler, 1968), 588.

[4] The term "konsequenter Naturalismus" was coined in 1902 by Adolf Bartels; Heinz-Georg Brands, *Theorie und Stil des sogenannten "Konsequenten Naturalismus" von Arno Holz and Johannes Schlaf* (Bonn: Bouvier, 1978), 9. For the "law of art," see Holz, "Die Kunst: Ihr Wesen und Ihre Gesetze," in Holz, *Werke*, vol. 5 (Neuwied: Luchterhand, 1962), 14–15.

[5] The term first appears in Adalbert von Hanstein's *Das jüngste Deutschland: Zwei Jahrzehnte miterlebter Literaturgeschichte* (Leipzig: Voigtländer, 1900), 157.

[6] Arno Holz and Johannes Schlaf, *Papa Hamlet. Ein Tod* (Stuttgart: Reclam, 1963), 62, 45.

[7] This feature is even more marked in Holz and Schlaf's drama *Die Familie Selicke* (The Selicke Family, 1890), where character's speech is so minutely dissected as to be pointillistic. See my "Dramatic Pointillism: The Examples of Holz and Schlaf's *Die Familie Selicke* and Maeterlinck's *L'Intruse*," *Comparative Literature Studies*, 30 (1993), 1–15.

[8] See Wolfgang Leppmann, *Gerhart Hauptmann: Leben, Werk und Zeit* (Bern: Scherz, 1986), 120–31.

[9] Gerhart Hauptmann, *Vor Sonnenaufgang*, in *Das Dramatische Werk*, vol. 1 (Frankfurt / Main: Ullstein / Propyläen, 1974), 222.

[10] Richard Evans, *The Feminists: Women's Emancipation Movements in Europe, America, and Australasia 1840–1920* (London: Croom Helm, 1977), 251.

[11] Hauptmann, *Einsame Menschen*, in *Das Dramatische Werk*, I, 362.

[12] Susanne Kord, *Ein Blick hinter die Kulissen: Deutschsprachige Dramatikerinnen im 18. und 19. Jahrhundert* (Stuttgart: Metzler, 1992), 78–92.

Sezession House, Vienna, exhibit building of the Vienna Sezession group.
Architecture by Joseph Maria Olbrich, 1897–98.
Photograph by Ernst Grabovzski.

Literary Movements of the 1890s: Impressionism, Symbolism, and fin-de-siècle Austria

Ernst Grabovszki

T HE LAST DECADE before the turn of the century was distinguished by a virtually unparalleled diversity of artistic movements. These broke with traditional ways of making of art, both stylistically and as to subject matter. The most important and defining trend — especially for literature — was the decay of naturalism and its replacement by impressionism and symbolism, though realist and nationalistic, even racist literature influenced the period as well. *Heimatkunst* (art idealizing rural life) and *Arbeiterdichtung* (writing by or about workers) arose at the same time, making the decade a conglomerate of several movements often running counter to each other: *Heimatkunst,* a fusion of political values approximating the later National Socialist ideals, was the climax of an anti-modern movement in the 1890s that abhorred the modern city and urban life. *Arbeiterdichtung* attacked the exploitation of workers by the modern economic system. Contrary to what the term suggests, *Arbeiterdichtung* was not exclusively written by members of the working class but was also produced by bourgeois authors. As can be seen, all of these movements were part of the broader, European literary landscape. Symbolism, impressionism, and the literature of decadence were international manifestations that crossed the boundaries between countries and the arts.

Impressionism

Literary impressionism especially owed much to French impressionist painting, a style that primarily confined itself to the still-life painting, to portraits, and landscapes. Artists such as Auguste Renoir (1841–1919) and Claude Monet (1840–1926) turned away from conventional subjects and left their studios to paint in the open air. They showed a strong interest in nature and, for instance, tried to capture the effects of light on a subject and the natural circumstances it was exposed to — the different times of a day, the weather, or the season — by using colors that reproduced the appearance of the subject at a given time of day rather than those customarily associated with that object. A tree painted at sunset might appear red, for example. They also eschewed realism, preferring instead to render their momentary impression of the object. Hence, the impressionist method tended towards reduction, simplification, and circumscription. With respect to literature, impressionism translated into a reduction of subject, plot, or action.[1] The founding of "secessions," groups of artists breaking with the artistic production and tradition, in Vienna (1887), Munich (1892), and Berlin (1898), supported from abroad by such artists as Edvard Munch (1863–1944) in painting or August Strindberg (1849–1912) in drama, opened venues for expressing this reorientation. Interestingly, impressionism arose in the field of literature when it had passed its zenith in the field of painting. The most important endeavor of impressionism both in the fields of graphic arts and literature was to differentiate between the concrete, specific object and its artistic representation since they considered the latter a mere repetition of nature. Impressionist authors considered naturalistic literature incapable of reproducing a true image of reality; a work of art, they argued, is designed to evoke a certain mood. The impressionist author dissected his perception, so that in typical impressionist works the reader is made fully aware both of the artificiality and of the highly subjective nature of the author's creation. Impressionist authors preferred novellas to novels, prose sketches to elaborate narrations, poetry to prose. The lyrical one-act play and the interior monologue gained importance and popularity among them.

The theoretical background of literary impressionism, symbolism, and *fin-de-siècle* art is not fully explored by merely considering painting or the graphic arts. As is pointed out elsewhere in this volume the philosophy of Friedrich Nietzsche (1844–1900) was highly significant not only for the movements discussed here but for the twentieth century as a whole. His "Umwertung aller Werte" (re-evaluation of all values), break with the Christian ethic, and subtle psychological insights into the real nature of human motivation helped to bring about a break with traditional value systems. Still, Nietzsche does not depict the human being as lost and exposed to involuntary forces but created a notion of a superior human being who set high goals not only for others but for himself as well. Artistic vanity probably helped make Nietzsche popular among writers, and a number of major literary figures were attracted to his praise of grandeur and superiority.[2] Nietzsche's influence varied, of course, from artist to artist. Whereas, for instance, his philosophy became a central intellectual and aesthetical impulse for Stefan George (1868–1933), Thomas Mann (1875–1955) and the expressionist poet Gottfried Benn (1886–1956), other writers were influenced only for a short time, and even cooled to Nietzsche in the course of time. The poet and dramatist Hugo von Hofmannsthal (1874–1929), for example, and the poet Rainer Maria Rilke

(1875–1926) altered their outlook toward the philosopher as they matured. Not so Stefan George. In his poem "Nietzsche" (1900), written in the year of Nietzsche's death, George depicts the philosopher as a savior and compares him to Christ: "Dann aber stehst du strahlend vor den zeiten / Wie andre führer mit der blutigen krone"[3] (but then you stand shining before the times / like other leaders with your blood-stained crown). Whereas George's admiration for Nietzsche's stylistic force in such works as *Also sprach Zarathustra* derived from his own idea of a poet's vocation, Hofmannsthal wrote in 1891: "Gut. Also da les' ich gestern Menschliches, Allzumenschliches und esse Kirschenkuchen dabei"[4] (Well, while I was reading *Menschliches, Allzumenschliches* yesterday I ate some cherry-tart). Hofmannsthal maintained an ironic distance to Nietzsche, accusing him of being pathetic and sentimental. Rilke revealed a similar attitude, although his narration *Ewald Tragy* (1898) in which he opposes established society, negates the conventional moral system and favors the creative subject's autonomy — ideas of Nietzschean origin.

Nevertheless, the Nietzschean experience marked a sense of awakening not only in the poets' role within society and within the arts but also in their ways of dealing with language. The poets of the naturalistic period had striven for new ways of expression, of course — writers such as Detlev von Liliencron (1844–1909) and Arno Holz (1864–1929) — but they did so by using everyday motifs and language. Liliencron's poem "Betrunken" (Drunk), for instance, tells of a man getting drunk and finally falling asleep: "Ich bin wieder im Zimmer. / Ich trinke mein achtes Glas Nordnordgrog. / Kinder, erklärt mir das Rätsel der Welt. / Aber Mine und Stine lachen. / Das Rätsel, bitt ich, / Das Rätsel der Welt" (I am in the room again. / I am drinking the eighth glass of northern grog. / Kids, explain the mystery of the world to me. / But Mine and Stine are laughing. / The mystery, please, / The mystery of the world).[5] Whereas naturalistic poetry avoids transcendence and detaches reality from any idealized view, Liliencron's poetry stands on the threshold of impressionism, resembling in style and manner the work of Stefan George, Hugo von Hofmannsthal, or Rainer Maria Rilke. As they break new ground in expression, artistic movements often tend to be inconsistent with politics and social values. Naturalism and impressionism were no exception in this respect. The cultural policies of Wilhelm II (ruled 1888–1918), made the "Pflege der Ideale"[6] (cultivation of ideals) its business and therefore did not approve of these new movements. In 1901, Wilhelm II stated that "die Kunst soll mithelfen, erzieherisch auf das Volk einzuwirken, sie soll auch den unteren Ständen nach harter Mühe und Arbeit die Möglichkeit geben, sich an den Idealen wieder aufzurichten" (art should have an educational effect on the population, it should give even the lower classes the possibility of living according to ideals after great effort and hard work).[7] But imperial authorities were not able to keep the arts on a short leash: the political climate became more and more liberal in the waning years of the century.

Writers grew increasingly self-confident about their role in society as they saw increasing opportunities for earning money in a changing literary market. The production of art increasingly accommodated itself to the market-oriented system around the turn of the century.[8] Publishers had gained increasing importance in the second half of the nineteenth century as mediators between foreign and German literature and as supporters of contemporary literary movements. In 1886 Samuel Fischer founded a publishing house in Berlin that, over time, became one of the most significant cultural forces in German-speaking Europe. He popularized not only major German and Austrian writers of the 1890s such as Gerhart Hauptmann, Hugo von Hofmannsthal, and Arthur Schnitzler (1862–1931) but also foreign authors such as Gabriele d'Annunzio (1863–1938) and Henrik Ibsen (1828–1906).[9] Without Fischer's efforts Ibsen probably would not have become the idol of German naturalism. Fischer also gave support to the next generation of writers who tried to transcend naturalism. He represented a new type of publisher, one who now acted not only as a mediator of literary developments but also as their initiator.[10]

In addition to Vienna, Berlin and Munich became centers of impressionism and symbolism. The development of impressionism and symbolism has to be judged within the context of the increasing urbanization at the end of the nineteenth century. Berlin had grown rapidly since the reunification of the German Empire in 1871. From 1871 until 1890 the number of inhabitants had nearly doubled from 826,000 to 1.57 million, and from 1890 to 1912 the number again increased by a million people. Building could not keep pace with the influx: around 1900, no less than 600,000 people were housed in overcrowded cellars, as shelters for the homeless were overrun. In any case, Berlin's industry had grown particularly in the fields of textiles, metal processing, and mechanical and electrical engineering.

Whereas Berlin represented the modern metropolis, Munich displayed a far more conflicted identity. Liberal and conservative forces clashed, because the programs of the avant-garde contrasted sharply with the *Heimatkunst* movement which distrusted the rapidly changing way of life and the increasing social mobility. Such oppositions, both in a literal and figurative sense, permeated the city's artistic atmosphere. While works of literature metaphorically crossed the border by venturing into other forms of art, the artist themselves literally crossed the border by emphasizing cultural exchange with France. The metropolis, particularly London and Paris, had early on become a popular topos in literature. The rise of the metropolis in Germany and Austria was relatively new, however, and contributed now to German-speaking literature. In Munich, for example the atmosphere and cultural diversity of the big city enabled a lifestyle free from social conventions: "die Verlockung der Anarchie, Geheimlehren als Gegentraditionen des Wissens — dies alles ist hier zu Hause" (the temptation of anarchy, occult doctrines as counter-traditions of knowledge — all this is at home here).[11] Rilke's short poem "Der Panther" lays bare an attitude towards the increasing urbanization and its consequences and effects. In it, Rilke tells of a panther put on display in a cage in the *Jardin des Plantes* in Paris. The insistent iambic rhythm of the verses expresses the animal's denaturalized existence far from its natural setting, its power and beauty reduced to a mere prop, an urban ornament to entertain the passersby. The poem suggests that the urban environment is inimical to human development, and effectively imprisons them and hardens their hearts. The last of the three strophes reads as follows: "Nur manchmal schiebt der Vorhang der Pupille / sich lautlos auf —. Dann geht ein Bild hinein, / geht durch der Glieder angespannte Stille — / und hört im Herzen auf zu sein" (Now and then the pupils' shutter lifts silently. — Then an image goes in, goes through the limbs' intensive stillness, and ceases to be in the heart).[12]

The poet most commonly associated with impressionism is Hugo von Hofmannsthal[13] who broke away from naturalism by emphasizing an active search for meaning, and who rather than using everyday language employed a musical language rich in images. His early poems are characterized by their musicality, by subtle, evocative imagery, and perfection in form. At the age of seventeen Hofmannsthal had not only published poems and plays but also had met Ibsen, had translated Nietzsche into French, read Baudelaire and Mallarmé, Poe, Swinburne, Turgenev, and Strindberg.[14] Hofmannsthal — who had studied Romance languages and literature and had traveled extensively in Italy, Greece, and northern Africa — was, as we see, a product not only of Viennese aestheticism, but of European culture. While in his early poems he strove for aesthetic perfection, l'art pour l'art, he came to realize after the turn of the century that mere aestheticism draws an all too arbitrary dividing line between life and art. He dealt with this problem in his short play *Der Tor und der Tod* (Death and the Fool, 1893) by focusing on a figure unable to cope with life. Claudio, the protagonist, believes that art is a means to manage life, but realizes ultimately that his choice to live in a house full of books and works of art constitutes isolation from life. Ironically, death brings him back to life: the ghosts in the play were, in fact, all once close to Claudio in life, but were eventually exploited by him. They force him to accept the fact that he had closed his mind to the world instead of opening and devoting himself to it. The figure of Claudio reveals Hofmannsthal's own grave doubts about empty aestheticism, culminating in the seminal fictitious letter, "Ein Brief"[15] (translated as *Letter of Lord Chandos,* 1902). Written by a character named Philipp Lord Chandos and addressed to Francis Bacon, the writer explains his abstinence from literary work as an increasing skepticism toward language. "Es ist mir völlig die Fähigkeit abhanden gekommen, über irgend etwas zusammenhängend zu denken oder zu sprechen" (I have utterly lost my ability to think and to speak coherently), the letter writer explains. He continues: "es zerfiel mir alles in Teile, die Teile wieder in Teile, und nichts ließ sich mit einem Begriff umspannen" (everything fell to pieces, and the pieces again fell to pieces, and nothing could be covered by a word).[16] The letter is symptomatic for at least two aspects of the turn of the century Zeitgeist: the *Sprachkrise* (crisis of language), discussed especially by Fritz Mauthner in his *Beiträge zu einer Kritik der Sprache* (Contributions to a Critique of Language, 1901–2), and the crisis of the ego and identity, an issue that became central to the theory of the Viennese *fin de siècle* and which was dealt with by the philosopher Ernst Mach in his work *Beiträge zur Analyse der Empfindungen* (Contributions for an Analysis of Sensations, 1886). Mauthner argues that language is incapable of grasping the world. It does not reproduce reality but creates illusions and deceptions because linguistic structures are always projected onto the world and not vice versa.[17]

In addition to poetry, narrative literature of the 1890s attempted to explore the interior landscape of its protagonists. The variety of narrative forms employed during the impressionist era derived from the decreasing relevance of traditional demarcations of literary genres and reflected a more general, all-pervasive loss of orientation in society and politics. The decline of traditional values and norms included rapid changes in living conditions as a consequence of rapid progress in the sciences and in technology, urbanization, the increasing relevance of the women's movement,[18] and finally, the gradual decline of the Habsburg Empire after the *fin de siècle*. In addition to the proliferation of narrative forms, elements of dramatic and poetic texts were often mixed with narrative elements.

In contrast to many impressionist authors Thomas Mann used narrative forms such as the novella and the novel in a deceptively traditional manner. Mann had grown up in an upper middle class family in Lübeck and, like Hofmannsthal, had begun writing while still in school.[19] In 1893 he became co-editor of the periodical *Frühlingssturm: Monatsschrift für Kunst, Litteratur und Philosophie* in which he published short poems and prose works under the pen name Paul Thomas. After moving to Munich in 1893 Mann worked as a trainee at an insurance company and published his novella *Gefallen* (Fallen) in 1894. In the following years Mann wrote several novellas such as *Enttäuschung* (Disappointment), *Der Bajazzo,* and in 1898 his novella *Der kleine Herr Friedemann* (translated as *Little Herr Friedemann*). In the summer of 1897 both Thomas Mann and his brother Heinrich moved to Italy living on the outskirts of Rome. Thomas had been invited by his publisher Samuel Fischer to write a novel and started preparations for his long novel *Buddenbrooks: Der Verfall einer Familie* (Buddenbrooks: The Decline of a Family, 1901). In this work the author depicts four generations of the wealthy merchant family Buddenbrook, living, like Mann's family, in Lübeck. The physical decline of the family, with a concomitant increase in its spirituality, culminates in the sensitive, artistically gifted, but weak Hanno Buddenbrook. Hanno's immersion in art is accompanied by a decrease in his ability to cope with life. With their weak mental condition and propensity for melancholy and depression, most of the Buddenbrook family members are archetypal *decadence* figures. In fact Schopenhauer's theory of negating the will of life in order to overcome the ailment of life finds literary expression in Mann's conception of these figures.

Symbolism

Like impressionism, symbolism also proceeded from the conception of the incompatibility of the "real" object and its depiction in a work of art. Contrary to impressionist theory, however, in symbolism the significance of the artistic representation goes beyond the visible reality and is, theoretically at least, not derived from a personal mood or sensation. Rather, it is split into several potential meanings, none of which makes a claim for any factual knowledge of the depicted reality. As Ingo Stoehr puts it, "while impressionism diffused reality into a series of sense impressions, symbolism focused it by way of a 'magic word' whose function was to lead to the secret truths."[20] A "realistic" or naturalistic image of the world is, in short, as foreign to symbolist art as it is to impressionism.

Impressionism and symbolism sought to reform not only the arts but life itself. Both movements explored life with particular attention to the increasing industrialization, mechanization, and modernization of everyday existence. Many impressionist artists lived in cities and were therefore concerned with urban themes and motifs. But impressionism did not focus exclusively on modern life and related concerns about the advantages and disadvantages of technical and scientific progress; rather, it championed a highly aestheticized way of life, one characterized by a passive and contemplative attitude focused on the fleetingness of being and the disobliging manner of experience. Stefan George, for instance, withdrew from everyday life to preside over an elitist circle of friends and followers who had established their own rules of admission.[21] Through this circle, George created a refuge from a world of whose ever increasing technical obsessions he could not approve. He saw himself as saving literature from the plebeian "decay" it had experienced in the period of naturalism. George's early artistic period was thus characterized by a cult of beauty and belief in *l'art-pour-l'art*. He wrote for a small group of readers instead of addressing the mass public, created his own eccentric orthography, punctuation, and saw to it that his books made use of *Jugendstil* font and design. In 1890 only 100 copies of his *Hymnen* were published. In this collection of seventeen solemn and esoteric, yet immature poems, he speaks of a realm of art to which only the enlightened have access. Although strophes, meters, and rhymes are designed in a traditional, even classical manner, these early poems betray a number of characteristics that have become typical for George's poetry: his tendency toward spare diction, in which every superfluous word is dropped. Articles, prepositions, conjunctions, prefixes, and even verbs are banished from these texts. Despite his minimalist use of such words, George drew on a rich, exotic vocabulary filled with unusual and archaic terms. George discussed with Hofmannsthal[22] the publication of a periodical devoted to this new kind of poetry he championed. In October 1892 the first volume of George's *Blätter für die Kunst* appeared containing works among others by George, Hofmannsthal, and the Belgian poet Paul Gérardy (1885–1974). In his introduction George states programmatically and in his characteristically lower-cased nouns: "Der name dieser veröffentlichung sagt schon zum teil was sie soll: der kunst besonders der dichtung und dem schrifttum dienen, alles staatliche und gesellschaftliche ausscheidend" (the title of this publication partly tells about its intention: to serve art, particularly poetry and literature, excluding all matters of state and society).[23] His literary magazine appeared until 1919. It was not sold in bookstores but was distributed solely among friends and followers. There arose a kind of George cult, one that to some extent exists still today.

While George's volumes of poems published in the 1890s — *Algabal* (1892), *Die Bücher der Hirten- und Preisgedichte, der Sagen und Sänge und der hängenden Gärten* (The Book of Pastoral and Poems of Praise, of Myths and Songs and Hanging Gardens, 1895), *Das Jahr der Seele* (The Year of the Soul, 1897), *Der Teppich des Lebens* (The Tapestry of Life, 1900) — followed the tradition of French symbolism and glorified an aristocratic human being in the Nietzschean sense, his best known poems were published in *Der siebente Ring* (The Seventh Ring, 1907) and praised a god named Maximin, an actual person who figured prominently in George's life. George was attracted to Maximilian Kronberger (1886–1904), a young man from Munich, whom he admitted into his poetic circle. The poems attack modern materialism and decry the teeming crowds of the Berlin megalopolis, contrasting them to the dignity and purity of the old Church and the aged Pope Leo XIII.

The early works of the Prague writer Rainer Maria Rilke (1875–1926), influenced by French authors as Stéphane Mallarmé (1842–1898) and Maurice Maeterlinck (1862–1949), demonstrate the extent to which symbolism was an international phenomenon.[24] Rilke's knowledge of several

European languages and his comprehensive education almost predestined him to a creative reception of foreign literatures. His work in the 1890s contrasted strongly with his later literary career. In the earlier period he was a prolific poet, having written several hundred poems for publication in local newspapers. In later years, though, Rilke withdrew from this busy urban and literary life, leaving behind bourgeois convention and devoting himself to his literary work.

A year before moving to Munich in 1896, Rilke began his study of philosophy, literature, art, and law in Prague. In 1895, Rilke also started to write plays, including the little-known *Im Frühlingsfrost* (In the Frost of Spring) and *Jetzt und in der Stunde unseres Absterbens* (Now and in the Hour of our Death, 1896). These works still followed naturalistic conventions — persons from lower class backgrounds were depicted in a realistic manner. Naturalistic elements can also be seen in *Höhenluft* (Mountain Air, 1897), in which the protagonist is a seamstress disowned by her family when she has an illegitimate child. In Munich Rilke was acquainted with the playwright Ludwig Ganghofer (1855–1920) and the then popular novelist Jakob Wassermann (1873–1934). The latter introduced him to the works of the Danish writer Jens Peter Jacobsen (1847–1885) who became a major influence on Rilke. The influence of Danish literature in general must not be underestimated in the poet's early years. Rilke read the works of the Danish poet, actor, and stage-director Hermann Bang (1857–1912) and Søren Kierkegaard (1813–1855) and it is not coincidental that the fictitious writer of *Die Aufzeichnungen des Malte Laurids Brigge* (translated as *The Notebooks of Malte Laurids Brigge,* 1910) is Danish. In 1897, Wassermann arranged an influential meeting with another of his acquaintances, the writer and feminist Lou Andreas-Salomé (1861–1937). This meeting turned out to be highly significant, as it initiated a long close personal as well as artistic friendship between the two. Andreas-Salomé had studied with Nietzsche in Rome, befriended Sigmund Freud in 1911, and established her own psychoanalytic practice in Göttingen in 1915. Together with Lou and the architect August Endell, Rilke moved to Wolfratshausen in Bavaria in 1897. His poems of this period were strongly influenced by his love for Andreas-Salomé.

From the mid-1890s on, Rilke immersed himself in Renaissance culture and in April 1898 went to Florence to deepen his knowledge of the period. Rilke's interest in foreign literature and culture was manifold: together with the aforementioned French and Danish influences, Russian language and literature became central for him. Together with Andreas-Salomé he traveled to Russia in 1899 and 1900, probably in the hope of creating a new sense of home and belonging for himself — yet another attempt to escape his bourgeois origin. His meeting with Leo Tolstoy both in 1899 and 1900 further increased his admiration for the Russian culture; Rilke developed a perception of pious Russian peasants and the boundless spaces of the Russian landscape that were more poetic and mystical than objective reality. Consequently, the poems written after this Russian sojourn are marked by an intensely religious tone, as though the poet found intimations of the divine in everything he saw. The literary result of this experience are the narrations collected in *Geschichten vom lieben Gott* (translated as *Stories of God*, 1904), the *Stunden-Buch* (translated as *The Book of Hours*, 1905), and the poem *Die Weise von Liebe und Tod des Cornets Christoph Rilke* (translated as *Lay of the Love and Death of Cornet Christoph Rilke*, 1906). Rilke's anti-bourgeois sentiments — to a great extent influenced by Nietzsche's elitist critique of society — are further reflected in his autobiographical short story *Ewald Tragy*, written in 1898 and published posthumously in 1929.

The 1890s saw remarkable developments in German-language drama. In *Frühlingserwachen: Eine Kindertragödie* Frank Wedekind (1864–1918) depicts the awakening sexuality of two young people falling victim to the moral values of their time. A fourteen-year-old school girl dies of an unsuccessful abortion and her equally young friend is expelled from school, escapes from a reformatory and contemplates suicide. The play calls the principles of bourgeois education into doubt and questions the prevailing moral prudishness of the time. Its structure — nineteen loosely connected scenes — is reminiscent of Georg Büchner's plays, for example, of *Woyzeck* (published 1875–78, first staged in 1913). Due to its attack on social grievances and frank portrayal of sexual matters, *Frühlingserwachen* was not performed until 1906, fifteen years after it had been written. Wedekind's plays *Erdgeist* (The Earth Spirit, 1895) and *Die Büchse der Pandora* (Pandora's Box, 1902) focus on the female protagonist Lulu, whose attraction is fatal. Dominated by her libido, she subjects men to her rule, dominates and exploits them, and finally perishes at the hands of Jack the Ripper. Again Wedekind thematizes the irruption of eros and irrationality into a seemingly neat and tidy world, and in so doing uncovers its hidden, socially destructive forces.

Analogous to the impressionists' preference for short prose sketches, the playwrights of this time were particularly fond of one-act plays (*Einakter*). Contemporary authors and theorists developed the concept of a *Konversationseinakter* and a *Katastropheneinakter,* a *Handlungseinakter* (action one-act play) and, most important, *Stimmungseinakter* (atmosphere one-act play).[25] The latter presents figures in a certain mood, emphasizes their fleeting thoughts and views and tends toward lyrical reflection rather than action. The most prominent authors using this form were Hugo von Hofmannsthal (*Gestern* [Yesterday, 1891], *Der Tor und der Tod* [The Fool and Death, 1894], *Das kleine Welttheater oder die Glücklichen* [The Small World Theater or The Happy Ones, 1903]) and Arthur Schnitzler (*Anatol* [1893], *Reigen* [Rondo, 1903], and *Marionetten* [Marionettes, 1906]).

Fin-de-siècle Austria

At the beginning of the 1890s a group of writers calling themselves "Junges Wien" (Young Vienna) — Arthur Schnitzler, Richard Beer-Hofmann (1866–1945), Peter Altenberg (1862–1919), Hugo von Hofmannsthal, and Leopold von Andrian — created with this organization a counterweight to German naturalism. A key figure for the Young Vienna group was Hermann Bahr (1863–1934), who provided the theoretical basis for turn-of-the-century literature in Austria and termed it the "Wiener Moderne." Bahr not only supported the Young Vienna group, particularly Hofmannsthal, but also supported the arts in general. He was born in Linz, had studied in Vienna and Berlin, and lived in Salzburg, Vienna, and Munich.[26] In one of his most renowned essays, *Die Überwindung des Naturalismus* (The Defeat of Naturalism, 1891), he criticized naturalistic literature for its lack of psychological insight. Modernism in Bahr's view entailed three phases: the first was naturalism, which depicts the outer social reality. The second phase analyses psychological issues, and in the third phase, which Bahr termed "Nervenkunst" (nerve art)[27] the *Seelenzustände* (conditions of the soul) were described with the purpose of presenting a highly personal, detailed, and subjective point of view. Therefore, Bahr's notion of *Seelenzustände* equates with the general notion of impressionism.

A survey of Austrian turn-of-the-century culture would be incomplete without a mention of the graphic arts, especially several artists' efforts to rejuvenate the field. The Vienna Secession, an organization of painters, designers, and architects, was founded by Gustav Klimt (1862–1918) in 1897. He became the group's first president but left in 1905 after a falling out with the architect Josef Hoffmann (1870–1956). The secessionists pleaded for freedom of individual artistic creation and argued against traditional academic art. Their most ambitious effort was to attempt to integrate art into everyday culture. Klimt, for instance, not only created a number of paintings, murals, and ceiling frescos but also provided the fashion and jewelry industry with models and designs. Egon Schiele (1890–1918), one of the most prominent Austrian painters in the twentieth century, owes his late fame to a Secessionist exhibition shortly before his death. He had become acquainted with Klimt in 1907 and developed his characteristic style — ornamental structure and the use of intense colors — under Klimt's influence and with the use of East-Asian models. Oskar Kokoschka's (1886–1980) early paintings and prints also show parallels to the linear style of the Secessionists, although he was soon recognized internationally as an important proponent of expressionist art. In his plays *Sphinx und Strohmann* (Sphinx and Strawman, 1907), *Mörder, Hoffnung der Frauen* (Murderer, Hope of Women, 1909), *Der brennende Dornbusch* (The Burning Bush, 1911), or *Orpheus und Eurydike* (1915) he minimized action, included pantomime and dance, and employed a pathetic, expressive language.

An author who decidedly did not turn his back on the historical reality of his time was the satirist, playwright, and editor Karl Kraus (1874–1936). In 1898 he created his own satirical and critical journal, the first issue of which appeared on April 1, 1899. *Die Fackel* (The Torch)[28] became Kraus's most long-term and important publication, in which he discussed political, social, economic, and literary issues. The periodical presented a highly critical and witty satire of Austrian culture. Kraus stated that "in der 'Fackel' eigentlich jahraus jahrein nichts anderes geschieht, als ein Ich mit der Zeit konfrontieren" (in the "Torch" nothing else happens year in, year out other than confronting an Ego with the times).[29] Kraus followed this intention until his death in 1936. *Die Fackel* appeared three times a month from 1899 until 1904 and thereafter at irregular intervals. Kraus's feat was to write all contributions completely by himself for the journal from February 1911 until 1936. He was also the author of a very lengthy and ambitious play, *Die letzten Tage der Menschheit* (The Last Days of Mankind, 1915–19), in which he analyzed the horrific events and consequences of the First World War.

One could argue that this form of "Nervenkunst" was fertile ground and an almost ideal prerequisite for the successful dissemination of Sigmund Freud's psychoanalysis in the field of artistic creation. Yet Freud was not met with unanimous approval, but with mistrust and rejection. Karl Kraus, for instance, argued that psychoanalysis was the disease pretending to be the cure, and the novelist Robert Musil remained skeptical as well. The physician and writer Arthur Schnitzler (1862–1931) was one of the authors closest to Freud's theories. His early stories such as *Frühlingsnacht im Seziersaal* (Spring Night in the Dissecting Room, 1880), *Der Sohn* (The Son, 1892), or *Der Empfindsame* (The Sentimental Man, 1895) show astonishing similarities to what Freud later described in his psychoanalytical works. Nevertheless their personal relationship remained distant throughout their lives.[30] They even used to write letters to each other rather than meet personally although they lived in the same Viennese district for some time.

Like his father Johann Schnitzler, Arthur Schnitzler[31] studied medicine and worked at the *Allgemeines Krankenhaus* in Vienna as a laryngologist. As a medical doctor Schnitzler was concerned with hypnosis and psychiatry.[32] In 1887 he had become the editor of the *Internationale Klinische Rundschau,* a medical journal founded by his father. His first literary publication dates back to November 1880 and in the following decade he published a number of prose works, poems and the comedy *Das Abenteuer seines Lebens* (The Adventure of His Life, 1891). In 1890 he came into contact with the Young Vienna group and in the years to come he published several plays such as *Die Frage an das Schicksal* (The Question to Fate, 1896), and *Anatols Hochzeitsmorgen* (Anatol's Wedding Morning, 1901). Schnitzler's most successful play of this period is *Liebelei* (translated as *Playing with Love*, 1895) which tells of the love of a young suburban woman for a wealthy man who does not reciprocate her affection. His most important plays, though, were staged after the turn of the century, such as *Reigen* (Rondo, 1900),[33] *Der einsame Weg* (translated as *The Lonely Way*, 1904), *Das weite Land* (The Wide Land), or *Professor Bernhardi* (1912). Whereas the protagonists of Schnitzler's early plays exemplify the superficiality of social types of the time, such as the young officer, the young girl from the lower classes, and so on, the later plays contain considerable social criticism. *Professor Bernhardi*, for instance, explores the anti-Semitism with which the Jewish director of a clinic has to cope.

Schnitzler's novellas, novels, and stories were overshadowed by his plays — with a few exceptions. Some of the prose, however, is still read today. *Leutnant Gustl* (translated as *Lieutenant Gustl*), published December 25, 1900 in the *Neue Freie Presse*, produced an unpleasant effect: The author was accused of defaming the Austrian military and as a consequence was stripped of his reserve officer rank. This novella is most memorable from a stylistic standpoint through its use of interior monologue. Gustl's story exemplifies not only the disintegration of a single person, but also that of society as a whole and further, as Magris suggests, symbolizes the crisis in the Austro-Hungarian world, its inconsistencies and instabilities.[34] In Schnitzler's *Traumnovelle* (translated as *Dream Story*, 1926), the literary project comes close to what Freud had discovered in the field of dream research. The story tells of a couple, Albertine and Fridolin, revealing their conscious and unconscious erotic lives and desires. As in psychoanalysis, the dreams in the novella serve as a medium for the characters to discover something new about one another.

Although Peter Altenberg[35] is commonly associated with the Young Vienna group, he remained an outsider to both that group and to society. His prose sketches, modest in length and unpretentious, describe Viennese characters, moods, and impressions. Having broken off several courses of study and an apprenticeship as a bookseller, Altenberg was diagnosed with the disability, "Überempfindlichkeit des Nervensystems" (hypersensitivity of the nervous system). As a regular guest at the famous Café Griensteidl in the 1890s, the major meeting-place for the Young Vienna group, Altenberg became friends with Schnitzler, the essayists Egon Friedell (1878–1938), Alfred Polgar (1873–1955), and especially Karl Kraus, who later became one of his most passionate promoters. In the last decade of his life, Altenberg was forced to spend much of his time in mental hospitals. His rhetorical talent and public life — he used to stay up in cafés and bars all night and slept in hotel rooms all day — gave him renown not only with the artists of his time but even with the tourists. Altenberg is the most prominent author associated with a genre typical for Viennese literature at the *fin de siècle, Kaffeehausliteratur,* though the term implies not so much a single literary genre as the place where literature was written. Short texts, commissioned works for newspapers, letters, reviews, aphorisms and the like comprised the literature itself. Analogous to Hofmannsthal's skepticism toward language, Altenberg's brevity and conciseness strive to leave things unsaid that cannot be said: "Was man 'weise verschweigt' ist künstlerischer, als was man 'geschwätzig ausspricht'!" (What is wisely kept secret is more artistic than what is expressed garrulously).[36]

The next decade saw literature continue to flourish in Germany and Austria by expanding and intensifying the artistic innovations of the 1890s.

Notes

[1] See Arnold Hauser, *Sozialgeschichte der Kunst und Literatur* (Munich: C. H. Beck, 1990; first edition 1953), 927–91.

[2] See Theo Meyer, *Nietzsche und die Kunst* (Tübingen / Basel: Francke, 1993) and Raymond Furness, *Zarathustra's Children: A Study of a Lost Generation of German Writers* (Rochester, NY: Camden House, 2000).

[3] Quoted in Theo Meyer, *Nietzsche und die Kunst,* 179.

[4] Quoted in Theo Meyer, *Nietzsche und die Kunst,* 189.

[5] Detlev von Liliencron, "Betrunken," in D. v. L., *Gedichte,* edited by Günter Heintz (Stuttgart: Reclam, 1997), 89–92, here 91. "Betrunken" was first published in *Neue Gedichte* (1892).

[6] Wolfgang Mommsen, "Die Kultur der Moderne im Deutschen Kaiserreich," in *Die Wiener Jahrhundertwende: Einflüsse — Umwelt — Wirkungen,* edited by Jürgen Nautz and Richard Vahrenkamp (Vienna / Cologne / Graz: Böhlau, 1993), 866.

[7] Franz Herre, *Jahrhundertwende 1900: Untergangsstimmung und Fortschrittsglauben* (Stuttgart: Deutsche Verlags-Anstalt, 1998), 45.

[8] For a comprehensive analysis of the economic situation of German writers see Britta Scheideler, "Zwischen Beruf und Berufung: Zur Sozialgeschichte der deutschen Schriftsteller von 1880 bis 1933," in *Archiv für Geschichte des Buchwesens* 46 (1997), 1–336.

[9] For a history of the S. Fischer Verlag see Peter de Mendelssohn, *S. Fischer und sein Verlag* (Frankfurt am Main: S. Fischer, 1970).

[10] Reiner Stach, *100 Jahre S. Fischer Verlag 1886–1986: Kleine Verlagsgeschichte* (Frankfurt am Main: S. Fischer, 1986), 19.

[11] Walter Schmitz, ed., *Die Münchner Moderne: Die literarische Szene in der "Kunststadt" um die Jahrhundertwende* (Stuttgart: Reclam, 1990), 19.

[12] Rainer Maria Rilke, "Der Panther," in Rainer Maria Rilke, *Werke,* vol. 1.2: Gedicht-Zyklen (Frankfurt am Main: Insel, 1986), 261.

[13] See Jacques Le Rider, *Hugo von Hofmannsthal: Historismus und Moderne in der Literatur der Jahrhundertwende* (Vienna: Böhlau, 1997).

[14] See Robert Vilain, *The Poetry of Hugo von Hofmannsthal and French Symbolism* (Oxford: Clarendon Press, 2000).

[15] Hugo von Hofmannsthal, "Ein Brief," in H. v. H., *Der Brief des Lord Chandos: Schriften zur Literatur, Kunst und Geschichte* (Stuttgart: Reclam, 2000), 46–59. The letter was first published in *Der Tag*, no. 489 and 491, October 18/19, 1902.

[16] Hofmannsthal, *Ein Brief*, 50, 52.

[17] See Dagmar Lorenz, *Wiener Moderne* (Stuttgart / Weimar: Metzler, 1995), 153.

[18] See Horst Thomé, "Modernität und Bewusstseinswandel in der Zeit des Naturalismus und des Fin de siècle," in *Naturalismus, Fin de siècle, Expressionismus, 1890–1918*, edited by York-Gothart Mix (Munich: Deutscher Taschenbuch Verlag, 2000), 15–27.

[19] See Gert Heine, *Thomas Mann Chronik* (Frankfurt am Main: Klostermann, 2004); Harald Höbusch, *Thomas Mann: Kunst, Kritik, Politik, 1893–1913* (Tübingen: Francke, 2000).

[20] Ingo Stoehr, *German Literature of the Twentieth Century: From Aestheticism to Postmodernism* (Rochester, NY: Camden House, 2001), 24.

[21] See Michael Winkler, "Der George-Kreis," in *Naturalismus, Fin de siècle, Expressionismus, 1890–1918*, edited by York-Gothart Mix (Munich: Deutscher Taschenbuch Verlag, 2000), 231–42; Robert E. Norton, *Secret Germany: Stefan George and His Circle* (Ithaca, NY: Cornell UP, 2002).

[22] See Jens Rieckmann, *Hugo von Hofmannsthal und Stefan George: Signifikanz einer "Episode" aus der Jahrhundertwende* (Tübingen: Francke, 1997).

[23] Quoted by Franz Schonauer, *Stefan George* (Reinbek: Rowohlt, 2000), 36.

[24] For a recent publication on Rilke see Rüdiger Görner, *Rainer Maria Rilke: Im Herzwerk der Sprache* (Vienna: Zsolnay, 2004); see also Helmut Naumann, *Rainer Maria Rilke: Stufen seines Werkes* (Rheinfelden: Schäuble, 1995).

[25] See Hartmut Vinçon, "Einakter und kleine Dramen," in *Naturalismus, Fin de siècle, Expressionismus, 1890–1918*, edited by York-Gothart Mix (Munich: Deutscher Taschenbuch Verlag, 2000), 369.

[26] For a biography on Bahr see Reinhard Farkas, *Hermann Bahr: Dynamik und Dilemma der Moderne* (Vienna / Cologne: Böhlau, 1989).

[27] See Dagmar Lorenz, *Wiener Moderne*, 44.

[28] See Heinz Lunzer, Victoria Lunzer-Talos, and Marcus G. Patka, eds., *"Was wir umbringen": 'Die Fackel' von Karl Kraus* (Vienna: Mandelbaum, 1999).

[29] *"Was wir umbringen,"* 9.

[30] Sigmund Freud, "Briefe an Arthur Schnitzler," edited by Heinrich Schnitzler, in *Neue Rundschau* 66 (1955), 95–106. For an analysis of the pre-Freudian aspects in Schnitzler's works see Frederick J. Beharriell, "Schnitzler, Freuds Doppelgänger," in *Literatur und Kritik* (1967), 546–55.

[31] For a recent analysis of Schnitzler's life and works see Konstanze Fliedl, *Arthur Schnitzler: Poetik der Erinnerung* (Vienna: Böhlau, 1997) and *Arthur Schnitzler: Zeitgenossenschaften / Contemporaneities*, edited by Ian Foster (Bern / Vienna: Lang, 2002).

[32] See, for instance, Arthur Schnitzler, *Über funktionelle Aphonie und deren Behandlung durch Hypnose und Suggestion* (Vienna: Braumüller, 1889).

[33] The play was written in 1896–97 and first staged in 1912. Schnitzler printed 200 copies in 1900 which were not intended for sale. For the play's reception see Alfred Pfoser, Kristina Pfoser-Schewig, and Gerhard Renner, *Schnitzlers 'Reigen': Zehn Dialoge und ihre Skandalgeschichte. Analysen und Dokumente.* 2 vols. (Frankfurt am Main: Fischer Taschenbuch Verlag, 1993).

[34] See Claudio Magris, *Der habsburgische Mythos in der österreichischen Literatur.*

[35] For Altenberg's biography see Andrew Barker, *Telegrams from the Soul: Peter Altenberg and the Culture of fin-de-siècle Vienna* (Columbia, SC: Camden House, 1996).

[36] Quoted in Dagmar Lorenz, *Wiener Moderne,* 179.

Part III

Genres

The Absence of Drama in Nineteenth-Century Germany

Benjamin Bennett

T HE TITLE OF COURSE puts me out on a limb, but in fact I would be
prepared to argue that the assertion it presupposes is a relatively
modest one. Under different circumstances I might have written on "The
Absence of Drama in the Nineteenth Century." This chapter attempts to
cover both the broad theoretical and historical points that support that
larger assertion, and the specific situation in German-speaking Europe,
including three particularly interesting cases from German literature.

The Literary-Historical Context

"Nineteenth-century German drama," as it is viewed by most German historians of literature, develops largely in relation to a central tradition of
works in the manner of Schiller's verse plays and, at a further remove, supposedly in the manner of Shakespeare. But even while the principal
upholders of this classical tradition, Franz Grillparzer (1791–1872) and
Friedrich Hebbel (1813–1863), spent most of their careers in Vienna —
although performances of Hebbel took place mainly in Germany, and
Grillparzer refused to show his work to a supposedly ungrateful public
after 1838 — Vienna is also the home of theatrical conventions that have
nothing to do with the classical. Especially prominent is the tradition of
Viennese popular comedy, which in the nineteenth century produced
two significant dramatic types, the "Zauberstück" (magical or fantasy
piece), represented mainly by Ferdinand Raimund (1790–1836), and
the "Lokalstück" or "Lokalposse" (dialect farce), represented mainly by
Johann Nestroy (1801–1862). Aspects of this whole complex of conventions, including the use of singing, still operate later in both the comic and
the more or less tragic works of Ludwig Anzengruber (1839–1889).

In the rest of German-speaking post-Napoleonic Europe, outside
Vienna, although there was a decent number of flourishing theaters, it is
safe to say that the practice of *drama*, the production of significant literary
works in the various theatrical genres, was at best sporadic. There were a
few major figures, but there is not much that connects them with one

another, historically, geographically, professionally or personally. Georg Büchner (1813–1837), now recognized as a dramatist of at least European stature and as one of the principal forerunners of modernism in drama, had no connection with any theater in his lifetime; no play of his was performed until 1910. Christian Dietrich Grabbe (1801–1836), whose experimental works were rediscovered by the expressionists, did see one of his plays performed, but drank himself to an early death. Otto Ludwig (1813–1865), by contrast, managed to put together a respectable literary career, which included several well-regarded if conventionally realist dramas, a couple of stage successes, and a series of Shakespeare studies. But once we get beyond these few names — assuming we leave to one side the works and projects of Richard Wagner — we find ourselves reduced to listing decidedly minor authors, and basing our choices mainly on the accidents of theatrical popularity. Most literary historians would find it impossible, for instance, to omit mentioning Gustav Freytag (1816–1895), because of the immense popularity of his comedy *Die Journalisten* (1852), even though neither this play itself nor Freytag's contribution, with *Die Technik des Dramas* (1863), to the theory of the well-made play, has any historical significance whatever in the development of the theatrical genres.

It is, in fact, not until the very end of the nineteenth century that theatrical life and practice in German-speaking Europe began once more to crystallize into what one can reasonably speak of as a "German drama." This development had two main centers: Vienna, of course, where in the 1890s the creative and critical work of Arthur Schnitzler (1862–1931), Hermann Bahr (1863–1934) and Hugo von Hofmannsthal (1874–1929) produced a drama that is generally regarded as early modernist and is referred more to the twentieth century than to the nineteenth; and Berlin, where, from the 1880s on, the *Deutsches Theater,* and especially the *Freie Bühne* (Free Stage) under Otto Brahm (1856–1912), provided a forum for forward-looking European drama in general, and in particular for emerging German naturalist playwrights like Gerhart Hauptmann (1862–1946). Although late-century German drama in Berlin is also regarded as early modernist and referred mainly to the twentieth century, I think a case can be made for treating at least early Hauptmann as nineteenth-century drama.

To recapitulate, the tradition of Schillerian verse drama is represented mainly by Grillparzer and Hebbel, the principal instances being: Grillparzer's *Sappho* (1818), the trilogy *Das goldene Vlieβ* (The Golden Fleece, 1822), *König Ottokars Glück und Ende* (King Ottokar's Prosperity and Demise, 1825), and *Des Meeres und der Liebe Wellen* (Waves of the Sea and of Love, 1831), plus the manuscript plays that were published posthumously, including *Libussa, Die Jüdin von Toledo* (The Jewess of Toledo), and *Ein Bruderzwist in Habsburg* (A Fraternal Conflict in Habsburg); and Hebbel's *Genoveva* (1843), *Herodes und Mariamne* (1850), *Gyges und sein*

Ring (Gyges and His Ring, 1856), and *Die Nibelungen* (1862), a dramatic trilogy. But both playwrights also produced works that do not fit the Schillerian mold. Grillparzer's early Gothic tragedy *Die Ahnfrau* (The Ancestress, 1817), and his later "dramatic fairy tale" *Der Traum ein Leben* (The Dream Is a Life, 1834), are written in a trochaic meter that alludes to Spanish dramatic conventions; several of Hebbel's major works are written in prose, including the early tragedy *Judith* (1841), the "bourgeois tragedy" *Maria Magdalene* (1844), and the "German tragedy" *Agnes Bernauer* (1855).

Of works associated with the traditions of Viennese popular theater, the most important are Raimund's *Der Bauer als Millionär oder Das Mädchen aus der Feenwelt* (The Peasant as Millionaire or The Girl from the Fairy World, 1826), *Der Alpenkönig und der Menschenfeind* (The Alpine King and the Misanthrope, 1828), and *Der Verschwender* (The Squanderer, 1834); Nestroy's *Der böse Geist Lumpacivagabundus oder Das liederliche Kleeblatt* (The Evil Spirit Lumpacivagabundus or The Three Wastrels, 1833), *Zu ebener Erde und erster Stock* (On the Ground Floor and One Floor Up, 1835), *Der Talisman* (1840), *Einen Jux will er sich machen* (He Wants to Have Himself a Time, 1842), *Der Zerrissene* (The Conflicted One, 1844), *Der Unbedeutende* (The Insignificant One, 1846), and *Freiheit in Krähwinkel* (Freedom in Krähwinkel, 1848); and Anzengruber's *Der Meineidbauer* (The Perjured Peasant, 1871), *Die Kreuzelschreiber* (The Signers with Their "X," 1872), *Doppelselbstmord* (Double Suicide, 1876), and *Das vierte Gebot* (The Fourth Commandment, 1877*)*.

For the rest: Büchner's entire dramatic output consists of two plays, *Dantons Tod* (Danton's Death) and *Leonce und Lena,* plus one fragmentary play, *Woyzeck.* Only *Dantons Tod* was published, in garbled form, during the author's lifetime. Grabbe's major works are: *Scherz, Satire, Ironie und tiefere Bedeutung* (Jest, Satire, Irony and Deeper Meaning, 1827), *Don Juan und Faust* (1829), and *Napoleon oder Die hundert Tage* (Napoleon or The Hundred Days, 1831). And in the field of drama, Otto Ludwig is remembered mainly for *Der Erbförster* (The Hereditary Forester, 1850) and *Die Makkabäer* (The Maccabees, 1854).

The Supposed Perfection of the Work of Art

Goethe was fond of using organic metaphors, especially from the realm of plant life, for processes in the domain of art or culture. But with regard to his own work, we must be careful not to take such metaphors too seriously. "[Er] wächst wie ein Orangebaum sehr langsam. Daß er nur auch wohlschmeckende Früchte trage" (It is growing very slowly, like an orange-tree, and let us hope that it bears good-tasting fruit), he writes to Duke Carl August (19 Feb. 1789), referring — of all things — to *Torquato Tasso,* a thoroughly unsettled and unsettling work, certainly one of the least "good-tasting" plays ever written in German. And with reference to *Faust,* he invokes the (for him) organically founded concept of completeness when he writes to Schiller (27 June 1797) that "das Ganze" (the whole) will remain a "Fragment," as if these concepts were not opposites.

But even if Goethe is either careless or (as I think) disingenuous when he uses the idea of the work's organic totality or unity, still it is true that at the time he was writing, this idea had already established itself firmly in European thinking. Winckelmann manages to combine the ideas of artistic unity and artistic imitation of nature when he suggests that one reason for the beauty of Greek sculpture might be that the actual natural bodies of the Greeks possessed more artistic unity than other bodies.[1] This same combination of the natural (including ideas like vitality and variety) with the thoroughly organized, which adds up to organic unity or perfection, in fact characterizes a great deal of eighteenth-century aesthetic thought, including Batteux's idea of the imitation of beautiful nature, Hutcheson's "uniformity amidst variety," and similar ideas in, say, Hemsterhuis and Hogarth. And the whole tendency reaches a theoretical climax in Germany: with Lessing's insistence, in *Laokoon,* on integrating the work's content and its mode of presentation; with Kant's and Schiller's insistence on the uniqueness and significance of aesthetic experience; and most obviously with Karl Philipp Moritz's "Versuch einer Vereinigung aller schönen Künste und Wissenschaften unter dem Begriff des *in sich Vollendeten"* (Attempt to Unify All of Beaux Arts and Belles Lettres under the Concept of *That Which Is Complete in Itself,* 1785), which insists not only on the organic integrity of the individual work, but also on the strict autonomy of the whole artistic domain.

In relation to literature, however, where it is much more difficult than in painting or sculpture or architecture to describe a work's unity, the idea of artistic perfection requires reinforcement, and receives it, especially in Germany, from the development of German systematic philosophy, as represented by Kant and Fichte and particularly by Hegel. The claim of perfect systematicity in texts like Kant's *Critique of Pure Reason* (whose basic content, Kant insists, cannot be contradicted without contradicting "reason itself") or Hegel's *Phenomenology of Mind* (whose own unfolding as an argument is supposed to be nothing other than the unfolding of consciousness that it describes), the claim, in other words, that a text can somehow gather up its own premises into its structure and thus exist and operate as an entirely self-contained unit, is of crucial importance in the history not only of philosophy, but also of our creative aims in producing, and our critical aims in studying, works of poetic literature. The idea of the perfectly self-contained work of poetry, I mean, is in large measure modeled after the idea of the perfectly systematic work of philosophy.

It is appropriate, therefore, that the one nineteenth-century author who unabashedly pretends to outdo Goethe in the matter of precisely that organicism with which Goethe himself was almost proverbially associated, should be Friedrich Hebbel (1813–1863), who was certainly a fervent (not to say rabid) Hegelian, and may in fact have managed to become such without benefit of any actual study of Hegel. In the foreword to his bourgeois tragedy *Maria Magdalene,* he compares Goethe, as author of the novel *Die Wahlverwandtschaften* (Elective Affinities, 1809), to "einem zerstreuten Zergliederer . . . der, statt eines wirklichen Körpers, ein Automat auf das anatomische Theater brächte"[2] (an absent-minded dissector who brings into his anatomical theater an automaton instead of a real body). This is an attack on Goethe's reputation at its very root, and Hebbel is therefore careful to explain exactly how the earlier author had failed. Goethe, he says, "konnte sich nicht in gläubigem Vertrauen an die Geschichte hingeben, und da er die aus den Übergangs-Zuständen, in die er in seiner Jugend selbst gewaltsam hineingezogen wurde, entspringenden Dissonanzen nicht aufzulösen wußte, so wandte er sich mit Entschiedenheit, ja mit Widerwillen und Ekel, von ihnen ab" (1:310; lacked the faith to surrender trustingly to history, and since he could not resolve the dissonances that arose from the transitional conditions into which he had been forcibly drawn in his youth, he turned away from them decisively, indeed with revulsion and disgust).

It follows that the true task of the literary author — in particular, of the dramatist — is to give himself over trustingly to the process of history, confident that by so doing, he will be enabled to "resolve the dissonances" that history itself seems to present him with. Harmony, unity, organic completeness, are thus the ultimate aims of literature; even the difference between the literary work and the unfolding of history itself must be minimized. Of "der welthistorische Prozeß" (the world-historical process) Hebbel says:

> die dramatische Kunst . . . soll ihn beendigen helfen, sie soll . . . in großen gewaltigen Bildern zeigen, wie die bisher nicht durchaus in einem lebendigen Organismus gesättigt aufgegangenen, sondern zum Teil nur in einem Scheinkörper erstarrt gewesenen und durch die letzte große Geschichts-Bewegung entfesselten Elemente, durcheinander flutend und sich gegenseitig bekämpfend, die neue Form der Menschheit, in welcher alles wieder an seine Stelle treten . . . wird . . . erzeugen. (1:310–11)

> [dramatic art should help bring it to an end, it should show in large, powerful images how the elements unleashed by the last great historical movement, elements that have not yet been finally resolved into a living organism but had merely in part congealed into a specious body, how these elements, in flux and struggle, generate the new form of humanity, in which everything will again find its place.]

Unlike Goethe's *Die Wahlverwandtschaften* — which Hebbel, without even pretending to account for genre distinctions, associates with the history of drama — the dramatic work must be a true organic "body," not a mere machine, and as such must contribute directly to the completion of history itself as an "organism" (1:308). There will be conflicts and oppositions in the work, as there are after all in history, but the task of the work, like that of history, is to resolve those conflicts in a new and more perfect "form" of humanity.

Drama and Its Inveterate Defect

Hebbel, then, is thoroughly committed to the idea of organic perfection, as it applies to the work of art, to the shape of history, and to the relation between the two. And it seems to me that this characteristic of his thought *disqualifies him as a dramatist* in any reasonable sense of the term. For the idea of organic perfection, or for that matter the idea of any type of perfection, is fundamentally inconsistent with a conception of drama that attempts honestly to account for both the literary aspect and the theatrical aspect of the form. The crucial point about Hebbel — despite the frequency with which his work was performed, and despite his marriage to a competent and respected actress — is that on the level of their basic conception, neither his theories of drama nor his dramatic texts are given a clear connection to the institution of the theater. This is not to say that his plays cannot be performed in a manner that is entertaining and perhaps even edifying; but at the level of *conception,* the connection is missing. It does not occur to him to worry about taking one of Goethe's *novels* as a principal instance in the history of drama.

The idea of perfection is inconsistent with any reasonable conception of drama, because drama is a radically imperfect or *defective* form. I have made this argument elsewhere, at considerable length, but the basic point is not difficult.[3] There are, to begin with, any number of passages in classical dramatic authors that show not only an awareness of the defective quality of their art, but a positive reveling in it. Shortly before the "rural fellow" arrives with his figs and asps, for instance, Cleopatra warns Iras of what will happen if they are taken to Rome as captives:

> Nay, 'tis most certain, Iras. Saucy lictors
> Will catch at us like strumpets, and scald rhymers
> Ballad us out o' tune. The quick comedians
> Extemporally will stage us and present
> Our Alexandrian revels. Antony
> Shall be brought drunken forth, and I shall see

> Some squeaking Cleopatra boy my greatness
> I' th' posture of a whore. (V, ii, 214–21)

On Shakespeare's stage, of course, the words "boy my greatness" were spoken *by a boy,* so that even if that boy is an excellent actor, still we are forced to recognize the gap between what he is and what he represents, and so are moved to ask ourselves whether his performance is not a kind of "squeaking" after all. Thus, we are put strongly in mind of the inescapably makeshift or provisional quality of theatrical art. And once we start thinking in this direction, it occurs to us that Antony *has* been "brought drunken forth" before us in the present performance, so that perhaps the rest of Cleopatra's scorn for Roman theatricalizing touches us as well. The play, in other words, positively insists upon the defectiveness of its art form.

Or to put the matter in general theoretical terms: there is no way for the dramatic work to be disclosed to us *as a whole.* If we position ourselves as readers of the text, then the quality of the work as an actual, ritual-like proceeding in an actual social setting is missing, a quality that is undeniably implied by the definition of the work as "drama." The readers of a novel know that they are doing with the text exactly the one thing that is meant to be done with it (namely, reading it); therefore, at least in principle, there is nothing to prevent the whole work's being disclosed in that process. But the reader of a drama knows that at least one thing that is clearly meant to be done with the text (that is, performance) is categorically different from what he or she is doing, that reading is but one avenue among several into the work, no more likely to disclose the work entirely than traveling any one street is likely to disclose an entire city. And the same consideration applies when we position ourselves as spectators at a performance. For acting and the directing of actors are arts, therefore subject to our critical scrutiny, which means that we cannot watch a performance without being aware of alternatives, of a whole range of other possible performances — aware, in fact, that tomorrow's performance, by the same actors now before us, could be different in any number of ways — and again, a total disclosure of the work cannot happen. But if the work as a whole, therefore, can never be disclosed, then in effect that perfect whole simply does not exist.

Drama, that is, defeats the organic metaphor by being a thoroughly *provisional* art, just as its stage is never accepted as more than a provisional reality. This provisional or defective character is also apparent in the operation of dramatic language. Ordinarily we expect literary language to be preponderantly *evocative,* and to have only a strictly minimal *referential* component. The word in literature means — it is generally agreed — not by referring to an object or idea, but by *bringing forth* that object or idea, by generating it (in our imagination, we sometimes say), not by merely responding to it. But in the theater, a great many of the objects (including people's bodies) that the play's literary language, left to itself, would be expected to evoke, are actually physically there as objects of reference. The dramatic poem says "rose" or "crown" or "tree," and instead of being permitted to develop these objects in imagination, we find our attention is drawn to an actual, rather paltry thing on the platform before us. Thus, the literary or poetic freedom of the language is seriously impaired. One can say, of course, that the language still evokes as long as we only read it, and begins to refer only when it is spoken in the theater. But if being spoken in the theater belongs to the work's very nature, which it must if the term "drama" has any real meaning, then the tendency of the language to operate in two categorically opposed and irreconcilable ways explodes any unified conception of the work we might wish to form. Again, this state of affairs suggests possibilities that dramatists have exploited in their plays. In Ionesco's *La Leçon,* for example, the repeated word "knife" apparently *creates* the implement by which the Pupil is killed (Ionesco says it makes no difference whether a real prop knife is used or not), in a procedure that suggests the absurdity of combining literary evocativeness with stage reality — even though precisely this combination *is* drama. And Kleist's Penthesilea, in a similar scene, creates out of sheer language the dagger with which she takes her life.

Drama, and every particular work of drama, is thus an absurdity, an impossibility; it is the combination of two arts, the literary and the theatrical, that are fundamentally different with respect to their very mode of existence. Or at least this combination is an impossibility as long as one insists that it stand the test of organic integrity, that it be in some sense perfect or perfectible. This is why someone with Hebbel's habits of thought has no business in any of the professions connected with drama. And although the same habits of thought may be less obvious in such authors as Grillparzer and Otto Ludwig, I think these authors' work can be shown to have the same basically anti-dramatic quality as Hebbel's. But what of Grabbe? Surely the irony of his work counts as a disruption of organic integrity. Actually, irony in drama, or in any type of literary fiction, can cut in two different directions. It can either disrupt the work's unity or attempt to *create* such unity, by incorporating into the work itself critical or productive perspectives that would normally be strictly external to it; it can be understood, in other words, as the work's attempt to gather up its own external premises into itself, in imitation of the systematics of Kant or Hegel. I will argue that in Grabbe's work, the latter is the case.

But why should the organic metaphor be defeated in the first place? What harm is there in our attributing organic integrity or perfection to the work of literature or drama, and then deriving enjoyment from the contemplation of that quality? This question will be opened in the discussion of Georg Büchner below, whom I will present, along with Nestroy and Hauptmann, as one of the few genuine dramatists of the nineteenth century writing in German. As for Heinrich von Kleist — as genuine and unsurpassed a dramatist as he unquestionably is — I exclude him from consideration here on the grounds that he does not really belong to the nineteenth century. One of the peculiarities of German literary historiography is that we do not ordinarily speak of "the nineteenth century" until some substantial distance from the shadow of Goethe has been attained.

Drama and Epic

When we read Hebbel's meditations on drama, and when we consider the extent to which they are consistent with a great deal of popularized Hegelian and neo-Hegelian thought in Hebbel's time, we perhaps begin to understand the relative lack of literary prestige enjoyed by realistic novels in nineteenth-century Germany. For realism presupposes reality, as what Hebbel would call "den äußeren Haken" (the external hook) that supposedly legitimizes it, whereas in truth (Hebbel implies) neither drama nor literature nor any social institution receives genuine legitimacy except by finding its own "inneren Schwerpunkt" (inner center of gravity, 1:310), by which it is made independent of everything external. And since it is difficult, in the nineteenth century, to disengage the novel as a genre from the artistic posture of realism, it appears to follow that for writers like Hebbel — including those whose ideas on literature and history are not as fully developed — the choice of drama as a form in which to present their literary fictions is practically dictated. But are these considerations really sufficient as the basis for a choice of form? Do they imply, or reflect, an adequate concept of drama?

If our attention is attracted, further, by the special German development of the *Novelle* — a genre that has been regarded by poets and critics as fundamentally "dramatic" in spirit, thus as a kind of substitute for theatrical drama — and if we recall that most of the major authors we are talking about — Hebbel for instance, Grillparzer, Otto Ludwig — did a substantial amount of work in that shorter narrative form, we must find it even more peculiar that these authors still insist on regarding themselves as dramatists. Let us listen to Hebbel again, in his essay "Mein Wort über das Drama!":

> Die Trennung zwischen Drama und Theater ist unnatürlich, sie sollte nicht sein. Aber sie ist, und sie wird schwerlich wieder beseitigt, denn die Ideal-Bühne ist nur einmal, bei den Griechen . . . verkörpert gewesen, das moderne Theater dagegen schwebte zu allen Zeiten mehr oder weniger in der Luft, da es sich wohl zuweilen zum National-Ausdruck erhob, aber nie im Sinne der Griechen ein National-Akt wurde, noch werden konnte. Es war von jeher Unterhaltungsmittel, Zeitvertreib. (3:555)

[The separation between drama and theater is unnatural, it ought not to be. But it is, and it is not likely to be eliminated, for the ideal stage has only been realized once, in ancient Greece. The modern theater, by contrast, has always more or less hovered in the air, occasionally achieving the status of a national expression, but never able to become, in the Greek sense, a national *act*. It has always been mere entertainment, a pastime.]

If we did not know who the author is, we would immediately take these words as the explanation of a decision *not* to write drama. And similarly, when we think of Grillparzer's positively pathological reaction to the public failure of his play *Weh dem, der lügt* (Woe to Him Who Lies, 1838) — after more than two decades of considerable success — we are prompted to ask ourselves what an individual of this temperament wanted with the theater in the first place.

The solution to these puzzles is suggested by Hebbel's theoretical concentration on the contiguity of drama and history. Neither he nor Grillparzer has any real aptitude or inclination for the theater. Their insistence on dramatic form is in truth — blind as they both were to it — the attempt to create *a viable modern version of epic poetry*. "Tantae molis erat Romanam condere gentem" (such hard work it was to found the Roman people), says Vergil (*Aeneid*, 1:33), speaking ostensibly of the Trojans' long labors, but also referring cryptically to his own hard work in writing the poem. And Hebbel, in exactly the same way, parallels his own writing with the historical work it evokes or records. In Grillparzer the spirit is perhaps more Homeric — οὐ γάρ πω τοίους ἴδον ἀνέρας οὐδὲ ἴδωμαι (never have I seen, nor shall I ever see again, men such as these) (*Iliad*, 1:262) — filled more with a sense of its object as irrecoverably past. But that he and Hebbel are both epic poets at heart is, in much of their work, almost too obvious to require comment — especially the vast trilogies that imitate the form of *Wallenstein*, Grillparzer's "Dramatisches Gedicht" *Das goldene Vlies*, and Hebbel's *Die Nibelungen*.

Admittedly there are works of Grillparzer and Hebbel that seem very distant from the epic in both form and content. But in the case of the domestic drama *Maria Magdalene*, for example, we are struck by the enormous amount of paratextual explanation, or self-justification, that Hebbel feels obliged to provide — in personal terms with the dedication to Christian VIII of Denmark, in theoretical terms with the foreword on drama and history that was quoted above — in order to give the play a context in which it might operate as more than merely an organ of bourgeois self-criticism or self-pity. And the case of Grillparzer's *Der Traum ein Leben* is perhaps even more interesting. For Calderón's *La vida es sueño*, which it parodies, is a genuine drama in the definition suggested earlier. Its hero is made to undergo "life" in the form of a staged dream, which is obviously parallel to the staged version of life being offered us in the theater, and from which that hero learns that *all* life is in truth theatrically fragile, fleeting, makeshift. The defective quality of drama as a form is thus exploited as a symbol of the defectiveness of life itself vis-à-vis the eternal. In Grillparzer, however, where the plot is similar, and where the parallel between dream vision and stage vision is just as central, only a small shift in emphasis produces a decidedly anti-dramatic meaning. Rustan, the hero, who is dissatisfied with the narrow scope of his existence and experience, has an actual dream in which he lives the adventurous and aristocratic life he had yearned for, and learns there of the treacherousness of such a life, of its penchant for disaster, whereby he is enabled to accept his original, relatively modest situation after all. The theater, in other words — considered as parallel to Rustan's dream — is a device that enables us to see beyond the limits of our own condition; the broad and complete view of life it offers provides us with a valid self-perspective that reconciles us to ourselves and to our actual existence, however inconspicuous. The defectiveness of dramatic form is thus, as far as possible, *concealed,* or *resisted,* for the sake of a type of transcendence, the supposed achievement of a balanced and reconciled world-view that is more easily associated with epic.

At least in Grillparzer and Hebbel, then, the works that are farthest from epic in their direct effect upon a reader or audience tend to serve as the vehicles for a *theory* of epic — ostensibly, that is, a theory of drama, unwittingly a theory of epic — by which audiences may be educated in how to respond to the other, larger works. The same range is also observable in Otto Ludwig, from the epic tendency that is evident in *Die Makkabäer* (and in the historical dimension of *Der Erbförster*) to the theoretical efforts of his later years, especially his Shakespeare studies. And in the case of Grabbe, finally, the question of how to take the irony of *Scherz, Satire, Ironie und tiefere Bedeutung,* and to a lesser extent of *Don Juan und Faust* — the question of whether to take it as a disruptive or as an integrating device — is probably decided in favor of the latter possibility by the obvious epic ambitions of such plays as *Napoleon oder die hundert Tage.*

The European Situation

It is still not clear, however, why a number of prominent German authors who are driven, mainly by their sense of history, in the direction of a revival of epic, should end up as the dramatists they are not really suited to be. Why are there not a few German versions of Victor Hugo, whose epic drive satisfies itself primarily in the form of the novel? Let us turn once more to Hebbel, who is more articulate on this point than the others we have mentioned, and reconsider his criticism of Goethe, whom he accuses of being too tolerant, too forgiving, vis-à-vis his own subject matter. Why, he asks, does Goethe simply accept the corrupt marriage of Eduard and Charlotte, in *Die Wahlverwandtschaften,* as if it were a justifiable union?

And why, in *Faust II*, when faced with the choice "zwischen einer unge-heuren Perspektive und einem mit Katechismus-Figuren bemalten Bretter-Verschlag" (1:309; between a vast perspective and a little shed painted with religious images), does Goethe perversely choose the latter as his final tableau? Not — Hebbel hastens to add — that he denies the "immeasur-able value" of those two works of Goethe; his aim is only to show "das Verhältnis, worin ihr eigener Dichter zu den in ihnen verkörperten Ideen stand . . . und den Punkt, wo sie formlos geblieben sind" (1:309; the rela-tion in which their own author stood to the ideas embodied in them, and the point where they remain formless).

The crucial concept is "perspective." What Hebbel cannot accept is the involved or sympathetic authorial perspective that in his view charac-terizes Goethe's works. What he misses in Goethe is what might be called a *commanding* perspective, from which one could perhaps pity the inno-cent victims of world-historical necessity, but without actually lowering oneself to their level, without becoming involved. At least in the case of *Die Wahlverwandtschaften*, in other words, Hebbel holds against Goethe the simple fact that he had written a novel, that here (and presumably even in *Faust*) he had entered into the novelist's inevitably *intimate* relation with his figures, a relation that is incompatible with the sovereign objec-tivity of the epic poet, which in turn is required if the work is to have an historical vision transcending the immediate conditions of its plot. Even irony or scorn toward the fictional figures in question would merely unbal-ance the novelist's attitude in another direction. The only real choice — since the actual epic narrator is no longer available as a convention — is that fictional form in which no narrating persona at all need be suggested, the drama.

In Grillparzer's case, an argument of similar structure would apply, though its terms would be different. Transcendence, or the commanding perspective, rather than involvement or intimacy, is required by Grillparzer as well, with respect to the fiction considered as potential experience; but it is required more for the sake of establishing a stable, non-despairing rela-tion with the past than for the sake of creating a new relation to some dialectically necessary future. And in both Grabbe and Ludwig it would be fairly easy to argue that an historical vision somewhere on the scale between Hebbel's and Grillparzer's produces their need for epic, hence for the commanding perspective apparently offered by drama.

In non-German-speaking Europe, finally — especially in English and French literature, where it is reasonable to characterize the spirit of most of the century as realistic — it is still the association of drama with an impersonal, commanding perspective that determines the fate of the genre, except that this association works in exactly the opposite direction. For precisely the involved perspective of the novelist, not the commanding per-spective of the dramatist or would-be epic poet, is required to legitimize a psychologically or socially realistic literature. No special narrative techniques are at issue here. The novelist's posture at its most basic, the unavoidable relation of intimacy that arises between novel characters and the author who is assumed to be in touch with them on a subjective level, is already sufficient to arm that author against any imputation of claiming to be exempt from the web of supposedly real conditions that his or her work depicts, an imputation that would be particularly damaging to a realist writer, since, by definition, there is no exemption from reality. Thus the question of basic perspective is useful in understanding the absence of drama in nineteenth-century Europe as a whole.

Büchner's Little Comedy

Why insist on an idea of what drama "is" extra-historically? Why not simply admit that drama *evolves* over time, that German drama of the nineteenth century is bound to be different — indeed, depending on what one considers the defining characteristics of drama, is likely to appear *fundamentally* different — from drama (even German drama) of, say, the eighteenth or the twentieth century? One could object to this objection that only the questionable application to literary phenomena of a metaphor of biological growth or evolution makes it possible to regard different institutions at different times as stages in the unfolding of a single underlying identity. But this argument would not get us anywhere. Instead, I will try to meet the objection head-on by showing that even in the nineteenth century, there are a number of scattered but unquestionably significant playwrights writing in German whose use of the theater corresponds to what I have called "genuine" drama, that the practice of authors like Grillparzer and Hebbel therefore does not simply represent what drama had "become" in nineteenth-century German literature. Of course this does not settle the matter completely. Some readers may prefer to speak of different "types" of drama in the period under consideration. I base my terminology on the theoretical argument I have suggested concerning drama's inherent defectiveness.

Georg Büchner, unlike Grabbe, Grillparzer, Hebbel or Ludwig, never had any professional connection at all with an actual theater. But I maintain nonetheless that he is more properly a dramatist, has a clearer sense of what the theater is good at, than any of those others. *Dantons Tod,* for instance, shows the founding political event of the nineteenth century, the French Revolution, as constituted mainly by acts of political theater, thus fundamentally corrupt, so that the inherent defectiveness of drama, in which the audience is participating here and now, is mobilized as an instrument of political awareness in the present. And in *Woyzeck* — where the plot is brutally simple, showing nothing but how

a typical nineteenth-century social dynamics forces an economically vulner-
able individual into the situation of having to murder his wife — there are
several theater-within-theater scenes, especially the Doctor's use of
Woyzeck as a demonstration to students, that reflect back at us the cor-
ruptness, the defectiveness, of the theatrical proceeding *we* are involved in.

But there is perhaps more to be gained by examining *Leonce und Lena,*
Büchner's little comedy, because it seems such a harmless piece of work. It
is, above all, a *little* comedy. Everything about it suggests littleness. The
basic plot, in which a prince finds his true love and gets to marry her without sacrificing his position, could be that of a children's story. The first act
contains two scenes that could conceivably serve as the basis for a play of
some substance: the first scene, in which Prince Leonce plays Hamlet to
the Tutor's Polonius and expresses a witty but still potentially dangerous
Wertherian *taedium vitae;* and the third, which is both a love scene and an
agonized lament for the absence of love. But both of these scenes are inter-
rupted by Valerio, whose arrival is entirely unmotivated. (In the love scene,
he crawls out from under a table where he had been, presumably, during
all of Leonce's melancholy interview with Rosetta.) We have no idea who
he is, what he is doing at the court of Popo, or why Leonce so readily
accepts his presence. His whole function, as far as we can tell, is to reduce
any large ideas or feelings to the stuff of witty mockery; and it seems,
accordingly, that he steps (or crawls) out onto the stage, at this or that
time, for no better reason than that the play's world (under his own influence) is too small to have room for him anywhere else.

Then, in the second and third acts, there are repeated references to the
small scale on which the fictional world is built. Valerio complains of having had to travel, on foot, through numerous principalities, grand duchies
and kingdoms, all in half a day.[4] King Peter asks for a report on the borders of his realm, which it turns out can all be seen from the palace windows; we hear that a dog has run through the kingdom, and that someone
is taking a walk on the northern frontier. And of course the basic plot presupposes an extremely small world, where the prince and the princess, each
fleeing a forced political marriage, must meet, fall in love, and then discover in each other the intended spouses from whom they had been fleeing. What shall we do — Leonce asks Lena when they have become king
and queen — with all the "dolls" we now possess? "Wollen wir ihnen
Schnurrbärte machen und ihnen Säbel anhängen? Oder wollen wir ihnen
Fräcke anziehen, und sie infusorische Politik und Diplomatie treiben lassen
und uns mit dem Mikroskop daneben setzen?" (Shall we give them mus-
taches and hang sabers on them? Or shall we dress them in frock coats and
turn them to practicing infusorial politics and diplomacy, and watch them
through a microscope?).

From the point of view of a theater audience, however, this insistence
upon the diminutiveness of the play's world is unmistakably a reminder of

the relation in size between the stage before us and the outside world it supposedly represents. What is shown us in the theater is literally a small world, because it is a world scaled down to fit into just this theater. Thus, the most utterly basic condition entailed by the work's *genre,* the reduction in scale of its fiction compared with reality, is incorporated on several different levels into the work's *structure* and *content.* And these correspondences in turn — that genre, conditions of presentation, artistic structure, plot content and rhetorical content all reflect one another — constitute practically a definition of artistic perfection, of exactly the sort of organic integrity that I have argued is excluded by the fundamentally defective character of drama.

In this respect, in fact, *Leonce und Lena* is as much a theoretical work as it is an imaginative work. The model of perfection that is suggested by the pervasive quality of littleness — which suggests in turn a reference to the illusion of perfect beauty associated with littleness in Swift's Lilliput — is re-imagined one last time in Leonce's and Valerio's visions of a perfect world at the play's conclusion:

> wir lassen alle Uhren zerschlagen, alle Kalender verbieten und zählen Stunden und Monden nur nach der Blumenuhr, nach Blüte und Frucht . . . und dann legen wir uns in den Schatten und bitten Gott um Makkaroni, Melonen und Feigen, um musikalische Kehlen, klassische Leiber und eine kommode Religion!

> [we shall have all clocks smashed, all calendars forbidden, and we shall count hours and months only by the clock of flowers, by blooming and fruit . . . and then we'll lie down in the shade and pray to God for macaroni, melons and figs, for musical throats, classical bodies and an accommodating religion.]

There is only one negative element in this vision of perfection, only one thing to which we must say "no." Leonce asks, "Wollen wir ein Theater bauen?" (Shall we build a theater?), and Lena, who does not say a single word in this scene of happy imagining, shakes her head negatively. In the perfect world, that is, there is no place for a theater, no place — we must infer — for a theater of the type we are sitting in, for drama as an instance of artistic perfection. Such a theater, such drama, has a function — a consoling or edifying function — only in an imperfect world, which means that the artistic perfection of the present play is also *a sign of imperfection* (in the world), and that the representation of organic integrity in littleness is also a representation of dissonance or incongruity on a larger scale. As a theater audience, we have no trouble understanding how this may be. For the more perfect the play is as poetic signification, the more glaring becomes its irreconcilability with *reality* in the form of the referentially constituted material theater in which its supposed perfection is communicated.

The more glaring becomes the contrast between poetic ideality and the provisional, makeshift quality of an actual stage.

Nor is this state of affairs neglected in the play's text. Even in the little world of the fiction, there is room for a great many things: sentimental love, Wertherian despair, a pair of comic policemen, the terminology of Kantian philosophy, the satirical description of a court ball. But is there room for *hunger?* "E la fama?" (And fame?), Alfieri is made to say in the play's first epigraph, to which Gozzi is made to reply, "E la fame?" (And hunger?). And in act 3, scene 2, the only scene in which the lower classes (except for servants) appear, this idea breaks into the play's fiction. The Administrator reminds the peasants of the role assigned them in the day's "program":

> Sämtliche Untertanen werden von freien Stücken reinlich gekleidet, wohlgenährt und mit zufriedenen Gesichtern sich längs der Landstraße aufstellen.

> [All the King's subjects, neatly dressed, well fed and with satisfied faces, will, on their own initiative, line up along the highway.]

This could almost be the author's voice speaking to his characters, drilling into them their little world's perfection. And the schoolmaster reinforces the point by admonishing his charges:

> Erkennt, was man für Euch tut: man hat Euch grade so gestellt, daß der Wind von der Küche über Euch geht und Ihr auch einmal in Eurem Leben einen Braten riecht.

> [See what's being done for you. You've been placed so that the breeze from the kitchen blows over you and you too, once in your life, get to smell a roast.]

Of course this is a joke, but it is also a crack, a fissure, a defect in the play's fiction, a violation of exactly the "program" we have just heard recited, according to which everyone in the play is to be "well fed." At this point, in other words, the façade of artistic perfection splits open for a moment to afford us a glimpse, a reminder of the grossly imperfect world beyond the theater. But *only* at this one point. If the idea of hunger, or of the world's real imperfection, were repeated, it would thereby become a *theme* in the fiction, subject to being incorporated into the artistic structure, thus co-opted and made harmless, no longer "beyond." What we have is an artistically perfect structure with a strictly singular, thus unanswerable defect (corresponding to the fundamental defectiveness of drama as a form) by which its littleness is instantly transformed from a kind of perfection into a kind of paltriness, not to say appalling inadequacy.

And yet the play continues to be amusing (in the schoolmaster's joke) even at the very instant of its becoming appalling. We cannot deny that it is amusing, any more than we can find Leonce suddenly unsympathetic because he intends to do the whole wedding ceremony over again — including presumably the tormenting of the hungry peasants — the next day. And this gulf, this huge incongruity of the amusing and the appalling, is yet another reflection of the double defect of genre and world that we experience in the theater. What Büchner has done, at least in effect, is insist as absolutely as possible on artistic perfection in drama, so that the depth of the defect, both artistic and social, that cannot be overcome, is displayed. That this procedure amounts to a refutation in advance of Hebbel's idea of drama, goes without saying.

Nestroy's Insignificance

I have made the argument elsewhere that in order to understand Nestroy's comedies, we must take into account the dynamics of three different societies: the fictional society, as it appears on the stage before us; actual Viennese or Austrian society; and the group of interacting people present here and now in the theater, including both actors and spectators.[5] The inclusion of that third group, however, the argument that the play cannot be understood fully except in the process of participating in that third society, has as a consequence the denial of any transcendent element whatever in Nestroy's work. Even for a Viennese theater audience in 1848, the "actual" Austrian society of 1848 (outside the theater) is still a kind of abstraction that can conceivably be duplicated in the minds of a theater audience of, say, 2003. But the process of belonging immediately to a theater audience of 1848 cannot be duplicated; and any element of the play's meaning that depends on that process, on the third society, is irretrievably lost as soon as the conditions of production have changed. My contention was, and is, that what is thus lost in Nestroy is what matters most in the play, its very reason for being. A similar contention could not be sustained with respect to any of the other major Viennese dramatists of the nineteenth century. Grillparzer's plays, and Raimund's, are obviously aimed at least as much at posterity as at the present. And even in Anzengruber's "folk" and "peasant" pieces, there is usually a character (Wurzelsepp, Steinklopferhanns, for example) whose pithy observations are clearly meant to give the work a philosophical dimension. Of course there are philosophically inclined characters in Nestroy as well, but I will argue that they are used in a diametrically opposed manner.

The play I will discuss here, *Der Unbedeutende* (The Insignificant One), is full of improbable plot complications. Secretary Puffmann requires an alibi for the evening of 7 September, when he had been betraying the trust of his employer Baron Massengold — in one of the subplots I won't go into here. Later that evening he happens upon a young boy asleep outside the tavern where his mother is making a purchase. He convinces the boy that he (the boy) had seen him (Puffmann) sneaking away from the house of Mamsell Klara Span across the way, and pays the boy handsomely for his promise not to say anything, a promise he knows the boy will not be able to keep. Thus, his alibi is assured, but Klara's reputation is ruined in the process once the boy's story makes the round of local gossips. Peter Span, however, Klara's brother and a master carpenter, traces the calumny to its source, uses the boy to identify Puffmann, and after contriving a test for Klara to eliminate his own lingering doubts about her virtue, confronts Puffmann directly, whereupon the subplots finish like a string of firecrackers going off: Klara is publicly vindicated, Puffmann is maneuvered by his own lies into marrying a woman he dislikes (he has called her a "Z'widere Bißgurn"[6] [repulsive shrew]), and Peter concludes the play by saying to Puffmann:

> Wenn Sie wieder einmal mit unbedeutende Leut' in Berührung kommen, dann vergessen Sie ja die Lektion nicht, daß auch am Unbedeutendsten die Ehre etwas sehr Bedeutendes ist.
>
> [If you should again come into contact with insignificant people, don't forget the lesson that even for the most insignificant, honor is still something very significant.]

Thus everything seems neatly wrapped up, all conflicts and dissonances resolved.

But the package quickly comes unglued if we poke at it a bit. "Honor," says Peter, is as important to "insignificant" people as it is to their supposed superiors. But the honor he is speaking of, as he well knows, means nothing more than the opinion in which one is held by the most vicious neighborhood busybodies. In Hebbel's *Maria Magdalene,* which is almost exactly contemporaneous with Nestroy's play, the dying Secretary accuses Meister Anton: "Er dachte…an die *Zungen,* die hinter Ihm herzischeln würden, aber nicht an die *Nichtswürdigkeit* der *Schlangen,* denen sie angehören" (You thought about the *tongues* that would whisper behind you, but not about the *baseness* of the *serpents* they belonged to). Peter Span, by contrast, is perfectly aware of the baseness of the people who determine his sister's standing in society, but he continues nevertheless to attach *value* to that social standing, which he calls by its exalted euphemism, "honor."

Peter (who of course was played by Nestroy) thus manages to despise what he values and to value what he despises. And more important, he does so *as our representative* in the fiction. For he is the play's philosophical commentator, its chorus, so to speak. In his first appearance on the stage — toward the end of the first act, but before we have any idea of who he is or how he functions in the plot — he sings a song and recites a monologue about carpentry as a specially philosophical trade. From his perch on the roof of the house he is building, says Peter, the carpenter has a perspective that is available to no one else. He looks down on all types of people and has a complete understanding of their follies. And it is only after the long, unmotivated meditation of act 1, scene 13, that we begin to learn how Peter fits into the story. It is as if we were observing his *descent* from a lofty philosophical detachment into the immediate reality of a life that by rights he should have disdained on intellectual grounds. Again, he apparently manages to disdain and affirm at the same time. But if he represents *us,* the audience, then how does this paradox characterize *our* situation?

Let us look again at the end of the play, where Peter suggests that when something really important is at stake, like "honor," even a socially "insignificant" person can summon up enough resolve and initiative to assert himself successfully, to carry the day even against those placed higher. The details of the plot do not bear him out in this suggestion. Peter succeeds against Puffmann only because he happens to be assisted by Packendorf — a socially "significant" person, a friend of the baron — who is working against Puffmann for reasons, mainly financial, that have nothing to do with Klara's honor. And even Packendorf's aid may not be enough. At the end of act 3, scene 33, Peter stands up defiantly to Baron Massengold, who is about to smooth over the affair to Puffmann's advantage. But in that very instant, the question of who will prevail in this unequal contest of wills is superseded (luckily for Peter) by the appearance of Thomas Pflökl, who distracts everyone's attention by re-introducing the farcical subplot of Puffmann's supposed suicide attempt. In fact, if the play shows anything, it shows that "insignificant" people are just that, that their success or failure is determined by sheer luck and by the coincidence or non-coincidence of their interest with that of more powerful people. When Peter suspects (correctly) that Puffmann is planning to have him arrested, he says to himself:

> Und die verdächtige Wisplerei — am End bin ich schon in eine Falle gegangen — hm — wenn auch — ich komm schon wieder heraus. Gott sei Dank, 's Mittelalter is beim Teufel — Hungerthürm, Torturvermummte, Bleidächer und eiserne Jungfrauen hat man in unserm milden Saeculum nicht mehr.

> [And that suspicious whispering — maybe I've fallen into a trap after all — but so what? — I'll get out again. Thank God, the Middle Ages are gone to the devil — dungeons, masked torturers, Venetian lockups and iron maidens are no longer in use in our mild century.]

It is true that there was no Inquisition, and no totalitarian regime, in Austria in the mid-1840s. But it is also true that little central legislative or judicial control was exercised over the local police, which meant that people with money and power could use the police to keep "insignificant" people out of their hair when necessary. In this case, at the last moment, Packendorf, who stands higher in the pecking order than Puffmann, uses the police officers who had come for Peter to arrest Puffmann's henchman instead. Again, Peter is saved only by an intervention from higher up in the social structure that renders him insignificant.

Peter suggests at the end that we ought to find in the play a measure of consolation for our insignificance in the real social world — an insignificance that practically all of us must suffer with respect to some level of established power. But the play actually offers us no such consolation. If anything, it rubs our nose in our helpless and humiliating condition. Which raises two questions: why do we need to be reminded of our daily humiliation in the first place? and why does the play not expose this quality of society more directly, with a clearer critical message? Both questions, I think, are answered by one of the inconspicuously pivotal scenes that are typical of Nestroy. As the final stage-setting appears, showing the second day of the church anniversary fair ("Kirchtag"), we hear:

KÜBLER:	Glaub aber doch nicht, daß der Nachkirchtag heut so lustig wird, als der Kirchtag war.
SCHMALZER:	Warum?
KÜBLER:	Es kommen hohe Herrschaften, und das is schenant.
WIRT:	Das ganze hochfreiherrliche Haus is angsagt.
KLOPF:	's is immer schmeichelhaft und ehrenvoll für uns, diese Herablassung.

[K: Don't think that the second day, today, will be as much fun as the first. S: Why? K: Their lordships are coming, and that puts a crimp in things. INNKEEPER: The whole baronial family is supposed to come. K: It's always flattering and an honor for us, this condescension.]

And when Baron Massengold then arrives with his party:

MASSENGOLD:	Da wären wir. — *(Grüßend zu den Anwesenden.)* Laßt Euch in Eurer Unterhaltung nicht stören, wackre Bürger.
KÜBLER *(mit tiefster Devotion):*	Dero glorreiche Gegenwart ist die schönste Unterhaltung für die unterthänigsten Kobelstädter.

[M: Here we are. (Greeting the others present.) Don't let us disturb you in your enjoyment, honest citizens. K (with extreme obsequiousness): Your worship's presence is the best enjoyment for us most submissive Kobelstädter.]

This scene obviously emphasizes the servility of "insignificant" people toward their betters. But it also illustrates *the influence of spectators' presence on what is shown them* — allegorically, by way of Massengold's unwitting influence on the citizens' behavior. And this point obviously applies to us as we sit in the theater. *Merely by being a theater audience,* we express a certain pretentiousness (which is echoed by Peter) about our critical ability vis-à-vis the society we live in. Insignificant though we may be in everyday life, here in the theater we transcend that humiliating condition at least for a short time and partake of "Bedeutung" in the sense of "meaning" (a socially critical fable that we can understand) as a substitute for "Bedeutung" in the sense of the social "significance" we lack. The play therefore cannot show us our insignificance directly, since *by* being an audience we are already denying or transcending that condition. And yet, of course, our real insignificance persists nonetheless, even as we sit in the theater; it persists, as it were, behind the scenes of the play we are watching. Thus — here and now, in the auditorium — we find ourselves in the position of adopting an affirmative attitude in a situation we also regularly despise or are ashamed of, which exactly replicates the position occupied by Peter with respect to the notion of "honor."

May we understand this replication of the fiction in the actual situation of the audience as the achievement of self-contained artistic perfection? Only up to a point. For this structural completeness, like the perfect littleness of *Leonce und Lena,* is pregnant with its own disruption. It reflects, in the first place, a painful anomaly in our condition; and it exists, in the second place, only for the play's first audiences, only while the play is still *new.* If we have the slightest bit of historical perspective, if we find ourselves thinking, "the social insignificance experienced by Nestroy's spectators," rather than simply "*our* insignificance," the structure no longer holds together; we are no longer actually trapped in the same type of paradox as Peter Span. But the whole point of artistic perfection is that it makes the work self-sufficient, independent of external conditions; a perfection that is restricted, say, to the year 1846 is *ipso facto* not perfect in the artistic sense. Thus, as in Büchner, perfection itself becomes a sign of imperfection. On one hand, the work's perfected structure only re-actualizes for us in the theater an ultimately intolerable contradiction in our social existence. On the other hand, that structure crumbles as soon as we gain enough perspective to begin deriving pleasure from it. And in case we lose track of the connection between these gaping incongruities and the fundamental defectiveness of dramatic form, one of Peter's songs has a stanza about the inconceivability of an artistically honest theatrical production.

Hauptmann's Reality

In both Büchner and Nestroy, then, at the very moment when the play seems to shape itself into a perfect whole, the wholeness of the audience's experience is irreparably ruptured, revealing the true, defective quality of both the work and its genre. Our experience as spectators is at some point no longer containable within the artistic space of the theater. Büchner's play splits open before a prospect of hunger and human suffering, Nestroy's exposes us to the merciless operation of historical time, where the immediate present is unconfrontable and conscious perspective proves to be nothing but a failure to understand.

It is in this respect, the uncontainability of theatrical experience within the theater, that I count Hauptmann at least as much a nineteenth- as a twentieth-century dramatist. The question about Hauptmann that is most interesting in this regard is why he spends as much effort as he does on the exact phonetic reproduction of dialect in his texts, especially Silesian dialect. For purposes of performance, that effort is wasted. If the actor does not already know the dialect, no amount of phonetic detail in the script will enable him to speak it convincingly. And if he does know it, then he does not need all the phonetic prompting Hauptmann provides. The reader of the printed text is in the same situation. If we know the dialect, we can imagine what the character sounds like; if we do not, then the dialect speeches are nothing but collections of orthographical puzzles for us.

From a reader's point of view, therefore, it must *seem* that the reproduction of dialect has a purely theatrical function, comparable to that of the detailed stage directions. From a performer's point of view — or from that of a spectator — the dialect spelling must *seem* to belong strictly to the text as a written document. The dialect thus operates as a kind of wedge between the theatrical aspect of the work and its literary aspect, as an insistence on the disjunction of semiotic modes at the work's heart, hence as a token of the defective or provisional quality that the work receives from its genre. Especially interesting, however, is the point of view that is thus presupposed for the work's recipient. For in order that the crucial artistic defect become apparent, it is necessary not only that the reader be inclined to imagine the text's theatrical realization (which we can probably assume most readers are), but also that the spectators in a theater be unable to exclude from their consciousness a broader cultural experience that includes knowledge of what Hauptmann's texts look like. The play, that is, like those of Nestroy and Büchner, presupposes the uncontainability of its relation with its audience inside the theater.

On a strictly formal level, therefore — given the basic exigencies of the genre, plus Hauptmann's use of dialect — the play has a tendency to break down as a structure and expose its audience, here and now in the theater, to an entirely extra-theatrical reality. And at least in early Hauptmann, it goes practically without saying that this formal deduction corresponds exactly to the intended effect of the plays on the level of content. Indeed, in specific plays this correspondence can be followed into considerable detail. In *Vor Sonnenaufgang* (Before Sunrise, 1889), for example, Helene's tragedy results from the failure of her experience to stay contained within the boundaries of a thoroughly unhappy but perhaps still supportable family situation. Her father is an alcoholic and passes this trait on to her sister, whose child is stillborn as a result. Her oafish prospective fiancé is her mother's paramour. Her brother-in-law is a money-hungry hypocrite involved in capitalist exploitation of the poor. But what finally destroys her is the arrival of Alfred Loth, a social progressive and a believer in women's rights, who opens her eyes to a world of possibilities beyond her unspeakable family.

Nor is it only Helene who shows this pattern. When Schimmelpfennig learns that Hoffmann — the brother-in-law — had been a member of Loth's political group at university, he says, "Also mit dir ist er umgegangen! Auf diese Weise wird mir der traurige Zwitter erklärlich"[7] (So he hung around with you! That explains his miserable half-and-halfness). Hoffmann, that is, like the recipient of drama, is obliged to think of himself in two different and inconsistent ways. And Loth himself, despite his contempt for Hoffmann, is in his own way no less a "half-and-half." He defends his love for Helene, to Schimmelpfennig, as a reconciliation between two opposed aspects of his own self:

> Du weißt nicht, wie ich mich durchgefressen hab' bis hierher. Ich mag nicht sentimental werden. Ich hab's auch vielleicht nicht so gefühlt, es ist mir vielleicht nicht ganz so klar bewußt geworden wie jetzt, daß ich in meinem Streben etwas entsetzlich Ödes, gleichsam Maschinenmäßiges angenommen hatte. Kein Geist, kein Temperament, kein Leben, ja wer weiß, war noch Glauben in mir? Das alles kommt seit . . . seit heut wieder in mich gezogen.

> [You don't know how I've survived till now. I don't want to get sentimental. Maybe I didn't feel it, maybe I wasn't so clearly aware of it till now, that in my striving I'd developed something horribly barren and machine-like in my character. No spirit, no temperament, no life, who knows if I still really believed in anything? All that is again clear to me after today.]

But this reconciliation is an illusion. Loth is forced by his "principles" (which prohibit marriage with a woman who might pass on genetic defects to her children) to choose after all:

> So steht es: es gibt drei Möglichkeiten! Entweder ich heirate sie, und dann . . . nein, dieser Ausweg existiert überhaupt nicht. Oder — die

bewußte Kugel. Na ja, dann hätte man wenigstens Ruhe. Aber nein! so
weit sind wir noch nicht, so was kann man sich einstweilen noch nicht
leisten — also: leben! kämpfen! — Weiter, immer weiter. (94–95)

[That's how it is, there are three possibilities! Either I marry her and
then . . . no, this way just doesn't exist. Or — a bullet you know where.
At least I'd have peace then. But no! we haven't come to that yet, we
can't yet afford that. So live! struggle! On and on.]

He has chosen, it appears, his principles and his duty to the human race
over his love for Helene. But then, why does he not stick to his plan to
study the local mining operations and their workers? Why does he assure
Hoffmann that he will be "über alle Berge" (long gone) the next day? In
fact he is still hung up between two irreconcilable ways of regarding himself, able to satisfy fully neither of them. And in this, he is yet another alle-
gory of the recipient of drama, for whom the corresponding gap of
irreconcilability in the genre is an opening through which reality itself is
exposed, a reality that would only be compromised and obscured by any
pretended artistic unity.

The Absence of Drama

I have tried to show some common tendencies in Büchner, Nestroy, and
Hauptmann, but I do not mean to suggest that these authors belong to a
single "type." In fact they are *aberrations*. In each case, the path to drama
probably begins with a sense of the utter political hopelessness of the situation in which the author finds himself, and the recognition that that sense
could not be expressed by any literary type in which structural perfection
or unity seemed a reasonable criterion of artistic adequacy. But exactly how
each author then reaches an understanding of the expressive possibilities
opened by the defectiveness of theatrical drama, is not clear. For Nestroy,
who operated within an established theatrical convention — but a convention whose techniques and purposes he soon radically alters — the
process was probably negative, a learning from the recognized failure of
the plays and styles he parodied. For Büchner it was probably a matter of
learning from positive models, mainly Shakespeare and Goethe. And
Hauptmann, besides being one of the first late-century rediscoverers of
Büchner, is also likely to have found the question of drama implied in his
wrestling with the theory of "consistent" realism.

In the end, however, we cannot get around attributing to each author
an independent theoretical meditation on drama. That such a meditation
should be necessary, that there is no basic background awareness of what
drama is — at least drama in the sense I have suggested — that drama is
thus absent in nineteenth-century Germany, is the main point of the first

part of this essay. But that a theoretical meditation on drama should still be possible in nineteenth-century Germany, presupposes the operation of a *tradition* of thinking about drama, which in principle should have been available to the century as a whole. That such widely separated and different writers as Büchner, Nestroy, Hauptmann should find themselves thinking similarly about the form of drama, is by no means naturally expectable, as it might be expectable that separate scientists should discover the same natural law. For drama is not in any respect a natural phenomenon. Its character, its very existence, is traditional in the sense of being formed by its history — by a specifically European history which, unlike Oriental theater traditions, yokes poetic art and theatrical art together and treats their combination as if it were nothing but a distinguishable type of poetry. Precisely this forcible amalgamation of categorically disparate art forms is what causes the defectiveness of drama.

The tradition that constitutes dramatic form, then, is demonstrably available to be tapped into in nineteenth-century German literature; but that literature, except for isolated aberrations, has no drama. On the basis of these observations, it is reasonable to ask, finally, what *prevents* the development of drama in the period under consideration. And although I have already suggested an answer to this question — an answer having to do with Hegelianism and the idea of the efficacy of consciousness in producing historical and artistic unities, an answer that, in being worked out, would probably involve the structure and content of a developing public education — still, perhaps the simple existence of the question is conclusion enough for the time being.

Notes

[1] Johann Joachim Winckelmann, *Kleine Schriften und Briefe*, 2 vols., ed. Hermann Uhde-Bernays (Leipzig: Insel, 1925), 1:71.

[2] Friedrich Hebbel, *Werke*, 5 vols., ed. Fricke, Keller, Pörnbacher (Munich: Hanser, 1963–67), 1:309. Further references are to this edition.

[3] See my *Theater As Problem: Modern Drama and Its Place in Literature* (Ithaca: Cornell UP, 1990), esp. pages 14, 51–54, 55–92, 172–78, 253–67.

[4] Georg Büchner, *Werke und Briefe*, Münchener Ausgabe, ed. Karl Pörnbacher et al. (Munich: dtv, 1988), 174. Further references are to this edition.

[5] See my *Theater As Problem*, chapter 3, 93–136.

[6] Johann Nestroy, *Sämtliche Werke: Stücke*, vol. 23/II, ed. Jürgen Hein (Vienna: Jugend und Volk, 1995), 78. Further references are to this volume.

[7] Gerhart Hauptmann, *Sämtliche Werke*, Centenar-Ausgabe, 11 vols., ed. Hans-Egon Hass et al. (Frankfurt / Main and Berlin: Propyläen, 1962–74), 1:90. Further references are to this volume.

Carl Spitzweg (1808–1885), The Reading from the Breviary, Evening. *Louvre, Paris. Courtesy of Reunion des Museés Nationaux/Art Resource, New York.*

The Nineteenth-Century German Novel

Jeffrey L. Sammons

THE HISTORY OF THE NINETEENTH-CENTURY novel in any Western nation is a topic of immense dimensions, for the novel became the dominant genre of modern Western literature; even today, someone who says that he or she is reading a "book" most likely means a novel. In view of the evident impossibility of miniaturizing this history into a compact space, it seems appropriate to venture some principles of procedure. My purpose will be to suggest trends within the development, pursuing less an orderly sequence than the diversity of possibilities. Thus, the absence of any author or title is not meant pejoratively.

In German literary history as with other topics the nineteenth century begins in the last quarter of the eighteenth and extends to the threshold of the First World War. More particularly than in other national literatures, the German-language novel has a fount in a single author's single exemplary work: Johann Wolfgang von Goethe's *Wilhelm Meisters Lehrjahre* (Wilhelm Meister's Apprenticeship, 1795–96), which radiated both inspiration and the anxiety of influence throughout most of our period. The chronicle of its descent, however, has been distorted and even somewhat obfuscated by a constrictive canonization process. No literary history, regardless of its magnitude, can be exhaustive because there is a great deal more literature than can be retained in any form of cultural memory. Canonization is therefore inevitable and necessary, although there is much to be said for not allowing it to petrify, and for maintaining options of inquiry into the less canonized. Even then, any literary history is a narrative that imposes an exclusionary order on the unruliness of evolving literary life.

In Germany canon was formed under the pressure of compelling nationalistic imperatives, one of which was to differentiate an idealistically elevated culture from the more worldly civilizations of other nations, especially of Western Europe.[1] One consequence of this was to create a myth of a definitive German genre in descent from *Wilhelm Meister,* the Bildungsroman, about which more will be said presently, and another was a systematic decanonization of the realistic social novel that came to be the core of the tradition in other national literatures. The result was a loss of awareness of the lively cosmopolitanism of German literary life, especially in the second half of the century, when Germans created literary works exportable to foreign lands and imported foreign literature in large volume.[2] Owing to the worldwide prestige achieved by German culture in the course of the century, the canonizers succeeded in persuading the larger learned community of their literary-historical narrative. One can see this most clearly in Erich Auerbach's still influential *Mimesis*,[3] which, notwithstanding its brilliance in the classical, medieval, and Romance precincts where he was most at home, is seriously deficient in its account of German matters. This essay will operate with contrasting examples, with the purpose of illustrating the variety of modes of the novel possible in Germany and to inhibit an impression of linear evolution.

To some extent a canonical anxiety about the novel was owing to an uneasiness about its status in the poetic system. Within the tripartite scheme inherited from antiquity it could only be located in the genre of the epic. But could the baggy, arbitrarily thematic modern novel, prosaic in both form and substance, be permitted succession to Homer? Friedrich Schiller, with his irritating forthrightness, just when he was accompanying the genesis of *Wilhelm Meister* with a running commentary, declared that the novelist was only the "Halbbruder" (half brother) of the poet.[4] In 1837, the quondam Young German novelist, Theodor Mundt (1808–61), attempted in *Die Kunst der deutschen Prosa* (The Art of German Prose) to rehabilitate prose fiction for the literary system, but the uneasiness about the novel persisted. Its very popularity was suspicious, a genre of romance that could be read by and probably depraved the imaginations of office clerks and servant girls. *Romanhaft* (novelistic) became a term of opprobrium; in Germany the novel may not be novelistic; it must strive to be something other than it is, an effort in which it can never succeed except in eccentric cases, which then come to be canonized and create the impression that the German novel tradition is essentially different from that of other nations.

Nowhere is this problematic more evident than in the literary-historical legend of the Bildungsroman, alleged to be a peculiarly German genre descended from the model of *Wilhelm Meister*. This is a long story, but the facts are, first, that, far from being the dominant genre of the nineteenth century, those major novels that can be denominated as Bildungsromane rarely in any account number more than half a dozen while the full range of novel types in Germany does not differ markedly from what is found in other countries; most of the novels in succession to *Wilhelm Meister* are unable to replicate its optimism about the successful formation of the self and some appear as anti-*Meisters;* and any known definition of the Bildungsroman applies equally well to any number of novels in other national literatures, so that the claim of German singularity cannot be sustained.[5] One indication that the dominance of the Bildungsroman is a mirage is that the authors of the acknowledged examples did not specialize in the genre but in most cases wrote only one, beginning with Goethe himself, whose sequel, *Wilhelm Meisters Wanderjahre* (Wilhelm Meister's Journeyman Years, final version, 1829) makes of Wilhelm less an internally developing personality than an observer of the fates of others recounted in incapsulated narratives while he discovers a craft as a surgeon. Of Goethe's other novels, the tragic *Die Leiden des jungen Werthers* (The Sufferings of Young Werther, 1774) might be regarded as a kind of anti-Bildungsroman *avant la lettre;* the *Unterhaltungen deutscher Ausgewanderten* (Conversations of German Emigrés, 1795) is a frame for recited novellas on the model of Boccaccio; and the intricate *Die Wahlverwandtschaften* (Elective Affinities, 1809) relates a chiastic love relationship among four characters whose personalities are already fixed.[6]

The problem of succession appears early on, with the Romantics. Although Friedrich Schlegel (1772–1829) famously declared *Wilhelm Meister* one of the great tendencies of the age, along with the French Revolution and Fichte's epistemology,[7] others found it earthbound and quotidian. Novalis (Friedrich von Hardenberg, 1772–1801), after much admiring preoccupation with it, declared it "durchaus *prosaïsch* — und modern," "eine Satyre auf die Poësie, Religion, etc.," "ein *Candide,* gegen die Poësie gerichtet" (thoroughly prosaic and modern; a satire on poesy, religion, etc.; a *Candide* directed against poesy).[8] His own novel, *Heinrich von Ofterdingen* (1802), is set in an imaginary late Middle Ages or early Renaissance, operates with fantasy tales and esoteric nature images, especially of minerals (he was by profession a mining engineer), and begins with a dream of the blue flower, which became the symbol of inchoate Romantic longing.[9] It remained a fragment. Although in this case it was cut off by the author's early death, other novels of the epoch also remained unfinished, either as a sign of Romantic openness to indeterminacy or owing to insoluble internal problems. An example of the latter is Ludwig Tieck's (1773–1853) *Franz Sternbalds Wanderungen* (1798), set in the time of Albrecht Dürer, in which a young artist never finds his way to creative work.[10] The tendency to make the protagonist an artist on the margin of society is just what Goethe avoided, abandoning the earlier version (*Wilhelm Meisters theatralische Sendung,* translated as *Wilhelm Meister's Theatrical Calling*)[11] in which Wilhelm was to realize himself in the theater for the definitive one in which he finds his way to service and citizenship. A distinctly Romantic anti-*Meister* is Joseph von Eichendorff's (1788–1857) *Ahnung und Gegenwart* (Presentiment and Present, 1815); it has a completely circular movement, its aristocratic protagonist passing through a series of ungratifying experiences in the fallen world of the present until he returns to his starting place, determined to become a monk and await better times.[12] A self that remains essentially unaltered through all ordeals and encounters like Eichendorff's protagonist can scarcely be said to have undergone *Bildung* in the Goethean sense. It is partly in consideration of such variants that Hartmut Steinecke has made the valuable and influential suggestion that we speak, instead of the Bildungsroman, of the *Individualroman,* to distinguish the novel focused on a single person from the more populated social novel.[13]

While there is no space here to trace the permutations of the *Individualroman,* something may be said of two apparently contrasting inheritors of the Bildungsroman tradition. One was the Austrian Adalbert Stifter (1805–68), in whose *Der Nachsommer* (Indian Summer, 1857) the protagonist Heinrich Drendorf successfully achieves *Bildung,* making the novel appear to be a lonely genuine successor to *Wilhelm Meister.*[14] But the integral self is formed at the cost of a renunciation of creativity, a suppression of passion, and a postponement of full adulthood — it has been estimated that Heinrich is around forty years old before he is permitted by his mentors to marry his sculpture-like beloved. Creativity is replaced with the admiration and maintenance of already existing works of art and craft, so that the forward thrust of Goethe's novel is halted in a museum-like stasis. Curiously, something similar happens in the more colorful, more emotionally charged, partly autobiographical novel of the Swiss author Gottfried Keller (1819–90), *Der grüne Heinrich* (Green Henry, first version, 1854–55, second version 1879–80), the evolution of which occupied years of his life and which was self-consciously in succession to Goethe.[15] But the aspiring artist Heinrich Lee never achieves his goal. In the first version he dies of grief and guilt over the coffin of his sacrificing mother; in the second he accommodates himself to a gray and sexually abstinent life as a civil servant. His problem throughout is defined as an excess of imagination recurrently rebelling from Goethean moderation, which would, if it could be internalized, have the effect of disciplining creativity within normative boundaries. Thus, the republican, civic-minded Keller comes into an unexpected contiguity with the conservative, politically detached Stifter.

With its few and often questionable examples, the Bildungsroman has had a curious fate for a genre alleged to be dominant in a national literature. In fact, it was in the twentieth century that it began to thrive in the hands of authors acculturated to believe that it *was* the peculiarly German genre, writers such as Thomas Mann (1875–1955) with *Der Zauberberg* (The Magic Mountain, 1924) and Hermann Hesse (1877–1962) with a series of novels from, among others, *Peter Camenzind* (1904) and *Demian* (1919) to *Siddhartha* (1922) and *Das Glasperlenspiel* (The Bead Game, 1943), and it finally came to generate inevitable parody in Günter Grass's (1927–) *Die Blechtrommel* (The Tin Drum, 1959).

The Romantic generation was not totally obsessed with Goethe and his visionary novel, for the activation of the modern imagination led not only into idealistic dreaming and the longing for the blue flower, but also into darker regions of the psyche. Less regarded than the high Romantics in his own nation but influential abroad was Ernst Theodor Amadeus (originally Wilhelm) Hoffmann (1776–1822), who narrated nightmarish fantasies in an eerily humoristic tone.[16] He attempted several novels, among them the unfinished, experimental *Lebensansichten des Katers Murr nebst fragmentarischer Biographie des Kapellmeisters Johannes Kreisler in zufälligen Makulaturblättern* (Views of Life of the Tomcat Murr along with a Fragmentary Biography of the Conductor Johannes Kreisler on Accidental Printing Scrap, 1819–21), in which the frustrating career of the musician alternates with the self-satisfactions of the biologically competent cat, but Hoffmann is better known for his grim tales, such as *Der Sandmann* (1816, the source of the first act of Jacques Offenbach's *Tales of Hoffmann*, 1880), *Nußknacker und Mausekönig* (Nutcracker and Mouse King, 1819, recommendable as an antidote to P. I. Tchaikovsky's *Nutcracker* ballet, 1892), or *Die Bergwerke zu Falun* (The Mines at Falun, 1819), where Hoffmann's nature imagery is more ambiguous than that of Novalis. The ambiguity of nature is evident also in Tieck's riddling tales, such as *Der blonde Eckbert* (Blond Eckbert, 1797) and *Der Runenberg* (The Rune Mountain, 1802).[17] Even more desolate is the mysterious, pseudonymously published *Die Nachtwachen. Von Bonaventura* (Nightwatches. By Bonaventura, 1804), in which there is a suggestion that God might exist but be insane.[18]

On the boundary of Romanticism there were experimental ventures into the novel genre that were not in every case seminal but look substantial in retrospect. The most remarkable nonconformist was Jean Paul (Johann Paul Friedrich Richter, 1763–1825), who became a celebrity with a series of complex, verbose novels with titles like *Blumen-, Frucht-, und Dornenstücke, oder Ehestand, Tod und Hochzeit des Armenadvokaten Fr. St. Siebenkäs im Reichsmarktflecken Kuhschnappel* (Flower, Fruit, and Thorn Pieces, or Marriage, Death, and Wedding of the Legal Aid Lawyer Fr. St. Siebenkäs in the Imperial Market Village of Kuhschnappel, 1796–97, commonly called *Siebenkäs*), in which the unhappily married protagonist fakes his death and marries another after his first wife dies; *Titan* (1800–3), an eccentrically complex narrative detailing how two geniuses devote themselves respectively to freedom of thought and to hedonism; or the unfinished, comic *Flegeljahre* (The Awkward Age, 1804–5), in which a young man must replicate the life stages of a benefactor in order to receive an inheritance as his path crosses with a long-lost brother. With whimsical chapter headings and the most exotic vocabulary seen in German literary writing since the seventeenth century, Jean Paul's arabesques are nevertheless full of genuine sentiment, humor, and ingenious irony.[19] With the younger generation he was more popular than the high Romantics because he was thought to express a cordial feeling for the common people, but after midcentury, when the tolerance for narrative experiment vanished, he came to be regarded by the tastemakers as the prime example of how not to do it.

Another novel on Romanticism's boundary of some originality but without detectable successors is Eduard Mörike's (1804–75) *Maler Nolten* (Painter Nolten, 1832). A shy, reclusive clergyman without much in the way of religious vocation or practical competence, Mörike is often thought of as the archetypal Biedermeier writer, domestic, private, unpretentious, and humorous, but the novel is evidence of instinctive depth. Although in clear succession to *Wilhelm Meister*, with interpolated poems and an engrossingly imaginative verse play, it is not a Bildungsroman but a fateful tangle among a psychopath and three neurotics; only the psychopath knows what she wants, while the others are imperfectly aware of their own, ultimately disastrous motives, among them unarticulable sexual repression.[20] More redolent of the future was the last phase in Tieck's career, rather amazingly, for, while he was typecast internationally as the "king of Romanticism," he moved toward an early form of realism with works that are still underestimated in their inventiveness because the superintending narrative of German literary history is unable to accommodate them. Among them were *Der junge Tischlermeister* (The Young Carpenter, 1836), a mini-Bildungsroman in which the young man, like Wilhelm Meister, gets involved with a theater troupe, but, unlike Wilhelm, obtains part of his *Bildung* from an adulterous relationship, enabling him to return to his wife and craft with greater maturity, a motif not often encountered on the threshold of the Victorian age. Tieck also undertook two ambitious historical novels, the unfinished *Der Aufruhr in den Cevennen* (The Rebellion in the Cevennes, 1826) about the struggles of the French Calvinists in the seventeenth century, and the crowning work of his career, *Vittoria Accorombona* (1840), placing one of the strongest female figures in German letters into an unidealized Renaissance setting of competing bands of gangsters. Tieck, in his time the outstanding German expert on Elizabethan drama, meant to rescue the tragically indomitable poet Vittoria Accorombona from her representation as a witch in John Webster's *The White Devil* (1612).[21]

With these works of his late phase Tieck joined the mode of historical fiction that had been growing in importance. Primarily it served two purposes. One was that it trained post-Romantic writers in realism. Germans long complained that they lacked the capital city and the self-aware social institutions on which the realistic novel in more advanced countries could be based; reaching back to historical materials could supplant the missing substance. Second, historical fiction was to supply a usable past for the nationalism that emerged in opposition to the repressive, static order imposed upon the German states after the defeat of Napoleon. The model for this endeavor was Sir Walter Scott, who was widely admired in Germany. In fact, it was with a pretended translation from Scott, *Walladmor* (1824), that one of the trendsetters, Willibald Alexis (Georg Wilhelm Heinrich Häring, 1798–1871), began his career as a historical novelist. Alexis launched upon a series of "Vaterländische Romane" (patriotic novels), patriotism in his usage referring less to an imagined Germany than to a real Prussia. These novels, such as *Der Roland von Berlin* (The Roland [an ancient statue] of Berlin, 1840), set in the fifteenth century, or *Der falsche Waldemar* (The Pretender Waldemar, 1842), set in the fourteenth century, were meant to define a tradition of Prussian values in a modern sense. But Alexis was to learn from bitter experience that the ruling order did not want from writers a patriotic discourse about the public weal; it did not want any intervention by writers in the public discourse at all. The consequence was an angry novel about the defeat of Prussia by Napoleon at the battle of Jena in 1806, *Ruhe ist die erste Bürgerpflicht* (Calm is the Citizen's First Duty, 1852), the title taken from a placard posted by the government after the humiliation: "Der König hat eine Bataille verloren. Jetzt ist Ruhe die erste Bürgerpflicht" (The king has lost a battle. Now calm is the citizen's first duty). Alexis ironically sets this complacent authoritarianism against the corruption in the ruling class of Berlin and the grotesque incompetence of the self-satisfied Prussian military in the face of Napoleon's underestimated military superiority.[22] Thus Alexis, against his instincts and intentions, was drawn into the dissidence of a younger generation of writers who had emerged in the 1830s.

This group of writers came to be known as Young Germany; like many literary-historical appellations, this one is inexact and misleading. It arose in part from Ludolf Wienbarg's (1802–72) dedication of his dissident lecture series, *Ästhetische Feldzüge* (Aesthetic Campaigns, 1834), "dem jungen Deutschland" (to the young Germany), adding in the preface: "nicht dem alten" (not to the old one), and in part from a confusion with a genuinely revolutionary movement, Young Italy. The writers did have a strong sense of belonging to a younger, post-Goethean generation, but they were not dangerous revolutionaries, whatever the governments may have thought. They were concerned in the first instance as writers with freedom of expression in opposition to the increasingly onerous censorship of the Metternichian restoration, as well as with the modernization of social relations among classes and, especially, between men and women, an interest modeled for them by the Saint-Simonian movement in France.[23] They pursued their aims mainly within the genres of the critical essay and the novel. The novels exhibit varying strategies. One is the encapsulation of sociopolitical discourses in melodrama, as in Ferdinand Kühne's (1806–88) *Eine Quarantäne im Irrenhaus* (A Quarantine in the Madhouse, 1835), in which a young man's uncle has him incarcerated in a madhouse for his deviant attitudes. Another was satire, as in Mundt's *Moderne Lebenswirren* (Confusions of Modern Life, 1834), in which the protagonist is sequentially persuaded by the "Parteiteufel" (devil of partisanship) of liberal, absolutist, and centrist ideologies. A third possibility was a first step in applying the techniques learned in historical fiction to the

Zeitroman, the novel of contemporary history, attempted by Heinrich Laube (1806–84) in the middle novel of his trilogy, *Das junge Europa* (Young Europe, 1833–37), *Die Krieger* (The Warriors, 1837), a thoughtful if disheartening assessment of liberal possibilities in the Polish revolution of 1830–31.

But the Young Germans became most notorious for their reconsideration of relations between the sexes, or, as commonly charged by their censorious enemies, for the "emancipation of the flesh." One earnest effort in this line was Mundt's *Madonna* (1835), which tells of a young woman with aspirations to emancipation who is being groomed for concubinage but gives herself to a theologian she truly loves, who then commits suicide out of shame. But the most spectacular event in this line was Karl Gutzkow's (1811–78) *Wally, die Zweiflerin* (Wally the Skeptic, 1835). Gutzkow was one of the most remarkable of writers to emerge from the stresses besetting nineteenth-century German intellectuals. Born in a stable to a lower-class father of doubtful mental health, he applied his powerful, energetic, and waywardly creative mind to a combative career throughout the middle half of the century. In his Young German phase it is difficult to untangle larger motivations from personal peeves. *Wally* is a muddled, ill-written novel that was meant as a vehicle for critical meditations on Christianity and the Bible; the plot, with icy eroticism, examines the conventions of love and marriage. In its most notorious episode, the title character Wally — it is difficult to call her a "heroine" — shows herself nude, in imitation of a scene in a medieval epic, to her friend on the day she is to marry another. The novel caused an uproar and gave the governments an opportunity to move against the literary movement without directly engaging its politics. Gutzkow served a jail term for blasphemy and lasciviousness, and at the end of 1835 the German Confederation issued a ban on the writings of Young Germany, listing in particular, along with Heinrich Heine, Wienbarg, Laube, Mundt, and Gutzkow.[24]

The ban had the intended effect of turning the writers against one another and interrupting their literary careers. By 1838 Young Germany had to all intents and purposes ceased to exist. But the ban was not the only reason for the failure of the movement. The novels were too intellectual and talky, too preoccupied with the concerns of a liberal literary subculture, to have much resonance; criticism in the later nineteenth century recalled the episode with repugnance. More promising for the future was a contemporary of the Young Germans, Karl Leberecht Immermann (1796–1840). He was a Prussian official loyal to his king, but his reputation as a conservative derived largely from a spat he had with a nationalistic student fraternity, then a sacred cow among the dissidents. Of his two clever novels, one, *Die Epigonen* (The Epigones, 1836), with by now stereotyped allusions to *Wilhelm Meister*, gave a name to a generation that felt diminished in its succession to the age of Goethe; it was also the first major German novel to portray an industrial milieu. The other, *Münchhausen: Eine Geschichte in Arabesken* (Münchhausen: A Story in Arabesques, 1838–39) is a comic novel that makes the famous liar a representative figure of the times. Unfortunately, a subsection of the work that satirically portrays a rural milieu was later excised and circulated, as though it were a straight-faced celebration of conservative values, as *Der Oberhof* (The Chief Farm), long displacing the whole novel and obscuring Immermann's true potential, cut short by his early death.[25]

A radically conservative alternative to the Young Germans was the Swiss clergyman Jeremias Gotthelf (Albert Bitzius, 1797–1854), whose novels of peasant life, such as *Wie Uli der Knecht glücklich wird* (How Uli the Farmhand Found Happiness, 1841) and its sequel, *Uli der Pächter* (Uli the Tenant Farmer, 1849), *Wie Anne Bäbi Jowäger haushaltet* (How Anne Bäbi Jowäger Keeps House, 1843–44), or *Geld und Geist* (Money and Spirit, 1843–44), can oppress the liberal-minded reader with their antihumanistic moralism and implacable insistence upon the subordination of the self to the religious and social order, but they are powerfully written, psychologically perceptive, and fearless in their defense of the welfare of the peasantry, as the author himself was in his sometimes embattled pastoral career. Ironically, the programmatically earth-bound realist with a deep suspicion of the seductive perils of the modern imagination has remained best known for a work of fantasy, *Die schwarze Spinne* (The Black Spider, 1842), in which a monstrous allegorical spider is attracted by immoral deviance and rebelliousness six hundred and four hundred years in the past, and lurks, vibrating with evil purpose, in the present. The narration rises to a pitch of terror unequalled in the German fiction of the century.[26]

Another ambitious experiment launched at mid-century had no immediate successors but has attracted a good deal of retrospective attention: the nine-volume epic by the former Young German scandalizer Gutzkow, *Die Ritter vom Geiste* (The Knights of the Spirit, 1849–51), a "Roman des Nebeneinanders" (novel of contiguity or simultaneity), attempting to give a full panorama of contemporary life and to sink a shaft through all the class levels from the royal court to the subproletariat at a moment in time. Apart from the question whether the linear art of narrative can reproduce simultaneity, the effort is impaired by its recurrence to the no longer modern mode of the secret society novel. Gutzkow made another valiant attempt with the equally vast *Der Zauberer von Rom* (The Sorcerer of Rome, 1859–61), in which a reforming pope rescues the Church from the papists by Germanizing it. But Gutzkow by then had lost much of his readership, having alienated it with a critical poison pen — he wrote of Keller that his characters had their lederhosen buttoned up to the throat[27] — that may have been a symptom of the mental illness in which he ended his life.[28]

Literary historians tend to see the Revolution of 1848, which failed to achieve for the bourgeoisie a political relevance commensurate with its cultural and intellectual merit, as a distinct caesura. While such chrono-logical boundaries are rarely as definitive as they are purported to be, after mid century one can often sense a tone of melancholy resignation and introverted passivity. In the conventional literary history, this tone has come to be known as "Poetic Realism." The canonizers have tried to make a virtue out of an allegedly idealistic realism more faithful to higher poetic purpose than the grittier, more urban, and socially critical realism of Western countries; contrarily, for the debunkers, Poetic Realism is the marker of the isolated provinciality of German writing in the second half of the century. In fact, Poetic Realism, insofar as there was such a thing, was not peculiarly German but imported from Denmark at a time when it, too, was suffering from national depression.[29] There is some reason to think that the concept of Poetic Realism might usefully be retired alto-gether in favor of one of "realism" comprehending differing literary strate-gies running parallel to one another. In any case, it would be well to get away from a notion of a domesticized, ameliorative, affirmative literary mode wholly occupying the literary scene.

One example might be the novella *Zwischen Himmel und Erde* (Between Heaven and Earth, 1856, revised 1858 and 1862) by one of the definers of Poetic Realism, Otto Ludwig (1813–65). It is a story of a family of roofers in which one assertive brother marries by deception the intended of the shy brother while he has been away on his apprenticeship. The ensuing tangle of guilt and hostility leads to a violent end for the older brother and a life of repressed desire for the other. The serious and severe tone is characteristic of the "Poetic Realism," as is the shorter form of the novella.

A great deal has been written about the history and theory of the German novella from Goethe to Thomas Mann, and there are many more examples and authors than can be accommodated here.[30] In part this has been another effort to claim particularity for German literature, in contrast to the dominance of the novel in other literatures, by decanonizing the more voluminous works and leaving out of consideration the tendency of the novella itself to get longer; while Heinrich von Kleist could write novellas in a few paragraphs, in the course of the century it is not unusual for them to reach 200 pages and more, as does, for example, *Zwischen Himmel und Erde.*

Even among the novellas by specialists in the genre, it is sometimes those converging to novel length that have the largest reputations. This is the case with Theodor Storm (1817–88), who wrote some fifty novellas, but his last and longest, *Der Schimmelreiter* (The White Horse Rider, 1888), about a dike reeve who fails to overcome the superstitions of his fel-low citizens, is his finest. Although it takes place in the eighteenth century, it is a cautionary tale about the imperfect vision of technological man.[31] It contains an austere, unsentimental but nevertheless moving love story proving that Poetic Realism need not be soft in head or heart. A similar case is that of the Swiss writer Conrad Ferdinand Meyer (1825–98), of whose aesthetically refined, mostly historical novellas, the best known is also one of the longest, *Der Heilige* (The Saint, 1879), which probes the puzzling character of Thomas à Becket. Meyer's employment of an imperfectly perceptive narrator, a Swiss crossbow craftsman in the service of Henry II, has generated interpretive enigmas that occupy critics to the present day.[32] Others, however, remained loyal to the form that some observers, surfeited with theoretical discourse, have defined bluntly as "a prose narrative of intermediate length." Probably one should mention in this connection Paul Heyse (1830–1914), who, for reasons today difficult to reconstruct, in 1910 became the first German imaginative writer to win the Nobel Prize for Literature. Heyse wrote more than a hundred novellas, but their relentlessly conventional plotting and sacrifice of substance to form make them hard to remember. Best known, perhaps not least because of its employment as a text for intermediate German teaching, is *L'Arrabbiata* (1855), about a fiercely independent girl whom we just know will learn love and subordination under the right circumstances.[33]

Sometimes a single work can make a reputation in prose fiction, as in the case of Baroness Annette von Droste-Hülshoff (1797–1848), the most gifted German religious poet in the middle half of the nineteenth century. She attempted, but was unable to complete, a novel, *Ledwina* (1824), but as a prose writer is best remembered for a novella, *Die Judenbuche* (The Jews' Beech Tree, 1842), a murder story that continues to perplex interpreters and exhibits an empathy with a criminalized underclass remarkable in an author of her social rank.[34] Droste-Hülshoff was long regarded as the only woman writer of distinction of her time, but much effort has been expended more recently on bringing others into view. Some of these have to be admitted as having been popular, or, in an older system of evaluation, subliterary writers, such as Theodor Mundt's wife Klara (1814–73), who as Luise Mühlbach wrote historical novels in more than a hundred volumes, many of which were widely read in English translation, or the family magazine author E. Marlitt (Eugenie John, 1825–87), but a friendlier view of them has been developing as authors who conveyed liberal and enlightened sentiments to a general readership.[35] Toward the end of the century, women writers of high refinement begin to emerge. One was the Austrian baroness Marie von Ebner-Eschenbach (1830–1916), who, after failing with ambitious dramas, turned to prose writing in the 1870s, where she had more success with a rapid series of novels and novellas, among them *Das Gemeindekind* (literally, The Ward of the Parish, translated as *Their Pavel,* 1887),[36] a grueling account of the son of a murderer who survives an upbringing as an ill-treated foster child to achieve a good character, and the charming, understated *Lotte, die Uhrmacherin* (Lottie the Watchmaker), with the unusual figure of a female artisan.[37] Another such writer who has come more clearly into view in recent times is Louise von François, whose best known work, *Die letzte Reckenbürgerin* (The Last Lady Reckenburg, 1871),[38] in which the protagonist with stoic dutifulness raises a girl wrongly believed to be the daughter of her illegitimate son and through patience restores a decent order to her life, is notable for its austerely disciplined style.[39]

The woman writer at midcentury beginning to attract the most attention is Fanny Lewald (1811–89), who struggled against her Jewish origin and her father's opposition to her writing to launch a substantial career of novels and travel books from the age of thirty; some of her novels have been recently republished. While in her time she was most successful with a historical novel, *Prinz Louis Ferdinand* (1849), a lively account of love liaisons, gallantry, and Jewish salon hostesses in the reign of Frederick William III, of particular interest today is her quasi-autobiographical novel *Jenny* (1843), giving a detailed portrayal of the struggle of a Jewish-born woman for emancipation and creative fulfillment. Lewald might remind us of her almost exact English contemporary George Eliot (1819–80) in her precision of social observation and earnest sense of duty, not, however, in suppleness of style or aphoristic wisdom.[40]

The most important German-Jewish writer between Heinrich Heine and the generation that emerged at the end of the century was Berthold Auerbach (1812–82), who rose from impoverished origins to national and international fame, though today he is barely remembered except by specialized literary historians and, occasionally, those who labor on the catastrophe that befell the German Jews. In his time, however, he was ubiquitously well connected in literary life and widely read abroad, especially in English-speaking countries and in Russia. He began his career with two ambitious novels with Jewish themes. The first of these, *Spinoza: Ein Denkerleben* (Spinoza: A Thinker's Life, 1837), is a fictionalized biography that follows the philosopher from his boyhood to the threshold of his intellectual work. Spinoza was a crucial figure for the formation of German-Jewish identity, a bridge to the great age of Goethe that had discovered him as an alternative to both traditional religion and modern materialism. Auerbach, though self-taught in philosophy and Latin, produced in 1841, when he was twenty-nine years old, a German translation of Spinoza's Latin works that was long standard. Auerbach was a fervid assimilationist, not out of opportunism but out of a conviction that Judaism could be rescued only by welding it to German culture. At the same time he was aware of the dangers and frustrations, as appears in his other Jewish novel, *Dichter und Kaufmann: Ein Lebensgemälde aus der Zeit Moses Mendelssohns* (Poet and Merchant: A Picture of Life from the Time of Moses Mendelssohn, 1840), which portrays the Jewish satirist Ephraim Kuh (1731–90), who, though at one time a protégé of Gotthold Ephraim Lessing (1729–81), ended in pathos and failure.[41] But Auerbach, having determined that he did not wish to specialize as a Jewish novelist, in 1843 turned to a long series of novels and novellas collectively known as the *Schwarzwälder Dorfgeschichten* (Black Forest Village Tales), which pioneered regional literature in Germany and laid the base of his international reputation. Among the best known are *Der Tolpatsch* (The Booby, 1843), *Die Frau Professorin* (The Professor's Wife, 1846), *Barfüßele* (Little Barefoot, 1856), and *Joseph im Schnee* (Joseph in the Snow, 1860). The *Dorfgeschichten* are not unworldly idylls, anti-modern in their values, or conspicuously reverential of the peasant class, and they are animated by Auerbach's moderate but fervent liberalism.[42]

Another of Auerbach's heroes, along with Spinoza, was Benjamin Franklin, a German translation of whose autobiography he edited in 1876. Franklin is the presiding genius over Auerbach's late novel, *Das Landhaus am Rhein* (The Villa on the Rhine, 1869), whose protagonists foil an evil slave-dealer returned to Germany and then sail to America to join a Negro regiment in the Civil War. The novel is a somewhat less significant example of a significant subgenre in nineteenth-century Germany, the novel of America, impelled in substantial part by the emigration, which touched the lives of millions of people and remained a topic of concern in public discourse for at least sixty years. Some authors, like Auerbach, had no experience of America, and sometimes anti-American stereotypes supervened; the most notorious case is *Der Amerika-Müde* (The America-Weary, 1855) by the Austrian liberal Ferdinand Kürnberger (1821–79), whose protagonist, modeled on Nicholas Lenau (Nicolaus von Strehlenau, 1802–50), who had a farcical American adventure in 1832, travels around the United States, disgusted by everything he sees.[43] But others had extensive and sometimes profound experience of America. The first important of these was the escaped Moravian monk who called himself Charles Sealsfield (Carl Postl, 1793–1864), who from 1829 to 1843 published a series of vigorous novels set mostly, though not exclusively, in Louisiana and the Republic of Texas, intensely partisan in the spirit of Andrew Jackson and of Manifest Destiny. The best known of these is a distillate from a section of *Das Kajütenbuch* (The Cabin Book, 1841) entitled *Die Prärie am Jacinto* (The Prairie on the Jacinto), which was further abridged into a novella, "Die Erzählung des Obersten Morse" (The Story of Colonel Morse), by Hugo von Hofmannsthal (1874–1929) in his widely employed anthology, *Deutsche Novellen* (originally published in 1912); it tells of a young man who foolishly rides out into the trackless Texas prairie, becomes hopelessly disoriented, and is saved from dying of thirst by a man who turns out to be a hallucinating murderer.[44]

Another such writer prominent in his time was Friedrich Gerstäcker (1816–72), who came to America in 1837 and remained for six years, much of the time as a backwoodsman in Arkansas, and produced a large body of fiction and expository writing about the United States. His most popular works were a pair of wild and woolly Westerns, *Die Regulatoren in Arkansas* (The Regulators in Arkansas, 1845) and *Die Flußpiraten des Mississippi* (The River Pirates of the Mississippi, 1848), but his most insightful novels about American life and the need for prospective German emigrants to be cautious as well as hopeful were *Nach Amerika!* (To America!, 1855), *Gold!* (1857–58), and *In Amerika* (1872).[45] These are major examples of a large area of German fiction that has been of growing interest since the United States Bicentennial of 1976, about which there is still much to learn. The topic reverted to fantasy at the end of the century in the hands of Karl May (1842–1912), who had not left Germany but for some time persuaded readers that he was identical with the invincible German superboy called, in his Westerns, Old Shatterhand, when, with his Apache companion Winnetou, he enforces justice in the American West, or Kara ben Nemsi in his North African and Balkan settings. Although May is by a large margin the best-selling fiction writer in the German language, still published in hundreds of thousands of copies, and has impacted German culture like no other writer, his comic-book quality may seem to place him outside the limit of literature as commonly understood.[46]

The model German-Jewish writer Auerbach was a good friend, ironically, of Gustav Freytag (1816–95), whose mid-century best seller, *Soll und Haben* (Debit and Credit, 1855), has acquired a reputation as the archetypal anti-Semitic German literary work. It is a double-plotted Bildungsroman contrasting a nice boy who succeeds in the world of commerce, because he is a nice boy endowed with an incorruptible set of bourgeois values, to a Jewish contemporary, who, though irritatingly resourceful and devoted to self-improvement, comes to a bad end with his intrigues, plots, and commercial manipulations. The novel is not very good, nor is it very bad; it is carefully constructed, modeled in considerable part on Charles Dickens's *David Copperfield*. The liberal Freytag, whose third wife was Jewish, had no notion that *Soll und Haben* was an anti-Semitic novel; he thought he was defending the unselfish work ethic of the German middle class against those who lacked it: the nobility, the Poles, and the Jews. He became apologetic when he realized that its popularity accompanied and perhaps fed the rising tide of anti-Semitism. But the fate of the book was out of his hands; its sixty-four editions by 1906 and 753,000 copies sold by the time the copyright expired in 1925 certainly owe something to its anti-Jewish reputation. It has been said that it became a standard confirmation gift for young people until it was displaced by Hitler's *Mein Kampf*. Freytag, of course, could not know what we know, but events have made of his mundane novel an ominous episode in the history of German culture.[47]

Within that history, *Soll und Haben* had one particularly regrettable consequence: it motivated Wilhelm Raabe (1831–1910), who quite rightly regarded himself as a more capable writer than Freytag and chafed at his greater success, to surpass it with a more finely executed novel on a similar plan, *Der Hungerpastor* (The Hunger Pastor, 1863–64). Here the German hero is not a boring commercial clerk like Freytag's protagonist but an idealistic, mentally agile young man who comes to serve an impoverished rural community as pastor, and his Jewish antagonist is not Freytag's grubby intriguer with a knack for manipulating commercial paper but a sharp-witted intellectual who rises to scholarly eminence and social elegance. The consequences, however, were distressingly similar; despite a slow start, over the years *Der Hungerpastor* became Raabe's best seller and the title that people who know one thing about him associate with him. Raabe was no more an anti-Semite than Freytag, and he tried, like Charles Dickens in the wake of *Oliver Twist,* to make amends by creating positive Jewish figures in other works. But to no avail; *Der Hungerpastor* escaped his grasp and became a major feature of one of the most peculiar reception histories in this period. His reputation was captured by a cult of aggressively unliterary and antimodern petty-bourgeois admirers determined to treat him as a wise man conformed to their own conservative, nationalist, and sometimes anti-Semitic biases, immune from literary criticism or even scholarly inquiry. Much effort has been expended since the 1960s to wrest him from the grasp of these false friends.[48]

Raabe began with what Friedrich Hebbel (1813–63), an acute critic as well as a major playwright, greeted as an "overture" to a conceivably larger career: *Die Chronik der Sperlingsgasse* (The Chronicle of Sparrow Alley, 1856), in which an elderly man mulls the loves and losses he has known with qualified optimism about the possibility of surviving misfortune and political oppression. Raabe, determined to make a living from writing only, then set out on what was to be a long struggle of trying to accommodate his particular imaginative vision and unusual formal sense to the less adventurous and less hospitable expectations of the public. A substantial part of his early work is historical fiction, recapitulating the evolution of realism. Later he repudiated this first phase as immature; critics have followed him in this judgment, but renewed attention may raise the standing of one or another of the novels and stories of his first phase.

In the 1860s he made an effort to conquer the public with three ambitious novels: *Der Hungerpastor, Abu Telfan* (1867), and *Der Schüdderump* (an untranslatable term for a cart carrying plague victims, 1869–70). The reception of the first was delayed and that of the others, less amenable to reader expectations, indifferent, turning Raabe for some time from novels to shorter prose. *Abu Telfan* is the sardonic story of a man who, having returned from enslavement in Africa, fails to reintegrate himself into his philistine, commonplace home town. *Der Schüdderump* tells of an effort of an invincibly jovial older man to sell his own granddaughter to a depraved aristocrat. What alienated Raabe from his readership more than these challenges to its expectations of poetic justice was his increasingly subtle experimentation with narrative perspective and unreliable narrators, the latter inspired by one of his model authors, William Makepeace Thackeray. Examples are *Drei Federn* (Three Pens, 1863), in which a conflicting story is told by three narrators in two segments apiece, or *Else von der Tanne* (Else of the Fir, 1865), a third-person narration enclosed within the consciousness of a pastor who is unable to articulate to himself his erotic attraction to an angelic girl he cannot protect from being stoned to death as a witch. As Raabe with bitter regret abandoned hope of finding a readership willing to do the work his inventiveness required of it, his art grew stronger. He returned to the historical mode with two subversive novels of the Seven Years' War, *Das Odfeld* (The Odin Field, 1888),[49] and his last published work, *Hastenbeck* (1899). Raabe's portrayals of war and violence are never about heroism and patriotic uplift but sorrowfully stress the waste and suffering the Germans inflicted upon themselves in the interest of foreigners and despotic rulers.

Two novels at the end of his career have come to be regarded as his finest: *Stopfkuchen: Eine See- und Mordgeschichte* (Stuffcake: A Sea and Murder Story, 1891), and *Die Akten des Vogelsangs* (The Documents of the Birdsong, 1896). In the first of these, a fat, apparently sluggish and self-complacent man, in whom dwells a competent and steely avenger, overruns with his garrulousness a boyhood acquaintance visiting from colonial Africa and pretending to memories of friendship. Stuffcake refuses to allow his visitor to evade his role of persecutor in their youth and sends him into flight with the discovery that his boyhood model had killed a man, allowing the blame to fall on Stuffcake's father-in-law. The abrasive tale is at once a parody of the Goethean ideal of *Bildung,* a self-critical reflection on Raabe's own authorial habits and fate, and a commentary on the harshness of human relations in the Germany of his time. *Die Akten des Vogelsangs* concerns the struggle of a firmly bourgeois, established official with an internal alter ego, a childhood companion who has disburdened himself of property, purpose, and worldliness in the utterly hopeless pursuit of a beautiful, frankly materialistic American girl they had both known in childhood, a quest that survives her remigration to the United States, her marriage, and her widowhood into total stasis. The narrator ultimately accepts his limitations and his fate while realizing how his split self has enriched and sensitized him beyond the commonplaces of bourgeois definition. The complex, multifaceted novel is a finely executed example of what has been called Raabe's "reminiscence technique."[50]

How differentiated and even disjointed the German literary culture in the age of realism could be is shown by a comparison of Raabe with another novelist prominent at the time, Friedrich Spielhagen (1829–1911). Though near contemporaries of similar social and geographical origin and comparable career evolution, Raabe and Spielhagen had, at least by surface appearances, nothing to do with one another; Raabe alludes to Spielhagen dismissively only a few times, whereas the exhaustively well-read Spielhagen, who produced an extensive corpus of literary criticism and theory, never mentions Raabe at all. In part this mutual silencing was owing to competitiveness in a literary economy that was less remunerative for authors than in Britain or France, but it may well have had a motive of aesthetic principle. Spielhagen was notorious as a theorist of the strictest narrative objectivity, by which he meant the silencing of the authorial voice as far as possible and which must have seemed to Raabe a direct repudiation of his garrulous, intrusive, visibly managing narrative habits with their wide variety of perspectives and recursive ironies. The careers of Raabe and Spielhagen came to be antitheses of one another. Raabe had constant, in his mind, related, struggles both with his public and with monetary compensation, while Spielhagen's writing propelled him promptly to prosperity. His novels were coveted by German and Austrian periodicals, appeared in many editions, and were highly regarded abroad, especially in the United States, while Raabe has never been an exportable author. But, while Raabe's prestige gradually improved in the latter part of his life, although for reasons that he did not find altogether gratifying, Spielhagen's crashed in midcareer; a ferocious attack on him by the naturalist Heinrich Hart in 1884 may have been partly a cause, partly a symptom of the decline of his reputation among the gatekeepers and tastemakers.

Spielhagen had begun with a sprawling sociopolitical novel of the loves and confusions of a young man in the period leading up to the Revolution of 1848, whose Goethean title, *Problematische Naturen* (1861–63), seemed to define the mood of a generation as Immermann's *Die Epigonen* had for the previous generation. This and four other novels form the remnant of Spielhagen's conventional reputation: *Die von Hohenstein* (The Hohensteins, 1864), a scathing portrayal of corruption in the aristocratic class, which was to be one of his enduring themes; *In Reih' und Glied* (In Rank and File, 1867), a first probe into the ideas of socialism, influenced by the skeptically regarded model of Ferdinand Lassalle; *Hammer und Amboß* (Hammer and Anvil, 1869), the first important German novel since *Die Epigonen* to attempt to deal with modern industry, in which the protagonist, after a disordered youth and an educational spell in prison, rises from the factory floor to self-taught engineering competence and profit-sharing ownership; and *Sturmflut* (Storm Surge, 1877), which parallels a natural disaster on Germany's north coast with the metaphoric flood of French gold reparations after the Franco-Prussian War. *Sturmflut,* for all its social and political critique, ends on a note hopeful for the future of social relations in the Wilhelminian Reich, which may be the reason it is the last work the canonization process has registered, even though Spielhagen had a quarter of a century of writing before him. For he became increasingly bitter and melancholy about the mean-spiritedness and materialism of postunification Germany, its squandering of the ideal capital of the Goethean age. Consequently he was dismissed as old-fashioned, but his most old-fashioned idea, as critics complained, was democracy. One can trace his disillusionment in a series of novels that converge ever more with the gritty, naturalistic realism of the French and the Scandinavians to which he was theoretically opposed and even to a kind of *fin-de-siècle* cynicism, among them *Platt Land* (Flat Country, 1879), *Ein neuer Pharoah* (A New Pharoah, 1889), *Sonntagskind* (Sunday's Child, 1893), and the paired final works, *Opfer* (Sacrifice, 1900) and *Frei geboren* (Born Free, also 1900), of which the second is the prequel of the first.[51]

Spielhagen accompanied these larger works with a series of shorter novels and novellas, towards the end grimly comic and bitingly satirical. Among these was a vignette of a sourly tragic intersection of upper-class depravity with bourgeois ambition, *Zum Zeitvertreib* (Killing Time, 1897), drawn from a scandal of adultery and lethal vengeance in the baronial Ardenne family. Unbeknownst to him, this event had already been the motive for one of the most celebrated novels of Theodor Fontane (1819–98), *Effi Briest* (1895).

It has been in no way advantageous to the disrespected Spielhagen's reputation that he stumbled onto the same territory as the author who has come to be regarded as the savior of the prestige of German realism.[52] Fontane had a career that can be an inspiration to late bloomers everywhere. He began as a pharmacist and then became a drama critic, a reporter from Britain, a war correspondent, a travel writer, and a specialist in ballads, pithy narrative poems that were a popular genre in his time. He published his first novel, *Vor dem Sturm* (Before the Storm), in 1878 at the age of fifty-nine. Again replicating the evolution of German realism, it is a historical novel about the rebellious initiative of the Prussian landed nobility against Napoleon. He wrote other works set in the past, among them the piquant *Schach von Wuthenow* (1883) about an early nineteenth-century nobleman who seduces a pockmarked but otherwise beautiful young lady, is obliged to marry her out of honor, and commits suicide after their wedding ceremony for fear of the disdain of his fellow officers.

Increasingly, however, Fontane set his works in the present, often, though not always, in Berlin. He began to specialize in gently comprehending stories about women, their unfulfilled loves, their nearly accidental adulteries, their achieved or unachieved yearning for elusive happiness and fulfillment, beginning with *L'Adultera* (1882), in which the husband loses his wife by tempting her with a young friend, and continuing with *Cécile* (1887), a triangle of a former mistress of a prince, her neglectful husband, and her admirer, ending in catastrophe; *Irrungen Wirrungen* (Errancies and Confusions, 1888), which shocked the public with an episode of unpunished extramarital sex across class boundaries; *Stine* (1890), even more shockingly a sympathetic portrayal of a kept woman; *Unwiederbringlich* (Irretrievable, 1891), a story of the deteriorating marriage of an older man to a younger wife, set in the Danish aristocracy; and the ineffably charming *Effi Briest,* which hovers delicately on the boundary of sentimentality without crossing it. Fontane's range extended to *Quitt* (Quits, 1891), a story, half of which is set in a Mennonite community in the American Southwest, of atonement for a killing; *Frau Jenny Treibel* (1893), a good-humored satire of bourgeois parvenus; and *Die Poggenpuhls* (The Poggenpuhl Family, 1896), about a widow of an officer and her children coping with genteel poverty. The last in the series, *Der Stechlin* (The Stechlin Lake, 1899), though his longest, comes as close as any German work to the Flaubertian ideal of a novel about nothing; depicting the latter days of a modest, minor nobleman, it is filled with conversation, old-age wisdom, ingenious if sometimes feckless social maneuvering, and events that do not happen. Fontane's carefully controlled narrative voice, observant and critical without becoming partisan or moralistically judgmental, his humorous and tolerant tone, the artistic "finesses" on which he prided himself, and a pioneering employment of leitmotif made him the most aesthetically satisfying of the German novelists at the end of the century and an acknowledged inspiration for Thomas Mann.[53]

The German novel was rather slow to accept the spirit of modernism. Naturalism was largely a matter of the drama. Most of the naturalistic prose experiments remained literary-historical curiosities; much of what we might call impressionism or neo-Romanticism expressed itself in poetry. Of the important careers of novelists that began at the end of the century one might mention that of Jakob Wassermann (1873–1934), whose oddly shaped *Die Juden von Zirndorf* (The Jews of Zirndorf, 1897) was the little-noticed prelude to a successful career, or of Arthur Schnitzler (1862–1931), whose *Leutnant Gustl* (1900), about an officer, who, having been insulted by a bourgeois who cannot honorably be challenged to a duel, very unwillingly faces the prospect of suicide until he is reprieved by the untimely death of his tormentor, both introduced the technique of stream-of-consciousness narration into German literature and cost Schnitzler his reserve-officer commission. In 1908 Wassermann published *Caspar Hauser oder die Trägheit des Herzens* (Caspar Hauser or the Lethargy of the Heart) about a boy of mysteriously incarcerated origins who turned up in Nuremberg in 1828 and was soon murdered, which became an international bestseller. In the same year Schnitzler published *Der Weg ins Freie* (The Way into the Open), one of the most thoughtful fictional probes into the Jewish situation in the new century. Structurally and narratively, however, both of these are fairly conventional novels. Rainer Maria Rilke's (1875–1926) delicately impressionist if not decadent

Die Aufzeichnungen des Malte Laurids Brigge (The Sketches of Malte Laurids Brigge) and the book version of Franz Kafka's (1883–1924) breakthrough work *Das Urteil* (The Judgment) did not appear until 1910 and 1916 respectively. There is a temptation, however, to think of Thomas Mann's *Buddenbrooks* (1901) as the last nineteenth-century German novel, inheriting the more English and French structure of the family saga along with Fontane's irony, more modernistically turned onto the narrative level itself.

Large stretches of the nineteenth-century German novel remain imperfectly explored territory, even to German literary history, and have come to be obscure to the interdisciplinary purview of comparative literature, although much of the corpus was once widely known in the larger world. Whether there are any means of reviving awareness of it beyond the intermittent scholarly inquiries of specialists is uncertain.

Notes

[1] See Jeffrey L. Sammons, "The Land Where the Canon B(l)ooms: Observations on the German Canon and Its Opponents, There and Here," in *Canon vs. Culture: Reflections on the Current Debate,* ed. Jan Gorak (New York and London: Garland, 2001), 117–33.

[2] See Norbert Bachleitner, ed., *Quellen zur Rezeption des englischen und französischen Romans in Deutschland und Österreich im 19. Jahrhundert* (Tübingen: Niemeyer, 1990); Bachleitner, *Der englische und französische Sozialroman des 19. Jahrhunderts und seine Rezeption in Deutschland* (Amsterdam and Atlanta: Rodopi, 1993); Bachleitner, ed., *Beiträge zur Rezeption der britischen und irischen Literatur des 19. Jahrhunderts im deutschsprachigen Raum* (Amsterdam and Atlanta: Rodopi, 2000).

[3] Erich Auerbach, *Mimesis: The Representation of Reality in Western Literature,* trans. Willard Trask (Princeton: Princeton UP, 1953).

[4] Friedrich Schiller, *Nationalausgabe* (Weimar: Böhlau, 1943–), 20:462.

[5] See Jürgen Jacobs, *Wilhelm Meister und seine Brüder: Untersuchungen zum deutschen Bildungsroman* (Munich: Fink, 1972); Jeffrey L. Sammons, "The Mystery of the Missing *Bildungsroman,* or: What Happened to Wilhelm Meister's Legacy?" in Sammons, *Imagination and History: Selected Papers on Nineteenth-Century German Literature* (New York, Bern, Frankfurt am Main, and Paris: Peter Lang, 1988), 7–31; Sammons, "The Bildungsroman for Nonspecialists: An Attempt at a Clarification," in *Reflection and Action: Essays on the Bildungsroman,* ed. James Hardin (Columbia: U of South Carolina P, 1991), 26–45.

[6] See Eric A. Blackall, *Goethe and the Novel* (Ithaca and London: Cornell UP, 1976); *Goethe's Narrative Fiction: The Irvine Goethe Symposium,* ed. William J. Lillyman (Berlin and New York: de Gruyter, 1983).

[7] Friedrich Schlegel, *Kritische Schriften,* ed. Wolfdietrich Rasch (Munich: Hanser, [1956]), 46.

[8] Novalis, *Schriften,* ed. Paul Kluckhohn and Richard Samuel (Darmstadt: Wissenschaftliche Buchgesellschaft, 1968), 3:638, 646.

[9] See John Neubauer, *Novalis* (Boston: Twayne, 1980), 126–52.

[10] On Tieck, see Wolfgang Rath, *Ludwig Tieck: Das vergessene Genie* (Paderborn, Munich, Vienna, and Zurich, 1996); on *Franz Sternbald,* Jeffrey L. Sammons, "Tieck's *Franz Sternbald:* The Loss of Thematic Control," *Studies in Romanticism* 5 (1965/66): 30–43.

[11] Goethe's manuscript, which arose in the 1770s and 1780s, was lost and the original version of the novel was not published until 1911, shortly after a manuscript copy of the work was found. Translated by John R. Russell. Columbia, SC: Camden House, 1995.

[12] On Eichendorff, see Egon Schwarz, *Joseph von Eichendorff* (New York: Twayne, 1972); on *Ahnung und Gegenwart,* Gerhart Hoffmeister, "Eichendorff's *Ahnung und Gegenwart* as a Novel of Religious Development," in *Reflection and Action,* ed. Hardin, 292–313.

[13] Hartmut Steinecke, *Romantheorie und Romankritik in Deutschland* (Stuttgart: Metzler, 1975–76), 1:27, 143–45.

[14] On Stifter, see Martin and Erika Swales, *Adalbert Stifter: A Critical Study* (Cambridge, Eng.: Cambridge UP, 1984); on *Der Nachsommer,* Christine Oertel Sjögren, *The Marble Statue as Idea: Collected Essays on Adalbert Stifter's* Der Nachsommer (Chapel Hill: U of North Carolina P, 1972).

[15] On Keller, see Gerhard Kaiser, *Gottfried Keller: Das gedichtete Leben* (Frankfurt am Main: Insel, 1981); on *Der grüne Heinrich,* Hartmut Laufhütte, *Wirklichkeit und Kunst in Gottfried Kellers "Der grüne Heinrich"* (Bonn: Bouvier, 1969).

[16] On Hoffmann see Peter von Matt, *Die Augen der Automaten: E. T. A. Hoffmanns Imaginationslehre als Prinzip seiner Erzählkunst* (Tübingen: Niemeyer, 1971); Horst S. Daemmrich, *The Shattered Self: E. T. A. Hoffmann's Tragic Vision* (Detroit: Wayne State UP, 1973).

[17] On this aspect of Tieck, see William J. Lillyman, *Reality's Dark Dream: The Narrative Fiction of Ludwig Tieck* (Berlin and New York: de Gruyter, 1979).

[18] See Jeffrey L. Sammons, *The Nachtwachen von Bonaventura: A Structural Interpretation* (The Hague, London, and Paris: Mouton, 1965); Andreas Mielke, *Zeitgenosse Bonaventura* (Stuttgart: Heinz, 1984). Authorship has been assigned, on internal and documentary grounds, to Ernst August Friedrich Klingemann (1777–1831), though it remains difficult to understand how so conventionally ordinary a mind could have produced such an adventurous and challenging text. On the authorship question, see Jost Schillemeit, *Bonaventura: Der Verfasser der "Nachtwachen"* (Munich: Beck, 1973), and Ruth Haag, "Noch einmal: Der Verfasser der *Nachtwachen von Bonaventura,*" *Euphorion* 81 (1987): 268–97, with an important correction, 448.

[19] See Dorothea Berger, *Jean Paul Friedrich Richter* (New York: Twayne, 1972).

[20] On Mörike, see Helga Slessarev, *Eduard Mörike* (New York: Twayne, 1970); on *Maler Nolten,* Jeffrey L. Sammons, "Fate and Psychology: Another Look at Mörike's *Maler Nolten,*" in Sammons, *Imagination and History,* 33–54.

[21] On the late Tieck, see Lillyman, *Reality's Dark Dream*, Chapter 6; on *Vittoria Accorombona*, Jennifer Cizik Marshall, *Betrothal, Violence, and the "Beloved Sacrifice" in Nineteenth-Century German Literature* (New York, Washington, DC / Baltimore, Bern, Frankfurt am Main, Berlin, Brussels, Vienna, and Oxford: Peter Lang, 2001), 116–26.

[22] See Wolfgang Gast, *Der deutsche Geschichtsroman im 19. Jahrhundert: Willibald Alexis* (Freiburg: Becksmann, 1972); Lionel Thomas, *Willibald Alexis: A Biography* (Oxford: Blackwell, 1964).

[23] See E. M. Butler, *The Saint-Simonian Religion in Germany: A Study of the Young German Movement* (Cambridge, Eng.: Cambridge UP, 1926; reprinted New York: Fertig, 1968).

[24] See Jeffrey L. Sammons, *Six Essays on the Young German Novel* (Chapel Hill: U of North Carolina P, 1972).

[25] See Peter Hasubek, *Karl Leberecht Immermann: Ein Dichter zwischen Romantik und Realismus* (Cologne, Weimar, and Vienna: Böhlau, 1996).

[26] All of Gotthelf's novels are exhaustively treated by Pierre Cimaz, *Jeremias Gotthelf (1797–1854): Der Romancier und seine Zeit* (Tübingen and Basel: Francke, 1998). See also H. M. Waidson, *Jeremias Gotthelf: An Introduction to the Swiss Novelist* (Westport, CT: Greenwood Press, 1978).

[27] Karl Gutzkow, *Liberale Energie: Eine Sammlung seiner kritischen Schriften*, ed. Peter Demetz (Frankfurt am Main, Berlin, and Vienna: Ullstein, 1974), 293.

[28] On Gutzkow's late novels see Peter Demetz, "Karl Gutzkows 'Die Ritter vom Geiste': Notizen über Struktur und Ideologie," *Monatshefte* 61 (1969): 225–31; Peter Hasubek, "Karl Gutzkow: Die Ritter vom Geiste (1850–51). Gesellschaftsdarstellung im deutschen Roman nach 1848," in *Romane und Erzählungen des Bürgerlichen Realismus: Neue Interpretationen,* ed. Horst Denkler (Stuttgart: Reclam, 1980), 26–39; Gustav Frank, *Krise und Experiment: Komplexe Erzähltexte im literarischen Umbruch des 19. Jahrhundert* (Wiesbaden: Deutscher Universitäts-Verlag, 1998), 113–266.

[29] See Clifford Albrecht Bernd, *Poetic Realism in Scandinavia and Central Europe 1820–1895* (Columbia, SC: Camden House, 1995).

[30] From the vast literature on this topic, among the recommendable titles in English are E. K. Bennett, *A History of the German Novelle*, 2nd ed. revised and continued by H. M. Waidson (Cambridge, Eng.: Cambridge UP, 1961); Martin Swales, *The German* Novelle (Princeton: Princeton UP, 1977); Henry H. H. Remak, *Structural Elements of the German Novella from Goethe to Thomas Mann* (New York, Washington DC / Baltimore, Bern, Frankfurt am Main, Berlin, Vienna, and Paris: Peter Lang, 1996).

[31] See David A. Jackson, *Theodor Storm: The Life and Works of a Democratic Humanitarian* (New York and Oxford: Berg, 1992).

[32] For a recent approach, see John Pizer, "The Oriental Alter Ego: C. F. Meyer's *Der Heilige,*" Pizer, *Ego-Alter Ego: Double and / as Other in the Age of German Poetic Realism* (Chapel Hill: U of North Carolina P, 1998), 60–75.

[33] See Charles H. Helmetag, "Paul Heyse (1830–1914)," in *Dictionary of Literary Biography,* vol. 129, *Nineteenth-Century German Writers, 1841–1900,* ed.

James Hardin and Siegfried Mews (Detroit and London: Gale Research, 1993), 143–58.

[34] See Heinz Rölleke, "Annette von Droste-Hülshoff: Die Judenbuche (1842)," in *Romane und Erzählungen zwischen Romantik und Realismus: Neue Interpretationen*, ed. Paul Michael Lützeler (Stuttgart: Reclam, 1983), 335–53; Pizer, "Gender, Childhood, and Alterity in Annette von Droste-Hülshoff's Doppelgänger Thematic," in *Ego-Alter Ego*, 20–39. Recent interpretations have become preoccupied with Droste's attitude toward the Jews; for one judicious consideration, see William Collins Donahue, " 'Ist er kein Jude, so verdiente er einer zu sein': Droste-Hülshoff's *Die Judenbuche* and Religious Anti-Semitism," *German Quarterly* 72 (1999): 44–73.

[35] On Mühlbach, see Brent O. Peterson, "Luise Mühlbach (Clara Mundt) (1814–1873)," in *Dictionary of Literary Biography*, vol. 133, *Nineteenth-Century German Writers to 1840*, ed. James Hardin and Siegfried Mews (Detroit, Washington, and London: Gale Research), 204–10; on Marlitt, Todd Kontje, *Women, the Novel, and the German Nation 1771–1871: Domestic Fiction in the Fatherland* (Cambridge, Eng.: Cambridge UP, 1998), 183–201.

[36] Translated by Lynne Tatlock. Columbia, SC: Camden House, 1996.

[37] See Ferrel V. Rose, *The Guises of Modesty: Marie von Ebner-Eschenbach's Female Artists* (Columbia: Camden House, 1994).

[38] Translated by Tiiu Laane as *The Last von Reckenburg* (Columbia, SC: Camden House, 1995).

[39] See Thomas C. Fox, *Louise von François and* Die letzte Reckenbürgerin: *A Feminist Reading* (New York, Bern, Frankfurt am Main, and Paris: Peter Lang, 1988).

[40] See Vanessa Van Ornam, *Fanny Lewald and Nineteenth-Century Constructions of Femininity* (New York, etc.: Peter Lang, 2002).

[41] See David Sorkin, "The Invisible Community: Emancipation, Secular Culture, and Jewish Identity in the Writings of Berthold Auerbach," in *The Jewish Response to German Culture from the Enlightenment to the Second World War*, ed. Jehuda Reinharz and Walter Schatzberg (Hanover and London: UP of New England, 1985), 100–19; Nancy A. Kaiser, "Berthold Auerbach: The Dilemma of the Jewish Humanist from *Vormärz* to Empire," *German Studies Review* 6 (1983): 399–419.

[42] See Jürgen Hein, *Dorfgeschichte* (Stuttgart: Metzler, 1976).

[43] See Jeffrey L. Sammons, "Nationalist Anti-Americanism of a Prussophile Austrian: Ferdinand Kürnberger's *Der Amerika-Müde* in the Context of his Career," in *History and Literature: Essays in Honor of Karl S. Guthke*, ed. William Collins Donahue and Scott Denham (Tübingen: Stauffenberg, 2000), 385–97.

[44] On Sealsfield, see Jeffrey L. Sammons, *Ideology, Mimesis, Fantasy: Charles Sealsfield, Friedrich Gerstäcker, Karl May, and Other German Novelists of America* (Chapel Hill and London: U of North Carolina P, 1998), 3–110.

[45] On Gerstäcker, see Sammons, *Ideology, Mimesis, Fantasy*, 113–200.

[46] Exhaustive information in Gert Ueding with Reinhard Tschapke, ed., *Karl-May-Handbuch* (Stuttgart: Kröner, 1987).

[47] See Michael Schneider, *Geschichte als Gestalt: Gustav Freytags Roman "Soll und Haben"* (Stuttgart: Heinz, 1980); T. E. Carter, "Freytag's *Soll und Haben*,

a Liberal National Manifesto as a Best-Seller," *German Life & Letters* N.S. 21 (1967–68): 320–29; Jeffrey L. Sammons, "The Evaluation of Freytag's 'Soll und Haben,' " in Sammons, *Imagination and History*, 193–216.

⁴⁸ See Hermann Helmers, ed., *Raabe in neuer Sicht* (Stuttgart, Berlin, Cologne, and Mainz: Kohlhammer, 1968); Horst Denkler, *Wilhelm Raabe: Legende–Leben–Literatur* (Tübingen: Niemeyer, 1989).

⁴⁹ Translated by Michael Ritterson as *The Odin Field*. Columbia, SC: Camden House, 2001.

⁵⁰ Roy Pascal, "The Reminiscence-Technique in Raabe," *Modern Language Review* 49 (1954): 339–48. See also Barker Fairley, *Wilhelm Raabe: An Introduction to his Novels* (Oxford: Clarendon P, 1961); Jeffrey L. Sammons, *Wilhelm Raabe: The Fiction of the Alternative Community* (Princeton: Princeton UP, 1987).

⁵¹ See Dirk Göttsche, *Zeit im Roman: Literarische Zeitreflexion und die Geschichte des Zeitromans im späten 18. und im 19. Jahrhundert* (Munich: Fink, 2001), 678–738; Jeffrey L. Sammons, *Friedrich Spielhagen: Novelist of Germany's False Dawn* (Tübingen: Niemeyer, 2004).

⁵² See, with caution, Thomas Tyrell, "Theodor Fontanes 'Effi Briest' und Friedrich Spielhagens 'Zum Zeitvertreib': Zwei Dichtungen zu einer Wirklichkeit" (Diss. Rice U, 1986); Anja Restenberger, *Effi Briest: Historische Realität und literarische Fiktion in den Werken von Fontane, Spielhagen, Hochhuth, Brückner und Keuler* (Frankfurt am Main, Berlin, Bern, Brussels, New York, Oxford, and Vienna: Peter Lang, 2001).

⁵³ From the vast literature on Fontane, see particularly Peter Demetz, *Formen des Realismus: Theodor Fontane. Kritische Untersuchungen* (Munich: Hanser, 1964; reprinted Munich: Ullstein, 1973) and Nancy A. Kaiser, *Social Integration and Narrative Structure: Patterns of Realism in Auerbach, Freytag, Fontane, and Raabe* (New York, Berne, and Frankfurt am Main: Peter Lang, 1986), 87–131; for an exemplary study of Fontane's expanding reputation, Helen Chambers, *The Changing Image of Theodor Fontane* (Columbia, SC: Camden House, 1997).

Between Sentimentality and Phantasmagoria: German Lyric Poetry, 1830–1890

Thomas Pfau

Während sich nun diese [romantische] Schule ihrem Ableben näherte, veränderte sich mehr und mehr die Physiognomie der Zeit. Die Revolution, der Liberalismus, die Technik, die materiellen Tendenzen, die Cultur, die Alles beleckt, die Philosophie, die den letzten Rest des Unmittelbaren in die Vermittlung des Denkens hereinzuziehen systematisch fortfuhr, der Geschäftsdrang, der uns von Morgen bis Abend an den Arbeitsstuhl fesselt und der zehnten Muse, der langen Weile, ihr bischen Lebenslust vollends zu erdrücken droht: Alles dieß verschwor sich gegen die poëtische Stimmung und stellte vor die letzte Wiese, auf der ein Dichter schlendern mochte, den Schlagbaum der Sorge. (Theodor Vischer)[1]

[As the Romantic school was nearing its end, the overall profile of the era seemed increasingly altered. Revolution; liberalism; technology; the material orientation of culture whose influence extends everywhere; a philosophy continually striving to storm the last bastions of immediacy with the mediations of systematic thought; and the pressure of an economic life that fetters us to our desks and threatens to throttle the last bit of pleasurable life out of the tenth muse — boredom: all these tendencies conspired against the poetic mood by erecting a gate of anxious concern in front of the pasture in which a poet might wish to roam one last time.]

Supplement or Impediment of Cognition: Emotion and Lyric Form after Hegel

WERE ONE PRESSED to name a single overarching and dominant feature of German lyric poetry after 1830, it would probably have to be the genre's enduring uncertainty as to its own social legitimacy and efficacy. The most comprehensive study of the *Biedermeier* period, by Friedrich Sengle, remarks on the uncertain cultural authority of the lyric in the post-Romantic era, in part because the genre appeared to lack a coherent poetic theory, and also because the poetics of the Jena Romantics had proposed the novel rather than the lyric as a new super-genre capable of amalgamating *Poesie* and *Kritik* in an infinite and universalizing progression. By contrast, traditional lyric forms appeared psychologically and formally ephemeral, something underscored by Goethe's at times casual approach to lyric and epigrammatic writing in his late years.[2] The bourgeois Revolution in Paris (July 1830) and Goethe's death (1832) appeared to signal not only the demise of Romantic aesthetics but also the emergence of an ideological constellation that posited art and aesthetics as prime movers of social change. In spite of these shifts, a number of prominent poets still mentioned today as among the most accomplished of their time (Eichendorff, Heine, Mörike, Storm) responded to the lyric's apparently declining authority by employing the lyric image and form to reflect on the waning authority of Romantic programs of literature. With its subdued, reticent, and often miniaturist emotionalism, the major lyric poetry after 1830 remembers and partially surrenders the prophetic or redemptive utopias of high Romanticism and comes to reflect on the causes for their collapse. Even at the end of the Romantic era, Heine's 1827 letters to his publisher Julius Campe, on the occasion of negotiating the first edition of his *Buch der Lieder,* reveal the young writer waxing self-conscious about the exhausted state of the lyric: "Das 'Buch der Lieder' ist nichts als eine Gesammtausgabe meiner bekannten Gedichte. . . . Es ist wunderschön ausgerüstet und wird wie ein harmloses Kauffartheyschiff unter dem Schutze des 2ten Reisebilderbandes ruhig ins Meer der Vergessenheit hinabsegeln" ("The 'Book of Songs' is nothing but a complete edition of my familiar poems. . . . It is beautifully equipped, and like a harmless trade-vessel it is destined to sail peacefully into the sea of oblivion under the protection of vol. 2 of my *Reisebilder* [Images of Travel]").[3]

In depicting the development of art as a dialectical progression from a symbolic via a classical toward a Romantic aesthetic, and consequently from a sensuous toward a progressively more abstract concept of representation, Hegel's Berlin *Vorlesungen zur Ästhetik* (*Lectures on Fine Art,* 1821–29) had posited Romantic poetry as the apotheosis of a more than two-thousand year long process in which the dialectical progression of *Geist* toward full self-awareness — ultimately bent on grasping the history of its own becoming — had continually availed itself of some sensuous, material scaffolding or other. To advance what Hegel's philosophy identifies as the core objective of *Geist* (spirit, intellect), lyric poetry had to "sublate" (*aufheben*) its primary focus on a subjective emotion and thus purify it from the theological stigmata of self-importance (*superbia*), melancholy (*acedia*), or narcissism (*vanitas*) that had long adhered to it:

> Indem nun aber dies Aussprechen, um nicht der zufällige Ausdruck des
> Subjektes als solchen seinem unmittelbaren Empfinden und Vorstellen
> nach zu bleiben, zur Sprache des *poetischen* Inneren wird, so müssen die

Anschauungen und Empfindungen, wie sehr sie auch dem Dichter als einzelnem Individuum eigentümlich angehören und er sie als die seinigen schildert, dennoch eine allgemeine Gültigkeit enthalten.

[But in order that this expression may not remain a merely casual expression of an individual's own immediate feelings and ideas, it becomes the language of the *poetic* inner life, and therefore *however intimately* the insights and feelings which the poet describes as his own belong to him as a single individual, they must nevertheless possess a universal validity.[4]]

Already in his 1817 *Enzyklopädie,* Hegel had identified as a salient goal of philosophy the ability to dialectically absolve emotions, like all other particulars, from their idiosyncratic, contingent, and indeterminate nature. "Die Form der selbstischen Einzelheit" (the form of self-absorbed singularity), which spirit maintains in feeling, "proves the lowest and most inferior; in it, spirit exists not as something free, as infinite universality but, on the contrary, holds its substance and content as something purely accidental, subjective, and particular."[5] Emotion here is posited as but a transitional step within an incomplete progression toward self-conscious universality. It is, in Hegel's characteristic parlance, "noch geistlos" (as yet devoid of spirit).[6] Later writers, such as the enormously successful Emanuel Geibel (1815–1884) or Friedrich Hebbel (1813–1863), would approach the lyric as a formal strategy for distilling the intellectual content from a supposedly amorphous feeling. For Geibel this meant that "der Dichter beichtet in Gesängen / Sich rein von Leidenschaft und Schmerz" ("The poet confesses [in the religious sense] and so purifies / Himself of all passion and pain"). By contrast, Theodor Storm's approach to lyric writing in the age of bourgeois realism aims at sculpting poetic form into a precise objective correlative for an equally unique and distinctive feeling:

> Poeta laureatus:
>   Es sei die Form ein Goldgefäß,
>   In das man goldnen Inhalt gießt
> Ein anderer:
>   Die Form ist nichts als der Kontur,
>   Der den lebend'gen Leib beschließt.[7]

> [Poet Laureate:
>   Let the form be a golden vase
>   Into which a golden content we pour.'
> A different view:
>   Form is nothing but the contour
>   That a living body shall encase.]

The programmatic title (*Lyrische Form*) and didactic form shows Storm rejecting the excessively "golden" poetry of *poeta laureatus* Geibel (at whose sumptuous state-funeral a copy of the 100th edition of his poems was placed inside his coffin) as little more than an eloquent affirmation of the bourgeois-industrial society under King Maximilian II of Bavaria and, later, Emperor Wilhelm I of Germany. The "universality" of Geibel's lyric images is but a rehashing of average and often complacent beliefs and feelings endemic to the socially dominant strata during the post-1848 era. While ultimately staying clear of political poetry, Storm distrusts the leveling impulse behind Geibel's quintessentially affirmative bourgeois style — with its eclectic deployment of traditional forms and nationalist, even jingoist overtones after 1871 — because such poetry preemptively insists on the purity and communicability of emotions that, as a result, appear generic and average.[8] More ambitiously than Geibel, Friedrich Hebbel approaches the lyric through an exacting psycho-epistemological framework that is to guide the writer in forging the passage from a contingent emotion to reflection to self-conscious thought: "Ein lyrisches Gedicht ist da, so wie das Gefühl sich durch den Gedanken im Bewußtsein scharf abgrenzt" (A lyric poem obtains as soon as feeling has been sharply delimited by conscious thought).[9] Focused on the same issue, though more circumspect in his position, Theodor Vischer (1807–87) remarks that poetry's innate tendency toward naïveté — that is, its longing for a "Zustand relativer Bewußtlosigkeit" (a state of relative unself-consciousness) — is accompanied by consciousness threatening "in diejenige Bewußtheit überzugehen, welche die Naivität zerstört und die Poësie in Prosa auflöst" (to destroy the naïveté in question and to dissolve poetry into prose).[10]

While the task of intellectualizing or "socializing" contingent emotions had appeared a principal objective of Hegelian thought and had clearly shaped the early work of writers such as Hebbel, Geibel or Theodor Vischer, Hegel's concept of feeling actually proves rather more intricate. For it is another, frequently ignored systematic imperative of Hegelian thought that any given disposition of mind, however deficient vis-à-vis the teleological objectives of philosophical thought, must contain within it fuel that will keep the dialectical machine running. Feeling, in other words, cannot be reduced to a simple, self-identical (quasi-narcissistic) state and hence amounts to more than the static opposite of self-conscious thought. For it contains within itself, however obliquely, a formal impetus toward self-reflection and externalization (*Entäußerung*). A latent measure of perceptual acuity or "Aufmerksamkeit" (attentiveness) must be contained within even the most ephemeral, hermetic, and seemingly oblique emotive state. For it is only out of such speculative seeds that speculative thought can acquire its energy and direction. To make that observation is to concede a peculiar, as it were, retroactive dependency of speculative thinking on supposedly contingent and inferior particularities, a dependency that speculative thinking itself can neither deny nor fully assimilate. Far from being an "immediate" and unreflective expression of feeling, lyric poetry according to Hegel presents itself as the medium most suited to extracting the intentionality and lucidity that supposedly lies dormant in a given feeling without simply discarding the emotive quality whereby such a different kind of knowledge attains phenomenal distinctness.

Perhaps most accomplished in developing a unique "Stimmung" (mood) toward objective clarity by meticulous prosodic and rhetorical means is the lyric oeuvre of Eduard Mörike (1804–75). His famous opening poem of *Gedichte* (1838) brilliantly correlates the transitional logic of conscious life, here captured as awakening "An einem Wintermorgen, vor Sonnenaufgang" (On a Winter-Morning, before Sunrise). Staying clear of expressive conventions and a hackneyed emotionalism that mars much of *Biedermeier* poetry, affect here is not the opposite of conscious existence but, rather, allows consciousness to grasp its own intrinsic dynamic in concrete form. Mörike captures such reflexivity in a meticulously sculpted image of the lyric self capturing and — with great phonetic, rhythmic, and lexical specificity — expressing its sensual "pleasure in being" as a moment of crystalline clarity:

> O flaumenleichte Zeit der dunkeln Frühe!
> Welch neue Welt bewegest du in mir?
> Was ist's, daß ich auf einmal nun in dir
> Von sanfter Wollust meines Daseins glühe.
>
> Einem Kristall gleicht meine Seele nun,
> Den noch kein falscher Strahl des Lichts getroffen;
> Zu fluten scheint mein Geist, er scheint zu ruhn,
> Dem Eindruck naher Wunderkräfte offen,
> Die aus dem klaren Gürtel blauer Luft
> Zuletzt ein Zauberwort vor meine Sinne ruft.[11]
>
> [O feathery light time of the dark dawn,
> What new world have you brought to life in me?
> What can this mean, so suddenly to be
> Aglow in you with joy to have been born.
>
> My soul is like a crystal in this moment,
> That no false ray of light as yet has stricken;
> My spirit seems to flow, and to be pent,
> Then to the touch of wondrous powers quicken
> Thronging before my senses, summoned there
> By magic out of the clear blue belt of air.]

Captured as an oceanic ("zu fluten scheint"), tranquil expectancy (*"er scheint zu ruhn"*), spirit manifests itself as an emotional potentiality, one not merely indulged as subjective pathos but, rather, scrupulously observed and formally captured by the simile of a crystal "den noch kein falscher Strahl des Lichts getroffen" (as yet undistorted by the spurious illumination of consciousness). With its ingenious alternation of phonetic values and its subtly lilting metrics, Mörike's lyric offers a formal analogue for its central epistemological claim: namely, that self-consciousness is not the other of emotion but can only be *felt* in its subtle dynamic. Not only does self-awareness originate in feeling but, as an ever-transitional "awakening," it constitutes a distinct "feeling," a momentary convergence of visual, tactile, and auditory impulses into a discreetly sensual emotion whose evanescence Mörike's neologism "flaumenleicht" conveys so incomparably. Knowledge thus inheres not in some abstract propositional content but, in the subject's feeling of its own faintly stirring transformation by the irreducibly particular manner in which the greatest of all abstractions, time, announces itself. Rather than succumbing to the alternate predicament of an abstract intellectualism or a regression into inconsequential private sentimentality, Mörike's poetry shrewdly balances afleeting emotion against a conscious existence subject to the vagaries of time. At the level of its specific images, as Kenneth Calhoon has so thoughtfully put it, Mörike's poetry "is photo- and phonographic in its manner of arresting the ephemeral — of at once defying and underscoring the impermanence that, more and more, defines the age."[12] Whereas philosophical thought can treat emotions only in a prosaic form (and medium) that denies them their essential qualities, lyric poetry is capable of grasping feeling *as* feeling. Fully cognizant of this key distinction, Hegel himself had specified that lyric poetry "[leiht] [d]iesem erfüllten Innern, um sich als Innerlichkeit auszudrücken, Worte und Sprache" (gives words and language to this enriched inner life so that *as inner life* it may find expression).[13]

Another lyric, only six lines long, shows Mörike's unrivaled skill in concentrating this awakening to what Rousseau had called "le sentiment de l'existence" through a single, meticulously chiseled objective image. Composed in 1827, "Septembermorgen" revives Goethe's early lyric idiom from the period at Sesenheim (1771–72), such as we find it in "Mailied."

> In Nebel ruhet noch die Welt,
> Noch träumen Wald und Wiesen:
> Bald siehst du, wenn der Schleier fällt
> Den blauen Himmel unverstellt,
> Herbstkräftig die gedämpfte Welt
> In warmem Golde fließen.[14]

> [Sleeps the world still
> In folds of mist.
> Meadow and woodland
> Still are dreaming.
> Soon when the veil
> Down has slid,

You shall see
Blue sky manifest
And autumn-vivid
The calm world amid
A warm gold streaming.]

Small-scale epiphanies here reestablish the image as the objective medium *through* (rather than *beyond*) which inwardness can achieve clarity. Without succumbing to allegorical, conceptually driven analogues for an otherwise diffuse emotion, Mörike achieves a classicist balance between the independent cogency of the image-as-object. Presaging the constructivist aesthetic of high modernism, Mörike's images not only undergo microscopic and quasi cubist exfoliation but, in their concreteness, also crystalize an otherwise formless subjective disposition. The luminous closing image, its Olympian confidence prepared by the rugged "herbstkräftig" ("autumn-vivid" — one of Mörike's countless innovative compounds) reflects what Adorno has called his "unwägbar feines, kaum definierbares, antikes odenhaftes Element" (inestimably subtle, scarcely definable *classical,* ode-like element). Facing that, in response to a "prosaic" life vitiated by innumerable "competing interests" and a consequently denuded notion of the human, "[d]er Begriff des Menschen, wie der Klassizismus ihn gewonnen hatte, zog darum in die private, einzelmenschliche Existenz und ihre Bilder sich zurück. . . . Die gesellschaftliche Kraft im Ingenium Mörikes jedoch besteht darin, daß er beide Erfahrungen, die des klassizistischen hohen Stils und der romantischen privaten Miniatur verband, und daß er dabei mit unvergleichlichen Takt der Grenzen beider Möglichkeiten inne ward und sie gegeneinander ausglich" (classicism's concept of the human being withdrew into private, individual existence and its images. . . . The social force of Mörike's genius, however, consists in the fact that he combined . . . the classicistic elevated style and that of the romantic private miniature, . . . and in doing so he recognized the limits of both possibilities and balanced them against one another with incomparable tact).[15] Inwardness in lyric form is not mired in its particulars but, through the quasi-providential operations of lyric (figural) language, has progressed toward expressing the perception of values and conflicts encrypted in emotional life, albeit without denying that this, their truth, is being experienced *as emotion.* Hence, in Hegel's precise diction, the lyric's task is

den Geist nicht *von* der Empfindung, sondern *in* derselben zu befreien. Das blinde Walten der Leidenschaft liegt in der bewußtseinslosen dumpfen Einheit derselben mit dem ganzen Gemüte, das nicht as sich heraus zur Vorstellung und zum Aussprechen seiner gelangen kann. Die Poesie erlöst nun das Herz zwar von dieser Befangenheit, insofern sie dasselbe sich gegenständlich werden läßt, aber sie bleibt nicht bei dem bloßen Hinauswerfen des Inhalts aus seiner unmittelbaren Einigung mit dem Subjekte stehen, sondern macht daraus ein von jeder Zufälligkeit der Stimmungen gereinigtes Objekt.[16]

[to liberate the spirit not *from* but *in* feeling. The blind dominion of passion lies in an unconscious and dull unity between itself and the entirety of a heart that cannot rise out of itself into ideas and self-expression. Poetry does deliver the heart from this slavery to passion by making it see itself, but it does not stop at merely extricating this felt passion from its immediate unity with the heart but makes it an object purified from all accidental moods.]

Poetry marks a unique phase in the evolution of philosophical self-consciousness, one potentially inimical to Hegel's overarching systematic view of art as but a dress-rehearsal for the ultimate telos of the idea of freedom as it is to be instantiated in "the prose of the world." And yet, in lyric poetry the kaleidoscope of social knowledge that lies dormant in emotional life is expressively reconstituted without simply "suspending" the emotional quality of that knowledge. It achieves this by embodying emotions in a language that is aware of its on its own medial character *as language*. Long before Roman Jakobson's conception of the "poetic function" as one principally focused on language as a medium, Hegel's theory of the lyric asserts poetry's reflexive relationship to its own, constitutive linguistic and rhetorical underpinnings.[17] Precisely because of its sustained reflexivity, poetry is capable of articulating the exemplary knowledge encrypted in what would otherwise remain nothing but contingent and transient emotional states of an individual. Building on Herder's postulate that "poetry is the perfected expression of a sentiment or intuition," Hegel's *Aesthetics* thus posits lyric as an intensely self-focused form of "late" art, one that hastens the demise of art as a medium within which the "Arbeit des Begriffs" (labor of the concept) has achieved all it can.[18]

Whereas Mörike largely regarded philosophical speculation about the dialectical mission of emotions and their objective mediation in the lyric image as a separate, even alien concern, other nineteenth-century writers often struggle with what they came to view as the lyric's dependence on sensory particulars. The titles of many poems by Friedrich Hebbel (1813–63) reveal this apologetic tendency for the transient and philosophically underdeveloped nature of the aesthetic, for example, "Die Sprache" (Language), "Welt und Ich" (World and Self) "Das Heiligste" (The Holiest), "Der Mensch und die Geschichte" (Man and History), "Unsere Zeit" (Our Times), and so on. Still, Hebbel's searching and imaginative diaries show him engaged in sustained reflection on the aporia of an intellectually consistent and conclusive poetry. If, as he dogmatically states, "der Mensch ist was er denkt" (man is what he thinks), poetry, including Hebbel's own, will suffer for it: "Meine Poesien aus der ersten Zeit sind unter allem Begriff schlecht, doch enthielten sie — was mich damals ordentlich plagte, da ich daraus den Schluß zog, daß es mir an Phantasie fehle, keinen Unsinn" (My earliest poetic efforts prove inconceivably bad, though they do not contain any nonsense — something that vexed me greatly at the time, since I concluded that I was lacking in imagination).[19] If Hebbel's quest for a poetry wholly accountable to and ideally determined by "thought" reveals a particular version of mid-nineteenth-century German philistinism — one might now call it "philosophical correctness" — his diaries and, at times, also his lyrics ponder the cost at which such an ascendancy of thought over emotions has been purchased. Reminiscent of Fichtean Idealism, Hebbel posits time and again that consciousness achieves distinctness *per se* only by reifying all otherness as "its" thought, with the consequence being that nothing primordially "Other" exists outside of it, ". . . daß es überall nichts Ursprüngliches für uns giebt, d.h., daß wir den Gedanken in dem Augenblick, wo wir uns seiner bewußt werden, schon zu Etwas gemacht haben" (". . . that nowhere there is anything primordial for us, i.e., that at the very moment when we become conscious of a thought as ours, we have already made it into a thing").[20] Applied to the insistent obliquity of emotions, Hebbel's view leads to a Stoicism bent on the intellectual containment of emotions and, hence, on stripping them of their sensory, particular force. With its opening image of pain as emotion reaching the lyric self only through the mediation of thought, Hebbel's long poetic meditation "Dem Schmerz sein Recht" (Giving Pain its Due) exemplifies this dilemma:

> Ewiger, der du in Tiefen wohnest,
> Die der jüngst geborene Gedanke,
> Der, weil du allein Gedanken sendest,
> Kam den Weg von dir zu mir durchmessen,
> Wenn er rückwärts blickt, nur schwindelnd nachmißt,
> Ewiger, vernimm in dieser Stunde
> Meines bang bewegten Herzens Flehen!
> . . .
> Ja, ein Weh giebt's, das man nicht ertrüge,
> Wenn es nicht sein eig'nes Maaß zerbräche,
> Und, wie einer abgeschmackten Lüge,
> Der Erinnerung selber widerspräche.
> Dann, vergessend in der innern Öde,
> Daß einst frisch das Herz geschlagen habe,
> Ist ein Mensch er Nessel gleich, die schnöde
> Wuchert über seinem eig'nen Grabe.[21]

> [Eternal one, who dwells in depths that
> The latest-born reflection — which, because you

Alone can assign thought its mission — could
Gauge only with dizziness when looking back:
Eternal one, learn in this hour
Of my anxious, heartfelt petition.
. . .
Yes, there is a pain that we could not bear
If it did not shatter its own measure and,
As in a jaded lie would
Contradict memory itself. Then,
Dwelling in the desert of the self and oblivious
Of its former, quickened pulse
Man resembles a nettle growing rancorously
Over his own grave.]

At once startlingly abstract and exacting, Hebbel's poem gauges the temporal distance between an enigmatic, though insistently painful emotion and the discipline of conscious thought that has sprung into existence only as a strategy for sheltering the self from a dizzying welter of feeling. In so establishing its authority by having shattered the sole authentic "Maaß" ("measure") of subjectivity — that is, the emotion of pain — thought has acquired clarity at the expense of a barren, poisonous, and denatured quality here figured as a "Nessel" (nettle). The metaphor of the plant no longer stands in the service of an organic poetics but, on the contrary, heightens the reader's awareness of the discontinuity between thought and emotion.[22] Hebbel's conscious self cannot escape self-awareness as an agency atrophied beyond recognition by conceptual thought. Perched between Hegel and Freud, lyric form appears to know of its intrinsically repressive logic vis-à-vis affective contents *from* which and in reaction *against* which it had dialectically acquired its concrete form. Hebbel's lyrics formally enact how the thinking subject becomes reflexively aware of (and tacitly mourns) its own constitutive belatedness.

Echo or Evasion: Lyric Emotion and Social Conflict in the Biedermeier and Vormärz

During the decades after 1830, several diverse, at times competing implications of Hegel's theory of the lyric as a uniquely transitional art form were to resonate in numerous writers and literary schools.[23] The first and, arguably most conspicuous involved drawing out the implication that, in jettisoning both its dependency on a material scaffolding and gradually overcoming its earlier absorption in pre-reflective emotive states, lyric poetry of the present age constituted the decisive factor in art's ongoing quest for self-transcendence. First published in 1835, Hegel's *Aesthetics* prove less the cause of this startling conception than that they offer a canny summation of tendencies readable in the dialectical evolution of art itself. Although the effects of his position for the nineteenth-century lyric and its aesthetic comprehension proved considerable, numerous writers of lyric poetry coming of age during the 1830s abandon the narrative and hence strictly transitional function that feeling had held in Idealist philosophy. Among this generation, typically grouped under the name of *Biedermeier* or the poets of *Weltschmerz* and *Zerrissenheit* (affliction), several secured a broad reading audience in their time — August von Platen, Justinus Kerner, Nikolaus Lenau, Emanuel Geibel, and Friedrich Rückert. In their lyric oeuvre, emotions appear less as encrypted meanings destined for philosophical comprehension than as psychological fetishes incessantly revisited and reworked by a voice whose subjective stance often appears overly mannered and generic. In the following passages from poems by Kerner, Lenau, and Rückert, we thus find the *Biedermeier* period's vast array of lyric writing, as well as its encyclopedic collecting and micro-scopic studying of lyric forms, to be centered around the core axiom of emotion:

[Kerner]

Könnt' ich mit meinem Gram
Mich in mich selbst versenken,
An was der Tod mir nahm,
Mit stiller Sehnsucht denken!

Könnt' in Waldeinsamkeit
Ich ein Einsiedler fliehen,
Dann würd' das herbe Leid
Mich minder heiß durchglühen.
. . .
Doch tiefer brennt die Glut
Indes mir still im Herzen.
Nicht schmerzlicher was tut,
Als ein verhaltenes Schmerzen.[24]

[Could I descend into my inner depths,
Holding close to my pain
And with quiet longing thin
Of what death had taken from me.

Could I flee, a hermit
Into a leafy solitude.

Even then the acrid pain
Should glow in me, undiminished.
. . .

Yet deeper still my heart
Remains quietly aglow.
No greater pain
Than a pain contained.]

* * *

[Lenau]
Sie ließ sich überraschen
Von diesem Trauerwort,
Und ihre Thränen waschen
Die rothe Schminke fort.

Das Leben täuscht uns lange,
Du zeigst der Schminke baar,
Des Lebens welke Wange,
O Schmerz; wie bist du wahr![25]

[She was surprised
By this one word of grief
And now her tears
Cleanse her cheeks' false bloom.

Life long has deceived us,
And now you lay bare of painted bloom
Life's faded cheeks,
O Pain, how true thou art!]

* * *

[Rückert]
Der Himmel hat eine Träne geweint,
Die hat sich ins Meer verlieren gemeint.
Die Muschel kam und schloß sie ein:
Du sollst nun meine Perle sein.
Du sollst nicht vor den Wogen zagen,
Ich will hindurch dich ruhig tragen.
O du mein Schmerz, du meine Lust,
Du Himmelsträn' in meiner Brust!
Gib, Himmel, daß ich in reinem Gemüte
Den reinsten deiner Tropfen hüte.[26]

[The heavens wept a tear
It was resigned to lose itself in the sea.
An oyster came and encased the tear
Henceforth thou shalt be my pearl.
Thou shalt not fear the lashing waves
But tranquil shall I bear thee.
O thou my pain, thou my joy.
Thou heavenly tear in my very own bosom!
Heaven grant that I in spirit pure
Shall keep this purest of thy tears.]

Entitled "*Verhaltnes Schmerzen*" (Suppressed Pain), Kerner's lyric meditates on the posthumous life of a pain or grief for which conventional society offers no outlet. Prescient of Freud's eventual analyses of repression and censorship, the lyric itself ruminates the psychological and social cost of a grief persistently attenuated or stifled only to emerge, with its palpable emotional reticence, as the very instrument of such prevarication. Though cherished with narcissistic intensity, the pain indexed in this lyric noticeably lacks all specific content and, consequently, any definitive causal explanation. Similar to Hegel's concept of the lyric form as the medium into which emotion *qua* emotion is sublated and so preserved, Kerner's titular *verhalten* (prevaricated) implies both, an attitude of prevarication and containment / preservation. In marked contrast to the far superior poetry of Eduard Mörike or Theodor Storm (1817–88), however, these lyrics exhaust themselves in coveting and holding fast to feeling as a merely *putative* meaning, that is, without any sustained attempt at infusing the affective state with a clarity and specificity that can only be effected by its transfiguration into a formal-rhetorical object construct.

Similarly, if in more compact form, Lenau's short lyric entitled "Schmerz" shows emotion as a symptomatic force slumbering in the word of mourning that, like Eichendorff's famous *Zauberwort,* possesses the magical power of unraveling the false painted bloom of the public persona. Containing with subtle but unmistakably misogynistic overtones, the (once generic) emotion of pain here strips the human subject down to its existential, temporal plight: as the painted face and the carefully composed social persona is stripped down to reveal the actual, "faded" countenance beneath, the core emotion of grief and melancholy (arguably Lenau's most recurrent topic) comes to be associated with experience, with life and the passage of time. The same enjambment of a vindictive and a possessive outlook on the emotion of pain also resonates in Rückert. A compulsive writer if ever there was one — he produced over 12,000 poems during his career — Rückert's lyric further develops the narcissistic dimensions of the Biedermeier lyric by converting it into a prized collector's item, a miniature, a pearl / tear contained within a "Muschel" ("shell") safely carried around by the lyric "I."

The pathos of the collector, even in the figural sense given to it by Rückert's poetry — groupings of which are often decoratively titled "Strauß" (bouquets) — constitutes, as Benjamin put it, "an attempt to overcome the wholly irrational character of the object's mere presence . . . through its integration into a new, expressly devised historical system: the collection." Rückert's poetry very plausibly aligns itself with Walter Benjamin's analysis of collecting as a type of "practical memory" whose "most deeply hidden motive" involves "a struggle against dispersion." What is collected and thus possessed in serial lyric form is emotion itself — with its volatile, external historical implications now defused. Like the porcelain cups and saucers of Wilhelm III, commented upon (via Max von Boehn) by Benjamin as vessels preserving "the memory of the most important events, the most precious hours, of his life," lyric writing of the kind Rückert, Lenau, Kerner and other epigones produce during the *Vormärz* period decontextualizes emotion by distilling it into "things [that] allow no mediating construction out of 'large contexts.'"[27] Pain beheld becomes pain held, possessed, and eventually coveted ("O du mein Schmerz, du meine Lust"). In their own way, each of these lesser-known writers — all of whom achieved more fame at the hand of composers setting their lyrics to music (Schumann, Brahms, Wolf, Mahler) — throw into relief a dead-end in the development of the lyric, a loss of the dialectical and speculative momentum which, according to Hegel, rendered the subjective, specifically emotive focus of lyric poetry a transitional stage toward a more prosaic and discursive self-knowledge. Instead of sublating emotion into something universal, each of the writers prizes it as an inalienable possession to be preserved in lyric, self-consciously formalized speech that resembles one of its miniature images (Rückert's "Muschel," for example).

Overall, the poetry of the 1830s and 1840s — except when committed to overtly political concerns — tends to agonize under the aura of its own belatedness, a predicament from which the lyric often retreats by fixating on precious, small-scale emotional states. Rückert's logic of poetic accumulation invariably renders emotions interchangeable and generic, constructs whose schematic imprecision ultimately deprives them of both, personal *and* universal significance. Yet in some of the best poets of the period (Eichendorff, Mörike, Heine, Storm), the lyric's intrinsic belatedness is itself converted into an explicit thematic concern and as a new formal-rhetorical possibility. Thus, when Heine laments the end of the "Nachtigallenwahnsinn" (nightingale madness) that had once given such delusive momentum to the Romantic movement, we quickly recognize his distinctive rhetorical pose. Commenting on the untimely position of the post-Romantic lyric in his late *Geständnisse* (*Confessions*) of 1854, Heine makes a point of figuring centrally in his equivocal farewell to Romantic lyric poetry: "Ich bin ihr letzter Dichter: mit mir ist die alte lyrische Schule der Deutschen geschlossen, während zugleich die neue Schule, die moderne deutsche Lyrik, von mir eröffnet ward" (I am the last poet [of the Romantic school]. With me, the old lyric school of the Germans has come to a close, just as with me the new school of modern German lyricism was being inaugurated).[28] To some extent, Heine's later poetry compensates for the lyric's seemingly anachronistic status by its commitment to longer narrative and often aggressively satiric modes: *Atta Troll* (1841–42), *Deutschland: Ein Wintermärchen* (1843), and the sub-set of poems entitled *Zeitgedichte* in Heine's *Neue Gedichte* (1844), for example.

And yet, the very perception that an imaginative and affective investment in poetry is no longer timely because no longer generative of new psychological or cultural meanings paradoxically also emerges as a dominant thematic and formal proposition in Heine's lyric poetry. With the end of the "Kunstperiode" (art-period) repeatedly pronounced by Heine after 1833, lyric writing recognizes itself as a pursuit both generically and historically over-determined. The modern writer, particularly of lyric poetry, appears burdened by an excess of knowledge; he is the epigone *par excellence,* "born too late" as Heine puts it when referring to his own generation as "wir Spätergeborenen."[29] Far from being an exclusive insight of Hegel's theory of Romantic art — presented in its second installment during Heine's 1823 residence in Berlin — the notion of the *Biedermeier* as a self-consciously belated historical phase reverberates in countless lyric poets after 1830. Oppressed by the abundance of aesthetic models generated since the age of Lessing and distressed by evident inadequacy of such models for the present age, the writers of the Restoration and *Biedermeier* era (1815–1848) struggle with a new adversary: the idea of culture as a monolithic and over-determined heritage. As Martin Greiner puts it, "Epigonen, das sind Reiche, die im Überfluß darben" and "Epigonentum ist das Kennzeichen einer Bildungskrise, das seelische Darben in einem problematisch gewordenen geistigen Reichtum" (the epigone is a wealthy subject starved by an excess of riches, [and] his is a psychological struggle with culture as heritage).[30] The point largely echoes Karl Immermann (1796–1840), author of the expansive novel *Die Epigonen* (1836), for whom literature resembles political life, since the middle-aged generation of the 1830s was compelled to compare "nur die unbedingten Erwartungen einer vollen und großen Nationalität, welche ihre Jugend beflügelt hatten, mit der bedingteren und mäßigeren Erfüllung" (the unconditional expectations of a plentiful, grand Nationalism that had inspired its youth [during the wars of liberation 1813–15] with the far more limited and modest fulfillment of those expectations).

Wir sind, um in einem Worte das ganze Elend auszusprechen, Epigonen und tragen an der Last, die jeder Erb- und Nachgeborenschaft anzukleben pflegt. Die große Bewegung im Reiche des Geistes, welche unsre Väter von ihren Hütten und Hüttchen aus unternahmen, hat uns eine Menge von Schätzen zugeführt, welche nun auf allen Markttischen ausliegen.

[We are, to put all the misery into one word, epigones and thus struggle with the burden that weighs down all those latter-born and to a rich bequest. The great intellectual movements which our fathers launched from their dwellings has brought us a cornucopia of treasures that now are strewn about on any variety of market-tables.]

Hence there prevails "eine gewisse Halbheit, ein Gespaltenes und Doppeltes im Bewußtsein von den öffentlichen Dingen, in den Begriffen von Recht, Eigentum und Besitz" (. . . a certain half-heartedness, something fragmented and doubled about our consciousness of public issues).[31] Immermann's dispiriting portrayal of Romanticism's cultural and intellectual achievements now being remaindered at market-stands everywhere is borne out by an unprecedented profusion of lyric writing and publishing during the 1830s, even as attempts at formal-aesthetic and socio-cultural definitions of lyric poetry seem to falter. Collections of poetry abound: Rückert, *Haus- und Jahrslieder* (1832–38); Platen, *Frühlingslieder* (1835); Eichendorff, *Gedichte* (1837); Mörike, *Gedichte* (1838); the crucially successful second and subsequent editions of Heine's *Buch der Lieder* (1837, 1839, 1844); Geibel, *Gedichte*, 1840; Lenau, *Polenlieder* (1832–35) and *Waldlieder* (1843); Hebbel, *Gedichte* (1842); Droste-Hülshoff, *Gedichte* (1844); Uhland, *Gedichte* (5th–9th edition, 1831–1835).[32] Likewise, the institution of the almanac presented a wide-ranging, often bewildering array of lyric forms and themes. Examples might include Nikolaus Lenau's *Frühlingsalmanach* (1835–36), the *Deutscher Musenalmanach*, edited by Gustav Schwab, Adalbert von Chamisso, and Franz von Gaudy between 1833–39, Friedrich Rückert's *Erlanger Musenalmanach* (1838), the Jung-Hegelian *Deutscher Musenalmanach* (1840–41) edited by Arnold Ruge and Theodor Echtermeyer, or O. L. B. Wolff's *Poetischer Hausschatz* (1843). The sheer profusion of lyric writing, printing, and publishing was materially reinforced by the increased efficiency of the printing process brought about by Koenig and Bauer's 1811 cylinder-based approach to printing (first applied by the London *Times* in 1814), their 1818 design of a "double cylinder press" for swift two-sided printing (further perfected by William Church in 1824), subsequently enhanced by Bullock's 1865 roll-fed rotary press, and Ottmar Mergenthaler's 1886 invention of the linotype machine. Such innovations reinforce Immermann's (and our own) sense of monotony within a literary genre confronting the loss of its "aura" as a unique instance of autographic expression. With a fatigue that presages the rise of major technological advances in the mechanical reproduction of text — and the book's consequent loss of its formerly sacred aura — readers of the Biedermeier era already agonized, as Christoph Herin has put it, under " . . . immer wieder . . . dieselben Bilder, dieselben Vergleiche, derselbe Tonfall, dieselbe Reime. . . . Die Variationen der gebräuchlichsten

Formeln ist so gering, daß der ermüdete Leser überall nur noch erstarrte Konvention findet" (the same metaphors, the same similes, the same tone, the same rhymes. So minor is the variation of the most widely used formulas that the fatigued reader encounters nothing but calcified, meaningless convention).[33] Reflecting the Biedermeier era's preoccupation with the collecting and inventory-taking of cultural artifacts, a number of poets (Platen, Lenau, Geibel, Rückert) explore a broad array of classical, modern, and experimental forms by scrupulously apprenticing themselves in a vast array of forms (Ghasel, terza rima, sestina, epigrammatic poetry, sonnet, alexandrine, ottava rima, canzone, ballad, ode, hymn) and then refining their prosodic possibilities.[34] Doing so could ensure lasting popularity, particularly in the case of Rückert and Geibel, with the latter's unfailingly conformist poetry earning him a lifetime of financial security and political approval.[35] However mediocre many of their lyric productions, writers such as Platen, Rückert, Schwab, Lenau, Kerner, Chamisso, Holtei, and Geibel secured a broad and enduring audience for lyric poetry well into the period of Realism and Naturalism.

At the same time, the implicit demand of so many emotively focused lyric poems, namely, as Adorno puts it, "die des jungfräulichen Wesens . . . impliziert den Protest gegen einen gesellschaftlichen Zustand, den jeder Einzelne als sich feindlich, fremd, kalt, bedrückend erfährt, und negative prägt der Zustand dem Gebilde sich ein" (that the lyric word be virginal, is itself social in nature . . . implies a protest against a social situation that every individual experiences as hostile, alien, cold, oppressive, and this situation is imprinted in reverse on the poetic work). A salient example of Adorno's thesis about lyric poetry's dialectical implication in complex historical forces — and hence, in Adorno's famous formulation, the lyric's inadvertent role as a "geschichtsphilosophische Sonnenuhr" (philosophical sundial telling the time of history) — can be found in the lyric oeuvre of Joseph von Eichendorff (1788–1857).[36] His extensive lyric corpus, much of which was first scattered throughout his novels, novellas, plays or occasional almanacs, only reached a broader audience with the publication of his collected poems (*Gedichte*) in 1837. By then the prophetic or utopian tone of Jena and Heidelberg Romanticism appeared but a distant, almost otherworldly memory. Yet Gutzkow's characteristic remark that "Eichendorff hat nur den Fehler, daß er zu spät kommt" (Eichendorff's only mistake is that he comes too late") fails to notice how persistently this very belatedness shapes the meditative structure of Eichendorff's lyric oeuvre and, indeed, constitutes its dominant affect.[37] As the memories and promises of his student days and subsequent involvement "Anfall von Patriotismus"[38] (in "a patriotic fit") with Lützow's patriotic effort against Napoleon (1813–14) receded, Eichendorff's lyrics condense history into a rich, albeit bewildering texture of affective states. A poem dating back to his participation in

Lützow's *Freikorps* (1814) attests to the phantasmagorical character of historical experience. Keeping watch, the lyric voice peers into the void, baffled by a landscape at once tantalizingly opaque and terminally uneventful:

> Mein Gewehr im Arme steh ich
> Hier verloren auf der Wacht,
> Still nach jener Gegend seh ich,
> Hab so oft dahin gedacht!
>
> Fernher Abendglocken klingen
> Durch die schöne Einsamkeit;
> So, wenn wir zusammen gingen,
> Hört ich's oft in alter Zeit.
>
> Wolken da wie Türme prangen,
> Als säh ich im Dunst mein Wien,
> Und die Donau hell ergangen
> Zwischen Burgen durch das Grün.
>
> Doch wie fern sind Strom und Türme!
> Wer da wohnt, denkt mein noch kaum,
> Herbstlich rauschen schon die Stürme,
> Und ich stehe wie im Traum.[39]
>
> [Weapon in arm, I stand
> Lost here at the guard,
> Quietly I gaze toward that region,
> Where my thoughts have often tended!
>
> Distant evening bells are sounding
> Through the beauteous solitude;
> Thus, when we jointly walked,
> I often heard it in old times.
>
> Clouds gleam like towers there,
> As if through mists I beheld my Vienna,
> And the Danube serenely wanders
> Amongst castles through the green.
>
> Yet how distant are the river and towers!
> Whoever lives there scarcely thinks of me,
> Autumnal storms already rustle,
> And I am suspended as in a dream.]

Eagerly sought after by the subject's gaze, history always appears to have already occurred elsewhere. As the soldier's vigilance is becalmed by distant church bells and inscrutable cloud formations, history bypasses the modern subject whose earnest watchfulness stands in ironic contrast to its quintessentially "lost" position. Above all, "Auf der Feldwacht" intimates the growing intuition that, rather than being constituted as a sequence of momentous events, history unfolds subterraneously, thus leaving the modern subject marooned in a purely imaginary zone where watchtowers and cloud formations seem fully interchangeable ("Wolken da wie Türme prangen").[40] Here, the similarity of the stony "watch tower" inhabited by the calcified representatives of the old *Herrschaft* ("Auf einer Burg") and the imaginary towering clouds brought into focus by the futile watchfulness of the young student turned anti-Napoleonic patriot works to richly ironic effect. Conceived as a missed and therefore "unclaimed experience," as Cathy Caruth's refers to it in her eponymous study on trauma, the enigma of history not only reaffirms the completed demise of feudal *Herrschaft,* but it also conceives of the ossified representatives of that order as equivalent to the alienated, hallu-cinatory condition of the modern subject: "Und ich stehe wie im Traum."[41] Eichendorff's poem thus attests to a basic asymmetry between views of history as a subterraneous, deep-structural transformation and an older, defunct model of history conceived as a series of conspicuous and heroic individual actions. Grouped among the subsection "Zeitlieder," Eichendorff's poem confirms a principal thesis of Hegel's aesthetics, namely, that contrary to epic poetry, "der lyrische Erguß steht zu der Zeit, als äußerem Elemente der Mitteilung, in einem viel näheren Verhältnis als das epische Erzählen, . . . [da] die Lyrik . . . die ver-schiedenartige zeitliche Bewegung selbst künstlerisch zu gestalten hat" (the lyric effusion stands in much greater proximity to *time* as an exter-nal frame for expression . . . because the lyric poet articulates the pre-sent).[42] Far from constituting an ephemeral, wholly subjective state, emotion here is imbued with a strong *representative* tendency. As an inad-vertent (perhaps serendipitous) reflex of historical forces extending toward and shaping the present, Eichendorff's post-Romantic lyricism quietly fuses the didactic and incidental objectives that until the end of the eighteenth century had still existed in separate forms (*Lehrdichtung, Gelegenheitsdichtung, Anakreontik*). In Eichendorff's self-consciously belated lyric productions, a central "feeling" or dominant, psycho-rhetor-ical *Stimmung* encrypts a deep-seated historical dissonance (*Verstimmung*). In so mediating feeling *qua* poetic writing, the seemingly incidental particulars of the here-and-now — such as Eichendorff's futile vigilance while on guard duty as a *Lützow* irregular, or the calcified knight sitting "eingeschlafen auf der Lauer" in the window of a medieval ruin (*Auf einer Burg*) — introduce their audience to a radically new concep-tion of both, history *and* lyric poetry. It now turns out, that the lyric voice's belatedness vis-à-vis the present is neither accidental nor reversible. Rather, the belatedness of a feeling and, consequently, of its embodiment in lyric form brings about a new kind of historical knowledge as a belated, often traumatic recognition whose acquisition is no longer convertible into remedial action.[43]

Lyric poetry of the Restoration and *Biedermeier* era does not constitute an imaginary refuge for a middle class alienated by its apparent stagnation and political irrelevance; rather, literary practice turned out to be co-originary with these very frustrations. In its hermetic, quasi-monastic formal presentation, lyric poetry seems so appropriate to articulate a disillusionment that Eichendorff, along with his ambitious reform-bureaucrat and superior, Theodor von Schön, felt after watching the defeat of administrative reformers driven by Romantic and late-Enlightenment ideals (*Reformbeamtentum*) at the hands of Prussian career bureaucrats.

> Zwischen Akten, dunkeln Wänden
> Bannt mich, Freiheitbegehrenden,
> Nun des Lebens strenge Pflicht,
> Und aus Schränken, Aktenschichten
> Lachen mir die beleidigten
> Musen in das Amtsgesicht.
>
> . . .
>
> Als der letzte Balkentreter
> Steh ich armer Enterbeter
> In des Staates Symphonie,
> Ach, in diesem Schwall von Tönen
> Wo fänd ich da des eigenen
> Herzens süße Melodie?
>
> Ein Gedicht soll ich euch spenden:
> Nun, so geht mit dem Leidenden
> Nicht zu strenge ins Gericht!
> Nehmt den Willen für Gewährung,
> Kühnen Reim für Begeisterung,
> Diesen Unsinn als Gedicht![44]
>
> [Amongst ledgers, dark walls
> I, longing for freedom, am now confined
> By life's strict sense of duty.
> And the muses, offended, mock my bureaucratic face
> Out of every cabinet and heap of files.
>
> . . .
>
> As the last cog in the wheel
> I, impecunious and disinherited
> Have joined the symphony of the state
> O! where in this deluge of sound

Would I find my own
Heart's sweet melody?

A poem I shall dedicate to you
Well then, do not deal too harshly
With the suffering bureaucrat!
Take resolve for achievement
Bold rhyme for enthusiasm
And this nonsense for a poem!]

Presaging Kafka's tormented protagonists, the claustrophobic space of the bureaucratic nation-state ("framing ledgers and dark walls") sets up the closing critique of the poem as a form whose political irrelevance aptly mirrors the speaking subject's political abjection. Such diffident, almost Stoic speech also counters the utopian longing of a wide array of political poetry written during the 1830s that would further intensify after 1840. Yet well beyond Eichendorff's model of an expressivity disillusioned with its cultural environment and hence with its limited formal possibilities, the next generation employed lyric poetry in a far more instrumental and overtly referential sense to indict a static and repressive political order. Among the first, Anastasius Grün (né Anton Alexander Graf von Auersperg, 1808–76) chose his pseudonym to express hopes for renewal in his widely read and acclaimed *Spaziergänge eines Wiener Poeten* (Strolls of a Viennese Poet, 1831). Often programmatically entitled ("Warum" and "Unsere Zeit), Grün's alternately satiric and combative indictment of the Metternich regime eventually prompted the political police to establish his identity. The Austrian chancellor in 1838 offered him the choice of exile or cessation of all publishing efforts. Although Grün would choose the latter, he was able to establish for himself a significant political role in Austro-German politics, particularly after 1848. His promising career as a writer of lyric poetry, however, was cut short by Metternich's early intervention. Here, as in the more prominent cases of Georg Herwegh (1817–75), Ferdinand Freiligrath (1810–76), and Franz Dingelstedt (1814–81), the latter's pronouncement that "Herwegh hat eine Zukunft wenn es in Deutschland eine Revolution gibt, sonst nicht" (Herwegh has a future if Germany undergoes a revolution, otherwise not)[45] turned out to be prescient. For political poetry after 1840 ultimately hankers after a political utopia whose attainment would render poetry, political or otherwise, wholly redundant. Such a model of literature abandons the Kantian claim to art's universality (*Allgemeinheitsanspruch*) — qualified by its non-conceptual and strictly hypothetical necessity — in favor of a model that enlists literature as a quotidian tool of representative speech by a prototypical, liberal and enlightened individual.

Arguably the most controversial poet of his time, Georg Herwegh (1817–75) predicated his political poetry on the emotional pathos of the *Freiheitslied* form that had risen to short-lived popularity during the 1813–15 patriotic insurgence against Napoleon. Yet in the absence of any external enemy, and with the political form of monarchy and rampant censorship and surveillance now the antagonist, Herwegh's strident calls for action lack any political framework or program. Rejecting Dingelstedt's argument that poetry must never be a matter of partisanship alone (*Der Dichter steht auf einer höhern Warte / Als auf den Zinnen der Partei*), Herwegh's poem, "*Die Partei*" (1843) seems uncompromising:

> *Partei! Partei!* Wer sollte sie nicht nehmen,
> Die noch die Mutter aller Siege war!
> Wie mag ein Dichter solch ein Wort verfehmen,
> Ein Wort, das alles Herrliche gebahr?
> . . .
>
> Sieh hin! dein Volk will neue Bahnen wandeln,
> Nur des Signales hart ein stattlich Heer;
> Die Fürsten träumen, laßt die Dichter handeln!
> Spielt Saul die Harfe, werfen *wir* den Speer!
> Den Panzer um — geöffnet sind die Schranken,
> Brecht immer euer Saitenspiel entzwei,
> Und führt ein Fähnlein ewiger Gedanken
> Zur starken, stolzen Fahne der *Partei*![46]
>
> [Party! Who would not take sides
> With partisanship, the source of all victory
> How can poets impugn such a word
> A word that has given birth to all things glorious?
> . . .
>
> Behold! Your people wants to forge new paths
> The splendid legion only awaits the signal
> As the nobility dreams, let poets act!
> While Saul plays the harp, let *us* wield the speer!
> Gird the armor — the barriers have come down
> Break the lyre
> And merge a banner of eternal thoughts
> With the strong, proud flag of the *Party*!]

Notwithstanding the poem's urgent rhetoric, Herwegh's politics remain oddly amorphous, buried beneath traditional allegorical and classical references and an ardent plea on behalf of divisive, adversarial politics whose concrete constitutional and civil-libertarian issues he is unable to integrate into the poetry. Not surprisingly, the conservative Friedrich Sengle dismisses Herwegh's poetry in particularly harsh terms: "Kein Wunder, daß Herwegh schon nach 1848 begraben wurde und die übrigen Lyriker, die sich mit Politik abgegeben hatten, gleich mit ins Grab geworfen wurden" (small wonder that Herwegh was consigned to oblivion after 1848, and along with him the other lyric poets who had embraced partisan politics in their work).[47] Arguably, Herwegh's confrontational conduct as writer and politician, often blamed for a reinforcement of censorship practices following his *Einundzwanzig Bogen aus der Schweiz* (1843), constitutes a low-point in the cooptation of lyric poetry for strictly political ends. As early as 1839, Theodor Vischer remarks on an enforced "political correctness" beginning to compromise the imaginative range of poetic writing:

> Man rief [den Dichter] an: halt! nicht so schnell! du mußt dich erst ausweisen, ob du auch die Fragen der Gegenwart, die großen speciellen Probleme in dein Gedicht aufgenommen hast. . . . und man übersah, daß es sich nicht darum handelt *ob* der Dichter die Zeitfragen, sondern *wie*, ob er sie auf poëtische Weise in sein Werk aufgenommen, ob er sie in ästhetischen Körper gewandelt hat."[48]

> [Poets were stopped in their tracks: "hold it; not so fast! You must first offer proof that you have incorporated into your poetry the questions of the present, its great and particular issues. . . . Yet in so doing, the most pivotal matter was being overlooked: namely, that it is not a question of *whether* but *how* the poet incorporates these issues into his oeuvre, and whether he has transfigured them into an aesthetic object.]

Heine's comments about Freiligrath — "Er gebraucht Hammer und Meißel und verarbeitet die Sprache wie einen Stein . . . Alles kann er machen, nur kein Lied" (he takes hammer and chisel to language as though it was a piece of rock. . . . He can make anything — except a poem) — would find their most witty and extensive articulation in *Atta Troll*.[49] They strike the mark far better for Herwegh. Generally critical of the co-optation of lyric forms for political ends, Heine's critique of Herwegh ("die eiserne Lerche" [the iron lark]) and his radical cohorts often assumes viciously satiric and mocking character, as can be seen in his "An einen politischen Dichter," occasioned by the 1841 publication of *Unpolitische Lieder* by Hoffmann von Fallersleben (1798–1874):

> Du singst, wie einst Tyrtäus sang,
> Von Heldenmut beseelet,
> Doch hast du schlecht dein Publikum
> Und deine Zeit gewählet.
>
> Beifällig horchen sie dir zwar,
> Und loben, schier begeistert:
> Wie edel dein Gedankenflug,
> Wie du die Form bemeistert.

Sie pflegen auch beim Glase Wein
Ein Vivat dir zu bringen
Und manchen Schlachtgesang von dir
Lautbrüllend nachzusingen.

Der Knecht singt gern ein Freiheitslied
Des Abends in der Schenke:
Das fördert die Verdauungskraft,
Und würzet die Getränke.[50]

[You sing as formerly Tyrtäus had
Intoxicated by heroic spirits;
Yet you have chosen poorly
Both your audience and your times.

Though they listen approvingly
And seemingly praise
How noble you marshal your thoughts
And command the form.

Also, they enjoy toasting you
With a glass of wine
And to recite, hoarse-roaring
Various battle-songs of yours.

The servant gladly recites a song of liberty
At night in his pub
For doing so enhances his digestive tract
And spices up his drink.]

As Nietzsche would later observe, reading Heine means following an invitation into the countless alleys and byways of *ressentiment,* and Heine's writings do indeed lay bare poetry's deeply antagonistic intellectual coordinates in an the era of political repression (under Metternich after 1819) and one of bourgeois dissipation and insincerity (under Louis Philippe after 1830).[51] The prime casualty is that of emotive authenticity. To stress that fact, Heine's poetry often incorporates the numbing inanity, judgmental arrogance, and brazen self-interest that informs the world of colloquial speech and printed discourse. And yet, once woven as subtly into the texture of Heine's lyric-satiric mode, such "Betrügen, Lüge, Schein" (deceit, lies, and semblance) cannot be isolated as the simple antithesis to an otherwise intact and authentic bourgeois subjectivity. Rather, Heine's "göttliche Bosheit" (divine malice), to recall Nietzsche's laudatory expression, generates a strange beauty all its own, a peculiarly urbane type of pleasure rooted in the bourgeois subject's tacit acquiescence in all things corrupt, deracinated, mendacious, or otherwise inauthentic. Of all the German nineteenth-century poets, many of whom stress their regional rather than national, let alone cosmopolitan moorings (Kerner, Droste-Hülshoff, Mörike, Lenau, Storm), the Jewish-born Heine is the most obviously European figure. Self-described as "der inkarnierte Kosmopolitismus" (cosmopolitanism incarnate), Heine can indeed be read as the most significant transitional poet between Goethe's emotionally and philosophically capacious poetry and Baudelaire's *Fleurs du Mal,* the ur-text of high Modernism published in the year after Heine's death.[52] The point emerges with full force in the very first line of the following short poem:

> In den Küssen welche Lüge!
> Welche Wonne in dem Schein!
> Ach, wie süß ist das Betrügen,
> Süßer das Betrogensein!
>
> Liebchen, wie du dich auch wehrest,
> Weiß ich doch, was du erlaubst;
> Glauben will ich, was du schwörest,
> Schwören will ich, was du glaubst.[53]
>
> [Ah, what lies are told by kisses!
> Bliss in false illusions, child!
> Sweet are beguiling artifices;
> Sweeter yet, to be beguiled!
>
> Your resistance I perceive, dear,
> Yet I know what you'll allow.
> I shall avow whatever you'll believe, dear,
> I shall believe whatever you'll avow.]

Besides startling us with its harsh affective dissonance, the opening line also produces a textual *déja vu* effect of sorts, in that it offers a parodic citation of the opening line from Goethe's "Willkommen und Abschied" ("In Deinen Küssen, welche Wonne"). From here on, all the way to the closing lines' chiasmic precision, this short incidental poem at once asserts and formally exemplifies the homology of affect and illusion, interiority and self-manipulation, sentimentality and *ressentiment* in Heine: "Believe I shall, whatever you'll swear, / Swear I shall whatever you'll believe." At its most extreme, Heine's style offers a deliberately grotesque amalgam of melodrama, sentimentality, and brazenly satiric indictment — designed, it seems, to sow confusion within an oppressively settled cultural landscape. Time and again, it confounds the declarative with the figural, the referential with the performative, and the vivid illustration of facts with the mocking recitation of sentiment.[54] To write and read literature after Goethe often induces in its subjects a vertiginous state of self-consciousness, not only because of the aristocratic, larger-than-life presence so scrupulously cultivated by the *Dichterfürst* himself, but because the epigone's ironic self-awareness is beyond stabilization. Gone is Goethe's unbridled, exuberant, and supremely self-assured dramatization of *eros,* as well as its underlying faith in the text's ability to reclaim the "source" of its inspiration. There is nothing gratuitous about contrasting the post-lapsarian and nervously self-conscious melancholy of the writer's persona in Heine with the statuesque charisma of Goethe's voice in his *Sesenheimer Lieder* (1771) or his hexametric expansiveness in *Römische Elegien* (1788). What makes Heine such a complex and intriguing transitional figure between Romanticism and Realism are characteristics that also link him to a Modernist aesthetic whose incipience can also, albeit in different form, be traced in the lyrics of Eichendorff, Mörike, Droste-Hülshoff, and C. F. Meyer. For Heine, the writer's identity is intrinsically hybrid. Half creator, half journalist, his lyric voices continually look back over their shoulder toward the aesthetic monuments of Germany's recent past, at once overwhelming and unhelpful and hence leaving no choice but to undo the untimely and oppressively "geläufige Zeichen der codierten lyrischen Rede der Romantik" (familiar inventory of Romanticism's lyric code).[55] Precisely this abrupt flourish of *ressentiment,* often found in epigrammatic form in the closing couplet of Heine's lyrics (including the one just quoted), is also a prompt to the reader to re-read and -evaluate the entire poem again and to gain distance on the delusive, at times narcissistic set of Romantic longings and identifications that he / she likely brought to a first reading of it. It is the dialectical nature of Heine's writing that such a revisionary reading can neither be avoided nor anticipated during a first "tour." For at first, Heine's dream-like images seduce readers into identifying with the melancholic surfaces of his idiom. Only as the reading process advances or, more likely, during a second reading, does the reader begin to grasp the language of *Empfindsamkeit* as one of stylistic artifice and, by extension, confronts the embarrassment of his or her earlier identification with that idiom. It is this confounding of affective dispositions previously held fundamental and inalienable for all beings — the ideological fantasy of a humanity untrammeled by divisions of class, education, religion, language — which Heine's lyrics fleetingly conjure and then dismantle. Yet to do so not only throws into disarray an empathetic mode of reading but, by extension, also the aesthetic foundations of these historically specific (Romantic) reading practices. Wolfgang Preisendanz rightly points out that the challenge issued by Heine's oeuvre involves less a formal accounting for his fracturing of lyric pathos by ironic means. For the more fundamental and pressing question concerns "how it is possible to speak of such an aesthetic borderline phenomena where the claims of aesthetics — as a philosophical and scientific theory of art and the beautiful — has already been shaken or proven irrelevant,

along with its self-image as a historical phenomenon." The truly "ago-
nizing" issue concerns the "historicity of aesthetics and its specific kind
of competency."[56] Throughout Heine's poetic oeuvre, feeling no longer
constitutes an unimpeachable origin or source for an expressive model of
writing but a spurious imposition and fraud perpetrated simultaneously
at the level of psychology and ideology. Heine perceives (and exposes)
such delusive dream worlds to be intimately entwined with a Romantic
paradigm of literature as authentic and deeply meaningful transposi-
tion of affect from the personal into the social realm. In recasting the
lyric, as Georg Lukács put it, as "eine besondere Form . . . in der die
Widersprüche sich lebendig bewegen können" (a particular form in
which contradictions may unfold dynamically), Heine exposes not only
the genre's "erdichteten und erlogenen Harmonie" (fictitious and false
harmony) but, on a larger scale, the deep-seated and unwholesome com-
plicity between formal and social values which, to him, was the very hallmark of Romantic aesthetics.[57] In this manner, Heine's poetry shows the
historical categories of literature and aesthetics growing acutely distrust-
ful of themselves and on the verge of suspecting their own, intrinsic
otherness. Through its deliberate formal *mésalliance* with the journalistic feuilleton, poetry in his view had begun to reveal its ideological
"impurity."

The Idyll Transformed:
Lyric Poetry and Modernity in the
Age of Realism and Naturalism

Following the failed 1848 revolution, lyric poetry in Germany evolved in
somewhat disparate ways. On the one hand, a number of writers seemed
unable to continue work in the genre at all. Their poetic efforts thus abandon the shorter form of the lyric in favor of the ballad or other narrative
verse forms of usually explicit historical content. Never entirely comfort-
able with lyric poetry, a genre he abandoned by 1847, Theodor Fontane
wrote extensive historical verse narratives, mostly drawn from Prussian,
British and Scottish history, to which his occupation as a Prussian press
attaché in London (1852, 1855–59) had further exposed him. With its
ideological spectrum ranging from Marx to Burckhardt, Wilamowitz-
Moellendorff, Ranke, and Treitschke, historicism had engendered a new
empirical methodology. Beyond that — as demonstrated in ballad collection such as Fontane's *Männer und Helden* (Man and Heroes, 1850), historical verse narratives by the Swiss writer C. F. Meyer (1825–98) and the
lesser, though immensely popular oeuvre of Felix Dahn — the historicist
movement, combined with the lasting European resonance of Sir Walter

Scott's historical novels after 1814, was also effecting a new amalgamation of poetry and history.[58] The aesthetically more successful instances of historical verse, such as C. F. Meyer's epic poem, *Huttens Letzte Tage* (Hutten's Last Days, 1871), describing the end in 1523 of Ulrich von Hutten, German humanist and supporter of the Reformation, rarely abide within a strictly empirical frame of reference; thus Meyer's poem derives much of its force from the *genius loci* of the island of Ufenau on Lake Constance, where the historical figure of Jakob Hutten had spent his final days in 1523 and where Meyer was to find inspiration for many of his own works some 350 years later. A fine example of the shorter lyric in the age of *Realismus,* Meyer's "Hohe Station" (Summit Station) shows how, rather than holding the lyric imagination to strictly empirical and inherently prosaic limits, the currents of contemporary history and the psyche of the educated middle-class individual at the margins of central European bourgeois society both reveal an otherworldly hue:

Hoch an der Windung des Passes bewohn ich ein niedriges Berghaus —
Heut ist vorüber die Post, heut bin ich oben allein.
Lehnend am Fenster belausch ich die Stille des dämmernden Abends,
Rings kein Laut! Nur der Specht hämmert im harzigen Tann!
Leicht aus dem Wald in den Wald hüpft über die Matte das Eichhorn,
Spielend auf offenem Plan; denn es ist Herr im Bezirk.
Jammer! Was hör ich? Ein schrilles Gesurre: "Gemordet ist Garfield!"
"Bismarck zürnt im Gezelt!" "Väterlich segnet der Papst!"
Schwirrt in der Luft ein Gerücht? Was gewahr ich? Ein schwärzliches
    Glöcklein!
Unter dem Fenstergesims bebt der elektrische Draht,
Der, wie die Schläge des Pulses beseelend den Körper der Menschheit,
Durch das entlegenste Tal trägt die Gebärde der Zeit.[59]

[High up at the winding mountain pass I dwell in a low-set chalet —
The mail has come and gone, and in solitude I find myself today.
Leaning on the windowsill I eavesdrop on the silence at dusk.
No sound anywhere except for the woodpecker hammering in the thicket
With sprightly motion, out of the forest and back across the moss, leaps
    the squirrel
Playing in the open, for it rules this demesne.
O grief! What shrill sounds reach my ear? "Garfield murdered!"
"Bismarck wrathful at his encampment!" "Papal blessing graciously
    bestowed!"
Does the air run wild with rumor? What do I behold? A blackened tiny
    bell!
Under my windowsill the electric wire trembles
As it carries, like the pulsations animating humanity's body,
The temper of history through the remotest of valleys.]

The disruption of a self-contained literary idyll by the static of history — faintly but insistently audible as it pulsates through telegraph wires — reproduces the aesthetic program of *Realismus* as a single, concise topos. Thus, it is with an unmistakable tone of satisfaction that Maximilian Bern's preface to his influential 1877 anthology, *Deutsche Lyrik seit Goethes Tode* notes "daß alle Errungenschaften der letzten Jahre auch an der Poesie nicht spurlos vorübergegangen sind. Manchem schönen Gedichte merkt man es an, daß es zu einer Zeit entstanden, in welcher der Dichter am Waldrande außer dem uralten Geflüster der Bäume auch das geheimnißvolle Klingen windbewegter Telegraphendrähte vernimmt" (. . . that all attainments of recent years have left their traces in poetry too. In many beautiful lyrics we sense that they originated in a time when, aside from the ancient rustling of trees, poets at the edge of the forest would also pick up on the furtive tinkle of telegraph wires swaying in the breeze).[60] And yet, in his focused and inquisitive auditory "belauschen" (scanning) of the silent mountain world, the speaker of Meyer's lyric poem betrays the dialectical bond between the Romantic *locus amoenus* and the hectic, inchoate, and often brutal convulsions of the historical world below. For what disrupts this idyll is the specter of an unintelligible history against which the idyll in the mountains sought to defend its authorial (and reading) subject. Cumulatively, the references to a political assassination in the United States, a papal blessing sought by worldly power (an apparent reference to Spanish king, Alfonso XII, soliciting such benediction by telegraphic communication with the Vatican in January 1875), and Bismarck's latest outbursts do not so much anchor (and hence justify) lyric writing within real material processes. Rather, the stenographic, coded refraction of historical processes serendipitously captured during its telegraphic transmission reinforces history's cryptic and inchoate nature and, in so doing, highlights the disorientation of the educated, middle-class individual caught up in that world.

Where the lyric resists notions of "political correctness" often harshly enforced by left-Hegelians, such as Arnold Ruge and Theodor Echtermeyer in their *Hallesche Jahrbücher* (1838–41), it startles its audience — both before and after 1848 — with its proto-Modernist, symbolist tendencies, even where it engages ostensibly "real-historical" subjects. With its incipient Modernism, Meyer's lyric oeuvre jettisons an older quasi-confessional model of "feeling" in favor of one grounded in an objective, constructivist aesthetics. Doing so, however, also exposed Meyer to the charge of mannerism, "excessive" craftsmanship. Keller's oft-quoted critical view of Meyer — "er hat ein merkwürdiges schönes Talent, aber keine rechte Seele; denn er ziseliert und feilt schon vor dem Gusse" (his is a talent of enigmatic beauty, yet he does not have soul, for he fine-tunes and files away even before pouring the cast) — was even more emphatically echoed by its epistolary addressee, Theodor Storm. Neither Keller nor Storm, who had ever held fast to the confessional and expressivist paradigm of *Gefühl* as the only legitimate ground for lyric writing, can quite fathom that "feeling" has become a simulacrum, the effect (rather than cause) of meticulously crafted lyric utterances.

There is no doubt that our receptivity to high-Modernist features stirring to life within certain strains of nineteenth-century poetry has been significantly shaped by the formalist agendas of high Modernism. One only need to think of the both poetic and critical impact of Gertrude Stein or T. S. Eliot on poetry in English, or that of Rilke in Germany, idioms subsequently developed further in the expressionist "Wortkunst" (verbal art) of Georg Heym, Richard Dehmel, Georg Trakl, and the Stefan George circle, as well as in new critical directions charted by Herwarth Walden, Karl Kraus, and Friedrich Gundolf, though these writers fall outside the period under consideration here.[61] The at times emphatic de-contextualizing view of the lyric poem advocated by symbolist and expressionist writers can also be seen as anticipating the eventual rise of the politically neutralized interpretive model of New Critical exegesis. As a result of the latter's once powerful, now much weakened role in the contemporary academy, the broadly discursive and at times prolix balladic and other narrative poetry (*Verserzählungen*) of Theodor Fontane, C. F. Meyer, or Gottfried Keller today commands far less attention than the oeuvre of Mörike, Eichendorff, or Droste-Hülshoff, which in often startling ways presages the compact, post-confessional expressiveness of the lyric in Rilke, Trakl, and George. Lest the Realist and Naturalist developments of lyric poetry after 1848 be dismissed as a temporary (and putatively naïve) aberration, it ought to be stressed that even here — particularly in the work of C. F. Meyer (in "*Schwarzschattende Kastanie*" [black-shadowing chestnut tree]) — strong "modernist" features are already in evidence. Therefore, any static juxtaposition of a "real" (because narrative) poetry first championed by Vischer — and subsequently reinforced in the naturalist *Großstadtlyrik* of Holz, Bleibtreu, and Hartleben — with the ostensibly esoteric poetics of high Modernism will prove misleading. It is rather the case that a tendency toward what Hugo Friedrich termed the "Entgegenständlichung" (dematerialization) of the empirical and historical world, as well as Friedrich's notion of the "Entpersönlichung" ("de-personalization") of Romantic interiority unfolding concurrently, constitutes a steadily intensifying *Leitmotif* of the entire nineteenth-century lyric.

. A few short examples may help illustrate the extent to which lyric poetry, almost before the onset of the *Realismus* period actually presages, perhaps even more acutely than contemporary prose fiction, the symbolist aesthetics of "Verfremdung" ("ostranenie") that the Russian formalists were to develop into a full-fledged theory of literature two generations later.[62] A late poem by Eichendorff, written in 1843 and entitled "Nachts in Danzig" (Nights in Danzig, 1842) shows the lyric's capacity for exposing the specious, phantasmagorical coherence of the empirical world and, in further consequence, the dystopic psyche bound up with that world.[63] Eichendorff, who was to die in the same year, 1857, that was to see the publication of literary Modernism's ur-text, Baudelaire's *Les Fleurs du Mal,* subtly throws into relief the phantasmagoric status of the bourgeois individual, politically abject, entangled in a web of irresolvable antagonisms of social mobility checked, notions of faith palpably out of sync with industrial and scientific modernization, and liberal-political hopes dashed by Frederick William's 1840 ascent to the Prussian throne. Though formally remote from Heine's viciously satiric political exposé of Germany's repressive and superannuated political and cultural landscape in *Deutschland: Ein Wintermärchen,* Eichendorff's lyric proves its contemporaneity with his far more notorious fellow poet. Its opening quatrains suspend life in pre-1848 Germany between the seductive, albeit apparitional quality of a fairy-tale world and a vision of wholly denatured life, an ominous cityscape whose material architectural features emerge only in proto-Cubist bits and pieces from the ideological haze that had settled over the Prussia of Frederick Wilhelm IV. and over Germany in general. Between the disjointed shapes of darkened gables and Gothic windows (*hohe Fenster*) pale statues loiter. Are we to read them as literal statues or as lethargic *Bürger,* the politically "undead" representatives of a developmentally stunted society?

> Dunkle Giebel, hohe Fenster,
> Türme tief aus Nebeln sehn,
> Bleiche Statuen wie Gespenster
> Lautlos an den Türen stehen.
>
> Träumerisch der Mond drauf scheinet,
> Dem die Stadt gar wohl gefällt,
> Als läg' zauberhaft versteinet
> Drunten eine Märchenwelt.[64]
>
> [Dark Gables, arch windows,
> Towers protruding from deep fog,
> Pale statues, ghostlike
> Standing silently in doorways.
>
> Dreamily the moon shines down,
> Well pleased with the townscape
> As if, magically transmuted into stone,
> There lies below an enchanted world.]

Given the poem's ominous, apparitional and fragmented opening, its second stanza cannot be read as a straightforward transfiguration or idealization. For the closing subjunctive construction — strikingly reminiscent of the one that suffuses Eichendorff's famous poem "Mondnacht" with an aura of mourning — the moon's gaze on sublunar "Danzig in 1842" suspends referential and symbolic readings of the lyric alike. Thus the closing image neither indexes an empirical, living and breathing city, nor does it symbolize a visionary idyll. Instead, the pale moonlight and the baroque emblem of the stone (*versteinet*) recast urban space as a scene where social ideals and political progress stymied by the course of pre-1848 history are being mourned;[65] any more naïve reading of the "fairytale" world of the city is contravened by Eichendorff's shrewd use of the subjunctive (*als läg*). A similarly phantasmagoric diction — again prescient of a Modernist aesthetic — also prevails in many of Annette von Droste-Hülshoff's later poems, such as "Neujahrsnacht" (New Year's Eve," 1841–42):

> Im grauen Schneegestöber blassen
> Die Formen, es zerfließt der Raum,
> Laternen schwimmen durch die Gassen,
> Und leise knistert es im Flaum;
> Schon naht des Jahres letzte Stunde,
> Und drüben, wo der matte Schein
> Haucht aus den Fenstern der Rotunde,
> Dort ziehn die frommen Beter ein.
> . . .
> Ich sehe unter meinem Fenster
> Sie gleiten durch den Nebelrauch,
> Verhüllt und lautlos wie Gespenster,
> Vor ihrer Lippe flirrt der Hauch;
> Ein blasser Kreis zu ihren Füßen
> Zieht über den verschneiten Grund . . .[66]

> [In gray flurries of snow forms
> Grow pale, space dissolves,
> Lanterns afloat in alleyways,
> The feathery white softly crunching;
> Already the year's final hour arrives,
> And yonder, where dull light
> Streams from the rotunda's windows,
> Pious pilgrims make their entrance.
> . . .
> Below my window they pass
> Gliding through smoky mists
> Robed and inaudible as ghosts,
> Exhalations flitting from their lips;
> A faded halo surrounding their feet
> Motions across the snow-covered earth.]

The modernity of such writing is rooted in Droste-Hülshoff's ability to unfold a seemingly realist scenario by connecting its imagistic components into a complex texture where the referential, the emblematic (*Bildchiffren*) and the emotive dimension of images are kept in careful balance. The opening proto-impressionist image of forms dissolving into snow thus betokens, like tropes of the desert (in "Am achten Sonntag nach Pfingsten" [On the Eighth Sunday After Pentecost], written 1839, published 1851) or of her native heath-landscape near Münster (in *Heidebilder*), a state of spiritual disorientation, even abjection. Her slightly later poem "Durchwachte Nacht" (Sleepless Night, 1845;) sharpens the dematerialization of the empirical world and, in consequence, the dissolving of clear boundaries between a reflexive consciousness and a self suspended in a meditative idiom that delicately balances textures of sensation against those of emotion:

> O wunderliches Schlummerwachen, bist
> Der zartren Nerve Fluch du oder Segen? —
> 's ist eine Nacht vom Taue wach geküßt,
> Das Dunkel fühl ich kühl wie feinen Regen
> An meine Wange gleiten, das Gerüst
> Des Vorhangs scheint sich schaukelnd zu bewegen,
> Und dort das Wappen an der Decke Gips
> Schwimmt sachte mit dem Schlängeln des Polyps.
> . . .
> Und drunten das Gewölke rollt und klimmt;
> Gleich einer Lampe aus dem Hünenmale
> Hervor des Mondes Silbergondel schwimmt,
> Verzitternd auf der Gasse blauem Stahle,
> An jedem Fliederblatt ein Fünkchen glimmt,
> Und hell gezeichnet von dem blassen Strahle
> Legt auf mein Lager sich des Fensters Bild,
> Vom schwanken Laubgewimmel überhüllt.[67]

> [O strange somnambulism, do you spell
> Blight or blessing for the delicate soul? —
> 'tis a night awakened by the kiss of dews,
> Like rainy spray I feel the dark
> Sliding along my cheeks; the fastenings
> Of the curtain seems in swaying motion
> On the stucco ceiling armorial ensigns
> Gently glide swim with the kraken's mazy motion.
> . . .
> And below the cloudy mass seethes and rises;
> Like a lamp issuing from pagan monument

The moon's silvery gondola swims into sight,
Trembling away in the steel-blue alley
On every elderleaf a sparkle glimmers,
And brightly drawn by the pale ray of light
The window's image reposes on my bed
Encased by a swaying confusion of leaves.]

If Droste-Hülshoff, like Eichendorff, was committed to a renewal of Catholicism in a predominantly secular age, such a seemingly conservative project gradually came to shape a poetics far more advanced than that of her politically "progressive" contemporaries (Freiligrath, Herwegh, Dingelstedt) or post-1848 realists such as Keller and Fontane. Drawing on her native province of Westphalia, now under Prussian administration, Droste-Hülshoff often integrated into her poems images, regional expressions, as well as cultural and religious practices characteristic of that region; as for the Lake Poets in England, the autochthonous is mobilized as a place uncorrupted by the capitalist and administrative abstractions of the modern nation and its anonymous subjects. Yet beyond that, the hallucinatory power of her images above (and more can be found in "Spiegelbild," "Doppelgänger," "Hünenstein," "Die Mergelgrube") makes it clear that a Catholic renewal *qua* poetry does not entail some simplistic fusion of religious dogma and aesthetics. Rather, it involves staging a defining confrontation of the self with a mystical, boundless region — a moment where, in ways later unfolded by Martin Buber — the self experiences and embraces its own otherness: "Wo eine Rechte . . . das Herz vom eignen Herzen nimmt, / Um freudig an das fremde es zu legen" (Where the right . . . takes the heart away from its own / So as joyfully to lay it alongside a foreign one).[68] Such a confrontation can only be imagined in a language committed to breaking down the reification and empirical distinctness of self and world that had been a premise shared by the political poets of the *Vormärz* era and by some realists after 1848 (Hebbel, Keller, Fontane, Dahn). As in Eichendorff, her image of the moon's "silver gondola swimming / And trembling away on the steel-blue alleyway" notably anticipates Trakl's spectral and faintly animated urban spaces.[69]

German lyric poetry between 1830 and 1890 exhibits a sustained, if diversely articulated struggle with the "Entgrenzung des Ichs" (delimitation of the self) that unfolds in the experience of emotion. Whereas Hegelians like Hebbel and Vischer, at times more emphatically than their philosophical progenitor, insist on the mastery of contingent emotions by thought and clearly delimited and decodable referential language, the more experimental writers of the period (Eichendorff, Heine, Mörike, Droste-Hülshoff, and at times C. F. Meyer) do not posit emotion as something to be remedied by reflexive consciousness. Rather, emotion is to be captured and developed in a proto-Modernist, constructivist aesthetic in which the lyric image functions as the central and most powerful echo of mystic experiences constantly threatened with extinction by the capitalist and spiritual bureaucracies that consolidated and entrenched themselves from the *Vormärz* era on into the *Gründerzeit* of Wilhelm II. Such vestigial and often disparaged mystic experience involves a voice staging the confrontation between a stable bourgeois self and its own, intrinsic otherness (contingent feelings, perceptions, phantasmagoric shifts of mood and proto-Freudian irruptions of the unconscious). Such a confrontation can only be mediated in a language open to the volatile and continually shifting boundaries between referential, symbolic, and outright irrational linguistic meanings. For that reason writers of such dissimilar character as Eichendorff, Heine, Mörike, Droste-Hülshoff, and Meyer ultimately agree on the need to jettison — be it by satiric or other means — the late-Romantic cliché of a confessional or sentimentalized emotionalism that prevails in epigones like Rückert, Lenau, Kerner, and Geibel. Because the latter remain largely content with a conventional model of affect, one grounded in a socially and culturally normative and largely fixed model of masculine, middle-class, and decorously melancholic subjectivity, they also, however inadvertently, precipitated a crisis of legitimacy in Romantic poetry. The most powerful lyric writers of the mid and late nineteenth century respond to that crisis by groping, in imagery and aesthetic theory, toward a conception of literariness whose lyric and critical articulation would only reach its point of culmination after 1890.

Notes

[1] Review of Eduard Mörike's poems, first published in *Jahrbücher für wissenschaftliche Kritik*, vol. 2, no. 14–17, column 108–36 (1839). Reprinted in *Eduard Mörike: Wege der Forschung*, ed. Victor G. Doerksen (Darmstadt: Wissenschaftliche Buchgesellschaft, 1975), 5–6.

[2] Friedrich Sengle, *Biedermeierzeit* (Stuttgart: Metzler, 1972), vol. 2, 467–71.

[3] Heinrich Heine, *Briefe*, ed. Friedrich Hirth (Mainz: Florian Kupferberg, 1950), vol. 1, 329.

[4] Friedrich Hegel, *Vorlesungen über Aesthetik*, ed. Eva Moldenhauer and Markus Michel (Frankfurt: Suhrkamp, 1993), vol. 3, 416. *Aesthetics: Lectures on Fine Art*, trans. T. M. Knox (Oxford: Clarendon Press, 1975), 1111.

[5] *Encyclopädie der philosophischen Wissenschaften*, in Hegel, *Theorie Werkausgabe* (Frankfurt: Suhrkamp, 1970), vol. 3, 247.

[6] *Enzyklopädie* 3, 249.

[7] Theodor Storm, *Storms Werke*, ed. Theodor Böhme (Leipzig: Bibliographisches Institut, n.d.), vol. 1, 217. See also Storm's assertion that "*jeder Ausdruck muß seine Wurzel im Gefühl oder der Phantasie des Dichters haben. Beispiel des Gegenteils:*

Geibel." Quoted in Ludwig Völker, "Bürgerlicher Realismus," in *Geschichte der deutschen Lyrik,* ed. Walter Hinderer (Würzburg: Königshausen & Neumann, 2001), 354. (Every expression must be rooted in a feeling or in the poet's imagination. For a contrary example, see Geibel). The Naturalist writer Arno Holz was the first of many to comment on Geibel's apparent and complete lack of development as a poet. "Eine totale Null in der Entwicklung" (A complete zero as regards artistic development), ibid. 355.

[8] For Storm's views on the relation between lyric form and political debate, see his short poem, "Antwort," which declines to comment on Prussia's successful retaking of his native province of Schleswig-Holstein, a development that for professional and emotive purposes proved very welcome to him: "Nun ist geworden, was du wolltest; / Warum denn schweigest du jetzund? / — Berichten mag es die Geschichte; / Doch keines Dichters froher Mund." *Storms Werke,* vol. 1, 189. (English translation: Now has come to pass what you wanted; / Why then do you now keep silent? / — History may report on it; a poet's serene voice cannot.)

[9] Friedrich Hebbel, *Tagebücher,* in *Sämtliche Werke,* ed. Richard Maria Werner (Berlin: Behr, 1905), part II, vol. 2, 58.

[10] Theodor Vischer, "Gedichte von Eduard Mörike," in *Eduard Mörike,* 3.

[11] Eduard Mörike, *Sämtliche Werke,* ed. Helmut Koopmann (Darmstadt: Wissenschaftliche Buchgesellschaft, 1997), vol. 1, 665. *Friedrich Hölderlin, Eduard Mörike: Selected Poems,* trans. and ed. Christopher Middleton (Chicago: U of Chicago P, 1972), 131.

[12] Kenneth Calhoon, "Reading and the Art of Leisure in Mörike's 'Wald-Idylle'." *MLN* 116 (2001): 536–50; quote from 543.

[13] Hegel, *Aesthetics,* 1111; German: *Vorlesungen über Ästhetik,* vol. 3, 416.

[14] Mörike, *Sämtliche Werke,* vol. 1, 743. *Friedrich Hölderlin, Eduard Mörike: Selected Poems,* trans. and ed. Christopher Middleton (Chicago: U of Chicago P, 1972), 143.

[15] Theodor Adorno, "Rede über Lyrik und Gesellschaft" in *Noten zur Literatur,* vol. 11 in *Gesammelte Schriften,* ed. Rolf Tiedemann (Darmstadt: Wissenschaftliche Buchgesellschaft, 1997), 61, 62, 63. English translation from *Notes to Literature,* trans. Shierry Weber Nicholsen (New York: Columbia UP, 1991), vol. 1, 49.

[16] Hegel, *Aesthetics,* 1111–12; German: *Vorlesungen über Ästhetik,* vol. 3, 417.

[17] See Roman Jakobson, "Linguistics and Poetics," in *Language and Literature* (Cambridge, MA: Harvard UP, 1987).

[18] J. G. Herder, *Werke,* ed. B. Suphan (Berlin: Weidmann, 1977–1913), vol. 27, 171.

[19] Friedrich Hebbel, *Tagebücher,* part II, vol. 1, 26, 38.

[20] Hebbel, *Tagebücher,* vol. 1, 144.

[21] Hebbel, *Werke,* Part I, vol. 6, 287; 290.

[22] On the concept of emotion, see Martha Nussbaum, *Upheavals of Thought: The Intelligence of Emotions* (New York: Cambridge UP, 2000), 19–88; Rei Terada, *Feeling in Theory: Emotion after the Death of the Subject* (Cambridge, MA: Harvard UP, 2001); Philip Fisher, *The Vehement Passions* (Princeton: Princeton UP, 2001).

See also my *Romantic Moods: Paranoia, Trauma, and Melancholy, 1780–1840* (Baltimore: Johns Hopkins UP, forthcoming). For a superb introduction on the concept of *Stimmung*, see David Wellbery, "Stimmung," in *Ästhetische Grundbegriffe*, ed. Barck, Fontius, Schlenstedt, Steinwachs, Wolfzettel (Stuttgart: Metzler, 2003), vol. 5, 703–33.

[23] It bears remembering that the first edition of Hegel's *Vorlesungen über Ästhetik oder Philosophie der Kunst* appeared in H. G. Hotho's 1835 edition of the philosopher's works. A second, improved edition was to follow in 1842.

[24] Justinus Kerner, *Kerners Werke*, part I (Berlin: Deutsches Verlagshaus, n.d.), 191.

[25] Nikolaus Lenau, *Werke und Briefe*, ed. Antal Mádl (Vienna: Deuticke, Klett-Cotta, 1995), vol. 2, 139.

[26] Friedrich Rückert, *Poetische Werke*, 12 vols. (Frankfurt: Sauerländer, 1868), vol. 1, 371.

[27] Walter Benjamin, *The Arcades Project*, trans. and ed. Howard Eiland and Kevin McLaughlin (Cambridge, MA: Harvard UP, 1999), 205, 211, 206. See also Susan Stewart, *On Longing: Narratives of The Miniature, The Gigantic, The Souvenir, The Collection* (Durham, NC: Duke UP, 1993).

[28] *Sämtliche Schriften*, vol. 6: I, 447. See also one of his posthumous poems: "Der Sangesvogel, der ist todt, / Du wirst ihn nicht erwecken! / Du kannst Dir ruhig in den Steiß / Die golden Feder stecken."

[29] Heine, *Sämtliche Schriften*, vol. 3, 425.

[30] Martin Greiner, *Zwischen Biedermeier und Bourgeoisie: Ein Kapitel deutscher Literaturgeschichte* (Göttingen: Vandenhoeck & Ruprecht, 1953), 79–80; see also Sengle, *Biedermeierzeit*, vol. 1, 93–98.

[31] Karl Immermann, *Werke* (Leipzig and Vienna: Bibliographisches Institut, n.d.), vol. 3, 136 and vol. 5, 290.

[32] Friedrich Rückert (1788–1866) is an extreme example, as he wrote more than 10,000 poems over nearly six decades.

[33] Christoph Herin, "Biedermeier" in *Geschichte der deutschen Lyrik*, ed. Walter Hinderer (Würzburg: Königshausen & Neumann, 2001), 283.

[34] See Sengle, *Biedermeierzeit*, vol. 2, 549–625, and Christoph Herin, "Biedermeier," 287–90.

[35] Following his first collection of poems, *Gedichte* (1840), Franz Emanuel Geibel received a life-long pension of 300 Taler from Friedrich Wilhelm IV of Prussia, followed by an even more lucrative appointment as honorary chair of German literature and poetics at Munich under Maximilian II. Following the Austro-Prussian conflict, the ardent nationalist Geibel relinquished the position in favor of a permanent sinecure of 1000 Taler by Wilhelm I. in 1868. On Geibel, see Walter Hinck, "Epigonendichtung und Nationalidee" in *Zeitschrift für deutsche Philologie* 85, 267–84 and Jürgen Link and Wulf Wülfling, eds. *Nationale Mythen und Stereotypen in der 2. Hälfte des 19. Jahrhunderts* (Stuttgart: Klett-Cotta, 1989). For a recent revaluation of Rückert's oeuvre, see Max-Rainer Uhrig, ed., *Gestörte Idylle* (Würzburg: Ergon, 1995).

[36] Adorno, "Rede über Lyrik und Gesellschaft," in *Gesammelte Schriften,* vol. 11, 52 and 60. English translation by Shierry Weber Nicholsen in Adorno, *Notes to Literature,* vol. 1, 39 and 46.

[37] Gutzkow, *Schriften,* vol. 2, 867. Echoing Goethe's *Dichtung und Wahrheit,* where the poet's punctual birth at the stroke of noon under a "genial planetary constellation" is recorded at the opening of chapter 1, Eichendorff recounts how "an event of great importance for me, namely, my birth" was elaborately orchestrated to take place precisely at midnight. A band is assembled in the freezing courtyard, fireworks have been prepared, and the midwife is to wave a white cloth at the appointed moment. Yet by a series of minute deviations and errors the ritual comes off "a minute and a half too late" and the ideal "constellation [of stars] had been missed" (*HKA,* 40). The baroque fascination with the constellation of the planets during the moment of one's birth serves here to highlight the protagonist's fall into a thoroughly historical world. No amount of feudal privilege and planning can restore the subject of modernity to the imaginary (maternal) shelter of a purely metaphysical order.

[38] Letter to Veit, *Briefe,* 14.

[39] Joseph von Eichendorff, *Werke,* ed. Ansgar Hillach (Darmstadt: Wissenschaftliche Buchgesellschaft, 1996), vol. 1, 163–64.

[40] See Eichendorff's letter to Otto H. von Loeben (4 August 1814), in which he remarks on the frustration of his military career. Having, in effect, "missed" the momentous departure of Lützow's troops for a front that was itself continually shifting, Eichendorff grew increasingly frustrated by the fact that military "action" continued to elude him. Before long, an armistice was declared and "in this abyss of inaction and boredom we soon began to ponder and brood about our fate" (*Briefe,* 28–29).

[41] On trauma, see Cathy Caruth, *Unclaimed Experience* (Baltimore: Johns Hopkins UP, 1996), 1–9; on Eichendorff's lyric oeuvre, see Richard Alewyn, "Ein Wort über Eichendorff" in Paul Stöcklein, ed. *Eichendorff Heute* (Darmstadt: Wissenschaftliche Buchgesellschaft, 1966); David Wellbery, "Verzauberung: Das Simulakrum in der romantischen Lyrik," in *Mimesis und Simulation,* ed. Andreas Kablitz and Gerhard Neumann (Freiburg: Rombach, 1998), 451–77; and Thomas Pfau, "Conjuring History: Lyric Cliché, Conservative Fantasy, and Traumatic Awakening in German Romanticism" in *South Atlantic Quarterly* 102:1 (2003): 53–91.

[42] Hegel, *Vorlesungen zur Ästhetik,* ed. Eva Moldenhauer and Karl Markus Michel, 447–48; English translation in Hegel, *Aesthetics: Lectures on Fine Art,* trans. T. M. Knox (Oxford: Clarendon Press, 1975), 1136.

[43] On reading habits in relation to the concept of *Bildung,* see Sheehan, 157–60, Nipperdey, 35–44.

[44] Eichendorff, *Werke,* vol. 1, 91–92. See also "*Der Isegrim,*" "*Der Unverbesserliche,*" or his "*Mandelkerngedicht.*" On the political struggles between reform-minded and politically opportunist sectors of the Prussian bureaucracy, particularly after the 1816 defeat of reforms launched by von Stein and continued under von Hardenberg, see James Sheehan (35–36, 252) who emphasizes how the narrow material base of this bureaucracy constrained its members to compromise their ambitions. See also Reinhart Koselleck, ed., *Bildungsbürgertum im 19. Jahrhundert* (Stuttgart:

Klett-Cotta, 1990). On Eichendorff's increasingly frustrating career as a member of the *Bildungsbeamtentum,* see the detailed account by Wolfgang Frühwald, "Der Regierungsrat Joseph von Eichendorff," in *Internationales Archiv für Sozialgeschichte der Deutschen Literatur* (1979), vol. 4, 37–67.

[45] Quoted in Bayerdörfer, "Vormärz," in Hinderer, ed., *Geschichte der deutschen Lyrik vom Mittelalter zur Gegenwart* (Würzburg: Königshausen & Neumann, 2001), 327.

[46] Georg Herwegh, *Werke,* part I (Berlin, Leipzig, Vienna: Deutsches Verlagshaus Bong & Co, n.d.), 121; In the "Preface" to his 1844 collection of poems, entitled "Ein Glaubensbekenntnis" (Credo), Dingelstedt was to reverse himself and confess to having descended down to the "ramparts of partisanship" (*Zinnen der Partei*) after all. *Freiligraths Werke,* ed. Julius Schwering (Berlin: Deutsches Verlagshaus, n.d.), Part 2, 10.

[47] Sengle, *Biedermeierzeit,* vol. 2, 543.

[48] Vischer, review of Eduard Mörike's poems in *Jahrbücher für wissenschaftliche Kritik,* reprinted in *Eduard Mörike: Wege der Forschung,* 6. Other poets, such as Annette von Droste-Hülshoff, share Vischer's misgivings. See influential opening grouping of poems, titled *Zeitgedichte,* in her 1844 volume *Gedichte,* where politically current topics such as the "Kölner Wirren" (Cologne Quarrels) regarding the status of Catholics in the Prussian and Protestant-dominated German Federation are being taken up in careful avoidance of outright political propaganda.

[49] See especially the *Vorrede* to *Atta Troll:* "Die Musen bekamen die strenge Weisung, sich hinfüro nicht mehr müßig umherzutreiben, sondern in vaterländischen Dienst zu treten, etwa als Marketenderinnen der Freiheit oder als Wächterinnen der christlich-germanischen Nationalität. Es erhub sich im deutschen Bardenhain ganz besonders jener vage, unfruchtbare Pathos, jener nutzlose Enthusiasmusdunst, der sich mit Todesverachtung in einen Ozean von Allgemeinheiten stürzte . . . " *Sämtliche Schriften,* ed. Klaus Briegleb (Munich: dtv, 1997), vol. 4, 494. (English translation: The muses received strict instructions that they were no longer to ramble about indolently but to enter into patriotic service, e.g. as sutlers of freedom or as a female honor-guard of the Christian-German nation. From the groves of German poetry there rose a peculiarly vague, sterile, and useless haze of enthusiasm that, without fear for life and limb, hurled itself headlong into an ocean of generalities.)

[50] Heine, *Sämtliche Schriften,* vol. 4, 485. See also Heine's letter of February 1842 to Julius Campe, who at that point had been saddled with *Betriebsverbot* by the Prussian authorities because of his publication of Dingelstedt's *Lieder eines kosmopolitischen Nachtwächters.*

[51] "*Den höchsten Begriff vom Lyriker hat mir Heinrich Heine gegeben. . . . Er besass jene göttliche Bosheit, ohne die ich mir das Vollkommne nicht zu denken vermag.*" Friedrich Nietzsche, *Sämtliche Werke,* ed. Giorgio Colli and Mazzino Montinari (Munich: dtv, 1980), vol. 6, 286. (Translation: "The highest concept of the lyrical poet was given to me by Heinrich Heine. . . . He possessed that divine malice without which I cannot imagine perfection." Nietzsche, *On the Genealogy of Morals & Ecce Homo,* trans. Walter Kaufman (New York: Vintage, 1967), 245.

[52] Heine, *Briefe,* vol. 2, 38.

[53] Heine, *Sämtliche Schriften,* vol. 1, 239; *Complete Poems,* trans. Hal Draper (Boston: Suhrkamp / Insel, 1982) 175, translation modified.

[54] As to the writing of this short lyric, an acquaintance of Heine's, Johann Peter Lyser (1803–1870) recalls how, at Heine's request during a meeting in 1830, he had written a short frivolous song. In reading it, Heine remarked that Lyser's closing couplet enjoining the beloved: "Lüge dreist — ich will's d'rauf wagen, / Weil ich Dich schon lieben muß" (Lie brazenly — I'll take my chances / For I am constrained to love you) — was too reminiscent of Goethe's style and sounded too innocent. In response, Heine then proceeded to write the lyric quoted above. Lyser's account is reprinted in *Begegnungen mit Heine: Berichte der Zeitgenossen,* ed. Michael Werner (Hamburg: Hoffmann und Campe, 1973), vol. 1, 196–99. On Heine's infusion of a proto-Nietzschean *ressentiment* into lyric poetry, see also my own "*Nachtigallenwahnsinn* and *Rabbinismus:* Heine's Literary Provocation to German-Jewish Cultural Identity," in *Romantic Poetry: Comparative History of Literatures in European Languages,* ed. Angela Esterhammer (Amsterdam: John Benjamins, 2002), 427–44.

[55] Peter von Matt, *Die verdächtige Pracht* (Munich: Hanser, 1998), 205.

[56] Wolfgang Preisendanz, *Heinrich Heine: Werkstrukturen und Epochenbezüge* (Munich: Fink, 1973), 68.

[57] Georg Lukács, *Deutsche Realisten des 19. Jahrhunderts* (Berlin: Aufbau Verlag, 1952), 130. English translation in Lukács, *German Realists in the Nineteenth Century,* trans. Jeremy Gaines and Paul Keast, ed. Rodney Livingstone (Cambridge, MA: MIT Press, 1993), 139.

[58] "Scott, in dem ich täglich lese, interessiert mich wieder aufs höchste" (Scott, whom I am reading daily, once again absorbs my attention to the utmost), Theodor Fontane, *Sämtliche Romane, Erzählungen, Gedichte, Nachgelassenes,* vol. 6, 1014n.

[59] C. F. Meyer, *Sämtliche Werke,* vol. 2, 64.

[60] Quoted in Ludwig Völker, "Bürgerlicher Realismus," in *Geschichte der deutschen Lyrik,* 342.

[61] On the George Circle, see Edward Norton's magisterial *Secret Germany: Stefan George and his Circle* (Ithaca: Cornell UP, 2002).

[62] See Viktor Sklovskij, "Kunst als Verfahren," in Jurij Striedter, ed., *Russischer Formalismus* (Munich: Fink, 1971), 5–35. On the concept of *ostranenie* or *Verfremdung,* see also Juri Striedter, "Transparenz und Verfremdung: Zur Theorie des Poetischen Bildes in der Russischen Moderne," in *Immanente Ästhetik, Ästhetische Reflexion: Lyrik als Paradigma der Moderne,* ed. Wolfgang Iser (Munich: Fink, 1966), 263–96.

[63] The word "phantasmagoria" only arises at the beginning of the nineteenth century, with early mentions in the Britain 1802 *Gentlemen's Magazine* and in the 1803 *European Magazine* and in essays by William Hazlitt. Though initially coined to describe optical illusions created by magic lanterns on display in London beginning in 1802 (OED), the term soon emerges as a descriptor for the operation of ideological fantasy. See Schopenhauer's *World as Will and Representation* (1819): "Solche deutliche Erkenntniß und ruhige, besonnene Darstellung dieser traumartigen

Beschaffenheit der ganzen Welt ist eigentlich die Basis der ganzen Kantischen Philosophie, ist ihre Seele und ihr allergrößtes Verdienst. Er brachte dieselbe dadurch zu Stande, daß er die ganze Maschinerie unsers Erkenntnisvermögens, mittelst welcher die Phantasmagorie der objektiven Welt zu Stande kommt, auseinandergelegte und stückweise vorzeigte, mit bewunderungswerther Besonnenheit und Geschicklichkeit. *Die Welt als Wille und Vorstellung* (Darmstadt: Wissenschaftliche Buchgesellschaft, 1990), vol. 1, 567. (English translation from *The World as Will and Representation,* trans. E. F. J. Payne [New York: Dover, 1969, 419–20]: "Such clear knowledge and calm, deliberate presentation of this dreamlike quality of the whole world is really the basis of the whole Kantian philosophy; it is its soul and its greatest merit. He achieved it by taking to pieces the whole machinery of our cognitive faculty, by means of which the phantasmagoria of the objective world is brought about, and presenting it piecemeal with marvelous insight and ability.") Hegel's review article of 1828 (*Rezensionen aus den Jahrbüchern für wissenschaftliche Kritik*), and Marx's critique of St. Max [Stirner] in the *German Ideology* (1845–46). Marx's argument particularly attends to the conjunction of de-personalization (*Entpersönlichung*) and de-materialization (*Entgegenstädlichung*) that Hugo Friedrich, in his *Struktur der modernen Lyrik,* posited as central to mid-nineteenth-century symbolism; as Marx puts it: "First comes the moral injunction to seek and, moreover, to seek oneself. This is defined in the sense that man should become something that so far is not, namely, an egoist, and this egoist is defined as being an 'all-powerful ego,' in whom the peculiar ability has become resolved from actual ability into the ego, into omnipotence, into the fantastic idea of ability. To seek oneself means, therefore, to become something different from what one is and, indeed, to become an all powerful, i.e., nothing, a non-thing, a phantasmagoria" (Marx, *The German Ideology* [Amherst, NY: Prometheus Books, 1998], 285; for the German text, see Karl Marx, *Werke,* 6 vols., ed. Hans-Joachim Lieber and Peter Furth [Darmstadt: Wissenschaftliche Buchgesellschaft, 1990], vol. 2, 316–17). See also Theodor Adorno, whose study of Richard Wagner nicely summarizes the relevant aspects of the term: "Where the dream is at its most exalted, the commodity is closest to hand. The phantasmagoria tends towards dream not merely as deluded wish-fulfillment of would-be buyers, but chiefly to conceal the labor that has gone into making it. It mirrors subjectivity by confronting the subject with the product of its own labor, but in such a way that the labor that has gone into it is no longer identifiable. The dreamer encounters his own image impotently, as if it were a miracle, and is held fast in the inexorable circle of his own labor, as if it would last forever." Theodor Adorno, *In Search of Wagner* (New York: Verso, 1981), 91; for the German text, see Adorno, *Gesammelte Schriften* (Darmstadt: Wissenschaftliche Buchgesellschaft, 1998), vol. 13, 87.

[64] Joseph von Eichendorff, *Werke* (Stuttgart: Cotta, 1953), 166; the new critical edition of Eichendorff produces a slightly different reading text, with the version printed here still supported by the manuscript. See Joseph von Eichendorff, *Historisch-Kritische Ausgabe* (Tübingen: Max Niemeyer, 1997), vol. 1,3, 230 and vol. 1,4, 415–17. For a reading of the poem, with just emphasis on its "never congruent perspectives," see Heinz Schlaffer, *Lyrik im Realismus* (Bonn: Bouvier, 1966), 14–16.

[65] On Baroque emblemata and the unsettling power of lyric cliché in Eichendorff, see my "Conjuring History."

66 Annette von Droste-Hülshoff, *Sämtliche Werke,* ed. Bodo Plachta and Winfrid Woestler (Frankfurt: Deutscher Klassiker Verlag, 1998), vol. 1, 148–49.

67 Droste-Hülshoff, *Sämtliche Werke,* vol. 1, 329–30.

68 Droste-Hülshoff, *Sämtliche Werke,* vol. 1, 300.

69 See a line such as "Ein kalter Glanz huscht über Straßen" ("Melancholie des Abends"), in Georg Trakl, *Das dichterische Werk,* ed. Walter Killy (Munich: dtv, 1972) 13; or "Zitternd flattern Glockenklänge" ("Die schöne Stadt"), 15, as well as Trakl's recurrent use of color adjectives to close in on otherwise ineffable emotive states; e.g., "Kleines Konzert," 25. On Trakl's modernity, see Wolfgang Preisendanz, "Auflösung und Verdinglichung bei Trakl" in *Immanente Ästhetik, Ästhetische Reflexion: Lyrik als Paradigma der Moderne,* ed. Wolfgang Iser (Munich: Fink, 1966), 227–61, esp. his claim that in Trakl "we no longer encounter images signifying something else but strictly self-referential ones" ("sich selbst meinende Bilder") 241.

Franz Stassen (1869–1949), Valhalla: The Valkyrie *(1914).*
Courtesy of Snark/Art Resource, New York.

Richard Wagner: Opera and Music Drama

Christopher Morris

T HE OLD CHESTNUT that more has been written about Richard Wagner (1813–83) than any historical figure bar Napoleon and Jesus Christ has been debunked many times. But legends are durable, and this one has been given a new lease of life thanks to the plethora of websites devoted to Wagner: typing the names of these three historical figures into a search engine will quickly reveal how widely this claim has been disseminated. The important point, of course, is not the veracity of the assertion, but the fact that it proves so popular. That such an exaggerated claim continues to flourish says something about the aura surrounding "der Meister" (as he was once known to his most ardent followers) and the hyperbole with which his name is associated, not least in Germany, where Wagner's quarrelling descendants can still generate more than their fair share of column inches in the national press.

In retrospect, the emergence of the Wagner phenomenon has an inevitability to it. Wagnerian theater is nothing if not extreme — in scale, in scope, in intensity — and the fact that it generated cultic enthusiasm is no more surprising than the (equally vigorous) hostility with which it was confronted. The one fate that Wagner's work has been spared is lack of interest. The cultural climate that nurtured Wagner's gargantuan and arrogant ambitions also granted an audience sympathetic to its pretensions and willing to subject itself to the considerable mental and physical rigors of five-hour music dramas. Perhaps only in the context of an ideology that presented art as the new religion — an ideology that Wagner doggedly promoted in his prose publications — could this zeal have manifested itself. At the same time, the partisan swagger of Wagner and his supporters was always bound to provoke opposition, and dissenting, polemically charged voices can be heard from many directions.

If this makes Wagner a fascinating subject and a vivid barometer of aspects of European culture in the nineteenth century, it does nothing to clarify the picture for the historian keen to sweep away layers of mythology, let alone biographers, who, perhaps more than usual, find themselves wading through second-hand accounts of second-hand accounts. In this respect Wagner is a humbling figure, perhaps one who forces the scholar to give up on naïve notions of "truth" or "objectivity" and to instead accept Friedrich Nietzsche's characterization of Wagner as the archetypal "actor" whose masks only conceal more masks. Equally, any attempt to come to terms with Wagner's work confronts an interpretational history of exceptional range, as though the operas (the term used to designate the works up to and including *Lohengrin* of 1848) and the later so-called *Musikdramen* meant all things to all people. Is *Der Ring des Nibelungen* (1876) a stinging Socialist indictment of the new industrial economy, as George Bernard Shaw would have it, or the aesthetic embodiment of commodification and division of labor, the view put forward by Theodor Adorno?[1] Is *Tristan und Isolde* (1865) a thoroughly literary mobilization of myth and psychology (Thomas Mann) or does it leave word and image behind in an overwhelming flood of music (Nietzsche)?[2] If any single interpretation seems to hang by a tenuous thread, this only seems to have added to the allure of Wagner's deeply ambiguous work, suggesting that the cultic characteristics of Wagner reception owe their origins partly to this perceived multivalency and indeterminacy.

This is not to say that Wagner encouraged or endorsed an openness of interpretation. Wagner sought unprecedented control over aspects of the performance and reception of his work, from lighting conditions to sightlines to the elimination of potential distractions. This need to leave nothing to chance reminded Adorno of the figure of the conductor: just as the orchestra is encouraged to express itself, but only according to the unifying will of the conductor, so Wagner's audience is offered the illusion of responding freely while in fact falling under the dominating spell of his music.[3] This desire for control is evident, too, in Wagner's writings. As David Levin recently observed, Wagner's correspondence and voluminous published writings on aesthetic theory suggest "an artist obsessed with anticipating, sealing, and reinforcing every imaginable breach in his aesthetic constructs."[4] It was critical to the project that Wagner began to develop in mid-career that he be understood not merely as a successor to the operatic tradition, not merely as the successful composer and librettist of *Der fliegende Holländer* (The Flying Dutchman, 1843) and *Tannhäuser* (1845). Rather, in a series of essays written while in exile from Germany after his participation in the failed Dresden uprising of 1849, Wagner announced nothing less than the end of opera and the beginning of the "Kunstwerk der Zukunft" (artwork of the future). This, Wagner claimed, would entail not merely revolutionizing the form and subject matter of the work of art, but the reform of the institutions through which it was disseminated, and the re-education of the German public so that new attitudes to art could be instilled. In short, Wagner was proposing a refashioning of German culture on his terms and with him at its center.

Revolutionary Aesthetics / Aesthetic Revolution

Are these merely the rantings of a megalomaniac artist? How could Wagner hope to have such claims taken seriously? The zeal and scope of these essays need to be understood, first of all, as an extension of the revolutionary fervor that had gripped Wagner since the mid-1840s. Although he was later to downplay his involvement in revolutionary activities in Dresden, it is clear from his correspondence and from the accounts of observers that Wagner, then court *Kapellmeister,* was actively involved both as a writer (in 1848 he published several inflammatory anonymous essays in Dresden's far-left *Volksblätter,* edited from 1848 to 1852 by the musician August Röckel) and as courier and lookout during the uprising itself. He was fortunate to escape Dresden after the collapse of the uprising, and was declared a wanted man in Saxony, a status that was only rescinded thirteen years later when he was granted a pardon. It was in the early months of exile in Zurich that Wagner wrote his first major essays on aesthetics: "Die Kunst und die Revolution" (Art and Revolution, 1849) "Das Kunstwerk der Zukunft" (The Artwork of the Future, 1850) and *Oper und Drama* (1852). In their language and tone, the essays often echo the publications and correspondence written during the revolutionary period. Indeed, the relationship between Wagner's revolutionary rhetoric and the Zurich essays works both ways. If Wagner's aesthetics took on the character of political revolution, his revolutionary ideas had announced the dawn of an aesthetic utopia, suggesting that Wagner's outrage at the political status quo had something to do with its antipathy to his goals as an artist.

Yet it would be unfair to reduce Wagner's overwhelming conviction solely to self-interest or to a hopelessly naïve aestheticism. For over a decade he had engaged publicly with political and philosophical discourse. During the late 1830s he had enthusiastically embraced the liberal politics of the *Junges Deutschland* circle (the poet Heinrich Laube had published some of his earliest essays) and his sympathies were to become increasingly radical through the 1840s. He appears to have been familiar with Max Stirner's *Der Einzige und sein Eigentum* (The Individual and his Property, 1845) and his anonymous publications during the revolutionary period espouse anarchist resistance (Mikhail Bakunin was among his acquaintances in Dresden). By the time he wrote the Zurich essays he had read Pierre-Joseph Proudhon's seminal *Qu'est-ce que la propriété?* (What is Property?, 1840) with its famous definition of property as theft.

Evident in his language, too, is the voice of Ludwig Feuerbach (1804–72), the philosopher of the Young Hegelian school to whom "Das Kunstwerk der Zukunft" is dedicated and on whose *Grundsätze der Philosophie der Zukunft* (Foundations of the Philosophy of the Future, 1843) Wagner clearly modeled his title. Feuerbach presents his work as an atheistic anti-philosophy — he characterized himself as having no religion and no philosophy[5] — devoted to the grounding of Hegel's all-too abstract idealism in notions of "Sinnlichkeit" (sensuality) and "Menschheit" (humanity), but he resists any labels that might threaten to reduce his position to a particular school of thought. When, in *Der Einzige und sein*

Eigentum, Max Stirner (1806–56) accused him of clinging to the very notions he appeared to reject, of investing his concept of materialism with idealism, Feuerbach published an anonymous reply insisting that he was "weder Materialist noch Idealist" (neither materialist nor idealist):

> Er ist mit Gedanken, was er der Tat nach, im Geiste, was er im Fleische, im Wesen, was er in den Sinnen ist — *Mensch:* oder vielmehr, da Feuerbach nur in die Gemeinschaft das Wesen des Menschen versetzt: Gemeinmensch, *Kommunist.*

> [He is in thought what he is in deed, in spirit what he is in the flesh, in essence what he is to the senses — a human being, or rather, since Feuerbach locates the essence of humanity in community, a communal human being, a *communist.*][6]

The passage delineates the radical subjectivity at the heart of Feuerbach's thought, but it also exposes a tendency to essentialize and totalize concepts, so that "Menschheit," for example, serves to ground other concepts in an opaque absolute that is never adequately defined. This is a characteristic, too, of Wagner's Zurich essays, as evident in his insistent mobilization of terms such as "reinmenschlich" (purely human), "Unwillkür" (instinct), "Natur," and the quintessential Feuerbachian opposition of *Egoismus* to *Kommunismus.*

In "Das Kunstwerk der Zukunft," for example, Wagner incorporates this binary into a dialectical history in which an original Hellenic unity has given way to a contemporary state of egoism that will find "Erlösung in den Kommunismus" (redemption in communal existence).[7] But if Feuerbach had focussed on the relationship of human "wholeness" to religion, Wagner's system proposes, not surprisingly, that art will be instrumental in undoing humanity's egoistic alienation. This, Wagner enthuses, will take the form of "das große Gesamtkunstwerk" (the great synthesis of the arts) that will absorb the individual arts into the common goal of the "unbedingte, unmittelbare Darstellung der vollendeten menschlichen Natur" (the unconditional, immediate representation of perfect human nature, *DS* 6, 28–29). Not only will this *Gesamtkunstwerk* unite previously isolated arts — a utopian aesthetic vision already articulated by Lessing, Novalis, Tieck and Schelling — but it will issue from the combined will of a united people, and here Wagner relates Feuerbach's *Kommunismus* to that most loaded of politico-cultural signifiers, *das Volk.* Tapping into the extensive nationalist discourse centered on the *Volk* as embodiment of untainted, traditional, and spontaneous cultural expression, Wagner called for a theater that would model itself on the practices of the common people, on folk festivals and singing societies. Revolution, then, would not brush aside tradition, merely the corrupt values of modern — and implicitly rootless — culture. And if the artist of the future is first and foremost Wagner himself, then the author of the Zurich essays is canny enough not to say it directly. Instead, the heroic artist figure will lead the *Volk* only by emerging from and being reabsorbed into a "freie künstlerische Genossenschaft" (free artistic fellowship, *DS* 6: 145).

Revolution's Other

But how is this fellowship defined? For Marc Weiner and David Levin a critical element here is the notion of constitutive exclusion. That is, the question of how this community is to be formed hinges on who will become its other, who will be excluded so that it can define itself as whole.[8] The major Zurich essays define this "fellowship" only in a general way, but, following Weiner and Levin, we might read them in the context of a short, vitriolic essay published under a pseudonym only a few months after "Das Kunstwerk der Zukunft." "Das Judentum in der Musik" (Jewishness in Music, 1850) makes no bones about exclusion, superimposing on the figure of the "Jew" the obverse of everything properly "human" and "creative" about the genuine *Volk*. As a perpetual "foreigner," the Jew is parasitic on any true culture, incapable not only of artistic creativity, but of language itself, defined here, of course, in terms of the natural, organic, and pure. As problematic and offensive as this is, it is compounded by Wagner's hypocrisy. If "Das Judentum in der Musik" needs to be read in the context of contemporary political discourse, and particularly the literature of the liberal and revolutionary circles in which Wagner had moved, it is also a critique of the misrepresentation of Jews in bourgeois liberal ideology. Paralleling Feuerbach's "grounding" of Hegelian idealism, Wagner claims that the liberals have formed a picture of Jews based on abstract concepts instead of developing an understanding "bei wirklicher, tätiger Berührung" (through actual, physical contact).[9] Wagner, then, offers to expose this misreading and its role in generating anti-Jewish attitudes by detailing "real" characteristics. Yet what we actually get in the name of this ideology critique is an exhaustive catalog of characteristics (actually vile stereotypes) that, as Wagner now craftily suggests, generate a quite rational and understandable "Abneigung" (revulsion) in the non-Jew (*SSD* 5: 67).

A similar slippage, this time between nationalist ideology and Wagner's appeal to universal values, is evident in his mobilization of the concept of myth. In *Oper und Drama*, the essay that most explicitly outlines the shape of the art of the future, Wagner argues that myth serves as a focused primal source of human experience in all its diversity, reducing mere history to its eternal essence and offering a model of rootedness in the *Volk* (*SD* 7: 154). By drawing on myth, the art of the future promises to rediscover these roots, and it is drama, he claims, that is the true vehicle of myth. If the novel articulates the superficial bourgeois reality of the "Staatsbürger" (citizen), true drama directly presents the inner reality of the human being (170). Drama is the mirror of the people, he adds, and he implies that he has no particular *Volk* in mind: "Das Unvergleichliche des Mythos ist, daß er jederzeit wahr, und sein Inhalt . . . für alle Zeiten unerschöpflich ist" (The incomparable thing about myth is that it is true for all time, and its content . . . is inexhaustible throughout the ages, 188). Wagner's claim is presented in the context of a discussion of Greek myth and culture, a rich — and highly idealized — pan-European model for Wagner, as it was for so many of his literary contemporaries and as it had been for the Romantics.

But Wagner's universalist aspirations are not what they seem. There is, he argues, a special quality to the mythology of the German people which transformed the religious myth of the Greeks into a truly human heroic saga, but which nevertheless maintained its roots in "*Urmythos*" (primal myth, 160). Wagner tries to stress the importance of the "Reinmenschliche" (purely human, 197), as opposed to nationalistic, aspects of Germanic myth, but his slippages imply, on the one hand, that the universal human spirit of the Greeks just happens to have been bequeathed to the Germans, while, on the other, Germanic myth is actually universal. Specifically, he privileges the German language, claiming that, in contrast to French and Italian, it maintains a connection with its roots (350). Wagner's interest in philology had led him to study older forms of German, and he had drawn on Middle High German sources for the libretto of his *Lohengrin* (1850). What he now proposed was the adoption of formal principles from earlier literary and linguistic traditions, above all the alliterative verse form of Old High German. Its pattern of verse-pairs of two or three accented syllables offered what Wagner considered a concentrated, immediate, and flexible framework for expression and signification. And unlike the end-rhyme of modern poetry, alliteration (*Stabreim*) preserves a connection to nature and the *Volk*, harking back, according to Wagner's by now familiar strategy, to an era in which the ordinary (German) people created poetry and myth (*SSD* 6: 309). In what Thomas Grey has tellingly termed a "utopia of regression," Wagner seeks the modern rejuvenation of an emotive immediacy lost as language strayed from its supposed sensual origins in the related root syllables of *Stabreim* and became ever more abstract and conceptual.[10]

Although Wagner presents his ideas as *sui generis*, Grey points to important Enlightenment precedents in Jean-Jacques Rousseau's *Essai sur l'origine des langues* (1754) and Johann Herder's *Über den Ursprung der Sprache* (1772), both of which seek to trace the proliferation of modern languages back to single sources rooted in nature and an unspoiled immediacy (Grey, 258–62). Central to Rousseau's model is the originally intimate relationship of language with music, a form of utterance that predates speech as such. This is a critical aspect of Wagner's thesis. What the modern poet has lost, he argues, is an awareness of the "Urmelodie" (original melody) that was once so intrinsic to language. Stabreim offers to reanimate this "Tonsprache" (musicalized speech, *DS* 7, 218), but this is not yet the dialectical synthesis of the arts toward which the Zurich essays gesture, for music, in turn, has something to learn from language. If words cry out for music's immediacy of expression, instrumental music (embodied in the symphony) yearns for "Erlösung . . . zur allgemeinsamen Kunst" (redemption into communal art, *DS* 6, 68). Music, too, has lost its way, condemned to a meaningless, vacuous self-sufficiency in which mere melodic pleasure — as opposed to real content rich in ideas — is the guiding principle. Modern music, he argues, ingratiates and adorns, but it means nothing. And opera, which should have resisted this empty music, gave itself over to it completely, turning its libretti into mere vehicles for elaborate stagings and vocal display. Again Wagner's xenophobia reveals itself, for although he is deeply critical of contemporary music practices throughout Europe, he singles out Italian and French opera for its presumed frivolity and vulgarity, this despite the fact that the formation of his own musical language owed much to the fusion of French and Italian with more characteristically German features. Above all, Wagner situates the artist of the future as heir to a German tradition, to the Beethoven symphony, which at least gestured, even if it ultimately failed, toward true poetic meaning. In his Ninth Symphony, the choral finale of which Wagner presents as a revolutionary union of poetry and music, Beethoven is seen to offer a model for a regenerative synthesis of the arts that will now be brought to fruition.

The term synthesis, though, might imply a merging of equals, but in Wagner's fascinatingly elaborate metaphors for the union of poetry and music, a more complex picture emerges. One passage in *Oper und Drama* presents Beethoven's gesture in the finale of the Ninth as the act of an individual who had to become "ein ganzer, d.h. gemeinsamer, den geschlechtlichen Bedingungen des Männlichen und Weiblichen unterworfener Mensch" (a complete, composite person, at once subordinate to the determinants of both male and female gender).[11] The suggestion is of androgyny, a metaphor that Jean-Jacques Nattiez has explored as a central trope in Wagner's aesthetics.[12] But, as Grey points out, the Feuerbachian and Young German slant of the Zurich essays together with Wagner's reliance on the contemporary discourse of the natural sciences results in a sometimes awkward collision of the abstract, symbolic implications of androgyny with strongly gendered metaphors centered on procreative union as a physical act (Gray, 143–46). This is startlingly evident a few pages later when Wagner opens yet another metaphorical passage with the phrase "Die Musik ist ein Weib" (Music is a woman, *DS* 7: 114). He then goes on to show that music, like woman, is aimless until it surrenders itself to the (rational, intellectual, masculine) embrace of poetry, that it has no identity until granted it in union with poetry. The result of this union is not adrogyny but procreation: poetry fertilizes the womb of music to give birth to music drama. The themes — feminine sacrifice, the incompleteness of woman, the rational vs. emotional binary of sexual difference — recall familiar contemporary cultural constructions, but it is the lengths to which Wagner pursues his metaphors and the sheer kaleidoscopic excess of the gender associations that distinguish his writing. And of course, Wagner's discussion would be incomplete without reference to the *Volk,* which, we are told, created melodies in the same way that the physical human being conceives through "den unwillkürlichen Akt geschlechticher Begattung" (the instinctive act of sexual coupling).[13]

Wagner's *Magnum Opus*

By the time the Zurich essays appeared in print (1849–52), Wagner had already embarked on the project intended to embody the theoretical principles they outlined. Combining aspects of several Norse myths and Germanic legends (including the Icelandic sagas and the Middle High German *Nibelungenlied*) and drawing on the work of scholars such as Karl Lachmann and Hans Joseph Mone, Wagner sketched out a prose résumé entitled *Nibelungensage (Mythus).* This he developed into a prose draft entitled "Siegfrieds Tod" (Siegfried's Death, written 1848), but when it became apparent that the events dramatized there required significant back-narration, Wagner decided to present its pre-history in dramatic form. The result was *Der junge Siegfried* (Young Siegfried, 1851), which was ultimately provided with its own "prequel" *Die Walküre,* itself preceded by a "Vorabend" (preliminary evening) titled *Das Rheingold.* Having originally centered the project on the guileless hero Siegfried, Wagner refocused what was now a mammoth tetralogy on the figure of Wotan (ruler of the gods in Valhalla) and his struggle with the corrupting influence of wealth and power.

Isolated musical sketches date from as early as 1850, but composition of the score began in earnest only in late 1853 with *Das Rheingold.* In his 1864 autobiography, *Mein Leben,* Wagner recalled that his inspiration for the work's orchestral prelude had appeared to him one afternoon during a semi-conscious state of reverie. He had experienced a sensation of sinking beneath waves, he tells us, and began to experience those waves as music. Awakening in terror, he realized that his musical realization of the opening of the *Ring* had appeared to him.[14] As autobiography the account is highly suspect, but as an elaborate and colorful dramatization of artistic creation, it suggests that Wagner's talent for myth and metaphor is not confined to his libretti or theoretical writings. It also suggests a strongly intertextual and reflexive element in Wagner's work, inviting us to consider how the opening of *Das Rheingold* might be related to other levels of creation and origin. That the prelude begins without discernible melodic or rhythmic shape and climaxes in wave-like surges of orchestral sound has prompted critics to interpret it as a musical *creatio ex nihilo,* a realization of the beginning of all things. Thomas Mann, for example, wrote of the "Urzelle" (primeval cell) and "Erzbeginn" (fundamental origin), and Warren Darcy has interpreted the prelude as a "musical metaphor for the creation of the world."[15]

But David Levin offers a more satisfying reading when he relates the *Rheingold* prelude to Wagner's *Tonsprache* concept, with its suggestion of an original musicalized language before words. What follows in the opening scene, Levin argues, is the extension of this linguistic evolution into verbal form (44–51). The curtain opens to reveal the coquettish Rhine daughters frolicking in the depths of *Vater Rhein.* Their opening "words" combine paeans to the waves with alliterative pre-semantic babble: "Weia! Waga! Woge, du Welle, walla zur Wiege! Wagala weia! Wallala weiala weia!" Even when the blissful innocence of their utterances suddenly transforms into conversation, their words retain what Levin calls the "wilfully archaic" character of *Stabreim* (alliteration, 44). And "wilful" is the operative word here, for Wagner's archaism is inextricably linked to an unprecedented investment in and development of the apparatus of the nineteenth-century orchestra and the techniques of scoring. The prehistory represented in the prelude and opening scene depends on a body of technically refined instruments deployed by a composer whose considerable experience as an opera and concert conductor had provided him with a sure touch and whose penchant for experimentation was evident long before he embarked on his post-revolutionary work. *Der Ring des Nibelungen,* as the tetralogy was ultimately titled, was to be a potent combination of the archaic and the modern, of atavism and technology.

It also arguably realized some of Wagner's other ideological fantasies. The opening scenes of *Das Rheingold* introduce us to two characters who seem to embody all the weaknesses against which Wagner's revolutionary zeal had been directed. Alberich and Mime, Nibelung brothers, are greedy, exploitive, and treacherous. They are the "egoistic" capitalists of the Ring, enslaving Nibelung workers to dig gold and silver in the depths of the earth. What is immediately striking, though, is how they look and sound. Following Adorno, Weiner draws attention to the (later suppressed) physical description of Mime in the verse draft of *Der junge Siegfried,* showing how Mime's dwarfish, deformed features play on contemporary Jewish stereotypes.[16] The Nibelungs are set apart, too, by their language and self-expression, their excited, rapid-fire exchanges delivered in stuttering, angular vocal lines with hurried, spurting rhythms. We can compare this, as Weiner does, with "das Judentum in der Musik" and its description of the supposedly agitated, restless quality of Jewish vocal music, a characteristic, Wagner informs us, derived from Jewish speech, with its "zischender, schrillender, summsender und murksender Lautausdruck" (hissing, shrill, buzzing, and gurgling sound).[17]

Are Mime and Alberich Jewish caricatures? And how should we interpret the figure of Beckmesser, the town notary in the "comic" *Die Meistersinger von Nürnberg*? Wagner's reflexive, and deeply nationalist, interpretation of the song contests of the sixteenth-century German singing guilds was first performed in June 1868, only months before Wagner ignored the advice of some of his closest supporters and republished "Das Judentum in der Musik." Is Beckmesser, whose distortions of true German song mark him as a parasitic outsider, a Jewish outsider?[18] These are without doubt among the most controversial questions in Wagner research. That Wagner was a zealous, even venomous, anti-Semite is not disputed. Where disagreement arises, however, is over the question of whether this anti-Semitism manifests itself in Wagner's operas and music dramas. On one side are scholars like Carl Dahlhaus, Martin Gregor-Dellin, Dieter Borchmeyer and Peter Wapnewski, each of whom refutes or downplays this possibility. Borchmeyer, for example, regards the interpretation above as an "unverifiable hypothesis" and finds "not a single trace in Wagner's music dramas" of his anti-Semitism.[19] Hans Rudolf Vaget, meanwhile, cites the "semantic indeterminacy" of music as "preclud[ing]" the representation of anti-Semitic characteristics in music.[20] On the other side are Paul Lawrence Rose, Marc Weiner, Barry Millington, Stewart Spencer and David Levin (among others), each of whom approaches the issue in quite different ways, but who nevertheless agree that the music dramas are not miraculously cordoned off, protected, like artistic national parks, from a deeply anti-Semitic cultural climate and from the intensity of what Borchmeyer acknowledges as Wagner's "violently anti-Semitic polemical writings" (184).

Certainly, Vaget's argument would be vigorously challenged by contemporary musicology, which has disputed the privileged autonomy accorded to music and has asserted its capacity to participate powerfully in ideological discourse. But the real problem here, as Lawrence Kramer observes, is the suggestion that anti-Semitism needs to be proven, as though it would somehow reside in the work like a specimen. What matters, Kramer counters, is the discursive framework of anti-Semitic ideology in which and against which Wagner's work has been performed, critiqued and disputed from the outset. What has emerged from this interpretative history is a powerful network of associations — and resistance to these associations — that will not be confirmed or denied merely through the positivistic scrutiny of texts. There is, in other words, a performative dimension to this history, a sense in which the supposed truth of any interpretation has hinged not on spurious notions of verifiable accuracy, but on its capacity to resonate with our experience of Wagner's work. Suggesting that the *Musikdramen* have been unjustly associated with the discourse of anti-Semitism misses the point because it is only within this contested discursive framework that the meaning of Wagner's work has been formed.[21]

Love-Death

The technology and scale of the *Ring* presented Wagner with a serious problem: where would it be performed? Confronting his mounting debts, Wagner concluded that he should postpone completion of the project and turn to something more readily performable. The result was that in 1857 Wagner broke off work on the score of *Siegfried*, as *Der junge Siegfried* was now called, and turned his attention to *Tristan und Isolde*, drawing on Gottfried von Strassburg's Middle High German epic version of the (probably) Celtic tale of adulterous love. If the primary impetus for writing *Tristan* was financial — Wagner's publisher even agreed to pay for and engrave each act before the next was begun — other, less mundane, motivations have tended to feature in the Wagner literature. One concerns Wagner's alleged tendency toward sudden and total enthusiasms. In 1854 fellow exile Georg Herwegh presented Wagner with a copy of *Die Welt als Wille und Vorstellung* (The World as Will and Idea, 1818) by the still relatively obscure German philosopher Arthur Schopenhauer (1788–1860). The metaphysical worldview of this quintessential pessimist seems to have immediately struck a chord with Wagner — later that year he described it to Franz Liszt as a "Himmelsgeschenk" (gift from heaven) — and it was ultimately to have a decisive bearing on Wagner's aesthetics and creative output.[22] Wagner's declaration to a patron in December 1856 that he had become alienated from the mood of *Siegfried* and that he now felt more at home in the "Reich der Schwermut" (realm of melancholy) was made shortly after he had penned sketches that would ultimately form part of *Tristan*, suggesting a link between *Tristan*, Schopenhauer, and the break from the *Ring*.[23]

Yet the linkage needs to be carefully placed in its context.[24] It would be misleading to represent *Tristan* as a pessimistic about-face to the *Ring*'s affirmative revolutionary politics. On the one hand the already completed portions of the *Ring*, especially *Die Walküre*, are dramatically and musically steeped in *Schwermut*, and on the other, *Tristan* is actually a defiant inversion of Schopenhauer's ascetic world-withdrawal. Wagner developed the *Tristan* legend into a celebration of metaphysical ecstasy incompatible with ordinary existence or with life itself — a sort of erotic Nirvana. Schopenhauer, by contrast, had advocated the renunciation of sexual love as a means of negating the effects of what he calls the "will," the noumenal reality that lies behind the phenomenal world and propels suffering through gratification. But Wagner seems to refuse to devalue the sensuality that formed an important part of his own experience — his personal extravagances are legendary — and that had been pivotal to his Feuerbachian sympathies. What he proposed, in short, was a misreading of Schopenhauer in which redemption from the will would come not by renouncing sexual love, but by taking it to its limit.

Nowhere is this excess more apparent than in the so-called *Liebestod* (love-death) — Wagner called it a *Verklärung* (transfiguration) — Isolde's final ecstatic release into the longed-for realm to which Tristan has already passed. As she stands over Tristan's lifeless body, Isolde asks if she alone can hear the music rising from his body, music that "envelopes" and "pierces" her, rising to an ecstatic climax. Tristan, in a sense, becomes Music, and thanks to what Friedrich Kittler aptly calls the "amplifier function" of Wagner's orchestra, we, the audience, share in the transfiguring sound.[25]

Partly as a result of its reduction to a concert item, the *Liebestod*'s reception history has often featured overwhelmed listeners unaware of its text or dramatic context, and this has tended to characterize the scene above all as a *musical* climax. The impression that *Tristan* assigns music a role more prominent — more "symphonic" even — than the Zurich essays allow is usually ascribed to the impact of Schopenhauer's aesthetics, which privileged music as the direct reflection of the Will. It is true that Wagner's compositional practices in *Tristan* seem to stray from the subservient, poetically motivated music advocated in the Zurich essays, but Wagner's ability, or willingness, to adhere strictly to the principles outlined there should not be taken for granted. The early parts of the *Ring* unleash a torrent of vocal and orchestral sound in a way that suggests a Wagner who can barely keep a check on the *Musik* in *Musikdrama*. So when *Tristan*, the supposedly straightforward commercial piece, turned out to be an almost five-hour drama with technical demands and an intensity considered unperformable by the musical standards of the day, it was as much an extension of Wagner's earlier practices as an embodiment of a new Schopenhauerian metaphysics of music.

Yet this flood of music should not blind us to the centrality of the *Liebestod*'s poetic text. Isolde's words bring the drama's metaphysical erotics to its conclusion; she sums up, in her poetry, the meaning of everything toward which the lovers have been striving. Might this alignment of Tristan with music and Isolde with poetry open up a subversive reading of Wagner's sexual metaphor, destabilizing the gender associations of music and poetry, or perhaps even question the gender polarities that had underpinned the metaphor. Certainly, there is a sense in which the work renders Tristan and Isolde, and their gender, interchangeable:[26]

Tristan

Tristan du,	Tristan thou,
ich Isolde,	I Isolde,
nicht mehr Tristan!	no more Tristan!

Isolde

Du Isolde,	Thou Isolde,
Tristan ich,	Tristan, I,
nicht mehr Isolde!	no more Isolde!

But there is another element here, one in which Wagner put a great deal of stock: *mise-en-scène*. As Slavoj Žižek points out, Isolde completes and makes meaningful the process of Tristan's own death, rising to a sustained erotic ecstasy that he was denied. Staring in wonder at Tristan's now radiant body, she asks if she is alone in seeing his transformation, and it is this summoning of the gaze, Žižek suggests, that situates the *Liebestod* as a proto-psychoanalytic fantasy scene.[27] It is as if Isolde embodies Tristan's fantasy vision of his own death, as if she is the gaze imagined to register his "self-obliteration," allowing him the impossible conflation of passing out of ordinary existence while simultaneously witnessing his own passing. Isolde, in other words, exists in this scene only as part of Tristan's dream, an interpretation memorably staged by director Jean-Pierre Ponnelle. In his staging the whole creative process is embodied in Tristan: his fantasy of total satisfaction is also a fantasy of total creation. This Tristan might be the embodiment of the androgynous figure Wagner associated with Beethoven, but it also suggests that the trope of the aimless woman who finds her identity only when she sacrifices herself to man has been totalized to the point at which she becomes a mere prop in his fantasy.

The Shrine at Bayreuth

Schopenhauer's name tends to be associated, as well, with the image of an increasingly resigned, post-revolutionary Wagner. But there are two sides to this Wagnerian withdrawal from the world. On the one hand, Wagner was forced to accept that no political revolution, least of all one carried out in the name of theatrical art, was going to clear the way for his utopian visions. Wagner's idealism, as strong as ever, divorced itself from the overt political sphere in which it had once been embedded and took on the character of a retreat from a modernity defined as commercialized, degenerate, and hostile to the German spirit. In "Deutsche Kunst und deutsche Politik" Wagner distinguishes between the un-German character of "Nützlichkeitswesen" (utilitarianism) and the essentially German desire to act for the sheer pleasure of the deed itself. In this way, he argues, the "Tugend der Deutschen" (virtue of the Germans) aligns with the "höchsten Prinzipe der Ästhetik" (highest principles of aesthetics, *DS* 8: 320).

This is the kind of aesthetic idealism that continued to guide Wagner's search for a venue to stage the *Ring*. No ordinary opera house would do, he insisted, not merely because existing technical facilities were inadequate to the task, but because the debased, purely commercial character of the theaters and their distracted, ill-informed audiences were precisely the features of operatic culture against which the *Ring* was directed. His vision, he wrote, was of an unadorned, perhaps temporary theater far from the big city (another un-German phenomenon), its audience of art lovers educated and well prepared for the performance. The auditorium would be steeply raked to remove visual obstructions, there would be no boxes, and the orchestra would be hidden in a deeply sunk pit so as to remove the distracting sight of the musicians. This invisible orchestra would transport the spectator to the "Unnahbarkeit einer Traumerscheinung" (remote world of dreams), inspiring a state of "Hellsehen" (clairvoyance) in which the events on stage would seem all the more real (*DS* 10: 38). And here we see the impact of Schopenhauerian aesthetics, which had marveled at music's capacity to penetrate to our "innersten Wesen" (innermost essence) while bypassing its realities, and which likened the composer to a "magnetische Somnambule" (magnetic somnambulist).[28]

On the other hand, "Deutsche Kunst und deutsche Politik" allowed that the theater might have its feet in two camps: it is the gateway to an aestheticized utopia, but it also offers to mediate between that realm and unavoidably utilitarian, worldly realities. Instead of revolution, then, we have a polarized combination of aestheticized nation and pragmatic pact with modernity, and in a sense this principle is mirrored in the new *Realpolitik* of Wagner's own strategy. A new theater required money, and Wagner was not above appealing to the wealthy bourgeoisie and to royalty (once the target of his wrath) to come to his aid. Middle-class support materialized in the form of patronage certificates bought by the public and by members of the first so-called Wagner Societies, one manifestation of the emergent Wagner cult. Modest royal support came in 1864 in the person of the eighteen-year-old Ludwig II, the newly crowned king of Bavaria whose fondness for Gothic Germanic fantasies (fairy-tale castles, forest legends) had already secured his devotion to Wagner's work. Rejecting offers from Berlin, Darmstadt, London and Chicago, Wagner settled on the provincial town of Bayreuth. It was a canny choice: located in northern Bavaria, it ensured that the enterprise would remain within Ludwig's jurisdiction but far from Munich, where Wagner's privileged relationship with Ludwig had generated considerable resentment.[29] Bayreuth also had longstanding cultural ties with Prussia, where Bismarck was being eyed (futilely, as it turned out) as a potential supporter. The fact that Wagner offered to stage the *Ring* as a quinquennial celebration of the Prussian victory over France in 1870 is a measure of the lengths to which he was prepared to go to secure funding for the cash-strapped project, and a reminder of its nationalist underpinnings. The offer was rejected, but sufficient funds were ultimately secured to begin construction in 1873, and the theater was completed just in time for the first staging of the now completed *Ring* in August 1876.

First-hand accounts and press reviews of the *Festspiele* reveal a spectrum of attitudes ranging from cultic enthusiasm suggestive of religious experience to profound disappointment and disgust with what was perceived to be a puffed up tourist trap. The features Wagner had envisaged were all incorporated, including a double proscenium with an inner frame designed to create a narrowing visual effect around the stage, so that characters and scenery would seem larger than life (*DS* 10: 37). Many critics drew particular attention to the extent of the darkness in the auditorium, a novelty at a time when partial light was still the norm. Eduard Hanslick, music critic for the *Neue Freie Presse* in Vienna, compared the effect of listening to the orchestral introductions in the dark to narcotics, and other critics described similar sensations of dreaming, floating and a loss of bodily awareness. The idealistic, Schopenhauerian Wagner should have reveled in the reaction, yet the reality of the performances had fallen far short of his vision, while Wagner the pragmatist was left confronting a crippling debt and a sense that his financial support had vanished now that the sensational promise of the Festival was a thing of the past. He was, in short, deeply disillusioned.

The Nietzsche Case

A similar sense of disillusionment caused Nietzsche (1844–1900) to flee Bayreuth during rehearsals. Or, at least, this is the popular interpretation of his hasty departure — in fact Nietzsche's ill health was probably the principal cause. This is not to say, though, that Nietzsche did not harbor profound reservations about the Bayreuth phenomenon and his own relationship to Wagner. Once a veritable disciple and an intimate in the Wagner household, Nietzsche had become increasingly alienated from Wagner's vision and ideology. For a brief period their relationship had been mutually beneficial: Nietzsche's academic credentials — he was appointed Professor of Classical Philology at Basel University in 1869 — clearly lent scholarly legitimacy to Wagner's cause, and with the publication of Nietzsche's *Die Geburt der Tragödie aus dem Geiste der Musik* (The Birth of Tragedy out of the Spirit of Music, 1872) Wagner found himself presented as nothing less than the inheritor and renewer of the promise of Hellenic culture. But Nietzsche's notebooks suggest that by 1874 he was having serious doubts, not least about the very question of Wagner's cultural legitimacy. Was it possible, he asked, that Wagner's desperate need to "adopt" potential successors (like Nietzsche) sprang from a fear that his project was merely a personal ambition and therefore destined to die with him? And did this insecurity not go hand in hand with his tyrannical attitude, his need to dominate friends and dismiss any form of criticism? (*NSW* 7: 764–65). Wagner, he concluded, was not merely contradictory, but thrived on extreme states, a sort of "Schauspieler" (actor) prone to histrionic affect (760). Nietzsche's growing, though still private, alienation was not lost on Wagner, and by 1876 their relationship had cooled substantially.

Strange, then, that Nietzsche should publish a tribute to Wagner to coincide with the festival. "Richard Wagner in Bayreuth" is filled with effusive praise for the Master, a tone that leads Nietzsche scholar R. J. Hollingdale to describe the essay as a "final effort to heal the split" between Wagner and Nietzsche. "Wagner," he adds, "has never been more sympathetically described."[30] But the very effusiveness of the language — Nietzsche describes the *Ring* as a "Himmelsgewölbe von Schönheit und Güte" (heavenly vault of beauty and goodness, *NSW* 1: 509) — should alert us to look beneath the façade of this ostensible tribute. The themes of the notebooks reappear too, but now carefully disguised as homage. Nietzsche imagines Wagner recognizing his *Volk* as those who share his own joys and sufferings, and he presents him as an artist who always tried to see and master the inner core of his audience, even if he was repulsed by what he found there. This, he suggests, is a sign of Wagner's "tyrannisches Übergewicht" (tyrannical superior force, 455). And turning then to the image of the actor, he describes the *Gesamtkunstwerk* as the product of "eine schauspielerische Urbegabung" (the primal talent of an actor, *NSW* 7: 467). Yet all of this is carefully couched in affirmative terms, implying, with subtle irony, that the German people would one day welcome a figure of such strength and purpose, even if they were as yet unprepared for him.

With *Menschliches, Allzumenschliches* (1878), however, the gloves were off, even if Wagner was not named. The identity of "the master" was clear, and the criticism of Schopenhauer left Wagner in no doubt as to the intent. Nietzsche was later to trace the open split to the publication of the libretto of *Parsifal*, Wagner's mystical *Weltabschiedswerk* (farewell work to the world). Its Christian morality, he claimed, disgusted him and left no room for turning back. In truth, Nietzsche was already quite familiar with *Parsifal* by the time it was published; there was no decisive moment or event, merely a gradual withdrawal and reassessment, and it was not until after Wagner's death in 1883 that Nietzsche fully vented his criticism. He now saw Wagner as an instructive symptom of modernity, his Schopenhauerian pessimism an embodiment of a spirit of sickness and decadence, his metaphysical pretensions a sign of an empty idealism, of the "bad conscience" of religious belief. But he also continued to develop the themes introduced in "Richard Wagner in Bayreuth": Wagner as tyrant, as seducer, as dilettante, and above all, as actor, "ein unvergleichlicher Histrio" (an incomparable histrion) as he described him in "Der Fall Wagner" (The Wagner Case, *NSW* 6: 630). Wagner, he argues, has taken the actor's desire for a mask to new heights of falsehood and deceptive appearance. Yet there is a telling ambiguity here, for what really seems to trouble Nietzsche is not so much the idea of masks as the use to which they are put. The problem with Wagner, it seems, is not his "Vielheit" (multiplicity, *NSW* 6: 37) but his determination to disavow it, the wilful ignorance of his own plurality, the hypocrisy of his blind "Widerspruch der Werthe" (contradiction of values, *NSW* 6: 52).

In fact, the mask can be seen as central in Nietzsche's work to a re-evaluation of identity in which the very superficiality of the mask becomes a release from notions of depth and authenticity.[31] In Pierre Klossowski's reading, for example, Nietzsche's pseudo-autobiography *Ecce Homo* becomes an account of a disengagement from the illusion of ego and its false sense of completeness and self-determination.[32] What *Ecce Homo* proposes instead, Klossowski argues, is affirmation of the dispersal of identity, an acknowledgement of the "arbitrary manner by which one feels existence" (12). "The phenomenon of the *actor*," Klossowski continues, "became, in Nietzsche, an analogue for the simulation of being itself" (223). Wagner's role in this is central in that he represents a model actor, but Nietzsche would attempt to make "authentic" what he had seen as "tainted and corrupt" in Wagner. That affirmative appropriation is clear when Nietzsche writes: "und so wie ich bin, stark genug, um mir auch das Fragwürdigste und Gefährlichste noch zum Vortheil zu wenden und damit stärker zu werden, nenne ich Wagner den grossen Wohlthäter meines Lebens" (and given the way I am, strong enough to turn even what is most questionable and dangerous to my advantage and thus to become stronger, I call Wagner the great benefactor of my life).[33] Wagner, then, stands as both a corrupt danger and a liberating stroke. More vividly than any other model, Nietzsche suggests, he gestures toward the figure of the actor whose shallow histrionics see through to the depth of things.

Guardian of Purity

Nietzsche's attacks on the contradictions and hypocrisy embodied in Bayreuth go beyond the works or their performance to confront what had by then become an institution. That process of institutionalization, a process both administrative and ideological, began in the period of relative solvency after the first festival when Wagner was working on *Parsifal*, the work that he hoped would benefit from the mistakes of the first festival. *Parsifal* was termed a "Bühnenweihfestspiel" (literally a Stage Dedication Festival Play), implying, with deliberate religious overtones, that the stage of the Festspielhaus would be dedicated to it, that *Parsifal* would be performed nowhere but in Wagner's temple to art. This fusion of the sacred and the aesthetic was fleshed out in theoretical terms in Wagner's late writings, above all in "Religion und Kunst" (1880), which opened with the view that "da, wo die Religion künstlich wird, es der Kunst vorbehalten sei, den Kern der Religion zu retten" (where religion becomes artificial, it is reserved for art to salvage the essence of religion, *SD* 10: 117). The article first appeared in the *Bayreuther Blätter*, a house journal set up in 1878 under the editorship of Hans von Wolzogen, one of the many sycophantic disciples who were gradually forming an inner circle at Bayreuth. Although it included Wagner Society reports and news from the festival, the *Blätter* was dominated by lengthy articles, like "Religion und Kunst," treating political and aesthetic themes. It was envisaged as a means of propagating Wagnerian ideology, and if Wagner seems occasionally to have been dismissive of its value, it nevertheless became the main outlet for his late ideas and a manifesto of a Bayreuth orthodoxy centered on a largely incoherent cocktail of *völkisch* nationalism, conservative social critique, vegetarianism, and anti-vivisectionism.

What really sets Wagner's late writings apart, though, is their commitment to biologically-rooted racial ideology, a commitment reinforced by Wagner's encounter with the theories of miscegenation and racial hierarchy put forward in Count Joseph-Arthur de Gobineau's *Essai sur l'inégalité des races humaines* (1853–55). It could be argued, in fact, that Wagner's endorsement of aspects of Gobineau's thought — the two corresponded and met personally several times between 1876 and 1882 — contributed significantly to its dissemination in the 1880s. Yet Wagner was sharply critical of Gobineau's failure to account for the unifying effect of Christianity. Racial inequality is a reality, Wagner conceded, but not irredeemable. The pure Aryan blood of Christ, he argues, offers to reverse racial degeneration and reunite humanity. Its absolute Other, of course, is Judaism, which opposes Christ's appeal to the poor with the glorification of exchange and ownership, perverting Christ's message of compassion to celebrate aggression and violence (*SD* 10: 139–41). This is no longer the anti-Jewish residue of his revolutionary years, but a recognizably modern, biologically-rooted anti-Semitism, Wagner's claims to the contrary notwithstanding. "Über das Weibliche im Menschlichen" (On the Feminine in Human Affairs, 1883), Wagner's final, unfinished, essay, maps this racial ideology onto the question of gender inequality. The regeneration of humanity will not be possible, Wagner claims, until the "Emanzipation" of woman is taken seriously, for women remain pawns in masculine, bourgeois traditions of marriage based on property rights. At its most noble, though, monogamous marriage based on love embodies racial purity and strength:

> Gewiß ist, daß die edelste weiße Rasse in Sage und Geschichte bei ihrem ersten Erscheinen monogamisch auftritt, als Eroberer durch polygamische Vermischung mit den Unterworfenen sofort aber ihrem Verderben entgegengeht.

> [It is certain that the noblest white race is monogamous at its first appearance in saga and history, but soon moves toward its own demise when it mixes polygamously with the races that it conquers.] (*DS* 10: 174)

Is this the key to the eponymous hero of *Parsifal*, a Christ-like figure whose compassion redeems and purifies the degenerate and corrupted community of knights at the temple of the Holy Grail? What are we to make of his ambiguous gender characteristics? Is the final resolution of sexual and racial difference to be found in this Aryan, androgynous redeemer?

Purity Defiled

From its earliest reception, the range and diversity of reactions to *Parsifal* suggests that such questions could only lead to more questions. The redemptive aspects of *Parsifal* seemed to many to mask what was in fact a hymn to an eroticized combination of sensual indulgence, affliction, and death. Far from turning its back on the ecstatic suffering and release central to *Tristan*, it had merely celebrated it by inversion, leaving its Pandora's box open too long to recover. Had Wagner's work not in fact always emphasized this decadent fusion of pleasure and pain, and did his music not draw the empathetic listener into this sensual realm? The idea that Wagner's work might celebrate decadence was no arbitrary association, for the very formation of an affirmative view of decadence had owed much to the reception of Wagner, particularly in France. Baudelaire's overwhelmed, *jouissant* reaction to *Tannhaüser* in 1860 can be seen to have initiated a strongly aestheticist Wagnerism that culminated in the *symboliste* and *décadent* contributions to the *Revue wagnérienne* (1885–87). Though short-lived, the *Révue* included contributions by notable literary figures including Stéphane Mallarmé, Paul Verlaine, and Joris-Karl Huysmans, whose celebrated novel *À Rebours* (1884) had done much to define *decadent* subjectivity. Ostensibly an explanatory account of the overture to *Tannhäuser*, Huysmans's contribution to the *Révue* interprets the music as a fantastic narrative of opium-induced visions and ecstatic sensual experience.

And how does this Wagnerian decadence intersect with questions of sexual orientation? Is there something queer about Parsifal's androgynous characteristics or the apparently homosocial bonds of the Grail brotherhood over which he assumes control? In what Mitchell Morris has called a subculture within the subculture, Wagnerism became associated with the issue of transgressive sexual desire and a focal point, both critical and affirmative, for discourse on homosexuality.[34] This hinged in part on a cult of personality in which Wagner himself came to be defined in terms redolent of contemporary, and stereotypical, constructions of homosexual behavior. Not that Wagner was being blatantly outed; rather, he was seen as a figure spiritually and intellectually sympathetic to homosexuality. Wagner's infamously extravagant sensuality and the "histrionic" tendency so emphasized by Nietzsche (not to mention his intimate relationships with Ludwig and Nietzsche) resonated with the image of the hyper-sensitive, nervous, flamboyant decadent, a figure whose defiance of normative morality and propriety went hand in hand with dissident sexuality.

But Wagner's work and audiences were critical here too. The physician and playwright Oskar Panizza went public with an open secret when he claimed in 1895 that the Bayreuth festival, now established as an annual event, was well known as a homosexual rendezvous. Four years later, Magnus Hirschfeld, a leading campaigner for the decriminalization of homosexuality in Germany, published a questionnaire intended to allow readers to evaluate their own homosexual inclinations. Included was the question "are you particularly fond of Wagner?"[35] And in *Richard Wagner und die Homosexualität* (1903) Hanns Fuchs, a novelist and homosexual rights activist, discussed at length the "geistige Homosexualität" (spiritual homosexuality) of Wagner's life and music dramas.[36]

It was in the wake of Oscar Wilde's sensational 1895 trials on charges of homosexual offenses (an event followed closely in Germany) that many of these associations were cemented. Although no uncritical devotee of the Master, Wilde nevertheless moved in literary and social circles saturated by Wagnerism, and the title figure of *The Picture of Dorian Gray* (1891) is the very embodiment of decadent — and discreetly homosexual — Wagnerism, a figure who, like Baudelaire, recognized in the Prelude to *Tannhäuser* "a presentation of the tragedy of his own soul."[37] This identification with tragedy raises the question of how the experience of Wagner's work might have drawn from and contributed to the discursive formation of homosexual subjectivity. For Morris the key lies in the representation of suffering, embodied above all in the wounded, seemingly emasculated, Tristan. Citing Nietzsche's characterization of Wagner as the "Orpheus alles heimlichen Elends" (Orpheus of all secret misery, *NSW* 6: 417–18), he wonders if Wagnerian suffering represented a means of "finding words for what hurts," of empowering the mute sufferer by offering a means of articulating pain — in short, a discourse for coming out (Morris, 283).

If the Bayreuth circle tended to respond to this Wagnerism by heroically ignoring it, other counter-arguments were not in short supply. In an intellectual climate increasingly focused on the pathologization of sexuality, characteristics associated with Wagnerism became a sign of deviancy: In *Entartung* (Degeneration, 1893) physician Max Nordau (1849–1923) drew on Wagner's libretti to diagnose their ten-year-dead author as suffering from hysteria, deranged erotic obsessions, and sadistic tendencies, and although he makes only passing reference to homosexuality, he refers the reader to sexologist Richard von Kraft-Ebbing's characterization of Wagnerians as sufferers of "konträre Sexualempfindungen" (contrary sexual instincts).[38] Here Wagner's personal pathology is mirrored by the perceived tendencies of his audience, and Wagnerism becomes symptomatic of a broader moral and spiritual decay that is intertwined with homosexuality. Not that Nordau was any friend of orthodox Bayreuth Wagnerism.

Mocking the preoccupations of Wagner's late writings and the Bayreuth circle, he dismissed what he saw as a cultish and bizarre combination of mysticism, anti-Semitism, and obsessions with bodily health and purity (Nordau, 210).

The ironies and contradictions of Wagner reception are nowhere better illustrated than in the complex relationships between these various Wagnerisms and anti-Wagnerisms. For example, Fuchs's discussion of the relationship between homosexuality and Wagnerism actually draws on and perpetuates the ideas found in both the Bayreuth orthodoxy and the denunciation of Wagnerian pathological decadence by the likes of Nordau and Kraft-Ebbing. His definition of a homosexual "type" relies on the sorts of stereotypical characteristics stressed by the critics of decadence. As Morris shows, Fuchs's work needs to be read in relation to the ideology of the *Gemeinschaft des Eigenen* (Fellowship of Individuals), a homophile reform movement that opposed the liberal, trans-gender focus of Hirschfeld's *Wissenschaftlich-humanitäres Komitee* (Scientific-Humanitarian Committee) with a separatist view of virile, masculine virtue (Morris, 272–77). In the pages of its journal *Der Eigene* (literally, The Individual) the virtues of homosocial fellowship, moral and physical health, and ancient Greek ideals were presented as the models for a renewed German masculinity. The echoes of Wagnerian nationalist ideology are all too clear, as are the traces of the *völkisch* cult of manhood and vitality that would gain increasing prominence with the rise of National Socialism. But, Morris adds, this pseudo-absorption would depend on a careful idealization that cleansed the ideology of overt homoeroticism, let alone any suggestion of actual sexual activity. If Fuchs's homosexual Wagnerism already depended on a deeply sublimated eroticism, it nevertheless presented a deeply ambiguous and troubling Wagner; with the help of a compliant and enthusiastic Bayreuth, National Socialism would suppress this Wagnerism and substitute an upright, heroic, and steadfastly moral cult of the German *Volk* (289).

Such contradictions and reversals show no sign of dissipating in our own time. Critical scholarship on Wagner has penetrated the popular press to the extent that the public is more aware than ever of the deeply reactionary, problematic, and occasionally hateful legacy of Wagner's work and followers. This, combined with postmodern skepticism toward the supposedly ennobling spirit of art and a broad liberal consensus against the politics of exclusion and discrimination ought to have spelled disaster for the dissemination of Wagner's work. But the seven-year waiting list for Bayreuth tickets shows no sign of shrinking, and even in an age of diminishing arts subsidies and spiraling production costs for these most demanding of works, the quantity, if not always the quality, of Wagner stagings grows from year to year. Audiences continue to subject themselves to marathon sessions in the theater, and the flood of literature on Wagner flows as it has done for almost a century and a half. The Wagner case, it seems, remains firmly open.

Notes

[1] George Bernard Shaw, *The Perfect Wagnerite: A Commentary on 'The Ring of the Niblungs'* (London: Grant Richards, 1898). Theodor W. Adorno, *Versuch über Wagner,* in *Gesammelte Schriften,* vol. 13, ed. Rolf Tiedemann (Frankfurt am Main: Suhrkamp, 1971). English translation: *In Search of Wagner,* trans. Rodney Livingstone (London: Verso, 1981).

[2] Thomas Mann, "Leiden und Größe Richard Wagners," in *Essays,* ed. Hermann Kurzke and Stephan Stachorski (Frankfurt: Fischer, 1995), vol. 4: 11–72. English translation: "The Sorrows and Grandeur of Richard Wagner," in Thomas Mann, *Pro and Contra Wagner,* trans. Allan Blunden (Chicago: Chicago UP, 1985), 91–148. Friedrich Nietzsche, *Sämtliche Werke: Kritischen Studienausgabe,* 15 vols., ed. Giorgi Colli and Mazzino Montinari (Berlin, New York: Deutscher Taschenbuch Verlag, 1980), vol. 1: 9–156. Subsequent references to this edition are cited in the text using the abbreviation *NSW* and volume and page number. English trans.: *The Birth of Tragedy,* in *Basic Writings of Nietzsche,* ed. and trans. Walter Kaufmann (New York: Random House, 1966), 29–144.

[3] Adorno, *In Search of Wagner,* 35.

[4] David J. Levin, *Richard Wagner, Fritz Lang, and the Nibelungen: The Dramaturgy of Disavowal* (Princeton, NJ: Princeton UP, 1998), 39.

[5] "Keine Religion! — ist meine Religion; keine Philosophie! — meine Philosophie." *Fragmente zur Charakteristik meines philosophischen Curriculum vitae* (1846), in Ludwig Feuerbach: *Werke in Sechs Bänden,* vol. 4, ed. Erich Thies (Frankfurt: Suhrkamp, 1975), 227.

[6] Feuerbach, "Über das *Wesen des Christentums* in Beziehung auf den *Einzigen und sein Eigentum*" (1845), in *Werke* 4: 80. Stirner had written: "Es ist schon gut, daß Feuerbach die Sinnlichkeit zu Ehren bringt, aber er weiß dabei nur den Materialismus seiner 'neuen Philosophie' mit dem bisherigen Eigentum des Idealismus, der 'absoluten Philosophie,' zubekleiden" (it is to his credit that Feuerbach honors sensuality, but he is only able to do this in a way that invests the materialism of his "new philosophy" with the established properties of idealism, of "absolute philosophy" *Der Einzige und sein Eigentum* [Leipzig, 1845; repr. Stuttgart: Reclam, 1972], 383 [translations are mine unless otherwise specified]). Feuerbach's response originally appeared in *Wigands Vierteljahrsschrift.* The Leipzig firm Otto Wigand published Wagner's Zurich essays and much of the work of Feuerbach and Stirner in the 1840s.

[7] Richard Wagner, "Das Kunstwerk der Zukunft," in *Dichtungen und Schriften,* 10 vols., ed. Dieter Borchmeyer (Frankfurt: Insel, 1983), vol. 6: 109. Subsequent references to this edition are cited in the text using the abbreviation *DS* and volume and page number. Wagner's use of the term "communist" is more in keeping with Feuerbach's idealistic sense of "community" and intersubjectivity than Marx's

radical social reform. Still, its revolutionary implications are plain, and in a footnote Wagner reminds his readers that use of the term constitutes a political crime.

[8] See Levin, 85–95 and Marc A. Weiner, *Richard Wagner and the Anti-Semitic Imagination* (Lincoln, NE and London: U of Nebraska P, 1995), 44–46.

[9] "Das Judentum in der Musik," in *Sämtliche Schriften und Dichtungen*, 12 vols., ed. Richard Sternfeld and Hans von Wolzogen (Leipzig: Breitkopf und Härtel, 1916), vol. 5: 67. Subsequent references to this edition will be given in the text with the abbreviation *SSD* and volume and page number.

[10] Thomas S. Grey, *Wagner's Musical Prose* (Cambridge: Cambridge UP, 1995), 257–69.

[11] *Oper und Drama, DS* VII, 110. The translation is Gray's (143–44).

[12] Jean-Jacques Nattiez, *Wagner Androgyne: A Study in Interpretation*, trans. Stewart Spencer (Princeton: Princeton UP, 1993).

[13] *Oper und Drama, DS* VII: 107. Gray's translation (150).

[14] Wagner, *Mein Leben*, ed. Martin Gregor-Dellin (Munich: List Verlag, 1963), 580.

[15] Mann, "Leiden und Größe Richard Wagners," 22. Warren Darcy, "Creatio ex nihilo: The Genesis, Structure, and Meaning of the *Rheingold* Prelude," *19th-Century Music* 13/2 (1989): 98.

[16] Adorno and Weiner also speculate on the implications of this description for Wagner's anxieties about his own appearance and paternity. See Weiner, 3–5 and Adorno, 24–25.

[17] "Das Judentum in der Musik," *SSD* 5: 71. The translation is Weiner's (116, 138).

[18] For more on Beckmesser and anti-Semitism see Levin, "Reading Beckmesser Reading: Antisemitism and Aesthetic Practice in *Die Meistersinger von Nürnberg*," *New German Critique* 69 (Fall 1996): 127–46. See also Weiner, especially pp. 66–72, 118–35, and 298–305, and Barry Millington, "Nuremberg Trial: Is There Anti-Semitism in *Die Meistersinger*?" *Cambridge Opera Journal* 3 (1991): 247–60.

[19] Dieter Borchmeyer, "The Question of Anti-Semitism," in *Wagner Handbook*, ed. Ulrich Müller and Peter Wapnewski, trans. and ed. John Deathridge (Cambridge, MA and London: Harvard UP, 1992), 183–4.

[20] Hans Rudolf Vaget, "Imaginings," *Wagner Notes* 18/6 (December 1995), n.p.

[21] Lawrence Kramer, "Contesting Wagner: The *Lohengrin* Prelude and Anti-anti-Semitism," *19th-Century Music* 25/2–3 (2001): 210–11.

[22] Wagner, letter to Franz Liszt (16 December 1854), in *Briefwechsel zwischen Wagner und Liszt*, vol. 2 (Leipzig: Breitkopf und Härtel, 1887), 45.

[23] Wagner, letter to Otto Wesendonck (22 December 1856), in *Briefe Richard Wagners an Otto Wesendonck, 1852–1870*, ed. W. Golther (Berlin, Alexander Duncker, 1904), 44.

[24] Much has been made, as well, of Wagner's relationship with Mathilde von Wesendonck, the wife of one of his patrons. The idea that a supposedly passionate affair with Mathilde is intertwined with the creation of the fictional adulterous pair in *Tristan* has all the hallmarks of the romanticised biographical legends that surround Wagner.

[25] Friedrich Kittler, "World-Breath: On Wagner's Media Technology," in *Opera Through Other Eyes,* ed. David J. Levin (Stanford CA: Stanford UP, 1993), 222.

[26] Lawrence Kramer, *Music as Cultural Practice, 1800–1900* (Berkeley, CA: U of California P, 1990), 165–66.

[27] Mladen Dolar and Slavoj Žižek, *Opera's Second Death* (New York, London: Routledge, 2002), 129–31.

[28] Arthur Schopenhauer, *Die Welt als Wille und Vorstellung,* in *Sämtliche Werke,* 5 vols., ed. Wolfgang von Löhneysen (Frankfurt, Stuttgart: Cotta-Insel, 1960), vol. 1: 363, 368.

[29] Ludwig commissioned the completion of the *Ring* in return for the rights to the work, an exchange Wagner was to regret when, to his horror, the king arranged for the completed dramas, *Das Rheingold* and *Die Walküre,* to be performed at the Court Opera in Munich. It was only one of a number of setbacks in an often fraught relationship and it was a spur to settle on a location and build the theater as quickly as possible, fundraising difficulties notwithstanding.

[30] R. J. Hollingdale, *Nietzsche: The Man and his Philosophy* (Cambridge: Cambridge UP, 1965; rev. 1999), 97.

[31] In *Jenseits von Gut und Böse* (Beyond Good and Evil) Nietzsche writes: "Jeder tiefe Geist braucht eine Maske: mehr noch, um jeden tiefen Geist wächst fortwährend eine Maske, Dank der beständig falschen, nämlich *flachen* Auslegung jedes Wortes, jedes Schrittes, jedes Lebens-Zeichens, das er giebt." (Every profound spirit needs a mask: even more, around every profound spirit a mask is growing continually, owing to the constantly false, namely *shallow,* interpretation of every word, every step, every sign of life he gives.) *NSW* 5: 58 (original emphasis). English trans.: *Basic Writings of Nietzsche,* ed. and trans. Kaufmann, 241.

[32] Pierre Klossowski, *Nietzsche and the Vicious Circle,* trans. Daniel W. Smith (Chicago: U of Chicago P, 1997), 224.

[33] *NSW* 6: 290. English trans.: *Basic Writings of Nietzsche,* ed. and trans. Kaufmann, 706.

[34] Mitchell Morris, "Tristan's Wounds: On Homosexual Wagnerians at the Fin de Siècle," in *Queer Episodes in Music and Modern Identity,* ed. Sophie Fuller and Lloyd Whitesell (Urbana and Chicago: U of Illinois P, 2002), 272.

[35] *A Categoric Personal Analysis for the Reader* (Leipzig, 1899), trans. Xavier Mayne, cited in Neill Bartlett, *Who Was That Man? A Present for Mr. Oscar Wilde* (Harmondsworth: Penguin, 1993), 72.

[36] Oskar Panizza, "Bayreuth und die Homosexualität," *Die Gesellschaft: Monatsschrift für Literatur, Kunst und Socialpolitik* 11 (1895): 88–92. English translation: *Wagner* 9 (April 1988): 71–5. Hanns Fuchs, *Richard Wagner und die Homosexualität* (Berlin: H. Barsdorf, 1903), cited in Morris, 276–7.

[37] Oscar Wilde, *The Picture of Dorian Gray,* ed. Isobel Murray (Oxford: Oxford UP, 1994), 135.

[38] Max Nordau, *Degeneration,* trans. anon. (Lincoln, NE and London: Nebraska UP, 1993), 181–82.

Works Cited

Adorno, Theodor W. *Versuch über Wagner.* In *Gesammelte Schriften,* vol. 13, ed. Rolf Tiedemann. Frankfurt am Main: Suhrkamp, 1971. English translation: *In Search of Wagner.* Trans. Rodney Livingstone. London: Verso, 1981.

Abbate, Carolyn. *Unsung Voices: Opera and Musical Narrative in the Nineteenth Century,* Princeton: Princeton UP, 1991.

——. *In Search of Opera.* Princeton NJ and Oxford: Princeton UP, 2001.

Dahlhaus, Carl. *Die Musikdramen Richard Wagners.* Velber: Friedrich, 1971. English translation: *Richard Wagner's Music Dramas.* Trans. Mary Whittall. Cambridge: Cambridge UP, 1979.

Dolar, Mladen and Slavoj Žižek. *Opera's Second Death.* New York, London: Routledge, 2002.

Feuerbach, Ludwig. *Werke in Sechs Bänden.* 6 vols. Ed. Erich Thies. Frankfurt: Suhrkamp, 1975.

Goehr, Lydia. *The Quest for Voice: Politics and the Limits of Philosophy.* Berkeley and Los Angeles: U of California P, 1998.

Grey, Thomas S. *Wagner's Musical Prose: Texts and Contexts,* Cambridge: Cambridge UP, 1995.

Grossmann-Vendrey, Susanna, ed. *Bayreuth in der deutschen Presse.* Regensburg: Gustav Bosse Verlag, 1977.

Hartford, Robert, ed. *Bayreuth: The Early Years,* London: Victor Gollancz, 1980.

Hollingdale, R[eginald] J. *Nietzsche: The Man and his Philosophy.* Cambridge: Cambridge UP, 1965; rev. 1999.

Klossowski, Pierre. *Nietzsche and the Vicious Circle.* Trans. Daniel W. Smith. Chicago: U of Chicago P, 1997.

Kramer, Lawrence. "Contesting Wagner: The *Lohengrin* Prelude and Anti-anti-Semitism," *19th-Century Music* 25/2–3 (2001): 190–211.

——. *Music as Cultural Practice,* 1800–1900. Berkeley, CA: U of California P, 1990.

Kittler, Friedrich. "World-Breath: On Wagner's Media Technology." In *Opera Through Other Eyes,* ed. David J. Levin. Stanford, CA: Stanford UP, 1993.

Lacoue-Labarthe, Philippe. *Musica Ficta: Figures of Wagner.* Trans. Felicia McCarren. Stanford CA: Stanford UP, 1994.

Levin, David J. *Richard Wagner, Fritz Lang, and the Nibelungen: The Dramaturgy of Disavowal.* Princeton, NJ: Princeton UP, 1998.

——. "Reading Beckmesser Reading: Antisemitism and Aesthetic Practice in *Die Meistersinger von Nürnberg.*" *New German Critique* 69 (Fall, 1996): 127–46.

——, ed. *Opera Through Other Eyes.* Stanford CA: Stanford UP, 1993.

——, ed. Special Wagner Issue, *New German Critique* 69 (Fall, 1996).

Mann, Thomas. "Leiden und Größe Richard Wagners." In *Essays*, ed. Hermann Kurzke and Stephan Stachorski. Frankfurt: Fischer, 1995. English trans.: "The Sorrows and Grandeur of Richard Wagner." In Thomas Mann. *Pro and Contra Wagner,* trans. Allan Blunden. Chicago: Chicago UP, 1985.

Millington, Barry. "Nuremberg Trial: Is There Anti-Semitism in *Die Meistersinger*?" *Cambridge Opera Journal* 3/3 (1991): 247–60.

———, ed. *The Wagner Compendium.* London: Thames and Hudson, 1992.

Morris, Mitchell. "Tristan's Wounds: On Homosexual Wagnerians at the Fin de Siècle." In *Queer Episodes in Music and Modern Identity,* ed. Sophie Fuller and Lloyd Whitesell. Urbana and Chicago: U of Illinois P, 2002, 271–91.

Morris, Christopher. *Reading Opera Between the Lines: Orchestral Interludes and Cultural Meaning from Wagner to Berg.* Cambridge: Cambridge UP, 2002.

———. "'Alienated From His Own Being': Nietzsche, Bayreuth and the Problem of Identity." *Journal of the Royal Musical Association* 127/1 (May, 2002): 44–71.

Müller, Ulrich, and Peter Wapnewski, eds. *Wagner-Handbuch.* Stuttgart: Alfred Kröner, 1986. English translation: *Wagner Handbook.* Ed. and trans. John Deathridge. Cambridge MA: Harvard UP, 1992.

Nattiez, Jean-Jacques. *Wagner Androgyne.* Trans. Stewart Spencer. Princeton: Princeton UP, 1993.

Nietzsche, Friedrich. *Sämtliche Werke: Kritischen Studienausgabe.* 15 vols. Ed. Giorgi Colli and Mazzino Montinari. Berlin, New York: Deutscher Taschenbuch Verlag, 1980.

———. *Unpublished Writings from the Period of* Unfashionable Observations. Ed. Giorgi Colli and Mazzino Montinari, trans. Richard T. Gray. Stanford CA: Stanford UP, 1999.

———. *Basic Writings of Nietzsche.* Ed. and trans. Walter Kaufmann. New York: Random House, 1966.

———. *Human, All Too Human.* Trans. R. J. Hollingdale. Cambridge: Cambridge UP, 1986.

———. *Untimely Meditations.* Trans. R. J. Hollingdale. Cambridge: Cambridge UP, 1983.

Nordau, Max. *Entartung.* 2 vols. (Berlin: Duncker und Humblot, 1893). English translation: *Degeneration.* Trans. anon. Lincoln NB and London: Nebraska UP, 1993.

Rose, Paul Lawrence. *Wagner: Race and Revolution.* New Haven CT: Yale UP, 1992).

Schopenhauer, Arthur. *Die Welt als Wille und Vorstellung.* In *Sämtliche Werke,* vol. 1, ed. Wolfgang von Löhneysen. Frankfurt, Stuttgart: Cotta-Insel, 1960. English translation: *The World as Will and Representation.* Trans. E. F. J. Payne. New York: Dover Publications, 1969.

Spencer, Stewart. "The Language and Sources of *Der Ring des Nibelungen*." In *Richard Wagner und sein Mittelalter,* ed. Ursula and Ulrich Müller. Salzburg: Ursula Müller-Speiser, 1989.

Stirner, Max. *Der Einzige und sein Eigentum.* Leipzig: Otto Wigand, 1845. Repr. Stuttgart: Reclam, 1972.

Tambling, Jeremy, *Opera and the Culture of Fascism,* Oxford: Clarendon Press, 1996.

Tomlinson, Gary, *Metaphysical Song: An Essay on Opera,* Princeton: Princeton UP, 1999.

Vaget, Hans Rudolf. "Imaginings," *Wagner Notes* 18/6 (December 1995), n.p.

Wagner, Richard. *Dichtungen und Schriften.* 10 vols. Ed. Dieter Borchmeyer. Frankfurt: Insel, 1983.

———. *Sämtliche Schriften und Dichtungen.* 16 vols. Ed. Richard Sternfeld and Hans von Wolzogen. Leipzig: Breitkopf und Härtel, 1916.

———. *Richard Wagner's Prose Works.* 8 vols. Trans. William Ashton Ellis. New York: Broude Brothers, 1966.

———. *Sämtliche Werke.* Ed. Carl Dahlhaus and Egon Voss. Mainz: Schott, 1970–.

———. *Mein Leben.* Ed. Martin Gregor-Dellin. Munich: List Verlag, 1963. English translation: *My Life.* Ed. Mary Whittall, trans. Andrew Gray. Cambridge: Cambridge UP, 1983.

———. *Briefe.* Ed. Hanjo Kesting. Munich and Zurich: Piper Verlag, 1983.

Weber, William. "Wagner, Wagnerism, and Musical Idelaism." In *Wagnerism in European Culture and Politics,* ed. David C. Large and William Weber. Ithaca, NY and London: Cornell UP, 1984.

Weiner, Marc A. *Richard Wagner and the Anti-Semitic Imagination.* Lincoln, NB and London: U of Nebraska P, 1995.

Žižek, Slavoj. *Tarrying with the Negative.* Durham: Duke University Press, 1993.

———. "There Is No Sexual Relationship." In *Gaze and Voice as Love Objects,* ed. Renata Salecl and Slavoj Žižek. Durham NC and London: Duke UP, 1996.

Part IV

Bibliographical Resources

Navigating the Nineteenth Century:
A Critical Bibliography

John Pizer

VIRTUALLY ALL PROFESSORS and graduate students of German in the United States today are aware that the gradual shift in emphasis from a focus on German literature and linguistics in their departments to a broader-based engagement with German Studies (and all the subdisciplines this term comprehends) has brought about major changes in curricular offerings and reading lists. Departments of German Studies offer a wide variety of courses on such topics as film, politics, German multiculturalism, and social histories of women and minorities, with correspondingly less emphasis on traditional works of German literature. Less well known and documented, but evident to anyone who discusses the issue of master and doctoral level general examinations with German Studies graduate students across the country, is the circumstance that these students are still expected to have a firm grasp of literary periods. To cite one personal example: in 2002 I was in contact with a former student who had graduated with a bachelor's degree in German from my university. She was preparing for an examination in nineteenth-century German literature, the last step in her quest for a master's degree at a different institution. She complained about the paucity of recent works treating German literature in a broad, comprehensive manner. She was particularly concerned that she had not attained a sufficient grasp of the various movements and periods that are used, then as now, to critically and chronologically organize the works composed during these roughly seventy years. She sought my advice on possible supplementary reading (having mainly relied, up to that point, on *Periods in German Literature,* edited by J. M. Ritchie in 1966), and wanted to know whether the cursory definitions she had formulated of terms such as "Biedermeier," "Poetic Realism," and "Young Germany" were accurate.

I relate these observations by way of explaining the approach taken in the following critical bibliography of scholarship on nineteenth-century German literature. The editors of the volume of which this essay is a part gave me broad latitude with respect to the choice of secondary materials to be examined. Their sole proviso was that most of them be of relatively recent vintage, written within the last twenty-five or so years. In considering that thousands of essays and books have been published on the subject,

I spent a great deal of time wondering how I could gain a purchase on so vast a subject. In other words, I reflected on what angle would enable me to validly engage in a radical winnowing process, a process that would allow me to eliminate from my discussion in a necessarily brief essay all but a tiny fraction of scholarship devoted to German literature composed between 1830 and 1899. My conversations with budding scholars in our discipline led to the reflection that the following bibliography would be of greatest benefit if addressed particularly to pre-doctoral level graduate students and others interested in seeking a general rather than specialized knowledge of nineteenth-century German literature and its various periods. The other essays composed for the present volume will no doubt greatly facilitate this process, but students and non-students alike will profit from a variety of perspectives. Indeed, the ten volumes comprising the *Camden House History of German Literature,* of which the current volume is a part, should help facilitate a broad acquaintance with all periods of German literature, from the earliest extant writings through the twentieth century. These ten volumes constitute the most detailed history of German literature written in English.

With a few exceptions, then, the works, composed in German or English selected for discussion in this essay, provide broad surveys of post-Romantic nineteenth-century German literature and its various movements. The first three books discussed offer general overviews of the entire period, from around 1830 to the fin de siècle. This section is followed by a discussion of works designed as comprehensive overviews of nineteenth-century German-language writers. Much work in recent German Studies is constituted by feminist scholarship focused on works by female authors, works neglected in the past but which have attracted considerable scholarly attention in recent years. An analysis of a work that surveys a wide range of well-known women writers as well as lesser-known women writers of the nineteenth century will supplement, therefore, the author-focused analysis. I will then examine works on the four figures singled out by the current volume who are not primarily associated with imaginative literature but who seminally influenced nineteenth-century German culture: Karl Marx, Friedrich Nietzsche, Richard Wagner, and the young Sigmund Freud. The rest of the essay will examine monographs that focus on the prominent movements of the German (as well as Austrian and Swiss) nineteenth century: Young Germany, Biedermeier, *Vormärz,* realism, and the several concurrent trends that encompass the oeuvre of what is broadly known as the Wilhelmine Age: impressionism, symbolism, aestheticism, and naturalism. Although this bibliography is primarily organized around movements rather than genres, most of the books discussed contain a preponderance of chapters devoted to the disparate literary forms. The essay takes note of these discussions and therefore may help guide those whose interests and examinations are organized around genres rather than around movements.

Throughout, this essay will focus on what in these works recommends them to those seeking a broad knowledge of nineteenth-century German literature and thought, and what, if any, are their drawbacks or weaknesses.

I should state at the outset that I may well have overlooked scholarship deserving of attention. Nevertheless, despite some effort, I was unable to locate any single-volume monographs of recent vintage that discuss the topic of post-Romantic nineteenth-century German literature in a truly comprehensive fashion. Thus, the three works I will discuss, Hermann Boeschenstein's *German Literature of the Nineteenth Century*, Eda Sagarra's *Tradition and Revolution: German Literature and Society 1830–1890*, and G. Wallis Field's *A Literary History of Germany: The Nineteenth Century 1830–1890*, were published some time ago, in 1969, 1971, and 1975, respectively. The lack of recent succinct but comprehensive critical surveys of the century no doubt reflects the age of specialization in which we live; again, the volume of which this essay is a part will no doubt help to compensate for this dearth.

Boeschenstein begins with an acknowledgement of the difficulties facing any scholar who would seek to treat post-Romantic German literature of the nineteenth century as an entirety, especially the problem of fixing periods chronologically. As he notes — and as we will see in subsequent works — some would situate the true beginnings of Biedermeier and Young Germany in 1815 (the end of the Napoleonic Age), others in 1830 (when the July Revolution in France took place), and still others in 1832 (the year of Goethe's death). Boeschenstein considers the burden of epigonality that psychologically tormented many authors in the wake of the Age of Goethe. Boeschenstein argues that epigonality was an especially prominent theme in the works of Karl Immermann, though he asserts (without offering substantiation) that one finds this perplexity in the work of Karl Gutzkow, Friedrich Spielhagen, and Gottfried Keller. An oddity in *German Literature of the Nineteenth Century* is the chapter title "Problematic Writers," by which Boeschenstein means those who fall outside the pale of the four categories constituting the remainder of his book: Marxist-socialist literature, peasant literature, Austrian literature, and bourgeois literature. Friedrich Hebbel, Annette von Droste-Hülshoff, Eduard Mörike, and Conrad Ferdinand Meyer are treated as such "outsiders." One may question such categories; Wilhelm Raabe and Keller are grouped together as "bourgeois" writers, but it seems doubtful that they were more bourgeois than Hebbel and Meyer in any but a superficial way. Nevertheless, Boeschenstein's book provides useful, if necessarily brief overviews of many of the century's still canonic works.

As is evident from its title, Sagarra's book treats nineteenth-century German literature within its social context, and will thus be of particular value to those with an interest in cultural studies. The opening section on "The Social Background 1830–1890" contains helpful information on topics such as daily life, societal hierarchies, and education. The second section focuses on the literature of the period, but the social circumstances informing this literature always remain in the foreground. Sagarra proceeds chronologically. She begins with a consideration of what the term "Biedermeier" signifies; in Sagarra's view, Biedermeier works concentrate on life's simple pleasures, and although they do not treat broad social issues, they are marked by an undercurrent of social unease and pessimism. Subsequent chapters in this section treat such domains as "peasant literature," "Young Germany," and the "German Form of Realism." Some of the book's chapters are organized around one writer or several writers whom Sagarra finds of particular import; for example, chapter ten is devoted to "Karl Gutzkow and the Nineteenth Century German Novel," while the penultimate chapter treats "Two Novelists of the Empire: Fontane and Raabe." Thus, the issue of genre also receives its due in *Tradition and Revolution,* though the various literary forms, as can be seen from these chapter titles, are not treated comprehensively but according to their respective significance for given epochs. Therefore, drama is only treated as a discrete genre in the chapter "Revolution in Drama: Grabbe, Büchner, Hebbel," so that drama in the Imperial Age is, relatively speaking, neglected. Overall, though, *Tradition and Revolution* offers a useful overview of post-Romantic nineteenth-century German literature because it is so well informed with respect to the social background of this body of works.

Field's *A Literary History of Germany: The Nineteenth Century 1830–1890* is particularly to be recommended for its biographic information. Although Boeschenstein does not entirely ignore this dimension and Sagarra actually emphasizes it in some cases, it receives more consistent attention in *A Literary History of Germany,* because most of this work's chapters are divided into sections on the individual authors. With respect to its more overarching structure, Field's book is organized both according to period and genre; for example, there are chapters on "Drama in the Nineteenth Century," "Heinrich Heine and *Das Junge Deutschland,*" and "Lyric Poetry from Poetic Realism to Impressionism and Symbolism." Additionally, two chapters respectively precede the two chronological halves — pre- and post-1848 — into which the book is informally divided. These two chapters provide an overview of the sociohistorical and philosophical undercurrents informing German, Austrian, and Swiss literature prior to and following the watershed political year, though with less social detail than one finds in Sagarra's book. Like Boeschenstein, Field offers a chapter on the problematic epigonality that was so consistent a factor following the end of the *Goethezeit,* but this chapter is not so exclusively focused on Immermann.

In concluding the discussion of broad overviews of nineteenth-century German-language literature, it should be stressed that each work has a somewhat different focus. Those seeking brief synopses of individual works should consult *German Literature of the Nineteenth Century. Tradition and Revolution* offers the most detailed examination of the literature's social background. *A Literary History of Germany: The Nineteenth Century* is particularly valuable if one is seeking succinct biographical information on most of the period's prominent writers.

To be sure, Field's book is not the authoritative source for information on individual authors. Prior to the publication of the *Dictionary of Literary Biography,* the main reference work for those seeking an overview of nineteenth-century German-language writers was *Deutsche Dichter des 19. Jahrhunderts: Ihr Leben und Werk* (1969), edited by Benno von Wiese. This comprises a collection of twenty-three essays, each dedicated to a single writer, composed by diverse scholars. Such a volume is necessarily selective, but contemporary readers will notice the absence of all but a single woman writer (Droste-Hülshoff) and two Jewish writers (Heine and Ludwig Börne). Disparate critical methodologies are evident. Some essays focus on psychological and sociocritical elements (for example, Roger Bauer's essay on Johann Nepomuk Nestroy), while others devote more attention to stylistic elements (Heinz Hillmann on C. F. Meyer). On the whole, however, *Deutsche Dichter des 19. Jahrhunderts* provides informative surveys of the still most widely read writers from the period.

A more consistent approach is evident in the two volumes of the *Dictionary of Literary Biography* that treat the German nineteenth century. *Nineteenth-Century German Writers to 1840* (1993), edited by James Hardin and Siegfried Mews, is volume 133 of the vast literary biography project. In all, seventeen volumes in the DLB are devoted to German-language literature. The introduction to volume 133 provides an informative survey of the historical events and political / social milieus that helped shape the era's literary output. The title is somewhat misleading, for many of the Romantic movement's leading luminaries produced their most significant works in the first two decades of the century. However, only post-*Goethezeit* authors are covered by the volume; not even the erstwhile Romantic Heine is included here (his entry is to be found in volume 90, *German Writers in the Age of Goethe, 1789–1832,* published in 1989). As with *Deutsche Dichter des 19. Jahrhunderts, German Writers to 1840* consists of individual articles on the various authors, written by leading Germanists (in this case, mainly North Americans rather than Europeans). The essays are necessarily brief, and this allowed for the inclusion of ten more writers than could be accommodated by Wiese's book (which treats the entire century). More women are covered (such as Louise von Gall and Ida Gräfin von Hahn-Hahn), as well as a number of intellectuals not primarily associated with imaginative literature (for example, the philosopher Ludwig Feuerbach and the theologian David Friedrich Strauss). Each essay is preceded by a list of the first editions of the authors' books, the first

English-language translation of the German work, critical or standard editions of their complete works, and significant shorter pieces. At the conclusion of each essay, letters, bibliographies, and a list of selected important secondary works are listed. As is to be expected in a biographic dictionary, these essays are limited to providing cursory overviews' of their subjects' life and works. However, their bibliographic apparatus — which means the list of the primary literature — is considerably more detailed than the list of primary and secondary works that conclude each contribution to Wiese's volume. Because they are obviously more up-to-date than those in Wiese's book, the essays in *Nineteenth-Century German Writers to 1840* are also more useful as a springboard for further study. The volume concludes with a helpful checklist of "Further Readings" that broadly treat the period under consideration.

As one would expect, *Nineteenth-Century German Writers, 1841–1900* (1993), also edited by Hardin and Mews and constituting volume 129 of the *Dictionary of Literary Biography,* employs the same structure and format as the volume discussed above. It covers the leading authors of Poetic Realism, philosophical and political thinkers such as Friedrich Engels, Marx, Nietzsche, and Wilhelm Dilthey, and includes an essay on Wagner. Turn-of-the-century writers associated with this period's diverse movements, such as Gerhart Hauptmann and Rainer Maria Rilke, are to be found scattered throughout a number of other volumes. The introduction repeats some of the information contained in the previous volume, but also provides a useful overview of major trends in the realist movement, which is justly termed "the dominant literary style of the second half of the nineteenth century" (xvii). This concluding assertion of the introduction is perhaps a valid, albeit tacit justification of the circumstance that prominent non-realists who were productive at the turn of the century were relegated to a variety of other volumes in the series. At any rate, a comprehensive index at the conclusion of each volume makes it easy to locate the essays on these and all the other authors included within the *Dictionary of Literary Biography*'s vast scope.

Though the *Dictionary* certainly cannot be accused of neglecting nineteenth-century women writers, it cannot provide a cohesive picture of this group as a whole, nor can it give a broad account of the particular conditions that shaped their oeuvre. Carol Diethe's *Towards Emancipation: German Women Writers of the Nineteenth Century* (1998), admirably fills in this gap. In her introduction, Diethe discusses the restrictions on education with which the female sex had to contend at that time, as well as key themes in women's writing during the century, such as religion, the struggles against class prejudices in matters of love (a theme obviously not foreign to male writers such as Gotthold Ephraim Lessing and Friedrich Schiller, but somewhat less a central focus in male nineteenth-century literature) and the idealization, unconsciously shaped by patriarchal priorities dominant during this period, of women who renounce true love. Diethe describes her own perspective as "mainstream feminist," but finds that "there are limits to the usefulness of feminism during the era under investigation," because, she implies, a purely feminist account does not adequately deal with class distinctions (14). The book's six chapters focus on twenty different writers. In discussing these women, Diethe strikes a balance between biographical detail, literary analysis, and the historical circumstances affecting their life and work. Each chapter is also introduced by a brief account of the social, political, and cultural matrices that shaped the lives and oeuvres of the authorial clusters as a whole. These clusters include the Romantic writers, those with "Weimar Connections," "The 1848ers," those who wrote "Popular Literature," authors particularly focused on "The Woman Question," and those who wrote "In Nietzsche's Shadow." Not all of these groupings are judicious. Droste-Hülshoff, for example, is included in the "Weimar Connections" cluster (along, more appropriately, with Johanna and Adele Schopenhauer, as well as Ottilie von Goethe), though she had little connection to the duchy's illustrious authors. In this regard, Diethe can only note that Droste-Hülshoff "heard about the Weimar circle at first hand" through Adele Schopenhauer (71). Including Marie von Ebner-Eschenbach with Ida von Hahn-Hahn and Eugenie Marlitt as writers of "popular literature" tacitly implies that they were her equals with respect to literary merit. Still, Diethe's analyses of the individual writers tend to be succinct yet not lacking in detail. These analyses deftly provide historical contextualization, an element essential to introductory overviews. Diethe's account of the life and works of Lou Andreas-Salomé, one of the women "in Nietzsche's shadow," is particularly well balanced, illustrating Andreas-Salomé's concomitant feminist and anti-feminist tendencies. Interestingly, Diethe is able to articulate this balance in the works of the putatively misogynist Nietzsche himself, so that she places him "within the camp of the 'moderate' feminists" (173). Such surprising twists make *Towards Emancipation* entertaining as well as informative.

Many academics deride the books published in the "Twayne's World Authors Series" for their lack of original scholarship. It is certainly true that most of these monographs offer little in the way of path-breaking interpretations and revelations to those who already possess a specialist's knowledge of a man or woman of letters, but criticism of the Twayne books on this account fails to consider the purpose of the series. Such books are written in order to provide a broad overview of the life, works, and historical background of the authors they examine. For this reason, they are ideal for those seeking a critical introduction to these authors. Because my bibliography was primarily composed with such an audience in mind, I recommend Twayne books on Marx and Nietzsche for those seeking an initial acquaintance with these prominent figures. The circumstance, however, that Richard E. Olsen's *Karl Marx* (1978) and Robert Holub's *Friedrich*

Nietzsche (1995) were published in the same series and aimed at the same audience does not signify that they are structurally identical. In the preface to *Karl Marx,* Olsen notes that his book is designed to lead the reader gradually into the increasing intricacies of Marx's thought. Though each chapter analyzes relatively discrete elements in his philosophy, the book treats "the most easily accessible aspects first in order to give the reader an overview which can provide the basis for an understanding of the relatively more complex ones to follow. Marx's theory fortunately lends itself easily to such an approach" (7).

Karl Marx opens with a brief biographical chapter. Particularly valuable here, in light of the polemics to which Marx is still subject on the part of both his detractors and followers, is Olsen's tendency to underscore the extreme caution with which Marx approached revolutionary insurrection in his time. The next two chapters summarize Marx's historiography, his belief that history's motor force was class struggle. In the "Asiatic mode," the relationship between the despot and his tribe was not class-driven, in Marx's view, and hence ahistorical. The "ancient mode" of Greece, Rome, and the Middle East, on the other hand, leads to a comprehensive division of social labor when the principle of private property emerges. This puts into play a series of contestations that Marx believed would bring about a classless, stateless, communist society. Hansen then examines Marx's views on materialism and his reworking of Hegelian dialectics into the paradigm of a class struggle. It may be argued that the discussion of dialectics should have been part of the chapter on Marxian history, but if Hansen had followed this procedure, he would have betrayed his promise to lead the reader gradually, step-by-step, through the complexities of Marx's thought.

Having established the general tenor of Marx's perspectives on history, Hansen can explore the complex relationships between ideology and materialism, dialectical predetermination and the efficacy of human agency in Marx's social theory in a manner that clarifies these historical views. Having addressed the broad thrust of Marxian methodology, Hansen turns his attention to the still politically charged issue of the young Marx's stand on humanism and alienation. The brief discussion of "Marx and the Contemporary World" with which the book concludes is obviously somewhat dated, since the Soviet Block's collapse and the emergence of almost unimpeded capitalist globalization has wiped out the "ectoplasmic fullness" Hansen saw in the "specter of communism" in the late 1970s (159). Nevertheless, *Karl Marx* offers a still relevant introduction to Marx's thought.

Holub's *Friedrich Nietzsche* does break some new ground in situating this iconoclastic philosopher's thought within its historical context. That is to say, Holub shows that much of Nietzsche's work was a response to, an engagement with, major trends in Wilhelmine Germany, a circumstance most previous scholarship had ignored. Like Hansen's book and others in the Twayne series, *Friedrich Nietzsche* begins with a biographical overview, but subsequent chapters treat developments in his thought as relatively discrete episodes, and are arranged typologically. The second chapter focuses on *Die Geburt der Tragödie,* on Nietzsche as a philologist, and on his relationship to Wagner. The next chapter discusses his pedagogical views; the elitist Nietzsche was opposed to universal education with its putative watering-down of the curriculum. His arguments against "monumental" history and his later anti-institutional ideas on education are emphasized here. Chapter four discusses Nietzsche's responses to then-current scientific discourses, such as thermodynamics and evolution. He used his engagements with these discourses in order to advance his own views on social decay and how it might be reversed. Nietzsche "The Social Observer" is the subject of the next chapter. Subsequent chapters focus on his moral theory, his views on religion, his critique of Wilhelmine culture, and his historical reception. *Friedrich Nietzsche* can be recommended to those seeking an acquaintance with the main currents of his thought, with how his beliefs are informed by trends in nineteenth-century Germany, and with how his writing attracted, repelled, and influenced intellectuals of subsequent generations.

Unquestionably, the most significant relationship among men of letters in Wilhelmine Germany for the development of that era's cultural life was the one between Nietzsche and Wagner. Dieter Borchmeyer's *Das Theater Richard Wagners: Idee – Dichtung – Wirkung* (1982) probes their relationship in detail, using Nietzsche's literary remains (*Nachlaß*) to explore Wagner's influence on *Die Geburt der Tragödie* in a novel way. Borchmeyer shows, for example, that Nietzsche's satiric broadside against Wagnerian metaphysics in *Zur Genealogie der Moral* is ironic considering that Nietzsche had adopted precisely this Wagnerian metaphysical stance during the genesis of the book on the birth of tragedy in 1872 (107). Borchmeyer's book is also quite valuable in its elucidation of the unique Wagnerian music-drama genre, and for its discussion of Wagner's reception by and influence on nineteenth-century German literature. For example, despite a relative paucity of utterances by Adalbert Stifter on music in general and on Wagner in particular, the Austrian's enthusiastic response to Alfred von Wolzogen's polemic against "Zukunftsmusik" leads Borchmeyer to illuminate subtle anti-Wagnerian tendencies in one of the most important works of nineteenth-century German-language literature, *Der Nachsommer.* This work, in turn, is shown to impact the language of Nietzsche's tirades against Wagner. Borchmeyer also examines the frequent references to Wagner in Theodor Fontane's novels. Fontane's antipathy toward Wagner is evident in the appellation "Hexenmeister," bestowed upon the composer in *L'Adultera.* Thomas Mann's and Hugo von Hofmannsthal's engagements with Wagner are also discussed. Given Borchmeyer's probing insights into Wagner's aesthetics and ambitions, his nuanced elucidation of the Nietzsche-Wagner relationship, his penetrating analysis of the music-drama genre, his useful interpretation of the poetics of Wagner's most well-known operas, and his discussion of Wagner's impact on Wilhelmine cultural life in general and on German literature in particular, *Das Theater Richard Wagners* is to be recommended over the Twayne book, Robert Raphael's *Richard Wagner* (1969) as an introduction to the famed composer, even though Borchmeyer's study is not intended to be a broad, introductory overview. While Raphael's book is, of course, written for a non-specialist audience, it has too many gaps, barely treating, for example, the Nietzsche-Wagner connection.

Most of Freud's most celebrated works were published in the twentieth century, and it is understandable that most critical engagements with the father of psychoanalysis focus on the later phase of his career. To be sure, comprehensive treatments of Freud analyze the origins of his thought in nineteenth-century Vienna, and the early influences which shaped his world view, but few recent works concentrate on the youthful Freud, the Freud with whom students of nineteenth-century German literature and thought are primarily concerned. An exception is Billa Zanuso's *The Young Freud: The Origins of Psychoanalysis in Late Nineteenth-Century Viennese Culture,* published in English translation in 1986 and in the original Italian in 1982. The first section of this book, "The Age of Freud," is focused on "Vienna, the Bourgeois City" and "Vienna, the Contradictory City," as its two chapters are titled. Zanuso's book offers a comprehensive overview of the paradigms central to Freudian thought: transference, the Oedipus complex, infantile sexuality, displacement, etc. However, *The Young Freud* is primarily concerned with the genesis of his thought, and articulates quite well the nineteenth-century Viennese context that shaped Freud's theories. Vienna in the age of Franz Joseph is shown to be a strongly contradictory city despite its glittering veneer of beauty and charm. On the one hand, it was swept up in scientific positivism and sustained by a bourgeois belief that thrift, hard work, and respect for civil authority and its institutions are the highest values, bound to meet with material success and spiritual well-being. On the other hand, Austria-Hungary's bureaucratic morass and unbridgeable ethnic divides imbued Vienna's rich intellectual currents with a sense of the nation's inevitable demise. Thus, when Zanuso aptly notes that "The social pessimism in his writings has no bearing on his typically nineteenth-century respect for progress" (59), we see this overarching strain in Freud's world view as rooted in the ambiguities of life and thought in nineteenth-century Vienna.

This does not explain what was revolutionary in Freud's views, but Zanuso explores these aspects as well. *The Young Freud* takes note of nineteenth-century society's deeply cherished myth concerning the absolute sexual innocence of children, and the resistance Freud met when he developed his ideas on infantile sexuality. Freud's perspectives reflected nineteenth-century Austria's dominant patriarchal precepts, but his theorems concerning the female sex drive are shown to challenge the patriarchal perspective as well. The book examines the development of Freud's thought under the influence of Jean Martin Charcot and Joseph Breuer in the late nineteenth century, and how Freudian analysis took an independent direction when Freud began to move away from his mentors' reliance on hypnotic suggestion and toward a form of psycho-analysis which focuses on conscious free association. Zanuso also touches on Freud's intellectual relationship with Arthur Schnitzler, and how fin-de-siècle Vienna's preoccupation with internal and external conflicts between "rational man" and "psychological man," reflected in the literature of Schnitzler and Hofmannsthal, also permeates Freud's early thought. Thus, *The Young Freud* is particularly valuable as a guide to the nineteenth-century forces that shaped his intellectual evolution.

The first literary movement fully anchored in the nineteenth century was Young Germany. Many scholars believe that the movement chronologically coincides with the era of Biedermeier literature. In his chapter on "Biedermeier — Young Germany," Boeschenstein notes: " 'Biedermeier' is inwardly directed, 'das Junge Deutschland' is out-going. The Metternich era elicited both these reactions, by frightening some people back into the shell of their private lives and by driving others to protest against the situation and to attempt to remedy it" (14). But it must be noted that the use of the term "Biedermeier" as a literary category is a twentieth-century convention designating an amorphous trend the common characteristics of which are only apoliticism and a focus on domestic, usually rural, life. "Young Germany," on the other hand, was a relatively cohesive cadre of politically oriented writers and an appellation stemming from the December 1835 edict that banned their works. The best recent overview of the movement is provided by Helmut Koopmann's *Das Junge Deutschland: Eine Einführung* (1993). This brief work begins with an examination of the factors that gave rise to Young Germany: the July Revolution in Paris, Goethe's death, the political disappointments of Germany in the Restoration Era. Each chapter of the book is preceded by brief excerpts from Young Germany texts that tend to sustain Koopmann's perspectives on its literary trends, styles, self-perception, and perspectives, as well as the views of its opponents and the results of the 1835 prohibition. Koopmann's most controversial position is undoubtedly his theory that Young Germany was far less "out-going" and socially activist than most scholars believe. Koopmann argues that its members hoped their writing itself, rather than direct political activism, would bring about progressive social change and German unification. In this, Koopmann distinguishes Young Germany from the *Vormärz*, which he situates in the 1840s. While Young Germany, in Koopmann's view, was essentially a literary movement preoccupied mostly by concerns innate to belles lettres, *Vormärz* writing is far more overtly political, both thematically and in its choice of genres. Koopmann asserts that "Der Aktivismus des Vormärz ist dem Jungen Deutschland verdächtig und fremd gewesen" (*Vormärz* activism was alienating and suspicious in the view of Young Germany, 3). Whether or not one agrees with Koopmann's thesis, *Das Junge Deutschland: Eine Einführung* provides what its title promises, an excellent introduction to the movements, its styles, aspirations, controversies, and sensibilities.

Another work worth consulting is *Das Junge Deutschland: Kolloquium zum 150. Jahrestag des Verbots vom 10. Dezember 1835,* edited by Joseph Kruse and Bernd Kortländer (1987). This collection of eleven essays creates a comprehensive overview of the period by individually treating the domains that shaped it: the battle against censorship, the early polemics against the classical constrictions of the Age of Goethe, later charges of pettiness leveled against its literary and political preoccupations by Engels and Vormärz writers, the central influence of Lessing and Luther on the movement, and the conflicted cosmopolitanism reflected in its engagement with the Goethean concept of *Weltliteratur.* Jost Hermand's essay "Jungdeutscher Tempelsturm. Zur Austreibung des Poetischen aus der Literatur" offers the interesting view that Young Germany was the first literary avant-garde of bourgeois liberal modernism. Hermand is critical of Young Germany's putatively vain, trivializing, aesthetically driven subjectivity, its pendulations between activism and elitism. Heine's intimate and seminal relationship with the movement's leading writers is stressed throughout the book (especially in essays by Jürgen Habermas and Manfred Windfuhr), as is Wolfgang Menzel's function as Young Germany's most significant and influential literary adversary.

Hermand and Koopmann are in agreement that the Young Germany movement was situated in the 1830s while the more resolutely political Vormärz authors dominated the 1840s. However, this view is not universally shared, and periodization is a notoriously inexact science. This is particularly evident in discussions of the so-called "Biedermeier." Certainly Boeschenstein is accurate in associating this term with contemporaries of the Young Germany authors who were preoccupied with home, nature, family life, and the inner working of the soul rather than with the hubbub of the external world. The signifier began to be engaged by literary historians in the 1920s and 1930s to characterize this politically countervailing trend during the Restoration Age. However, writers associated with Biedermeier — and virtually every other literary period for that matter — often display a tendency highly disadvantageous to literary historians, namely, to live long and productive lives that extend beyond the period into which they are pigeon-holed, and to compose works that defy strict categorization. A case in point is Stifter. Not without reason, the editors of the anthology *Von der deutschen Klassik bis zum Naturalismus,* used by teachers in survey courses of nineteenth-century German literature, place

Stifter in the Biedermeier rubric. Stifter exhibited most of the attributes associated with this trend: a turn to the private sphere, an immersion in the natural world, a renunciation of fame and social engagement but a concomitant preoccupation with rustic village life. Yet it is equally just to consider Stifter's famous preface to the *Bunte Steine* "an early document of poetic realism," as Eric Downing does in his *Double Exposures: Repetition and Realism in Nineteenth-Century German Fiction* (25), published in 2000. Downing shows that the consistent chiastic reversals in the preface betray a distinct political agenda. He finds that Stifter engages in a pattern of repetition and self-contradiction; this recognition enables Downing to place Stifter in the company of writers firmly situated within the pantheon of Poetic Realism, such as Theodor Storm, Raabe, and Keller.

Where does this leave us with respect to books providing an overview of Biedermeier? Certainly, *Begriffsbestimmung des literarischen Biedermeier* (1974), edited by Elfriede Neubuhr, contains a number of essays (most of which were written in the first half of the twentieth century) which help to define the period, but the most authoritative work on Biedermeier is Friedrich Sengle's three-volume *Biedermeierzeit: Deutsche Literatur im Spannungsfeld zwischen Restauration und Revolution 1815–1848* (1971–80). As is obvious from the subtitle, Sengle does not restrict his term to works from the period marked by inwardness and political quietism. Instead, he uses "Biedermeier" to characterize the entire corpus of literature produced between the fall of Napoleon and the onset of the mid-century revolution. The first volume is focused on general tendencies constellating this period: its intellectual background, its moods, influences, literary techniques, and language trends. The second volume deals with issues of genre. It contains chapters devoted to drama, lyric, epic, and narrative prose, but also to subgenres and forms that fall outside traditional categories, such as travel literature and autobiographical modes. The third volume consists of individual chapters on those authors of the period whom Sengle finds of greatest significance, and concludes with a comprehensive overview that seeks to define and demarcate the "Biedermeierzeit." The fifteen writers covered in this volume are all primarily associated with imaginative literature, so that authors identified most closely with Young Germany, such as Ludolf Wienbarg, Heinrich Laube, and Theodor Mundt are excluded. Even Karl Gutzkow, a leading writer and author of the most famous novel connected to Young Germany, *Wally, die Zweiflerin,* does not receive sustained attention, though he and the other Young Germany authors are the object of scattered commentary. Thus, though progressive, politically oriented writers like Heine, Georg Büchner, and Nestroy are the focus of individual chapters, most of the other fifteen writers are associated with Biedermeier in the narrower sense of the term: Stifter, Ferdinand Raimund, Jeremias Gotthelf, etc.

Despite this shortcoming, *Biedermeierzeit* is to be recommended as the most comprehensive guide to German literature of the Restoration Age. Its organization into three volumes has obvious advantages if one's quest for information is specifically focused on genre, individual authors, or broad intellectual and aesthetic trends. It should also be pointed out that the third chapter of the first volume offers an overview of Biedermeier in the narrower sense of the term, as a conservative, anti-cosmopolitan, politically disengaged tendency within the period (I: 118–54). Sengle explores here the origins of the term, trends in previous Biedermeier research, and the period's basic characteristics. "Heimat" (homeland) and nature are viewed as constituting the rather narrow experiential frame-of-reference favored by the Biedermeier authors not so much because the Restoration era instilled a fear of engagement with the broader sociopolitical realm due to Metternich's draconian repressions, as Boeschenstein implies, but because of the transparency with which the divine order manifests itself in these domains. To be sure, that praise of self-confidence, of individual subjectivity shown by Hermand and Koopmann to be valorized by Young Germany authors is seen by Sengle's Biedermeier authors as leading to isolation and sin; virtue is only to be found in rustic communal and family life. Sengle also offers a discerning account of Biedermeier rhetoric and its choice of genres, so that those seeking knowledge of Biedermeier as a discrete trend within the period between 1815 and 1848 will find *Biedermeierzeit* of value.

There are compelling reasons for agreeing with the hypothesis of Koopmann and Hermand that, with respect to the political left, one should distinguish between a Young Germany literature of the 1830s, progressive in tenor but still bourgeois in outlook, focused on aesthetic issues and the desirability of artistic individuation, and a *Vormärz* group in the 1840s, socialistically inclined, overtly political, directly occupied with the proletariat, and little concerned with formal and stylistic issues. An example of such uniquely *Vormärz* writing could be found in the radically tendentious poetry of Georg Herwegh, Georg Weerth, and Ferdinand Freiligrath composed between 1840 and 1850. Nevertheless, it is difficult to find any secondary works that treat the *Vormärz* period as a distinctive decade, even though Hermand laid the groundwork for such a possibility by editing the collection *Der deutsche Vormärz. Texte und Dokumente* (1967) after bringing out, under separate cover, *Das Junge Deutschland: Texte und Dokumente* (1966). Part of the problem is terminological: the "März" of "*Vormärz*" refers to the month in 1848 when the revolution is said to have truly begun, so that the "Vor" would encompass the entire period between 1815 and 1848, when the historical, social, and intellectual matrices that climaxed in the revolution were taking shape. Viewed in this light, the *Vormärz* epoch is chronologically identical to what Sengle termed the "Biedermeierzeit." Representative of this still dominant critical trend is Peter Stein's *Epochenproblem "Vormärz" (1815–1848)* (1974). Despite this drawback, Stein gives a creditable account of the history of *Vormärz* research, the term's treatment as a problematic pendant to "Biedermeier," as well as the term's materialistic valorization in Marxist circles. Particularly illuminating is an excursus on the Austrian Vormärz as a distinct phenomenon; underscoring such a distinction is a strong tendency in critical studies of the period. Here as elsewhere, Stein employs a materialistic methodology to resolve periodization dilemmas, a not always convincing approach.

The realist period in German literature, almost universally situated by scholars between 1848 and the century's end, is usually referred to as "Bourgeois Realism" or "Poetic Realism." The former category refers to the circumstance that virtually all of Germany's realist writers were of the middle class. The most significant study that analyzes the literary half-century from this viewpoint is Fritz Martini's monumental *Deutsche Literatur im bürgerlichen Realismus, 1848–1898* (1981), a work to be recommended to those who wish to know the epoch in detail. "Poetic Realism" was the term of choice for the movement's chief theorists; in Germany, these were Julian Schmidt and Otto Ludwig. The two best relatively recent overviews of the period which adopt this model are Clifford Bernd's *German Poetic Realism* (1981) and Roy Cowen's *Der Poetische Realismus. Kommentar zu einer Epoche* (1985). Bernd's book argues that German Poetic Realism's origins are to be situated in Scandinavia, a thesis he developed in much greater detail in his follow-up study *Poetic Realism in Scandinavia and Central Europe 1820–1895* (1995). In *German Poetic Realism,* Bernd shows how Schmidt advanced his literary theory through a series of polemics against earlier nineteenth-century writers, whose work Schmidt either found too fantastic (the Romantics), too political (the pre-1848 progressives Schmidt called *Märzpoeten*) or somehow too narrowly focused. Poetic Realism is thus defined through negation, as an approach that steers between extremes: "On the one hand, literary excesses of fancy and escapism were condemned; on the other, realistic literature was to be shunned if its poetic substance had withered to a state of artificial incrustation" (26–27).

Cowen's book is more detailed than that of Bernd. It opens with an account of the terminological and chronological difficulties involved with the periodization of German literature in the nineteenth century, particularly with respect to realism. Cowen characterizes the "poetic" realists as a discrete group characterized by esteem for individualism in art, which causes them to reject the leveling tendencies they saw in the "bourgeois" values of contemporaries. This critical distance toward non-individuation, together with personal feelings of inability and discouragement in the face of widespread belief in post-1848 Germany that the most communal of the genres was also the most elevated, are together seen to create what Cowen regards as a major criterion of Poetic Realism: the relative absence of dramatic writing among its leading luminaries. From such a perspective, Hebbel, the most prominent pre-naturalism dramatist of the age, would have to be considered a "bourgeois" rather than a "poetic" realist. Cowen's book also offers an account of the nonliterary influences that promoted Poetic Realism's growth, as well as its antecedents, literary influences, and internal relationships, its development, style, and preferred themes and genres. *Der Poetische Realismus* concludes with individual examinations of some of the movement's most canonic works, an analysis of two works by each of the following authors: Keller, Storm, Meyer, Raabe, and Fontane. Cowen recognizes that Poetic Realism is a direct consequence of the revolution's collapse, but he focuses primarily on the epistemological consequences the movement drew from its failure: a rejection of idealistic speculation and of Romantic musings on the natural / supernatural dialectic, a refusal to ponder the deeper "meaning" of the world (and thus a turning away from the philosophical ruminations Cowen associates with Christian Dietrich Grabbe, Büchner, Mörike, and Hebbel).

The recently published *A Companion to German Realism 1848–1900* (2002) is of interest for its focus on domains that are attracting the most sustained attention of contemporary German Studies scholars, domains such as feminism, colonialism, German-Jewish discourse, homosexuality, regionalism, and emigration. The book's title, as well as individual contributions on Karl May's reception during the Wilhelmine Empire and on male-male desire in the early fiction of Thomas Mann, indicate the editorial view that realism can be seen to encompass the entire second half of the nineteenth century, a position widely but not universally shared. There are fresh treatments of canonic authors such as Fontane and Freytag, but authors largely neglected by contemporary research, such as May and Marlitt, are discussed as well. Although such a book cannot give a comprehensive survey of the period, it is to be recommended as a cohesive example of how contemporary priorities and approaches can produce novel insights into the German realist period. Editor Todd Kontje's introduction provides a useful overview of the age.

The optimism and positivism in Germany sustained by a belief in scientific progress in the second half of the century received a dramatic boost with the founding of the Second Empire in 1871. Many scholars justifiably distinguish the political period from 1870 up to the end of the First World War, when imperial Germany collapsed, as a distinct literary period as well. Rapid urbanization and industrialization during this era, the impoverishment of the proletariat, and the increasing facelessness and anonymity of city life undermined Poetic Realism's quest for individuation and aesthetic and psychological totality in literature. Social unrest and a sense of spiritual fragmentation led to the flowering of new literary trends during this age. The politically engaged writers turned to naturalism, while symbolism, impressionism, and aestheticism are terms for the intertwined tendencies pursued by more ethereal, inwardly directed souls, particularly the George Circle and the Viennese Modernists. The most recent comprehensive treatment of German literature during the nineteenth-century years of this Wilhelmine Age is Peter Sprengel's *Geschichte der deutschsprachigen Literatur 1870–1900: Von der Reichsgründung bis zur Jahrhundertwende* (1998). The first section of this work provides an overview of the epoch's political, scientific, technological, and intellectual foundations. It opens with an account of the generally enthusiastic response to the Franco-Prussian War on the part of Germany's leading literary figures, though Sprengel notes Raabe's bitter disappointment at the consequences of empire. The work highlights the contrasting sense of trauma in the years of Austria's Dual Monarchy, a trauma stemming from ethnic / linguistic conflicts and the dashed hopes of greater-Germany adherents. He finds the resulting crises in identity and legitimation highly conducive to the emergence of the Young Vienna movement as a creative force around 1890.

Particularly valuable for our purposes is Sprengel's analysis of impressionism on the one hand, and aestheticism and symbolism on the other. I say this because there is a relative paucity of works on these movements in German-speaking lands, a deficit that Ernst Grabovszki's essay in the present volume will no doubt help to correct. Reading Sprengel's analysis makes it clear why critical treatment of the three tendencies in Germany and Austria is a difficult undertaking. He notes that impressionism was not a literary movement per se, but that certain works betray the influence of French impressionist painting. While it is said that impressionism constitutes a subjective counterpoint to naturalism, the Parisian Impressionists maintained close contact with Emile Zola, and, like the French Naturalist, saw objectivity as their highest goal. Thus, Sprengel recommends caution when using the term "impressionistic" in connection with literature, though he notes Hermann Bahr's enthusiastic embrace of a literary impressionism.

Sprengel regards "aestheticism" as the all-embracing term for the epoch's anti-naturalist trends. He finds that the circle of German-language authors engaged with the aesthetic movement, which had strong support in England and France, was relatively small. Its adherents were Stefan George and his circle, Hofmannsthal, and certain Berlin Bohemians and representatives of Young Vienna. He traces the emergence of symbolism in Germany to the influence of Charles Baudelaire's symbol-laden poem "Correspondances," as well as to the hermeticism of Stéphane Mallarmé and Maurice Maeterlinck. Citing a confused essay by Bahr, Sprengel argues that symbolism was generally misunderstood among German literati, even by George, minimizing its impact (113–19). With respect to Young Vienna, a thorough overview of this movement's origins at the end of the nineteenth century is provided by Jens Rieckmann's *Aufbruch in die Moderne: Die Anfänge des Jungen Wien: Österreichische Literatur und Kritik im Fin de Siècle* (1985).

After his discussion of literary movements, Sprengel examines the various institutions of literary life in the last decades of the nineteenth century. The rest of the book, the sections that encompass most of its content, are organized around the following genres: narrative prose and verse epic, drama, lyric poetry, and non-fiction prose. With the exception of the last-named category, each of these sections consists primarily of chapters on how these genres were exemplified by individual writers in Switzerland, Austria, and Germany, respectively. The volume closes with an extensive bibliography of works on the genres, trends, literary life, etc., of the last decades of the nineteenth century.

Naturalism was the most dominant literary tendency at the end of the century in Germany, but before turning our attention to the most useful overview of this period, an examination of two other works which treat turn-of-the-century German literature as a whole is in order, for they contribute unique dimensions toward an understanding of this era. Roy Pascal's *From Naturalism to Expressionism: German Literature and Society 1880–1918* (1973) is an exemplar of cultural studies *avant la lettre*. That is to say, Pascal situates the literature of the period within the broad sociopolitical and cultural nexus that shaped it. One may call this book an early instance of cultural studies because the nexus is as much the focus of Pascal's attention as the literature itself. *From Naturalism to Expressionism,* as its subtitle suggests, treats the Wilhelmine Age as a whole rather than stopping at the century's end. Pascal analyzes such domains as family life, sexuality, increasing polemics against organized religion, nationalism, imperialism, Jewish identity, intellectual directions such as positivism and *Lebensphilosophie,* and how cultural life was differently constellated in the epoch's leading German-speaking cities: Berlin, Munich, Vienna, and Prague. Pascal frequently and cogently utilizes the work of Georg Simmel in order to elucidate the age's intellectual trends. For example, he draws on Simmel in order to illustrate how symbolism and expressionism are strongly linked; adherents of both movements regarded the artist as the guardian of spiritual welfare, maintaining the relatively novel position that "only the artist is without a private interest" (26–27). Pascal's attempts to define literary trends sometimes fall short. For example, he prefers the term "small-town realism" as a substitute for Poetic Realism, and he equates naturalism with "great-city realism." Even with the proviso that "such designations do not mean that writers merely reflect a specific social environment" (124), Pascal's categories would imply that Fontane's Berlin novels do not belong to realism, and that Hauptmann's *Die Weber* is not a work of naturalism. Despite this shortcoming, *From Naturalism to Expressionism* provides an excellent cultural overview of the age.

Deutsche Literatur der Jahrhundertwende (1981), edited by Viktor Žmegač, contains a number of essays that provide broad introductions to the turn of the century and its literary trends. The book's three sections consist of a "panorama" of the epoch, an examination of its social history, and an analysis of its stylistic categories. Among the topics covered are "Heimatkunst," symbolist drama, "Jugendstil," and the Viennese Modernism of Schnitzler and Hofmannsthal. In the introduction, Žmegač notes that the main literary currents associated with the last decades of the nineteenth century developed simultaneously. For this reason, naturalism and impressionism betray similar rhetorical and stylistic ambitions, and this circumstance explains the formal eclecticism found in many works of the period. *Deutsche Literatur der Jahrhundertwende* is, overall, more focused on issues of style and form than *From Naturalism to Expressionism,* and therefore provides a helpful pendant to the latter work in aesthetic matters.

The most cohesive (with respect to form, theory, and style) literary movement in Germany during the Wilhelmine Age was naturalism. Günther Mahal's *Naturalismus* (1996[3]) provides a comprehensive overview of this movement. Mahal traces naturalism's complex historical definitions and diverse applications; for example, the term was used in connection with prehistoric art styles and with the philosophy of the Greek Stoics (16). Most of the book consists of many brief discussions of the central domains important to any literary school: what and who seminally influenced it, its approach to genres, its supporters and critics, its approach to language and style, etc. Particularly illuminating is Mahal's discussion of naturalism's problematic relationship to socialism and social democracy. Given the way Mahal describes the naturalists' stress on individualism and individual achievement, their preference for writing as opposed to direct social engagement, their many internal battles over aesthetic issues, and the fact that they were seen as a conspiratorial group from the outside when, in fact, they were too fractious for any genuinely revolutionary activity, one is reminded of the Young Germany writers as described by Koopmann and Hermand. Mahal himself alludes to the fact that both the naturalists and the "Jungdeutschen" constituted a unity more in the eyes of the external world than from their own perspective (147). Nevertheless, Mahal is able to articulate common elements that allow German naturalism to emerge as a coherent school. For example, he argues that thoroughgoing naturalists deliberately assumed the stance of objective presenters of truth through their precision and self-assumed neutrality. Thus, the naturalist is unconcerned with steering the reader to an "acceptable" interpretation; the reader must proceed from the evidence to draw his or her own conclusions. German naturalists rejected realism's tendency to engage in "amateur speculations" about psychological matters, and did not imbue their heroes with a complex "inner life." Naturalists were primarily interested in the precise delineation of both internal and external "reality," so that individual details and observations, the distillation of a "small slice of reality," were more important to them than the cultivation of broadly drawn concepts (160). In the brief section on genre, Mahal characterizes naturalist lyric as statically descriptive, underscores the emphasis on milieu and discrete scene construction in the movement's imaginative prose, as well as the non-idealistic, quotidian focus and the embrace of social / biological predetermination in its drama, an embrace which works to the detriment of dramatic climax. *Naturalismus* concludes with a somewhat in-depth analysis of several significant works associated with the movement: the lyric anthology *Moderne Dichter-Charaktere* and Arno Holz's poetry collection *Buch der Zeit,* Holz and Johannes Schlaf's *Die papierne Passion,* which defies conventional genre-based categorization, and Hauptmann's drama *Das Friedensfest.*

Navigating one's way through the secondary works devoted to almost an entire century of a nation's literature can be a difficult undertaking. As was indicated at the outset, this critical bibliography was primarily directed toward those seeking a broad acquaintance with German literature from 1830 to the end of the nineteenth century, with its movements, thematic, stylistic, and generic trends, and its prominent individuals. Nevertheless, many of the works discussed will also serve as a starting point for more specialized research. Aptly, perhaps, the most famous phrase in the most famous novel of the seventy or so years under consideration reflects the sentiments of many students of nineteenth-century German literature who are preparing to study for general exams, composing a research paper, or just attempting to attain a comprehensive overview of a rich domain: "Das ist ein *zu* weites Feld," the judgment pronounced at the conclusion of Fontane's *Effi Briest* by the deceased title heroine's father in response to the mother's musings on how they might have prevented her tragic demise. By consulting the relatively few works covered in this essay, one will be able to gain a sense of this broad field without allowing it to seem intimidating in its vastness.

Works Cited

Bernd, Clifford Albrecht. *German Poetic Realism.* Boston: Twayne, 1981.

———. *Poetic Realism in Scandinavia and Central Europe 1820–1895.* Columbia, SC: Camden House, 1995.

Boeschenstein, Hermann. *German Literature of the Nineteenth Century.* New York: St. Martin's Press, 1969.

Borchmeyer, Dieter. *Das Theater Richard Wagners. Idee–Dichtung–Wirkung.* Stuttgart: Reclam, 1982.

Cowen, Roy C. *Der Poetische Realismus. Kommentar zu einer Epoche.* Munich: Winkler, 1985.

Diethe, Carol. *Towards Emancipation: German Women Writers of the Nineteenth Century.* New York: Berghahn, 1998.

Downing, Eric. *Double Exposures: Repetition and Realism in Nineteenth-Century German Fiction.* Stanford: Stanford UP, 2000.

Field, G. Wallis. *A Literary History of Germany: The Nineteenth Century 1830–1890.* London: Benn, 1975.

Hardin, James, and Christoph E. Schweitzer, eds. *German Writers in the Age of Goethe, 1789–1832. Dictionary of Literary Biography.* Vol. 90. Detroit: Gale, 1989.

Hardin, James, and Siegfried Mews, eds. *Nineteenth-Century German Writers to 1840. Dictionary of Literary Biography.* Vol. 133. Detroit: Gale, 1993.

———, eds. *Nineteenth-Century German Writers, 1841–1900. Dictionary of Literary Biography.* Vol. 129. Detroit: Gale, 1993.

Hermand, Jost, ed. *Das Junge Deutschland. Texte und Dokumente.* Stuttgart: Reclam, 1966.

———. *Der deutsche Vormärz. Texte und Dokumente.* Stuttgart: Reclam, 1967.

———. "Jungdeutscher Tempelsturm. Zur Austreibung des Poetischen aus der Literatur." Kruse 65–82.

Holub, Robert C. *Friedrich Nietzsche.* New York: Twayne, 1995.

Kontje, Todd, ed. *A Companion to German Realism 1848–1900.* Rochester: Camden House, 2002.

Koopmann, Helmut. *Das Junge Deutschland: Eine Einführung.* Darmstadt: Wissenschaftliche Buchgesellschaft, 1993.

Kruse, Joseph A., and Bernd Kortländer, eds. *Das Junge Deutschland: Kolloquium zum 150. Jahrestag des Verbots vom 10. Dezember 1835.* Hamburg: Hoffmann und Campe, 1987.

Mahal, Günther. *Naturalismus.* 3rd ed. (1st ed. 1982). Munich: Fink, 1996.

Martini, Fritz. *Deutsche Literatur im bürgerlichen Realismus* 1848–1898. 4th ed. (1st ed. 1962). Stuttgart: Metzler, 1981.

Neubuhr, Elfriede, ed. *Begriffsbestimmung des literarischen Biedermeier.* Darmstadt: Wissenschaftliche Buchgesellschaft, 1974.

Olsen, Richard E. *Karl Marx.* Boston: Twayne, 1978.

Pascal, Roy. *From Naturalism to Expressionism: German Literature and Society 1880–1918.* London: Weidenfeld and Nicolson, 1973.

Raphael, Robert. *Richard Wagner.* New York: Twayne, 1969.

Rieckmann, Jens. *Aufbruch in die Moderne. Die Anfänge des Jungen Wien: Österreichische Literatur und Kritik im Fin de Siècle.* Königstein / Ts.: Athenäum, 1985.

Ritchie, J. M., ed. *Periods in German Literature.* N.p.: Dufour, 1967.

Sagarra, Eda. *Tradition and Revolution: German Literature and Society 1830–1890.* London: Weidenfeld and Nicolson, 1971.

Sengle, Friedrich. *Biedermeierzeit. Deutsche Literatur im Spannungsfeld zwischen Restauration und Revolution 1815–1848.* 3 vols. Stuttgart: Metzler, 1971–1980.

Sprengel, Peter. *Geschichte der deutschsprachigen Literatur 1870–1900. Von der Reichsgründung bis zur Jahrhundertwende.* Munich: Beck, 1998.

Stein, Peter. *Epochenproblem "Vormärz" (1815–1848).* Stuttgart: Metzler, 1974.

Vivian, Kim, Frank Tobin, and Richard H. Lawson, eds. *Von der deutschen Klassik bis zum Naturalismus: An Anthology of German Literature, Volume 2.* Prospect Heights, IL: Waveland, 1998.

Wiese, Benno von, ed. *Deutsche Dichter des 19. Jahrhunderts: Ihr Leben und Werk.* Berlin: Schmidt, 1969.

Zanuso, Billa. *The Young Freud: The Origins of Psychoanalysis in Late Nineteenth-Century Viennese Culture.* Oxford: Blackwell, 1986.

Žmegač, Viktor, ed. *Deutsche Literatur der Jahrhundertwende.* Königstein / Ts.: Hain, 1981.

List of Primary Sources

Compiled by Thomas Spencer

Alexis, Willibald (Georg Wilhelm Heinrich Häring). *Walladmor,* 1824. Translated anonymously by Thomas de Quincey as *Walladmor.* 2 vols. London: Taylor & Hessey, 1825.

———. *Der Roland von Berlin,* 1840. Translated by W. A. G. as *The Burgomaster of Berlin.* 3 vols. London: Saunders & Otley, 1843.

———. *Der falche Waldemar,* 1842.

———. *Ruhe ist die erste Bürgerpflicht,* 1852.

Anzengruber, Ludwig. *Der Pfarrer von Kirchfeld,* 1870.

———. *Der Meineidbauer,* 1871. Translated by Adolf Busse as *The Farmer Forsworn,* in *The German Classics of the Nineteenth and Twentieth Centuries,* vol. 16, edited by Kuno Francke and W. G. Howard. New York: German Publication Society, 1914.

———. *Die Kreuzschreiber,* 1872.

———. *Die G'wissenswurm,* 1874.

———. *Das vierte Gebot,* 1878.

———. *Der Sternsteinhof,* 1885.

Auerbach, Berthold. *Spinoza: Ein historischer Roman,* 1837. Translated by E. Nicholson as *Spinoza: A Novel.* 2 vols. Leipzig: Tauchnitz; London: Low, Marston, Searle & Rivington, 1882.

———. *Dichter und Kaufmann: Ein Lebensgemälde,* 1840. Translated by Charles T. Brooks as *Poet and Merchant: A Picture of Life from the Time of Moses Mendelssohn.* New York: Holt, 1877.

———. *Schwarzwälder Dorfsgeschichten,* 1843. 2 vols. Excerpts translated by Meta Taylor as *Village Tales from the Black Forest.* 2 vols. London: Bogue, 1846–47. First complete edition in English translated by Charles Goepp as *Black Forest Village Stories.* New York: Leypolt & Holt, 1869.

———. *Die Frau Professorin,* 1846. Translated by Maria Howeitt as *The Professor's Lady.* New York: Harper, 1850.

———. *Schwarzwälder Dorfgeschichten: Neue Folge,* 1849. Mannheim: Bassermann, 1849.

———. *Barfüßele,* 1856. Translated by Edward H. Wehnert as *The Barefooted Maiden.* London: Low, 1857.

Auerbach, Berthold. *Joseph im Schnee,* 1860. Translated anonymously as *Joseph in the Snow.* New York & London: Lovell, 1867.

———. *Das Landhaus am Rhein,* 1869. Translated by James Davis as *The Villa on the Rhine.* New York: Leypoldt & Holt, 1869.

Bernstein, Elsa. *Wir drei,* 1891.

Büchner, Georg. *Der Hessische Landbote,* 1834.

———. *Dantons Tod,* 1835.

———. *Lenz,* 1839.

———. *Leonce und Lena,* 1842.

———. *Woyzeck,* 1877.

Note: All of these works translated by Henry Schmidt in *Complete Works and Letters.* German Library. Vol. 28. New York: Continuum, 1986.

Deutscher Musenalmanach. Eds. Adalbert v. Chamisso, Gustav Schwab und Franz von Gaudy. 1833–39.

Deutscher Musenalmanach. Eds. Theodor Echtermeyer und Arnold Ruge. 1840–41.

Dingelstedt, Franz. *Lieder eines kosmopolitschen Nachtwächters,* 1842.

Droste-Hülshoff, Annette von. *Ledwina,* 1824.

———. *Des Arztes Vermächtnis,* 1838.

———. *Die Judenbuche,* 1842. Translated by Lionel and Doris Thomas as *The Jew's Beech* in *Novellas of Realism,* vol. 1. New York: Continuum, 1989.

———. *Gedichte,* 1844. Selected poems translated as *Poems* [by] *Annette von Droste-Hülshoff.* Ed. Margaret Atkinson. London: Oxford UP, 1964.

———. *Das geistliche Jahr,* 1851.

Ebner-Eschenbach, Marie von. *Das Gemeindekind,* 1887. Translated by Lynne Tatlock as *Their Pavel.* Columbia, SC: Camden House, 1996.

———. *Lotte, die Uhrmacherin,* 1880.

Eichendorff, Joseph Freiherr von. *Aus dem Leben eines Taugenichts,* 1826. Translated by F. G. Nichols as *Life of a Good-For-Nothing.* London: Hesperus, 2003.

———. *Gedichte,* 1837. Selected poems translated in *The Penguin Book of German Verse.* Ed. Leonard Forster. Baltimore: Penguin, 1957.

Erlanger Musenalmanach. Ed. Friedrich Rückert. 1838.

Fallersleben, Hoffmann von. *Unpolitische Lieder,* 1841.

Feuerbach, Ludwig. *Grundsätze der Philosophie der Zukunft,* 1843. Translated and abridged by Zawar Hanfi as *Principles of the Philosophy of the Future* in *German Socialist Philosophy.* New York: Continuum, 1997.

Fontane, Theodor. *Gedichte,* 1851. Enlarged editions in 1875, 1889, 1891, and 1898.

———. *Vor dem Sturm: Roman aus dem Winter 1812 auf 13,* 1878. Translated by R. J. Hollingdale as *Before the Storm: A Novel of the Winter of 1812–13.* Oxford: Oxford UP, 1985.

Fontane, Theodor. *L'Adultera*, 1880. Translated by Gabriele Annan as *The Woman Taken in Adultery*. Chicago: Chicago UP, 1979.

———. *Schach von Wuthenow*, 1882. Translated by E. M. Valk as *A Man of Honor*. New York: Ungar, 1975.

———. *Cécile*, 1887. Translated by Stanley Radcliff as *Cecile*. London: Angel, 1993.

———. *Irrungen Wirrungen*, 1888. Translated by William L. Zwiebel as *Delusions, Confusions* in *Delusions, Confusions; and, The Poggenpuhl Family*. Ed. Peter Demetz. New York: Continuum, 1989.

———. *Stine*, 1890. Translated by Harry Steinhauer as *Stine* in *Twelve German Novellas*. Berkeley: U of California P, 1977.

———. *Quitt*, 1891.

———. *Unwiederbringlich*, 1891. Translated by Douglas Parmée as *Beyond Recall*. London: Oxford UP, 1964.

———. *Frau Jenny Treibel oder Wo sich Herz zu Herzen findt*, 1893. Translated by Ulf Zimmerman as *Jenny Treibel* in *Short Novels and Other Writings*. Ed. Peter Demetz. New York: Continuum, 1982.

———. *Effi Briest*, 1895. Translated by William A. Cooper as *Effi Briest* in *The German Classics of the Nineteenth and Twentieth Centuries*, vol. 12, edited by Kuno Francke and William Guild Howard. New York: German Publications Society, 1914.

———. *Die Poggenpuhls*, 1895–96. Translated by Gabriele Annan as *The Poggenpuhl Family* in *Delusions, Confusions; and, The Poggenpuhl Family*. Ed. Peter Demetz. New York: Continuum, 1989.

———. *Der Stechlin*, 1897–98. Translated by William Zwiebel as *The Stechlin*. Columbia, SC: Camden House, 1995.

François, Louise von. *Die letzte Reckenbürgerin*, 1871. Translated by Tiiu Laane as *The Last von Reckenburg*. Columbia, SC: Camden House, 1995.

Freiligrath, Ferdinand. *Ein Glaubensbekenntnis*, 1844.

———. *Gedichte*, 1838, enlarged 1839. Translated by Käthe Freiligrath-Kroeker as *Poems from the German*. London: Low, Marston; Leipzig: Tauchnitz, 1869.

———. *Ça ira*, 1846.

Freytag, Gustav. *Soll und Haben*, 1855. Translated by L. C. Cummings as *Debit and Credit*. New York & London: Harper, 1855.

Frühlingsalmanach. Ed. Nikolaus Lenau. 1835–36.

Geibel, Emanuel. *Gedichte*, 1840. Enlarged 1843. Select poems translated by Henry John Dayrell Stowe in *Adaptations from the German of Emanuel Geibel, by the Late Henry John Dayrell Stowe*. London: Bowden, Hudson, 1879.

Gerstäcker, Friedrich. *Nach Amerika!*, 1855.

———. *Die Flußpiraten des Mississippi*, 1848. Translated as *The Pirates of the Mississippi*. London: Routledge, 1856.

Gerstäcker, Friedrich. *Die Regulatoren in Arkansas,* 1845. Chapters 1–13 translated anonymously as *The Regulators of Arkansas.* New York: Dick & Fitzgerald, 1857. Chapters 13–25 translated anonymously as *Bill Johnson; or, The Outlaws of Arkansas.* New York: Dick & Fitzgerald, 1857. Translated as *The Feathered Arrow; or, The Forest Rangers.* London: Routledge, 1857.

———. *Gold!* 1857–58.

———. *In Amerika: Amerikanisches Lebensbild aus neuer Zeit. Im Anschluß an "Nach Amerika!,"* 1872.

Gotthelf, Jeremias. *Wie Uli der Knecht glücklich wird: Eine Gabe für Dienstboten und Meisterleute,* 1841. Revised as *Uli der Knecht: Ein Volksbuch,* 1846. Translated by Julia Firth, revised by John Ruskin as *Ulric the Farm Servant: A Story of the Bernese Lowlands.* Orpington: Allen, 1886; New York: Dutton, 1907.

———. *Die schwarze Spinne,* 1842. Translated by B. O. Adefope as *The Black Spider.* London: Atlanta, 1992.

———. *Geld und Geist oder Die Versöhnung,* 1843–44. Translated anonymously as *Wealth and Welfare.* London & New York: A. Strahan, 1866.

———. *Wie Anne Bäbi Jowäger haushaltet, und wie es ihm mit dem Doktern geht,* 1843–44.

———. *Uli der Pächter: Ein Volksbuch,* 1849.

———. *Käthi die Großmutter,* 1846. Translated by L. G. Smith as *The Story of an Alpine Valley: or, Katie the Grandmother.* London: Gibbings, 1896.

Grabbe, Christian Dietrich. *Herzog Theodor von Gotland,* 1827.

———. *Marius und Sulla,* 1827.

———. *Scherz, Satire, Ironie und tiefere Bedeutung,* 1827. Translated by Maurice Edwards as *Jest, Satire, Irony and Deeper Significance: A Comedy in Three Acts.* New York: Ungar, 1966.

———. *Die Hohenstaufen,* 1829–30.

———. *Don Juan und Faust,* 1829. Translated by Maurice Edwards as *Don Juan and Faust* in *The Theater of Don Juan: A Collection of Plays and Views, 1630–1963.* Ed. Oscar Mandel. Lincoln: U of Nebraska P, 1963.

———. *Napoleon oder Die hundert Tage,* 1831. Excerpts translated by Max Spalter as *Napoleon; or, The Hundred Days* in *Brecht's Tradition.* Baltimore: Johns Hopkins UP, 1967.

———. *Hannibal,* 1835.

———. *Die Hermannsschlacht,* 1838.

Grillparzer, Franz. *Die Ahnfrau,* 1817. Translated by Letitia Elizabeth Landon as *The Ancestress: A Dramatic Sketch* in *The Venetian Bracelet, The Lost Pleiad, A History of the Lyre, and other Poems.* London: Longman, Rees, Orme, Brown & Green, 1828.

———. *Sappho,* 1818. Translated by John Bramsen as *Sapho.* London: Black, 1820.

Grillparzer, Franz. *Das Goldene Vlies*, 1821. Translated by Arthur Burkhard as *The Golden Fleece*. Yarmouth Port, MA: Register, 1942. The third part of the work, *Medea*, translated by F. W. Thurstan and Sidnez A. Wittmann as *Medea*. London: Nisbet, 1879.

———. *König Ottokars Glück und Ende*, 1825. Translated by Henry Stevens as *King Ottocar's Rise and Fall* in *Nineteenth Century German Plays*. New York: Continuum, 1990.

———. *Ein treuer Diener seines Herrn*, 1828. Translated by Arthur Burkhard as *A Faithful Servant of his Master*. Yarmouth, MA: Register Press, 1941.

———. *Des Meeres und Der Liebe Wellen*, 1831. Translated by Henry Stevens as *Hero and Leander*. Yarmouth Port, Mass.: Register, 1938.

———. *Der Traum, ein Leben*, 1834. Translated by Henry Stevens as *A Dream is Life*. Yarmouth Port, MA: Register Press, 1946.

———. *Weh dem, der lügt*, 1838. Translated by Henry Stevens as *Thou Shalt Not Lie*. Yarmouth Port, MA: Register Press, 1939.

———. *Der arme Spielmann*, 1848 (1847). Translated by A. Remy as *The Poor Musician* in *The German Classics of the Nineteenth and Twentieth Centuries*, vol. 6, edited by Kuno Francke and William Guild Howard. New York: German Publication Society, 1913.

———. *Die Jüdin von Toledo*, 1872. Translated by George Henry Danton and Annina P. Danton as *The Jewess of Toledo* in *The German Classics of the Nineteenth and Twentieth Centuries*, vol. 6, edited by Kuno Francke and William Guild Howard. New York: German Publication Society, 1913.

———. *Ein Bruderzwist in Habsburg*, 1872. Translated by Arthur Burkhard as *Family Strife in Habsburg*. Yarmouth Port, MA: Register Press, 1940.

———. *Libussa*, 1872. Translated by Henry Stevens as *Libussa*. Yarmouth Port, MA: Register, 1941.

Grün, Anastasius. *Spaziergänge eines Wiener Poeten*, 1831.

Gutzkow, Karl. *Briefe eines Narren an eine Närrin*, 1832.

———. *Wally, die Zweiflerin*, 1835. Translated by Ruth-Ellen Boetcher-Joeres as *Wally the Skeptic*. Bern: Herbert Lang, 1974.

———. *Das Urbild des Tartüffe*, 1846.

———. *Zopf und Schwert*, 1844. Translated by Grace Isabel Colbron as *Sword and Queue* in *The German Classics of the Nineteenth and Twentieth Centuries*, vol. 7, edited by Kuno Francke and William Guild Howard. New York: German Publication Society, 1914.

———. *Uriel Acosta*, 1846. Translated by M. M. as *Uriel Acosta*. New York: Ellinger, 1860.

———. *Die Ritter vom Geiste*, 1850–51.

———. *Der Zauberer von Rom*, 1858–61.

Halbe, Max. *Jugend*, 1893. Translated by Sara Tracy Barrows as *Youth*. Garden City, NY: Doubleday, 1916.

———. *Der Strom*, 1903.

Hauptmann, Gerhart. *Bahnwärter Thiel,* 1888. Translated by A. S. Seltzer as *Flagman Thiel* in *Great German Short Novels and Stories,* edited by Bennett A. Cerf. New York: Huebsch, 1914. Reprinted in *German Novellas of Realism.* Vol. 2. Ed. Jeffrey Sammons. New York: Continuum, 1989.

———. *Vor Sonnenaufgang,* 1889. Translated by Peter Bauland as *Before Daybreak* in *Gerhart Hauptmann: Plays.* New York: Continuum, 1994.

———. *Das Friedensfest: Eine Familienkatastrophe,* 1890. Translated by Janet Achurch and C. E. Wheeler as *The Coming of Peace: A Family Catastrophe.* Chicago: Sergel, 1900.

———. *Einsame Menschen,* 1891. Translated by Mary Morison as *Lonely Lives.* New York: De Witt, 1898.

———. *Die Weber,* 1892. Translated by Theodore H. Lustig as *The Weavers* in *Gerhart Hauptmann: Plays.* New York: Continuum, 1994.

———. *Der Biberpelz,* 1893. Translated by Theodore H. Lustig as *The Beaver Coat* in *Gerhart Hauptmann: Plays.* New York: Continuum, 1994.

———. *Hannele Matterns Himmelfahrt,* 1893. Translated by Charles Henry Meltzer as *Hannele.* New York: Doubleday, Page, 1908.

———. *Florian Geyer,* 1896. Translated by Bayard Quincy Morgan as *Florian Geyer* in *The Dramatic Works of Gerhart Hauptmann,* edited by Ludwig Lewisohn. Vol. 9. New York: Viking, 1929.

———. *Fuhrmann Henschel,* 1898. Translated by Marion A. Redlich as *Drayman Henschel.* Chicago: Dramatic Publishing Co., 1910.

———. *Michael Kramer,* 1900. Translated by Ludwig Lewisohn as *Michael Kramer* in *The Dramatic Works of Gerhart Hauptmann.* Ed. Ludwig Lewisohn. Vol. 5. New York: Huebsch, 1916.

———. *Rose Bernd,* 1903. Translated by Ludwig Lewisohn as *Rosa Bernd* in *The Dramatic Works of Gerhart Hauptmann.* Ed. Ludwig Lewisohn. Vol. 2. New York: Huebsch, 1913.

———. *Die Ratten,* 1911. Translated by Ludwig Lewisohn as *The Rats* in *The Dramatic Works of Gerhart Hauptmann.* Ed. Ludwig Lewisohn. Vol. 2. New York: Huebsch, 1913.

———. *Gabriel Schillings Flucht,* 1912. Translated by Ludwig Lewisohn as *Gabriel Schilling's Flight* in *The Dramatic Works of Gerhart Hauptmann.* Ed. Ludwig Lewisohn. Vol. 6. New York: Huebsch, 1916.

Hebbel, Friedrich. *Judith,* 1840. Translated by Marion Sonnenfeld as *Judith.* In *Three Plays.* Lewisburg, PA: Bucknell UP, 1974.

———. *Genoveva,* 1843.

———. *Maria Magdalene,* 1844. Translated by Paul Bernard Thomas as *Maria Magdalena* in *The German Classics of the Nineteenth and Twentieth Centuries,* vol. 9, edited by Kuno Francke and William Guild Howard. New York: German Publication Society, 1914.

———. "Mein Wort über das Drama!" 1843.

———. *Der Diamant,* 1847.

Hebbel, Friedrich. *Herodes und Mariamne,* 1849. Translated by Marion Sonnenfeld as *Herod and Mariamne.* In *Three Plays.* Lewisburg, PA: Bucknell UP, 1974.

————. *Agnes Bernauer,* 1852. Translated by Loueen Pattee, adapted by Hannelore Spencer as *Agnes Bernauer* in *Nineteenth Century German Plays.* Ed. Egon Schwarz. New York: Continuum, 1990.

————. *Gyges und sein Ring,* 1856. Translated by Marion Sonnenfeld as *Gyges and his Ring.* In *Three Plays.* Lewisburg, PA: Bucknell UP, 1974.

————. *Gedichte,* 1857.

————. *Mutter und Kind,* 1859.

————. *Die Nibelungen,* 1861. Translated by G. H. McCall as *The Niebelungs.* London: Siegle, 1903.

————. *Demetrius,* 1864.

Heine, Heinrich. *Harzreise,* 1824. Translated by Frederic Wood and adapted by Robert Holub and Martha Humphreys as *The Harz Journey* in *Heinrich Heine: Poetry and Prose.* New York: Continuum, 1982.

————. *Ideen. Das Buch Le Grand,* 1826. Translated by Frederic Wood and adapted by Robert Holub and Martha Humphreys as *Ideas — Book Le Grand* in *Heinrich Heine: Poetry and Prose.* New York: Continuum, 1982.

————. *Buch der Lieder,* 1827.

————. *Zur Geschichte der Religion und Philosophie in Deutschland.* 183?. Translated by Helen Mustard as *Concerning the History of Religion and Philosophy in Germany.* In *The Romantic School and Other Essays.* New York: Continuum, 1985.

————. *Die romantische Schule,* 1835. Translated by Robert Holub as *The Romantic School.* In *The Romantic School and other Essays.* New York: Continuum, 1985.

————. *Florentinische Nächte,* 1836. Translated as *Florentine Nights* in *The Works of Heinrich Heine.* Vol. 1. London: Heinemann, 1891–1905; New York: Dutton, 1906.

————. *Der Rabbi von Bacharach,* 1840. Translated as *The Rabbi of Bacharach* in *The Works of Heinrich Heine.* Vol. 1. London: Heinemann, 1891–1905; New York: Dutton, 1906.

————. *Atta Troll. Ein Sommernachtstraum,* 1843.

————. *Deutschland. Ein Wintermärchen,* 1844.

————. *Neue Gedichte,* 1844.

————. *Romanzero,* 1851.

————. Hal Draper, translator. *The Complete Poetry of Heinrich Heine.* Cambridge, MA: Suhrkamp/Insel, 1982.

Herwegh, Georg. *Gedichte eines Lebendigen,* 1841.

————. *Einundzwanzig Bogen aus der Schweiz,* 1843.

Heyse, Paul. *L'Arrabbiata,* 1855. Translated by G. H. Kingsley as *La Rabbiata* in *Four Phases of Love.* London: Routledge, 1857.

Holz, Arno. *Das Buch der Zeit,* 1884. Revised 1886, 1892, 1905, 1921.

———. *Papa Hamlet,* 1889. (with Johannes Schlaf)

———. *Die Familie Selicke,* 1890. (with Johannes Schlaf)

———. *Phantasus,* 1898–99. Revised 1913, 1916.

———. *Die Blechschmiede,* 1902. Revised 1917, 1921.

Immerman, Karl Leberecht. *Merlin. Eine Mythe,* 1832.

———. *Die Epigonen: Familienmemoiren in neuen Büchern,* 1836.

———. *Münchhausen: Eine Geschichte in Arabesken,* 1838–39.

Keller, Gottfried. *Gedichte,* 1846.

———. *Neuere Gedichte,* 1851.

———. *Der grüne Heinrich,* 1854–55. Revised edition, 1879–80. Translated by A. M. Holt as *Green Henry.* London: Calder, 1960; New York: Grove Press, 1960.

———. *Die Leute von Seldwyla,* 1856. Enlarged edition, 1874. Excerpts translated by Wolf von Schierbrand as *Seldwyla Folks: Three Singular Tales by the Swiss Poet Gottfried Keller.* New York: Brentano's, 1919. Includes "Three Decent Combmakers," "Dietegen," "Romeo and Juliet of the Village." Selections translated in *Gottfried Keller: Stories.* Ed. Frank G. Ryder. New York: Continuum, 1982. Includes "The Three Righteous Combmakers," translated by Robert Browning; "A Village Romeo and Juliet" translated by Paul Bernard Thomas and adapted by Frank Ryder; "Mirror, the Cat," translated by Robert Browning; "Clothes Make the Man," translated by Harry Steinhauer; "The Lost Smile," translated by Frank Ryder.

———. *Sieben Legenden,* 1872. Translated by Martin Wyness as *Seven Legends.* London & Glasgow: Gowans & Gray, 1911. Selections translated in *Gottfried Keller: Stories.* Ed. Frank G. Ryder. New York: Continuum, 1982. Includes "The Virgin as Knight" and "The Virgin and the Nun," translated by Robert Browning.

———. *Züricher Novellen,* 1878. "Das Fähnlein der sieben Aufrechten" translated by B. Q. Morgan as "The Banner of the Upright Seven" in *Gottfried Keller: Stories.* Ed. Frank G. Ryder. New York: Continuum, 1982.

———. *Das Sinngedicht,* 1881.

———. *Martin Salander,* 1886. Translated by Kenneth Halwas as *Martin Salander.* London: Calder, 1964.

Kühne, Ferdinand Gustav. *Eine Quarantäne im Irrenhaus,* 1835.

Kürnberger, Ferdinand. *Der Amerika-Müde,* 1855.

Laube, Heinrich. *Das Junge Europa,* 1833–37. Comprises *Die Poeten,* 1833; *Die Krieger,* 1837; *Die Bürger,* 1837.

———. *Reisenovellen,* 1834–36.

———. *Die Karlsschüler,* 1847.

Lenau, Nikolaus. *Gedichte,* 1832. Selections translated in the *Penguin Book of German Verse.* Ed. Leonard Forster. Baltimore: Penguin, 1957.

———. *Polenlieder,* 1832–35.

———. *Faust: Ein Gedicht,* 1835.

Lenau, Nikolaus. *Waldlieder,* 1843.

Lewald, Fanny. *Jenny,* 1843. *Prinz Louis Ferdinand,* 1849. Translated by Linda Rogols-Siegel as *Prinz Louis Ferdinand.* Lewiston, NY: Mellon, 1988.

Liliencron, Detlev von. *Adjutantenritte und andere Gedichte,* 1883.

———. *Poggfred,* 1896.

Ludwig, Otto. *Der Erbförster,* 1853–54. Translated by Paula Green as *The Forest Warden.* Boston: Badger, 1913.

———. *Die Makkabäer,* 1853–54.

———. *Zwischen Himmel und Erde,* 1856. Translated and condensed by Muriel Almon as *Between Heaven and Earth.* New York: Ungar, 1965.

Mann, Thomas. *Buddenbrooks,* 1900. Translated by John Woods as *Buddenbrooks.* New York: Knopf, 1994.

Marx, Karl. *Deutsche Ideologie,* 1845–46. Translated as *The German Ideology.* Amherst, NY: Prometheus Books, 1998.

———. *Manifest der Kommunistischen Partei,* 1848. Translated as *Manifesto of the Communist Party.* In *The Marx-Engels Reader.* Ed. Robert C. Tucker. 2nd ed. New York: Norton, 1978.

———. *Die großen Männer des Exils,* 1852.

———. *Der 18. Brumaire des Louis Bonaparte,* 1852. Selections translated as *The Eighteenth Brumaire of Louis Bonaparte.* In *The Marx-Engels Reader.* Ed. Robert C. Tucker. 2nd ed. New York: Norton 1978.

Meyer, Conrad Ferdinand. *Huttens letzte Tage,* 1871; enlarged edition, 1881; revised edition, 1884.

———. *Georg Jenatsch,* 1874. Translated by David B. Dickens as *Jürg Jenatsch* in *The Complete Narrative Prose of Conrad Ferdinand Meyer.* Lewisburg, PA: Bucknell UP, 1976.

———. *Der Heilige,* 1879–80. Translated by M. V. Wendheim as *Thomas à Becket, the Saint.* Leipzig: Haessel, 1885.

———. *Gedichte,* 1882; enlarged 1887, 1891, 1892. Selections translated by Charles Wharton Stork and Margarete Münsterberg in *The German Classics of the Nineteenth and Twentieth Centuries,* vol. 14, edited by Kuno Francke and William Guild Howard. New York: German Publication Society, 1914.

———. *Kleine Novellen,* 1882–83.

———. *Die Hochzeit des Mönches,* 1883–84. Translated by Sarah Holland Adams as *The Monk's Wedding.* Boston: Cupples & Hurd, 1887.

———. *Die Richterin,* 1885. Translated by Marion W. Sonnenfeld as *The Judge* in *The Complete Narrative Prose of Conrad Ferdinand Meyer.* Lewisburg, PA: Bucknell UP, 1976.

Meyer, Conrad Ferdinand. *Die Versuchung des Pescara,* 1887. Translated by Clara Bell as *The Tempting of Pescara.* New York: Gottsberger, 1890.

———. *Angela Borgia,* 1891. Translated by Marion W. Sonnenfeld as *Angela Borgia* in *The Complete Narrative Prose of Conrad Ferdinand Meyer.* Lewisburg, PA: Bucknell UP, 1976.

Mörike, Eduard. *Maler Nolten,* 1832. Translated by Raleigh Whitinger as *Nolten the Painter.* Rochester, NY: Camden House, forthcoming 2005.

———. *Gedichte,* 1838; enlarged 1848, 1856, 1867. Translated by Norah K. Cruickshank and Gilbert F. Cunningham as *Poems.* London: Methuen, 1959. Selections translated by David Luke and Gibert McKay in *Mozart's Journey to Prague* [*and*] *Selected Poems.* London: Libris, 1997.

———. *Idylle vom Bodensee oder Fischer Martin und die Glackendiebe,* 1846.

———. *Das Stuttgarter Hutzelmännlein,* 1853.

———. *Mozart auf der Reise nach Prag,* 1856. Translated by Florence Leonard as *Mozart's Journey from Vienna to Prague.* Philadelphia: Presser, 1897. Translated by David Luke as *Mozart's Journey to Prague* in *Mozart's Journey to Prague* [*and*] *Selected Poems.* London: Libris, 1997.

Selected poems translated by Christopher Middleton in *Selected Poems.* Chicago: U of Chicago P, 1972.

Mundt, Theodor. *Moderne Lebenswirren,* 1834.

———. *Madonna,* 1835.

———. *Die Kunst der deutschen Prosa,* 1837.

Nestroy, Johann. *Der böse Geist Lumpacivagabundus oder Das liederliche Kleeblatt,* 1835.

———. *Zu ebener Erde und erster Stock oder die Launen des Glückes,* 1838.

———. *Der Talisman,* 1843. Translated by Robert Harrison and Katharina Wilson as *The Talisman.* In *Nineteenth Century German Plays.* Ed. Egon Schwarz. New York: Continuum, 1990.

———. *Einen Jux will er sich machen,* 1844. Translated anonymously as *The Matchmaker.* New York: French 1957.

———. *Der Unbedeutende,* 1849.

Nietzsche, Friedrich. "Der Fall Wagner," 1888. Translated by Walter Kaufmann as *The Case of Wagner.* New York: Vintage, 1967.

———. *Die Geburt der Tragödie aus dem Geiste der Musik,* 1872. Translated by Ronald Spiers as *The Birth of Tragedy.* Cambridge: Cambridge UP, 1999.

———. "Ueber Wahrheit und Lüge im außermoralischen Sinn," 1873. Translated by Maximilian Mügge as "On Truth and Falsity in Their Extramoral Sense." In *Friedrich Nietzsche: Philosophical Writings.* Eds. Reinhold Grimm and Caroline Molina y Vedia. New York: Continuum, 1995.

———. *Ecce Homo.* Translated by Walter Kaufmann. In *On the Genealogy of Morals & Ecce Homo.* New York: Vintage, 1967.

Nietzsche, Friedrich. *Menschliches, Allzu menschliches,* 1878. Translated by R. J. Hollingdale as *Human, All Too Human.* Cambridge: Cambridge UP, 1986.

———. "Richard Wagner in Bayreuth," 1876. Selections translated by Anthony Ludovici as *Richard Wagner in Bayreuth.* In *Friedrich Nietzsche: Philosophical Writings.* Eds. Reinhold Grimm and Caroline Molina y Vedia. New York: Continuum, 1995.

———. *Zur Genealogie der Moral,* 1887. Translated by Walter Kaufmann. In *On the Genealogy of Morals & Ecce Homo.* New York: Vintage, 1967.

Platen-Hallermünde, August Graf von. *Frühlingslieder,* 1835. Selected poems translated by Edwin Morgan in *Platen: Selected Poems.* West Linton, Peebles, Scotland: Castlelaw Press, 1978.

Prutz, Robert. *Rheinlieder,* n.d.

Raabe, Wilhelm. *Else von der Tanne,* 1865. Translated by James C. O'Flaherty and Janet K. King as *Elsa of the Forest.* Tuscaloosa: U of Alabama P, 1972.

———. *Die Chronik der Sperlingsgasse,* 1857.

———. *Abu Telfan oder Die Heimkehr vom Mondgebirge,* 1868. Translated by Sophie Delffs as *Abu Telfan; or, The Return from the Mountains of the Moon.* London: Chapman & Hall, 1881.

———. *Drei Federn,* 1863.

———. *Die Leute aus dem Walde, ihre Sterne, Wege, und Schicksale,* 1863.

———. *Der Hungerpastor,* 1864. Translated by Arnold Congdon as *The Hunger-Pastor.* London: Chapman & Hall, 1885.

———. *Der Schüdderump,* 1870.

———. *Pfisters Mühle,* 1884.

———. *Das Odfeld,* 1888. Translated by Michael Ritterson as *The Odin Field.* Rochester, NY: Camden House, 2001.

———. *Stopfkuchen: Eine See- und Mordgeschichte,* 1891. Translated by John Woods and Barker Fairley as *Tubby Schaumann* in *Wilhelm Raabe: Novels.* Ed. Volkmar Sander. New York: Continuum, 1983.

———. *Die Akten des Vogelsangs,* 1896.

———. *Hastenbeck,* 1899.

Raimund, Ferdinand. *Der Diamant des Geisterkönigs,* 1824. Translated by Edmund Kimball as *The Diamond of the Spirit King.* New York: Lang, 1996.

———. *Das Mädchen aus der Feenwelt oder Der Bauer als Millionär,* 1826.

———. *Der Alpenkönig und der Menschenfeind,* 1828. Translated by John Baldwin Buckstone as *The King of the Alps.* London: T. H. Lacy, 1831.

———. *Der Verschwender,* 1834. Translated by Erwin Tramer as *The Spendthrift.* New York: Ungar, 1949.

Reuter, Fritz. *Läuschen un Rimels,* 1853.

———. *Kein Hüsung,* 1858.

Rückert, Friedrich. *Haus- und Jahrslieder,* 1832–38.

Sealsfield, Charles (Carl Postl). *Die Prärie am Jacinto,* n.d.

———. *Das Cajütenbuch oder Nationale Charakteristiken,* 1841. Translated by C. F. Mersch as *The Cabin Book; or Sketches of Life in Texas.* New York: Winchester, 1844; translated by Sarah Powell as *The Cabin Book; or, National Characteristics.* London: Ingram, Cooke, 1852.

Spielhagen, Friedrich. *Problematische Naturen,* 1861–63. Translated by Maximilian Schele De Vere as *Problematic Characters.* New York: Leypoldt & Holt, 1869.

———. *Die von Hohenstein,* 1864. Translated by Maximilian Schele De Vere as *The Hohensteins.* New York: Leypoldt & Holt, 1870.

———. *In Reih' und Glied,* 1867.

———. *Hammer und Amboß,* 1869. Translated by William Hand Browne as *Hammer and Anvil.* New York: Leypoldt & Holt, 1870.

———. *Sturmflut,* 1877. Translated by S. E. A. H. Stephenson as *The Breaking of the Storm.* London: Bentley, 1877.

———. *Platt Land,* 1879.

———. *Ein neuer Pharoah,* 1889.

———. *Sonntagskind,* 1893.

———. *Zum Zeitvertreib,* 1897.

———. *Frei geboren,* 1900.

———. *Opfer,* 1900.

Stifter, Adalbert. *Studien,* 1844–1850. Includes *Die Mappe meines Urgroßvaters,* 1841–42, translated by Maria Norman as *My Great Grandfather's Notebook* in vol. 1 of *Rural Life in Austria and Hungary.* London: Bentley, 1850. *Abdias, Brigitta,* and *Der Waldsteig (The Forest Path)* translated by Helen Watanabe-O'Kelly. London: Angel, 1990.

———. *Bunte Steine,* 1853. Preface, *Granit (Granite)* translated by Jeffrey Sammons; *Kalkstein (Limestone)* translated by David Luke in *German Novels of Realism,* vol. 1. New York: Continuum, 1989.

———. *Der Nachsommer,* 1857. Translated by Wendell Frye as *Indian Summer.* New York: Lang, 1985.

———. *Witiko,* 1865–67.

———. *Erzählungen,* 1869.

Stirner, Max. *Der Einzige und sein Eigentum,* 1845. Translated as *The Ego and its Own.* Cambridge; New York: Cambridge UP, 1995.

Storm, Theodor. *Immensee,* 1850. Translated by Helen Clark as *Immensee, or the Old Man's Reverie.* Münster: Brunn, 1863. Translated by Jonathan Katz as *The Lake of the Bees.* London: Hesperus, 2003.

———. *Gedichte,* 1852; enlarged 1856, 1864, 1868, 1875, 1885. Selected poems translated in *The Penguin Book of German Verse.* Ed. Leonard Forster. Baltimore: Penguin, 1957.

———. *Am Kamin,* 1857.

———. *Auf dem Staatshof,* 1858.

Storm, Theodor. *Aquis submersus,* 1876. Translated by Geoffrey Skelton as *Beneath the Flood.* London: New English Library, 1962.

———. *Der Schimmelreiter,* 1888. Translated by Muriel Almon as *The Rider of the Pale Horse* in *The German Classics of the Nineteenth and Twentieth Centuries,* vol. 11, edited by Kuno Francke and William Guild Howard. New York: German Publication Society, 1914.

Tieck, Ludwig. *Der Aufruhr in den Cevennen,* 1826. Translated by Mme. Burette as *The Rebellion in the Cevennes.* London, 1845.

———. *Der junge Tischlermeister,* 1836.

———. *Vittoria Accorombona,* 1840. Translated anonymously as *The Roman Matron: or, Vittoria Accorombona.* London: Bury St. Edmunds, 1845.

Uhland, Ludwig. *Gedichte,* 1815. Enlarged 1820, 1831. Translated by Alexander Platt as *Poems of Uhland.* Leipzig: Volckmar, 1848.

Wagner, Richard. *Der fliegende Holländer,* 1843.

———. *Tannhäuser,* 1845.

———. *Lohengrin,* 1848.

———. "Die Kunst und die Revolution," 1849.

———. "Das Judentum in der Musik," 1850.

———. "Das Kunstwerk der Zukunft," 1850.

———. *Oper und Drama,* 1852. Translated by William Ashton Ellis as *Opera and Drama* in vol. 2 of *Richard Wagner's Prose Works.* 8 vols. London: K. Paul, Trench, Trübner, 1892–1899.

———. *Mein Leben,* 1864.

———. *Tristan und Isolde,* 1865.

———. *Der Ring des Nibelungen,* 1876.

———. "Deutsche Kunst und deutsche Politik," 1867.

———. "Religion und Kunst," 1880.

———. *Parsifal,* 1882.

———. "Ueber das Weibliche im Menschlichen," 1883.

Selected prose works translated by H. Ashton Ellis in *Wagner on Music and Drama: A Compendium of Richard Wagner's Prose Works.* New York: Dutton, 1964.

See also Richard Wagner. *Richard Wagner's Prose Works.* Trans. W. A. Ellis. 8 vols. London: K. Paul, Trench, Trübner, 1892–1899. Vol. 1 reprinted as *The Art-Work of the Future, and Other Works.* Lincoln: U of Nebraska P, 1993.

Numerous translations of all the Wagner libretti exist.

Wienbarg, Ludolf. *Ästhetische Feldzüge,* 1834.

Selected Secondary Works Cited

1. General

Auerbach, Erich. *Mimesis: The Representation of Reality in Western Literature*. Trans. Willard Trask. Princeton: Princeton UP, 1953.

Bachleitner, Norbert. *Der englische und französische Sozialroman des 19. Jahrhunderts und seine Rezeption in Deutschland*. Amsterdam and Atlanta: Rodopi, 1993.

——, ed. *Beiträge zur Rezeption der britischen und irischen Literatur des 19. Jahrhunderts im deutschsprachigen Raum*. Amsterdam and Atlanta: Rodopi, 2000.

——, ed. *Quellen zur Rezeption des englischen und französischen Romans in Deutschland und Österreich im 19. Jahrhundert*. Tübingen: Niemeyer, 1990.

Blackbourn, David. *The Long Nineteenth Century: A History of Germany, 1780–1918*. New York & Oxford: Oxford UP, 1998.

Boeschenstein, Hermann. *German Literature of the Nineteenth Century*. New York: St. Martin's Press, 1969.

Breuilly, John, ed. *Nineteenth-Century Germany: Politics, Culture and Society 1780–1918*. London: Arnold, 2001.

Craig, Gordon A. *The Politics of the Unpolitical: German Writers and the Problem of Power, 1770–1871*. Oxford, New York: Oxford UP, 1995.

Diethe, Carol. *Towards Emancipation: German Women Writers of the Nineteenth Century*. New York: Berghahn, 1998.

Field, G. Wallis. *A Literary History of Germany: The Nineteenth Century 1830–1890*. London: Benn, 1975.

Fisher, Philip. *The Vehement Passions*. Princeton: Princeton UP, 2001.

Furst, Lilian R. *Counterparts*. London: Methuen, 1977; Detroit: Wayne State UP, 1977.

Greiner, Martin. *Zwischen Biedermeier und Bourgeoisie: Ein Kapitel deutscher Literaturgeschichte*. Göttingen: Vandenhoeck & Ruprecht, 1953.

Häntzschel, Günter, et al. *Zur Sozialgeschichte der deutschen Literatur von der Aufklärung bis zur Jahrhundertwende: Einzelstudien*. Tübingen: Niemeyer, 1985.

Hardin, James, and Christoph E. Schweitzer, eds. *German Writers in the Age of Goethe, 1789–1832. Dictionary of Literary Biography*. Vol. 90. Detroit: Gale, 1989.

Hardin, James, and Siegfried Mews, eds. *Nineteenth-Century German Writers to 1840. Dictionary of Literary Biography*. Vol. 133. Detroit: Gale, 1993.

Hardin, eds. *Nineteenth-Century German Writers, 1841–1900. Dictionary of Literary Biography.* Vol. 129. Detroit: Gale, 1993.

Hermand, Jost. "Allgemeine Epochenprobleme." In *Zur Literatur der Restaurationsepoche 1815–1848,* ed. Jost Hermand and Manfred Windfuhr. Stuttgart: Metzler, 1970. 3–61.

Kord, Susanne. *Ein Blick hinter die Kulissen: Deutschsprachige Dramatikerinnen im 18. und 19. Jahrhundert.* Stuttgart: Metzler, 1992. 78–92.

Koselleck, Reinhart, ed. *Bildungsbürgertum im 19. Jahrhundert.* Stuttgart: Klett-Cotta, 1990.

Kreis, Georg. *Der Weg zur Gegenwart: Die Schweiz im 19. Jahrhundert.* Basel and Boston: Birkhäuser, 1986.

Lukács, Georg. *Deutsche Realisten des 19. Jahrhunderts.* Berlin: Aufbau Verlag, 1952. English translation in Lukács, *German Realists in the Nineteenth Century,* trans. Jeremy Gaines and Paul Keast, ed. Rodney Livingstone. Cambridge, MA: MIT Press, 1993.

Morgan, Bayard Q. *A Critical Bibliography of German Literature in British Translation 1481–1927, with a supplement for 1928–35.* Stanford: Stanford UP, 1938.

Nussbaum, Martha. *Upheavals of Thought: The Intelligence of Emotions.* New York: Cambridge UP, 2000. 19–88.

Pascal, Roy. *From Naturalism to Expressionism: German Literature and Society 1880–1918.* London: Weidenfeld and Nicolson, 1973.

Paulin, Roger. "'In so vielseitiger Wechselwirkung': Some Problems in Nineteenth-Century Anglo-German Literary Relations." In *Das schwierige neunzehnte Jahrhundert,* ed. Jürgen Barkhoff, Gilbert Carr, and Roger Paulin. Tübingen: Niemeyer, 2000. 567–78.

Pfau, Thomas. *Romantic Moods: Paranoia, Trauma, and Melancholy, 1780–1840.* Baltimore: Johns Hopkins UP, forthcoming.

Ritchie, J. M., ed. *Periods in German Literature.* N.p.: Dufour, 1967.

Sagarra, Eda. *Germany in the Nineteenth Century: History and Literature.* Frankfurt: Peter Lang, 2001.

———. *Tradition and Revolution: German Literature and Society 1830–90.* London: Weidenfeld and Nicolson; New York: Basic Books, 1971.

Sammons, Jeffrey L. "The Land Where the Canon B(l)ooms: Observations on the German Canon and Its Opponents, There and Here." In *Canon vs. Culture: Reflections on the Current Debate,* ed. Jan Gorak. New York and London: Garland, 2001. 117–33.

Scheideler, Britta. "Zwischen Beruf und Berufung: Zur Sozialgeschichte der deutschen Schriftsteller von 1880 bis 1933." *Archiv für Geschichte des Buchwesens* 46 (1997): 1–336.

Sprengel, Peter. *Geschichte der deutschsprachigen Literatur 1870–1900. Von der Reichsgründung bis zur Jahrhundertwende.* Munich: Beck, 1998.

Sked, Alan. *The Decline and Fall of the Habsburg Empire, 1815–1918.* London: Longman, 1989.

Stark, Susanne. *"Behind Inverted Commas": Translations and Anglo-German Relations in the Nineteenth Century*. Clevedon, UK: Multilingual Matters, 1999.

Stein, Peter. "Sozialgeschichtliche Signatur 1815–1848." In *Zwischen Restauration und Revolution 1815–1848*, edited by Gert Sautermeister and Ulrich Schmid. Munich: Hanser, 1998. 16–37.

Terada, Rei. *Feeling in Theory: Emotion after the Death of the Subject*. Cambridge, MA: Harvard UP, 2001.

Vinçon, Hartmut. "Einakter und kleine Dramen." In *Naturalismus, Fin de siècle, Expressionismus, 1890–1918*, edited by York-Gothart Mix. Munich: Deutscher Taschenbuch Verlag, 2000. 367–80.

Webber, Andrew. "Traumatic Identities: Race and Gender in Annette von Droste-Hülshoff's *Die Judenbuche* and Freud's *Der Mann Moses*." In *Harmony in Discord: German Women Writers in the Eighteenth and Nineteenth Centuries*, ed. Laura Martin. Bern: Lang, 2001. 185–205.

Wiese, Benno von, ed. *Deutsche Dichter des 19. Jahrhunderts: Ihr Leben und Werk*. Berlin: Schmidt, 1969.

2. Genres

2.1. Drama

Bennett, Benjamin. *Theater as Problem: Modern Drama and Its Place in Literature*. Ithaca: Cornell UP, 1990.

2.2. The Novel

Hardin, James, ed. *Reflection and Action: Essays on the Bildungsroman*. Columbia: U of South Carolina P, 1991.

Jacobs, Jürgen. *Wilhelm Meister und seine Brüder: Untersuchungen zum deutschen Bildungsroman*. Munich: Fink, 1972.

Sammons, Jeffrey L. "The Bildungsroman for Nonspecialists: An Attempt at a Clarification." In *Reflection and Action: Essays on the Bildungsroman*, ed. James Hardin. Columbia: U of South Carolina P, 1991. 26–45.

Sammons, Jeffrey L. "The Mystery of the Missing *Bildungsroman*, or: What Happened to Wilhelm Meister's Legacy?" In Sammons, *Imagination and History: Selected Papers on Nineteenth-Century German Literature*. New York, Bern, Frankfurt am Main, and Paris: Peter Lang, 1988. 7–31.

Steinecke, Hartmut. *Romantheorie und Romankritik in Deutschland*. Stuttgart: Metzler, 1975–76.

2.3. The Novella

Bennett, E. K. *A History of the German Novelle*. 2nd ed. revised and continued by H. M. Waidson. Cambridge, Eng.: Cambridge UP, 1961.

Remak, Henry H. H. *Structural Elements of the German Novella from Goethe to Thomas Mann*. New York, etc.: Peter Lang, 1996.

Swales, Martin. *The German Novelle*. Princeton: Princeton UP, 1977.

2.4. Poetry

Herin, Christoph. "Biedermeier." In *Geschichte der deutschen Lyrik,* ed. Walter Hinderer. Würzburg: Königshausen & Neumann, 2001. 287–90.

Iser, Wolfgang, ed. *Immanente Ästhetik, Ästhetische Reflexion: Lyrik als Paradigma der Moderne.* Munich: Fink, 1966.

3. Periods and Movements

3.1. Biedermeier

Neubuhr, Elfriede, ed. *Begriffsbestimmung des literarischen Biedermeier.* Darmstadt: Wissenschaftliche Buchgesellschaft, 1974.

Sengle, Friedrich. *Biedermeierzeit: Deutsche Literatur im Spannungsfeld zwischen Restauration und Revolution 1815–1848.* 3 vols. Stuttgart: Metzler, 1971–80.

3.2. Das Jahrhundertwende

Lorenz, Dagmar. *Wiener Moderne.* Stuttgart / Weimar: Metzler, 1995.

Rieckmann, Jens. *Aufbruch in die Moderne. Die Anfänge des Jungen Wien: Österreichische Literatur und Kritik im Fin de Siècle.* Königstein / Ts.: Athenäum, 1985.

Schmitz, Walter, ed. *Die Münchner Moderne: Die literarische Szene in der 'Kunststadt' um die Jahrhundertwende.* Stuttgart: Reclam, 1990.

Stoehr, Ingo. *German Literature of the Twentieth Century: From Aestheticism to Postmodernism.* Volume 10 of *Camden House History of German Literature.* Rochester, NY: Camden House, 2001.

Thomé, Horst. "Modernität und Bewusstseinswandel in der Zeit des Naturalismus und des Fin de siècle." In *Naturalismus, Fin de siècle, Expressionismus, 1890–1918,* edited by York-Gothart Mix. Munich: Deutscher Taschenbuch Verlag, 2000. 15–27.

Zanuso, Billa. *The Young Freud: The Origins of Psychoanalysis in Late Nineteenth-Century Viennese Culture.* Oxford: Blackwell, 1986.

Žmegač, Viktor, ed. *Deutsche Literatur der Jahrhundertwende.* Königstein / Ts.: Hain, 1981.

3.3. Naturalism

Maurer, Warren R. "Naturalism." In *Encyclopedia of German Literature,* edited by Matthias Konzett. Chicago: Fitzroy Dearborn, 2000. Vol. 2, 750.

Mahal, Günther. *Naturalismus.* 3rd ed. (1st ed. 1982). Munich: Fink, 1996.

3.4. Realism

Bernd, Clifford Albrecht. *German Poetic Realism.* Boston: Twayne, 1981.

———. *Poetic Realism in Scandinavia and Central Europe 1820–1895.* Columbia, SC: Camden House, 1995.

Cowen, Roy C. *Der Poetische Realismus. Kommentar zu einer Epoche.* Munich: Winkler, 1985.

Downing, Eric. *Double Exposures: Repetition and Realism in Nineteenth-Century German Fiction.* Stanford: Stanford UP, 2000.

Hauser, Arnold. *Sozialgeschichte der Kunst und Literatur.* Munich: C. H. Beck, 1990; first edition 1953.

Holub, Robert. *Reflections of Realism: Paradox, Norm, and Ideology in Nineteenth-Century German Prose.* Detroit: Wayne State UP, 1991.

Kontje, Todd, ed. *A Companion to German Realism 1848–1900.* Rochester: Camden House, 2002.

Martini, Fritz. *Deutsche Literatur im bürgerlichen Realismus* 1848–1898. 4th ed. (1st ed. 1962). Stuttgart: Metzler, 1981.

Schlaffer, Heinz. *Lyrik im Realismus.* Bonn: Bouvier, 1966.

Smith, Duncan. "Realism." In *Encyclopedia of German Literature,* edited by Matthias Konzett. Chicago: Fitzroy Dearborn, 2000. Vol. 2, 806.

Swales, Martin. *Epochenbuch Realismus: Romane und Erzählungen.* Berlin: Erich Schmidt, 1997.

3.5. Romanticism

Furst, Lilian R. *Romanticism in Perspective.* London: Macmillan, 1969; New York: Humanities Press, 1970.

Vida, E. M. *Romantic Affinities.* Toronto, Buffalo, and London: U of Toronto P, 1993.

3.6. Vormärz

Hermand, Jost. *Der deutsche Vormärz. Texte und Dokumente.* Stuttgart: Reclam, 1967.

Stein, Peter. *Epochenproblem "Vormärz" (1815–1848).* Stuttgart: Metzler, 1974.

Bayerdörfer. "Vormärz." In *Geschichte der deutschen Lyrik vom Mittelalter zur Gegenwart,* edited by Walter Hinderer. Würzburg: Königshausen & Neumann, 2001. 308–39.

3.7. Young Germany

Butler, E. M. *The Saint-Simonian Religion in Germany: A Study of the Young German Movement.* Cambridge, Eng.: Cambridge UP, 1926; reprinted New York: Fertig, 1968.

Hermand, Jost, ed. *Das Junge Deutschland. Texte und Dokumente.* Stuttgart: Reclam, 1966.

Koopmann, Helmut. *Das Junge Deutschland: Eine Einführung.* Darmstadt: Wissenschaftliche Buchgesellschaft, 1993.

Sammons, Jeffrey L. *Six Essays on the Young German Novel.* Chapel Hill: U of North Carolina P, 1972.

4. Individual Writers and Poets

Altenberg, Peter

Barker, Andrew. *Telegrams from the Soul: Peter Altenberg and the Culture of fin-de-siècle Vienna.* Columbia, SC: Camden House, 1996.

Alexis, Willibald

Gast, Wolfgang. *Der deutsche Geschichtsroman im 19. Jahrhundert: Willibald Alexis.* Freiburg: Becksmann, 1972.

Thomas, Lionel. *Willibald Alexis: A Biography.* Oxford: Blackwell, 1964.

Auerbach, Bertold

Kaiser, Nancy A. "Berthold Auerbach: The Dilemma of the Jewish Humanist from *Vormärz* to Empire." *German Studies Review* 6 (1983): 399–419.

Sorkin, David. "The Invisible Community: Emancipation, Secular Culture, and Jewish Identity in the Writings of Berthold Auerbach." In *The Jewish Response to German Culture from the Enlightenment to the Second World War,* ed. Jehuda Reinharz and Walter Schatzberg. Hanover and London: UP of New England, 1985. 100–119.

Bahr, Hermann

Farkas, Reinhard. *Hermann Bahr: Dynamik und Dilemma der Moderne.* Vienna / Cologne: Böhlau, 1989.

Bonaventura

Mielke, Andreas. *Zeitgenosse Bonaventura.* Stuttgart: Heinz, 1984.

Sammons, Jeffrey L. *The Nachtwachen von Bonaventura: A Structural Interpretation.* The Hague, London, and Paris: Mouton, 1965.

Droste-Hülshoff, Annette von

Donahue, William Collins. " 'Ist er kein Jude, so verdiente er einer zu sein': Droste-Hülshoff's *Die Judenbuche* and Religious Anti-Semitism." *German Quarterly* 72 (1999): 44–73.

Pizer, John. "Gender, Childhood, and Alterity in Annette von Droste-Hülshoff's Doppelgänger Thematic." In Pizer, *Ego-Alter Ego: Double and / as Other in the Age of German Poetic Realism.* Chapel Hill: U of North Carolina P, 1998. 20–39.

Rölleke, Heinz. "Annette von Droste-Hülshoff: Die Judenbuche (1842)." In *Romane und Erzählungen zwischen Romantik und Realismus: Neue Interpretationen,* ed. Paul Michael Lützeler. Stuttgart: Reclam, 1983. 335–53.

Ebner-Eschenbach, Marie von

Rose, Ferrel V. *The Guises of Modesty: Marie von Ebner-Eschenbach's Female Artists.* Columbia: Camden House, 1994.

Eichendorff, Joseph Freiherr von

Alewyn, Richard. "Ein Wort über Eichendorff." In *Eichendorff Heute,* ed. Paul Stöcklein. Darmstadt: Wissenschaftliche Buchgesellschaft, 1966. 7–18.

Frühwald, Wolfgang. "Der Regierungsrat Joseph von Eichendorff." In *Internationales Archiv für Sozialgeschichte der Deutschen Literatur* (1979). Vol. 4, 37–67.

Hoffmeister, Gerhart. "Eichendorff's *Ahnung und Gegenwart* as a Novel of Religious Development." In *Reflection and Action,* ed. Hardin. 292–313.

Pfau, Thomas. "Conjuring History: Lyric Cliché, Conservative Fantasy, and Traumatic Awakening in German Romanticism." In *South Atlantic Quarterly* 102:1 (2003): 53–91.

Schwarz, Egon. *Joseph von Eichendorff.* New York: Twayne, 1972.

Wellbery, David. "Verzauberung: Das Simulakrum in der romantischen Lyrik." In *Mimesis und Simulation,* ed. Andreas Kablitz and Gerhard Neumann. Freiburg: Rombach, 1998. 451–77.

Fontane, Theodor

Chambers, Helen. *The Changing Image of Theodor Fontane.* Columbia, SC: Camden House, 1997.

Demetz, Peter. *Formen des Realismus: Theodor Fontane. Kritische Untersuchungen.* Munich: Hanser, 1964; reprinted Munich: Ullstein, 1973.

Kaiser, Nancy A. *Social Integration and Narrative Structure: Patterns of Realism in Auerbach, Freytag, Fontane, and Raabe.* New York, Bern, and Frankfurt am Main: Peter Lang, 1986. 87–131.

Restenberger, Anja. *Effi Briest: Historische Realität und literarische Fiktion in den Werken von Fontane, Spielhagen, Hochhuth, Brückner und Keuler.* Frankfurt am Main, etc.: Peter Lang, 2001.

François, Louise von

Fox, Thomas C. *Louise von François and* Die letzte Reckenbürgerin: *A Feminist Reading.* New York, etc.: Peter Lang, 1988.

Freud, Sigmund

Young, Robert J. C. "Freud's Secret: *The Interpretation of Dreams* was a Gothic Novel." In *Sigmund Freud's The Interpretation of Dreams: New Interdisciplinary Essays,* ed. Laura Marcus. Manchester / New York: Manchester UP, 1999. 206–31.

Freytag, Gustav

Carter, T. E. "Freytag's *Soll und Haben,* a Liberal National Manifesto as a Best-Seller." *German Life & Letters* N.S. 21 (1967–68): 320–29.

Sammons, Jeffrey L. "The Evaluation of Freytag's 'Soll und Haben.'" In Sammons, *Imagination and History,* 193–216.

Schneider, Michael. *Geschichte als Gestalt: Gustav Freytags Roman "Soll und Haben."* Stuttgart: Heinz, 1980.

Geibel, Franz Emanuel

Hinck, Walter. "Epigonendichtung und Nationalidee." In *Zeitschrift für deutsche Philologie* 85 (1966): 267–84.

Link, Jürgen, and Wulf Wülfling, eds. *Nationale Mythen und Stereotypen in der 2. Hälfte des 19. Jahrhunderts.* Stuttgart: Klett-Cotta, 1989.

George, Stefan

Norton, Robert E. *Secret Germany: Stefan George and His Circle.* Ithaca, NY: Cornell UP, 2002.

Winkler, Michael. "Der George-Kreis." In *Naturalismus, Fin de siècle, Expressionismus, 1890–1918,* edited by York-Gothart Mix. Munich: Deutscher Taschenbuch Verlag, 2000. 231–42.

Gerstäcker, Friedrich

Sammons, Jeffrey L. *Ideology, Mimesis, Fantasy: Charles Sealsfield, Friedrich Gerstäcker, Karl May, and Other German Novelists of America.* Chapel Hill and London: U of North Carolina P, 1998. 113–200.

Goethe, Johann Wolfgang von

Blackall, Eric A. *Goethe and the Novel.* Ithaca and London: Cornell UP, 1976.

Bruford, Walter H. "Goethe and some Victorian Humanists." *Publications of the English Goethe Society* 18 (1949): 34–67.

Fuchs, Albert. *Goethe et l'esprit français.* Paris: Les Belles Lettres, 1958.

Guthke, Karl S. *Goethes Weimar und "Die grosse Öffnung" in die Welt.* Wiesbaden: Harrassowitz Verlag, 2001.

Lillyman, William J., ed. *Goethe's Narrative Fiction: The Irvine Goethe Symposium.* Berlin and New York: de Gruyter, 1983.

Proescholt-Obermann, Catherine W. *Goethe and his British Critics: The Reception of Goethe's Works in British Periodicals 1795–1855.* Frankfurt, Bern, & New York: Peter Lang, 1992.

Simpson, J. *Matthew Arnold and Goethe.* London: Modern Humanities Research Association, 1979.

Gotthelf, Jeremias

Cimaz, Pierre. *Jeremias Gotthelf (1797–1854): Der Romancier und seine Zeit.* Tübingen and Basel: Francke, 1998.

Waidson, H. M. *Jeremias Gotthelf: An Introduction to the Swiss Novelist.* Westport, CT: Greenwood Press, 1978.

Gutzkow, Karl

Demetz, Peter. "Karl Gutzkows 'Die Ritter vom Geiste': Notizen über Struktur und Ideologie." *Monatshefte* 61 (1969): 225–31.

Frank, Gustav. *Krise und Experiment: Komplexe Erzähltexte im literarischen Umbruch des 19. Jahrhundert.* Wiesbaden: Deutscher Universitäts-Verlag, 1998. 113–266.

Hasubek, Peter. "Karl Gutzkow: Die Ritter vom Geiste (1850–51). Gesellschaftsdarstellung im deutschen Roman nach 1848." In *Romane und Erzählungen des Bürgerlichen Realismus: Neue Interpretationen,* ed. Horst Denkler. Stuttgart: Reclam, 1980. 26–39.

Hauptmann, Gerhart

Leppmann, Wolfgang. *Gerhart Hauptmann: Leben, Werk und Zeit.* Bern: Scherz, 1986.

Heine, Heinrich

Boek, Oliver. *Heine Nachwirkungen.* Göppingen: Kümmerle, 1972.

Pfau, Thomas. "*Nachtigallenwahnsinn* and *Rabbinismus:* Heine's Literary Provocation to German-Jewish Cultural Identity." In *Romantic Poetry: Comparative History of Literatures in European Languages,* ed. Angela Esterhammer. Amsterdam: John Benjamins, 2002. 427–44.

Preisendanz, Wolfgang. *Heinrich Heine: Werkstrukturen und Epochenbezüge.* Munich: Fink, 1973.

Werner, Michael, ed. *Begegnungen mit Heine: Berichte der Zeitgenossen.* Hamburg: Hoffmann und Campe, 1973.

Heyse, Paul

Helmetag, Charles H. "Paul Heyse (1830–1914)." In *Dictionary of Literary Biography,* Vol. 129, *Nineteenth-Century German Writers, 1841–1900,* ed. James Hardin and Siegfried Mews. Detroit and London: Gale Research, 1993. 143–58.

Hoffmann, E. T. A.

Daemmrich, Horst S. *The Shattered Self: E. T. A. Hoffmann's Tragic Vision.* Detroit: Wayne State UP, 1973.

Matt, Peter von. *Die Augen der Automaten: E. T. A. Hoffmanns Imaginationslehre als Prinzip seiner Erzählkunst.* Tübingen: Niemeyer, 1971.

Teichmann, Elizabeth. *La Fortune de Hoffmann en France.* Geneva: Droz, 1961.

Webber, Andrew. *The Doppelgänger: Double Visions in German Literature.* Oxford: Clarendon, 1996.

Hofmannsthal, Hugo von

Le Rider, Jacques. *Hugo von Hofmannsthal: Historismus und Moderne in der Literatur der Jahrhundertwende.* Vienna: Böhlau, 1997.

Rieckmann, Jens. *Hugo von Hofmannsthal und Stefan George: Signifikanz einer "Episode" aus der Jahrhundertwende.* Tübingen: Francke, 1997.

Vilain, Robert. *The Poetry of Hugo von Hofmannsthal and French Symbolism.* Oxford: Clarendon Press, 2000.

Holz, Arno, and Johannes Schlaf

Brands, Heinz-Georg. *Theorie und Stil des sogenannten "Konsequenten Naturalismus" von Arno Holz und Johannes Schlaf.* Bonn: Bouvier, 1978.

Immermann, Karl

Hasubek, Peter. *Karl Leberecht Immermann: Ein Dichter zwischen Romantik und Realismus.* Cologne, Weimar, and Vienna: Böhlau, 1996.

Keller, Gottfried

Kaiser, Gerhard. *Gottfried Keller: Das gedichtete Leben.* Frankfurt am Main: Insel, 1981.

Laufhütte, Hartmut. *Wirklichkeit und Kunst in Gottfried Kellers "Der grüne Heinrich."* Bonn: Bouvier, 1969.

Kraus, Karl

Lunzer, Heinz, Victoria Lunzer-Talos, and Marcus G. Patka, eds. *"Was wir umbringen": 'Die Fackel' von Karl Kraus.* Vienna: Mandelbaum, 1999.

Lewald, Fanny

Van Ornam, Vanessa. *Fanny Lewald and Nineteenth-Century Constructions of Femininity.* New York, etc.: Peter Lang, 2002.

Mann, Thomas

Heine, Gert. *Thomas Mann Chronik.* Frankfurt am Main: Klostermann, 2004.

Höbusch, Harald. *Thomas Mann: Kunst, Kritik, Politik, 1893–1913.* Tübingen: Francke, 2000.

Marlitt, E.

Kontje, Todd. *Women, the Novel, and the German Nation 1771–1871: Domestic Fiction in the Fatherland.* Cambridge, Eng.: Cambridge UP, 1998. 183–201.

May, Karl

Ueding, Gert, with Reinhard Tschapke, ed. *Karl-May-Handbuch.* Stuttgart: Kröner, 1987.

Meyer, C. F.

Pizer, John. "The Oriental Alter Ego: C. F. Meyer's *Der Heilige.*" In Pizer, *Ego-Alter Ego: Double and / as Other in the Age of German Poetic Realism.* Chapel Hill: U of North Carolina P, 1998. 60–75.

Mörike, Eduard

Sammons, Jeffrey L. "Fate and Psychology: Another Look at Mörike's *Maler Nolten.*" In Sammons, *Imagination and History,* 33–54.

Slessarev, Helga. *Eduard Mörike.* New York: Twayne, 1970.

Mühlbach, Luise

Peterson, Brent O. "Luise Mühlbach (Clara Mundt) (1814–1873)." In *Dictionary of Literary Biography,* Vol. 133, *Nineteenth-Century German Writers to 1840,* ed. James Hardin and Siegfried Mews. Detroit, Washington, and London: Gale Research. 204–10.

Nietzsche, Friedrich

Furness, Raymond. *Zarathustra's Children: A Study of a Lost Generation of German Writers*. Rochester, NY: Camden House, 2000.

Hollingdale, R. J. *Nietzsche: The Man and his Philosophy*. Cambridge: Cambridge UP, 1965; rev. 1999.

Holub, Robert C. *Friedrich Nietzsche*. New York: Twayne, 1995.

Klossowski, Pierre. *Nietzsche and the Vicious Circle*. Trans. Daniel W. Smith. Chicago: U of Chicago P, 1997.

Meyer, Theo. *Nietzsche und die Kunst*. Tübingen / Basel: Francke, 1993.

Novalis (Friedrich von Hardenberg)

Neubauer, John. *Novalis*. Boston: Twayne, 1980.

Raabe, Wilhelm

Denkler, Horst. *Wilhelm Raabe: Legende–Leben–Literatur*. Tübingen: Niemeyer, 1989.

Fairley, Barker. *Wilhelm Raabe: An Introduction to his Novels*. Oxford: Clarendon P, 1961.

Helmers, Hermann, ed. *Raabe in neuer Sicht*. Stuttgart, Berlin, Cologne, and Mainz: Kohlhammer, 1968.

Pascal, Roy. "The Reminiscence-Technique in Raabe." *Modern Language Review* 49 (1954): 339–48.

Sammons, Jeffrey L. *Wilhelm Raabe: The Fiction of the Alternative Community*. Princeton: Princeton UP, 1987.

Richter, Jean Paul Friedrich

Berger, Dorothea. *Jean Paul Friedrich Richter*. New York: Twayne, 1972.

Rilke, Rainer Maria

Görner, Rüdiger. *Rainer Maria Rilke: Im Herzwerk der Sprache*. Vienna: Zsolnay, 2004.

Naumann, Helmut. *Rainer Maria Rilke: Stufen seines Werkes*. Rheinfelden: Schäuble, 1995.

Rückert, Friedrich

Uhrig, Max-Rainer, ed. *Gestörte Idylle*. Würzburg: Ergon, 1995.

Schiller, Friedrich

Ludwig, Otto. "Shakespeare und Schiller." In *Otto Ludwigs Werke in sechs Bänden,* ed. Adolf Bartels. Vol. 6. Leipzig: Hesse, 1906. 156–59.

Schnitzler, Arthur

Fliedl, Konstanze. *Arthur Schnitzler: Poetik der Erinnerung*. Vienna: Böhlau, 1997.

Foster, Ian, ed. *Arthur Schnitzler: Zeitgenossenschaften / Contemporaneities.* Bern / Vienna: Lang, 2002.

Sealsfield, Charles

Sammons, Jeffrey L. *Ideology, Mimesis, Fantasy: Charles Sealsfield, Friedrich Gerstäcker, Karl May, and Other German Novelists of America.* Chapel Hill and London: U of North Carolina P, 1998. 3–110.

Spielhagen, Friedrich

Göttsche, Dirk. *Zeit im Roman: Literarische Zeitreflexion und die Geschichte des Zeitromans im späten 18. und im 19. Jahrhundert.* Munich: Fink, 2001. 678–738.

Sammons, Jeffrey L. *Friedrich Spielhagen: Novelist of Germany's False Dawn.* Tübingen: Niemeyer, 2004.

Staël, Mme. de

Furst, Lilian R. "Mme. de Staël's *De L'Allemagne* A Misleading Intermediary." *Orbis Litterarum* 31 (1976): 41–58.

Stifter, Adalbert

Sjögren, Christine Oertel. *The Marble Statue as Idea: Collected Essays on Adalbert Stifter's* Der Nachsommer. Chapel Hill: U of North Carolina P, 1972.

Swales, Martin and Erika. *Adalbert Stifter: A Critical Study.* Cambridge, Eng.: Cambridge UP, 1984.

Storm, Theodor

Jackson, David A. *Theodor Storm: The Life and Works of a Democratic Humanitarian.* New York and Oxford: Berg, 1992.

Tieck, Ludwig

Lillyman, William J. *Reality's Dark Dream: The Narrative Fiction of Ludwig Tieck.* Berlin and New York: de Gruyter, 1979.

Marshall, Jennifer Cizik. *Betrothal, Violence, and the "Beloved Sacrifice" in Nineteenth-Century German Literature.* New York, etc.: Peter Lang, 2001.

Rath, Wolfgang. *Ludwig Tieck: Das vergessene Genie.* Paderborn, Munich, Vienna, and Zurich, 1996.

Sammons, Jeffrey L. "Tieck's *Franz Sternbald:* The Loss of Thematic Control." *Studies in Romanticism* 5 (1965 / 66): 30–43.

Wagner, Richard

Adorno, Theodor W. *Versuch über Wagner.* In *Gesammelte Schriften,* Vol. 13, ed. Rolf Tiedemann. Frankfurt am Main: Suhrkamp, 1971. English translation: *In Search of Wagner,* trans. Rodney Livingstone (London: Verso, 1981).

Borchmeyer, Dieter. *Das Theater Richard Wagners. Idee–Dichtung–Wirkung.* Stuttgart: Reclam, 1982.

Dolar, Mladen, and Slavoj Žižek. *Opera's Second Death.* New York, London: Routledge, 2002.

Grey, Thomas S. *Wagner's Musical Prose.* Cambridge: Cambridge UP, 1995.

Kramer, Lawrence. *Music as Cultural Practice, 1800–1900.* Berkeley, CA: U of California P, 1990.

Levin, David J. *Richard Wagner, Fritz Lang, and the Nibelungen: The Dramaturgy of Disavowal.* Princeton, NJ: Princeton UP, 1998.

Mann, Thomas. "Leiden und Größe Richard Wagners." In *Essays,* ed. Hermann Kurzke and Stephan Stachorski. Frankfurt: Fischer, 1995. Vol. 4, 11–72. English translation: "The Sorrows and Grandeur of Richard Wagner." In Thomas Mann, *Pro and Contra Wagner.* Trans. Allan Blunden. Chicago: Chicago UP, 1985. 91–148.

Nattiez, Jean-Jacques. *Wagner Androgyne: A Study in Interpretation,* trans. Stewart Spencer. Princeton: Princeton UP, 1993.

Raphael, Robert. *Richard Wagner.* New York: Twayne, 1969.

Shaw, George Bernard. *The Perfect Wagnerite: A Commentary on "The Ring of the Niblungs."* London: Grant Richards, 1898.

Weiner, Marc A. *Richard Wagner and the Anti-Semitic Imagination.* Lincoln, NE and London: U of Nebraska P, 1995.

Contributors

BENJAMIN BENNETT is Kenan Professor of German at the University of Virginia. His special interests include drama (history, theory, criticism), German literature of the eighteenth, nineteenth, and early twentieth centuries, European literature of the same periods, and literary theory. Among his major publications are *Modern Drama and German Classicism: Renaissance from Lessing to Brecht* (1979); *Goethe's Theory of Poetry: Faust and the Regeneration of Language* (1986); *Hugo von Hofmannsthal: The Theaters of Consciousness* (1988); *Theater as Problem: Modern Drama and Its Place in Literature* (1990); *Beyond Theory: Eighteenth-Century German Literature and the Poetics of Irony* (1993); *Goethe as Woman: The Undoing of Literature* (2001); and *All Theater Is Revolutionary Theater* (forthcoming in 2005).

ERIC DOWNING is Associate Professor of Comparative Literature at the University of North Carolina, Chapel Hill, where he also holds an adjunct position in Classical Studies. His interests include literary theory, aestheticism, realism, ancient-modern relations, and German literature with particular emphasis on narrative fiction from the late eighteenth through the early twentieth century. He has also worked on Nietzsche, Freud, Benjamin and, more recently, W. G. Sebald. His publications include *Artificial I's: The Self as Artwork in Ovid, Kierkegaard, and Thomas Mann* (1993) and *Double Exposures: Repetition and Realism in Nineteenth-Century German Fiction* (2000).

GAIL FINNEY has been Professor of Comparative Literature and German at the University of California, Davis since 1988. Her publications include *The Counterfeit Idyll: The Garden Ideal and Social Reality in Nineteenth-Century Fiction* (1984), *Women in Modern Drama: Freud, Feminism, and European Theater at the Turn of the Century* (1989, 1991), *Look Who's Laughing: Gender and Comedy* (ed., 1994), *Christa Wolf* (1999), and numerous articles on nineteenth- and twentieth-century German and comparative literature. She has also edited a volume of essays entitled *Visual Culture in Twentieth-Century Germany: Text as Spectacle* which will appear with Indiana UP in 2006. She is currently working on a book entitled *Children of Oedipus: Staging Family Trauma in Contemporary Film.*

LILIAN R. FURST is Marcel Bataillon Professor of Comparative Literature at the University of North Carolina, Chapel Hill. She has a particular interest in European literature of the nineteenth century and has published widely on romanticism, realism, naturalism, and irony. Her more recent books include *Through the Lens of the Reader* (1992); *All Is True: The Claims and Strategies of Realist Fiction* (1995); *Between Doctor and Patient: The Changing Balance of Power* (1998); *Just Talk: Narratives of Psychotherapy* (1999); *Medical Progress and Social Reality* (2001); and a dual-voice auto-biography, *Home Is Somewhere Else* (1994).

ERNST GRABOVSZKI is Lecturer in the Department of Comparative Literature at the University of Vienna. His most recent books are *Literature in Vienna at the Turn of the Centuries* (Camden House, 2003; co-edited with James Hardin) and a biography of Charles Sealsfield (forthcoming).

ROBERT C. HOLUB has been teaching German literary, cultural, and intel-lectual history at the University of California at Berkeley since 1979. His research includes volumes on Heine, Habermas, Nietzsche, literary theory, and German realism. He is currently serving as Dean of the Undergraduate Division in the College of Letters and Science.

ARNE KOCH is Assistant Professor of German at the University of Kansas. He has written articles on Fritz Reuter and Berthold Auerbach, on Reinhold Solger, and on translation practices in Poetic Realism. His cur-rent research projects are centered on the tensions between regional and national identity in nineteenth-century literature, and on the Low German works of Ernst Moritz Arndt.

CLAYTON KOELB is Guy B. Johnson Professor of German and Comparative Literature and Chair of the Department of Germanic Languages at the University of North Carolina, Chapel Hill, where he teaches and conducts research on modern European literature and culture. He has a special interest in German literature from 1750–1950. Among his book publica-tions are *The Incredulous Reader: Literature and the Function of Disbelief* (1984); *Inventions of Reading: Rhetoric and the Literary Imagination* (1988); *Kafka's Rhetoric: The Passion of Reading* (1989); and *Legendary Figures: Ancient History in Modern Novels* (1998).

CHRISTOPHER MORRIS is Lecturer in Music at University College Cork, Ireland, where he also teaches in the Department of Drama and Theatre Studies. He has published a number of articles on opera and film music in Austro-German culture and is author of *Reading Opera Between the Lines: Orchestral Interludes and Cultural Meaning from Wagner to Berg* (2002).

THOMAS PFAU is Associate Professor of English and German Literature at Duke University. He is author of *Friedrich Hölderlin: Essays and Letters on Theory* (1987); *Idealism and the Endgame of Theory: Three Essays by F. W. J. Schelling* (1994); *Wordsworth's Profession* (1997); and *Romantic Moods: Paranoia, Trauma, Melancholy — 1780–1840* (Johns Hopkins UP, forthcoming). In addition, he has published essays in numerous journals and essay collections and is the co-editor of *Lessons of Romanticism* (1998).

JOHN PIZER is Professor of German and Comparative Literature at Louisiana State University. He has published numerous articles on nineteenth-century German literature. His two most recent books are: *Toward a Theory of Radical Origin: Essays on Modern German Thought* (1995) and *Ego-Alter Ego: Double and / as Other in the Age of German Poetic Realism* (1998). His next book, *The Idea of World Literature: History and Pedagogical Practice,* will be published by LSU Press.

JEFFREY L. SAMMONS, Leavenworth Professor of German Emeritus at Yale University, has published primarily on German literature of the nineteenth century. His books include: *Heinrich Heine: A Modern Biography* (1979); *Wilhelm Raabe: The Fiction of the Alternative Community* (1987); *Ideology, Mimesis, Fantasy: Charles Sealsfield, Friedrich Gerstäcker, Karl May, and Other German Novelists of America* (1998); and *Friedrich Spielhagen: Novelist of Germany's False Dawn* (2004).

ANDREW WEBBER is Reader in Modern German and Comparative Culture at the University of Cambridge. He has published widely in German and comparative literary and film studies. His books include *The Doppelgänger: Double Visions in German Literature* (1996) and *The European Avant-Garde* (2004). He is currently working on a cultural topography of Berlin, with the support of a Leverhulme Major Research Fellowship.

Index